Carluccio's

COMPLETE ITALIAN FOOD

Carluccio's

COMPLETE ITALIAN FOOD

ANTONIO AND
PRISCILLA CARLUCCIO

PHOTOGRAPHY BY ANDRÉ MARTIN
ILLUSTRATIONS BY FABRICE MOIREAU

ALHAMBRA EDITIONS

Dedication

We dedicate this book to all our Italian suppliers who still struggle to produce delicious and genuine food against the tide of mass production. A. & P. C.

In the recipes both metric and imperial quantities are given. Use either all metric or all imperial, as the two are not necessarily interchangeable.

The author and publishers believe the information contained in this book to be correct and accurate at the time of going to press. Cooking and eating wrongly identified mushrooms can be fatal. If ever in doubt, don't. Neither the author nor the publishers can accept any legal responsibility or liability for any errors, omissions or mistaken identification of fungus species that may be made.

Publishing Director: Anne Furniss
Editor & Project Manager: Lewis Esson
Designer: Paul Welti
Photographic Art Director: Priscilla Carluccio
Recipe Editor: Jane Middleton
Indexer: Hilary Bird
Typesetter: Peter Howard
Production Controller: Candida Lane

This edition first published in 2005 by
Alhambra Editions,
Alhambra House,
27–31 Charing Cross Road,
London WC2H 0LS

Reprinted in 2005, 2006
10 9 8 7 6 5 4 3

Cataloguing-in-Publication Data: a catalogue record for this book is available from the British Library.

ISBN-13: 978 184400 297 9
ISBN-10: 1 84400 297 7

Printed and bound in China

Endpapers: pan di San Giuseppe (page 294).
Half-title page: a vegetable stall at Turin market.
Title page: the Altesino vines, Montalcino, in late autumn.
Right: grapes drying for vin santo in Montalcino.

CONTENTS

INTRODUCTION

The twenty regions of Italy provide a gastronomic feast which is unsurpassed. Although the geography of these regions is immensely diverse, the basic principles of Italian cooking are the same – culinary simplicity and the use of the finest, freshest ingredients available. Italy can in many respects be seen as the perfect market garden, with sweet milk and meat from the mountains of the Alps in the North to the freshest fish, sun-ripened fruit and vegetables of the South.

Geography apart, each region of Italy is also culturally different and each bears the distinctive marks of its past settlers and invaders, Barbarians, Arabs, Carthaginians, Etruscans, Phoenicians, Turks, Normans, Bourbons, Spaniards and Austrians. Each civilization tried to reproduce its own home cooking, as we all do today when living in other countries. Among early examples of these culinary invaders were the Islamic Saracens, who invaded Sicily, bringing with them the exotic sweetmeats like marzipan and nougat, and giving birth to that island's famous tradition in this area.

In the days of the Ancient Romans, sophisticated dishes and many fine wines were produced to please the Emperors and their courts, and eating became a fashionable pursuit at that time. From this period up until the Middle Ages, it was the monasteries that preserved the culinary arts and the spices that had once accompanied returning travellers disappeared, only to reappear with the rise of the great maritime republics in the eleventh to thirteenth centuries. The *Quattro Repubbliche Marinare* – Venice, Genoa, Pisa and Amalfi – became the culinary centres of Italy, with the introduction of elegant tableware and customs.

Obviously some of the most important Italian food we know today was introduced from outside. Olive oil was brought to Puglia and Sicily by the Ancient Greeks; and, in the North, polenta or maize came by boat from the New World to Venice, swiftly becoming the staple diet of Northerners. Also from the New World came the now ubiquitous tomato. The cultivation of rice began in the fifteenth century, in Lombardy where the Po Valley's abundant water made it ideal for the crop. Germanic and Nordic influences are also very strong in the heavier dishes of the Alto Adige.

Within Italy itself, migration from the South to the North has been considerable in this century and

the traditions of Puglia, Campania and Calabria have brought a new culinary experience to be shared. *Pasta al pomodoro* is now eaten in Milan and Turin instead of their more traditional rice or polenta.

If the largest part of Italy was poor it was not in its food and wine; these were then – and are now – treated as precious commodities as well as basic parts of Italian culture. It is the very strong desire to consume good food and drink that has given the farmers, winemakers and fishermen the courage to cultivate and bring to market the best. Italians are motivated and inspired by the culture of their food and wine and will go to amazing lengths to source the best ingredients to achieve a perfect dish. The resourcefulness born out of this desire has generated the produce so admired worldwide today.

In this journey through Italy we have investigated and sought out the products of traditional methods of agriculture, livestock husbandry and fishing. Italian food is about flavour, something that has sadly disappeared from much of our mass-produced food in recent years. It is about ripe fruit picked off the tree and eaten while still warm from the sun, fish straight from the water, meat reared and butchered with skill, wine made with the genuine local grapes and matured in ancient barrels, organic vegetables just dug from richly manured fields with the earth still clinging to their roots. This is not a romantic vision, it is how our food should be!

Producing this book has been a fascinating experience. Travelling together, as we do, my wife and I have the rare privilege of sharing with our producers their inherited knowledge of food growing and processing – as most of our producers are growers as well. They have helped us to understand more about the local ingredients, the methods of cultivation and the care with which the product is 'manufactured'. With the trend towards laboratory- and factory-prepared food, the skills these people inherited from their families are in danger of disappearing. This book is an attempt to recall these good traditions of the past and marry them with the culinary needs of a different age, in which people do much less physical labour and therefore have different dietary requirements.

Above all, however, this book is a personal view of real Italian food, where it comes from and why it tastes the way it does. The simplicity of the recipes relies on one thing – genuine and excellent products! *Buon appetito!*

PREVIOUS PAGES AND THIS PAGE: VARIOUS VIEWS OF THE WONDERFUL KITCHEN OF A FRIEND IN NAPLES.

OPPOSITE: MAP SHOWING THE REGIONS OF ITALY AS USED IN THIS BOOK.

TRENTINO-
ALTO ADIGE
VALLE
D'AOSTA
Milano
LOMBARDIA
FRIULI-
VENEZIA
GIULIA
PIEMONTE
VENETO
Venezia
Po
Po
Adige
Torino
Genova
LIGURIA
EMILIA-ROMAGNA
Parma
Bologna
Arno
Firenze
TOSCANA
MARCHE
Mar Mediterraneo
Tiber
Mar Adriatico
UMBRIA
LAZIO
Roma
ABRUZZI
MOLISE
CAMPANIA
Napoli
Bari
PUGLIA
SARDEGNA
BASILICATA
Cagliari
CALABRIA
Palermo
SICILIA

Fish & Shellfish

Pesci e Frutti di Mare

Fish is becoming more and more popular worldwide and is replacing meat in the diet of many. Indeed one reason for its popularity is its healthier qualities when compared to meat. In general fish contain significantly less fat than meat and the fat, or oil, they do contain has, in fact, been found to be actively beneficial.

However, with growing demand for fish there is greater pressure on available stocks and this means that finding a supply of the best fish is becoming increasingly difficult. As anxieties about the pollution of our seas and rivers grow, stocks are put under even greater pressure, so that we are now in real danger of over-fishing to such an extent that we are likely to deny ourselves this splendid natural resource in the very near future. As fish wars break out between neighbouring countries and everyone fishes to the limit of their allowance, the whole issue of fishing and eating the fruits of the sea has become a political problem. We will soon have to decide whether we can continue to gather and eat so vigorously, so we can plan to continue having the valuable stocks available to us in the future.

Italy is thankfully blessed with a particularly good supply of fish and the coastal regions of Liguria, Tuscany, Lazio, Campania, Calabria, Basilicata, Apulia, Abruzzo e Molise, Marche, Emilia-Romagna, Veneto, Friuli-Venezia Giulia, Sicily and Sardinia all have a part of the Mediterranean to themselves. This does not mean, however, that Piedmont, Lombardy, Trentino-Aldo Adige and Umbria do not enjoy fish too, as they have their own supply of wonderful freshwater lakes providing a good number and variety of freshwater fish. Modern transportation methods also mean that fresh sea fish are available in these regions, reaching their destination within hours of being pulled from the sea.

Funnily enough, of all the regions Sardinia is the one with the most recent tradition of eating fish. The earlier inhabitants occupied more of the interior of the island, preferring to live on game rather than fish. However, the development of tourism in the last century has ensured that a lot of fish is available on the coast, and it has become highly prized.

Despite having a healthy supply of fresh and saltwater fish all over the country, Italy – like Spain and Portugal – also enjoys and uses a great deal of *baccalà* and stockfish in its cooking. Both

Top left: Lake bream air-drying for missoltit on Isola dei Pescatori in Lake Maggiore.

are forms of preserved cod; *baccalà* being salted at sea and then dried in large chunks when it is landed, and stockfish being whole air-dried fish. One or the other is eaten in all the regions of Italy, partly for economic reasons and partly for religious ones. It used to be the fish of the poor, and was eaten on Fridays by fasting Catholics who did not have access to fresh fish. Now, though, it is valued by many for its distinctive flavour and versatility.

Other fish preserved in salt include anchovies and sardines, both of which have given birth to many dishes. Preserved anchovies are particularly valued, being used in a huge number of dishes – from the ancient Roman condiment *garum* to today's pizza. Fish are also pickled in vinegar and this gives the flesh of freshwater fish like carp, goregone, eels and trout, an almost Oriental sweet-and-sour tang.

Another traditional method of preserving fish is by smoke-curing it. In Italy, this method was used in the past only for meat such as hams, but in top restaurants it is now possible to be served very thinly sliced smoked swordfish, tuna fish and sturgeon, as well as air-dried and salted cod or mullet roe (known as *bottarga*), a very expensive speciality from Sardinia and Sicily. Salted and air-dried fillets of tuna fish, known as *mosciame*, are a delicacy to compare with the finest of foods, while the smoked swordfish, tuna and sturgeon are of a high enough quality to be exported to the connoisseurs of fish in the Nordic countries, alongside their locally smoked salmon, mackerel, eel and herring.

Today, however, the most popular way of preserving many foods, including fish, is by freezing it, and a wide variety of frozen fish is offered conveniently prepared in supermarkets. What this means is that fish can be eaten fresh all year round and all over the country, as it can be frozen and packaged at the coast immediately after it has been caught. In my opinion, however, this is no service to lovers of fish as the taste and texture of any dish is compromised by using frozen fish. At least in Italy if frozen fish is served in a restaurant it has to be declared as such on the menu, giving the diner an opportunity to make an informed decision about what he or she eats.

Good fresh fish remains the highest prize and it is therefore important to know what you are looking for when you buy it. It is crucial to have some knowledge of the flesh of the type of fish you are buying so you know the exact characteristics you are looking for and then, of course, to know the best way to cook it in order to make the most of both the dish and the fish.

It is essential that a fish is at its absolute freshest when it is bought so the first priority is to find a trustworthy supplier. Good indications of freshness for whole fish are clear, bright eyes and bright red gills. It is also important that it smells of the sea and that it does not smell of fish, this is a sure sign that it is old and will not taste fresh. Finally, the flesh of the fish should be firm to the touch, springing back to its former shape when touched. Some fish like tuna and swordfish are, however, 'hung' like game to develop the flavour and tenderness of the flesh.

If buying shellfish, the main points to look for are that the shell of molluscs such as mussels, clams and scallops, are tightly closed. If they are even very slightly open, and don't close when tapped sharply on a hard surface, they are dead and should not be used. Other shellfish like crabs and lobster should be heavy and fresh-smelling. If they smell of fish it means they are not fresh, so reject them.

Above all, when buying seafood, trust your instincts and do not be afraid to reject anything that does not look, feel or smell right. Good fish, when it is fresh and well cooked, is a wonderful experience. It is no surprise that it has been such a staple part of the Mediterranean diet for so long and reassuring that its popularity is developing once again all over the world.

Right: On Lake Maggiore, Paolo preparing lake bream prior to drying on the boat of the Battista family.

Below: Camogli Madonna and child casting their protective gaze over the sea and the fishermen.

A-Z of Fish & Shellfish

Acciuga, Alice / Anchovy
Probably the best-loved and most versatile of Italian fish, anchovies are small saltwater fish which live in deep waters and approach the shore only during the spring mating season. The fishing of this speciality is strictly controlled to avoid damaging stocks. Being a lovely blue-green colour, they are classified by Italians as among the *pesce azzurro*, or blue fish, along with sardines and mackerel.

Newly hatched anchovies, called *neonati*, *latterini* or *bianchetti*, are caught with very fine nets and eaten bones and all with just a little lemon juice or used for very delicate salads and fritters, while the adult fish grow to a maximum of 20 cm (8 inches) in length and are either used fresh in a variety of regional dishes or preserved in salt and olive oil. At their best, these preserved anchovies have all the flavour and aroma of freshly caught and filleted fish.

Left: neonati

Anchovies are central to the cuisine of the southern coastal regions of Italy and so command a high price. The best fresh *acciughe* or *alici*, as they are sometimes called in the South, can be found in the Gulf of Naples – Salerno is particularly well-known for producing high-quality preserved anchovies and in Sicily, where Cefalu is at the centre of the anchovy industry.

Fresh anchovies should be used very quickly as the delicate and fragrant flesh deteriorates quickly. The fillets can be eaten raw with just a few drops of lemon juice sprinkled over them; or marinated in a mixture of lemon juice, parsley and olive oil, then served with a green parsley sauce made with olive oil, chilli and garlic, and accompanied by lots of crusty bread.

When it comes to cooking fresh anchovies there are many different regional recipes to choose from, but my favourite is stuffing the boned fish with a mixture of breadcrumbs, herbs, eggs and Parmesan cheese, sprinkling them with olive oil and baking them in the oven.

How Anchovies are Prepared for Bottling

Fresh anchovies are layered in coarse sea salt, weighted and left for 3 months to mature. During this time the anchovies exude oil, which is skimmed off at regular intervals and the brine is topped up. The anchovies are judged 'ripe' and ready when they develop a very pleasant smell and the flesh is a good pink colour.

Then comes the rinsing process: the first rinse takes place in brine at 80°C (175°F). The second is done in fresh brine at 40°C (105°F) and the last in cold water. By this stage most of the excess salt and oil will have been washed away.

The fish are then filleted by hand and the fillets wrapped in porous cloths and put in a centrifugal spinner for 2-3 minutes to eliminate all the excess water. They are then carefully packed by hand into jars and covered with olive or vegetable oil.

Above: acciughe

Anchovies to be preserved in oil are first cured in salt to make *acciughe sotto sale*, or salted anchovies. To do this the fish are layered with rock salt and left to mature for at least three months (see opposite). When they are ready, they are removed from the salt, any excess brushed off, their heads removed and the backbone cut away with a small knife. On no account should the salted fish be washed. In Alba, salted anchovies are layered with very thickly sliced white truffle before being steeped in oil. Anchovy fillets (*filetti di acciughe*) are also available in cans; those that are a good size and canned in olive oil are the best.

Preserved anchovies have an infinite number of uses in Italian cuisine, one of the best known being *bagna caôda*, a speciality from Piedmont (see page 33). This famous sauce, used as a hot dip for crudités, is made from just anchovies, garlic and oil. Anchovies are also used in the classic *salsa verde*, or green sauce, for *bollito misto*, as well as many other sauces, and of course are familiar to all the world on pizzas.

Another classic use of the fish is *burro di acciughe* (anchovy butter), which is made by mashing preserved anchovies to a paste then mixing this with butter. This preparation is excellent in sauces or delicious spread on bread or *crostini*. *Pasta d'acciuga* (anchovy paste) can also be bought in jars, tins or tubes.

Acciugata, a Ligurian sauce made by dissolving fillets of anchovies in olive oil, is used to give a sharp, distinctive flavour to otherwise bland food such as boiled or steamed fish, and boiled eggs. It can also be used with tomatoes, oregano and garlic, as a sauce for either pasta or meat.

ALBORELLA / FRESHWATER FISH

This is a very common freshwater fish, mostly found in Lake Como, which grows up to 20 cm (8 inches) in length and has a silvery skin. It is easily scaled and skinned and the flesh has a sweetish taste. The favoured cooking method for it is to flour the whole fish or fillets and deep-fry them. The fish is sometimes marinated in vinegar and wine with bay leaves, then sautéed in oil with onions. The fish is often air-dried to make the speciality of Lake Maggiore, Missoltit, see page 21.

ALIOTIDE AND PATELLA REALE / LIMPET

Limpets are single-shelled molluscs, looking like small pyramids, which are found attached to rocks. You need to have good eyes to spot them and a knife with a pointed tip to detach them. As long as you know it has come from unpolluted waters, you can eat this shellfish raw with just a few drops of lemon juice. Limpets have a very nutty flavour and are delicious in fish soups. The best dish I ever tasted with limpets was a truly memorable linguine with mussels and limpets at the Cambusa restaurant in Positano.

ANGUILLA, BISATO / EEL

This remarkable creature is both a sea fish and a freshwater fish. But the most impressive thing about the eel is the fact that they all begin their life in the Sargasso Sea off the American Coast and within 2 hours of being hatched are transported by the Gulf Stream thousands of miles to Europe, where they are caught and speedily consumed. In Italy, these elvers (as they are called at this stage of their life) are known as *cieche* (meaning 'blind'), not because they cannot see but because they are so easy to catch that the fishermen say they are blind to the nets.

The fish that are not caught as elvers from the sea swim into freshwater lakes and rivers to spend 6 or 7 years maturing, before swimming back to their birthplace to breed and end their life. Eels from the Comacchio Valleys at the mouth of the Po are especially good. There the elvers are trapped in artificial lakes when they enter the Po Estuary south of Venice and are then effectively farmed until they reach maturity.

Right: anguilla

Eels are traditionally eaten fried, grilled, baked and stewed. In Sardinia, they are cooked with tomatoes. One of the most memorable dishes I have had with eel was one in which it was simply baked with bay leaves and no other flavouring (see the recipe for Anguilla alla Luciana on page 35).

The *capitone*, a large female eel which has reached its maximum weight, is perhaps worth a special mention. It is traditionally eaten at Christmas and is a delicacy in Rome and all over the south. The fish is cut into sections, cured with olive oil, garlic, mint and vinegar, then grilled on charcoal.

ARAGOSTA, ASTICE / SPINY OR ROCK LOBSTER, LOBSTER
Of the many varieties of this crustacean in existence, the spiny or rock lobster *aragosta nostrana*, the one without claws, is the most common. The larger darkish blue/green true lobster with claws is called *astice* and is similar to the American Maine lobster.

The best way to cook lobster is to boil it in water, when the shell turns bright red. There is considerable debate about what is the most humane way to cook a live lobster and the current consensus seems to be that the swiftness of plunging it in rapidly boiling water is preferred. Once cooked it can be halved and, while still warm, sprinkled with good olive oil (preferably the most delicate Ligurian) and a few drops of lemon juice. Don't forget to provide your guests with the appropriate tools so they can extract the juicy meat from the claws.

I think the sweetish taste of lobster meat is particularly good when cooked with tomatoes to make a sauce for linguine (see page 155).

LEFT: PRESOAKED BACCALÀ IN THE MARKET

ARINGA / HERRING
This North Atlantic fish is not caught in the Mediterranean but is widely used in Italy, generally in *antipasto*, once it has been salt-cured and smoked. One of the most remarkable recipes for it I have tasted comes from Sicily, where it is eaten in a salad with grapefruit and orange (see page 29).

ARSELLA, SEE VONGOLA

ARZILLA, SEE RAZZA

ASTICE, SEE ARAGOSTA

BACCALÀ, STOCCAFISSO / SALT COD, STOCKFISH
Baccalà and *stoccafisso* are respectively salted and air-dried cod. Like herring, this is another preserved northern fish which has successfully found its way into Italian cuisine. Some attribute its introduction to Christopher Columbus, who found it in his ship's supplies when on the way to America. For a long time, in fact, stockfish was the staple diet of navigators as it would last out long journeys. Both types of preserved cod come from the Lofoten Isles in Norway, where a whole industry and way of life has grown up around the fishing, salting and drying of cod.

Two regions of Italy are famous for their *baccalà* recipes, Liguria and Veneto, from whence it spread all over Italy. In the past it was the food of the poor and was especially useful because it could be eaten on religious fast days in the landlocked valleys of the Italian Alps where access to fresh fish was difficult. Today, as with many other traditional peasant foods, it is enjoying a renaissance in Italian cuisine.

Baccalà, or salt cod, can only be used after having been soaked in frequent changes of fresh water for at least 24 hours in order to soften the flesh and remove the salt. Salt cod is usually sold dry in halves or sometimes quarters, but in some places you can buy it presoaked and ready for use.

Stockfish, on the other hand, is air-dried and sold whole. Although it is unsalted, it requires lengthy soaking before cooking to rehydrate, as well as vigorous beating with a mallet in order to tenderize it and break up the fibres. Strangely, it is called *baccalà* in Vicenza and Venice although it is known as *stoccafisso* elsewhere in Italy. In fact Vicenza is famous for its *baccalà alle vicentina* which is usually eaten with white polenta.

Other regional specialities using stockfish and *baccalà* are *frittelle di baccalà* (fritters), *insalata di baccalà* (a salad of *baccalà* cooked with parsley, lemon juice and chilli flakes) and *stocco alla Genovese* (a long-cooked stew, see page 40).

BARBO / BARBEL
This freshwater fish can be found all over Italy, where it lingers in the muddy beds of many rivers and lakes. It is a very delicate fish, with few bones, and is best eaten fried or poached. It must, however, never be eaten raw as the uncooked flesh is toxic.

BELOW: STOCCAFISSO

ABOVE: [LEFT] MOSCIAME (SEE TONNO, PAGE 26); [RIGHT] BOTTARGA

FAR RIGHT: THE INGREDIENTS ASSEMBLED FOR CACCIUCCO.

BIANCHETTI, SEE ACCIUGA

BISATO, SEE ANGUILLA

BOTTARGA, BUTTARIGA / ROE OF GREY MULLET AND TUNA

Bottarga is the name given to the roe of both the grey mullet (*bottarga di muggine*) and tuna (*bottarga di tonno*). The mullet roe is much smaller than that of the tuna and is pressed then cured in brine before being hung up to dry. Sicily and Sardinia are the main producers and consumers of this speciality, and there it is eaten in thin slices seasoned with lemon juice and olive oil as an appetizer, and on scrambled eggs.

The much bigger tuna roe can weigh up to 2 kilos (4 lb) and is traditionally pressed into an oblong shape once cured. It is mostly used grated over pasta and eggs, the bland accommodating flavour of which is the perfect foil for the strong flavours of the salted fish. It commands very high prices and can only be found in the best delicatessens.

BRANZINO, SPIGOLA / SEA BASS

When Italians hear the words *spigola* or *branzino* their culinary hearts start to beat a little faster, for sea bass is one of the best-loved fish in Italy. It is widely available, as it can be caught off any coast where the sea is fairly rough. It can reach up to 1 metre (3 ft) in length and 10 kg (22 lb) in weight.

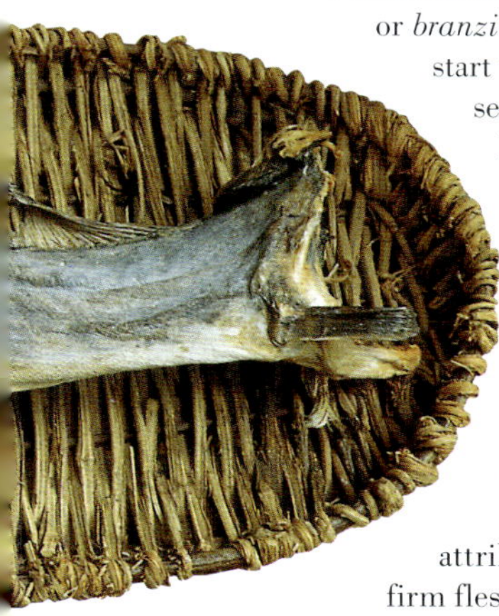

Its popularity can be attributed to its delicate but firm flesh, which is enormously versatile and easy to cook. Whether boiled, baked or grilled, sea bass always delivers its promise. Because it is so well liked, this fish has to be farmed to meet the demand. This means that the size and weight of the fish can be controlled for culinary use. Wild sea bass are a wonderful silver colour, whereas their cultivated cousin is darker and never quite matches up in terms of flavour.

The fish is often baked whole in a salt crust or in foil parcels with parsley, garlic, lemon and fennel. The Sicilians cook it in sea water, see Branzino all'Acqua di Mare, page 35.

BURIDDA, SEE CACCIUCCO

CACCIUCCO / FISH SOUP

This classic Livornese fish soup, also called *buridda* in Liguria, is made using a wide variety of fish, but usually *murena* and *scorfano*, with wine, garlic, parsley, olive oil and tomatoes (see page 29).

CALAMARO / SQUID

There is quite a lot of confusion about these very popular cephalopods, related to the octopus. They come in many varieties which look very similar and share similar preparation and cooking methods. The differences between the varieties are more to do with size and shape than taste or texture. The *totano seppia*, or flying squid, is notable for its habit of leaping from the water and gliding for some distance. Found mostly off the Ligurian coast, it is treated in much the same way as other squid, but has coarser flesh.

Squid have tube-like bodies with two fins, and a head with ten short tentacles attached. Two of these tentacles are much longer than the others and are lined with small suckers. The skin of the *calamaro* (squid) or *calamaretto* (baby squid) is generally pinkish in hue with flashes of white.

The squid carries ink in its body, which it ejects to confuse enemies when they are in pursuit. Italians, especially Venetians, have managed to prepare wonderful dishes using the black ink, *risotto nero* being perhaps the best-known.

To prepare squid for cooking, the skin is first removed. Then the transparent quill inside the tube is

removed and discarded. The black ink sac inside the body should be removed carefully and reserved if you want to use it to colour a dish.

Once cleaned, squid can be cooked in a variety of ways. They are often poached whole very briefly in sea water and eaten in salads dressed with olive oil and lemon. In Apulia, they use very little water for the broth and then drink it as a tonic after cooking the squid. Alternatively, whole small squid or large ones cut into rings are dusted with flour and deep-fried until crispy. They may also be grilled or stuffed whole – usually with the chopped tentacles, breadcrumbs or rice and flavourings like garlic and parsley or pecorino and pine nuts – and baked in the oven, and they often feature alongside other seafood in soups.

CANESTRELLO, SEE CAPASANTA

CANNOCCHIA, PANNOCCHIA / SQUILL FISH

This most Mediterranean of shellfish, which vaguely resembles a langoustine, is very much an Italian affair. Especially common in the Adriatic, it lives in the sand and mud on the seabed. It can reach 20 cm (8 in) in length and has a sort of fortified shell on its back and tail that has two black marks on it which look like a pair of eyes. This crustacean has many different names and uses, depending on where it is fished. In Venice it is called *canoci*, in Puglia *caratiedde*, *spanocchio* in Naples and *cicala* in Tuscany.

To get at the tender meat, it is best to cut two small strips down each side of the body with scissors so that the meat can be extracted in one piece. It is mostly used in fish soups, but is also served freshly boiled and dressed with olive oil and lemon juice.

CANNOLICCHIO, CAPPALUNGA / RAZOR-SHELL

This is a very peculiar mollusc which has two shells shaped like an old-fashioned cut-throat razor. It lives on the bottom of sandy sea beds and is quite difficult to fish because it sits in an upright position and the sharp shells can cut nets and hands. It is easiest to fish when the tide is low and you can gently pull the shells out of the sand.

Razor shells can reach 30 centimetres (1 foot) in length, but the smaller ones are more tender. They can be grilled, added to fish soups or used in seafood salads. They are usually sold in bundles and go for those that are heavy for their size. To get at the meat without cutting yourself on the shells the *cannolicchi* must first be steamed open in a pan with a little olive oil and water.

CAPASANTA, CONCHIGLIA DI S. GIACOMO, PETTINE / SCALLOP

Many different names have been given by various Italian regions to this popular and most distinctive of shellfish. In Italy it is usually cooked without the pinkish coral or roe.

One of the best varieties, the *canestrello* or queen scallop, is particularly common in the Venice region, where it lives on the sandy sea beds and is harvested by divers all year round. It is no surprise then, that it is from Venice that some of the best recipes have evolved, including *risotto ai canestrelli*, an Italian version of Spanish *paella*, although the finest scallops are rightly reserved for a simple but exquisite seafood salad. The fine flavour of the scallop suits the simplest of treatments, say with a little white wine, garlic and parsley.

CAPITONE, SEE ANGUILLA

LEFT: CAPASANTA

CAPONE, CAPPONE / GURNARD

This is a strange fish that looks like a red mullet with a large head surrounded by bony scales and two very large fins just beneath the head. It lives in the sand on the seabed at various depths. There are several varieties which range from small to quite large, reaching up to 75 cm ($2^{1}/_{2}$ feet) in length.

The flesh is very good, tender but not too firm. Cut into steaks, it can be grilled, but its best use is to flavour fish soups.

CARPA / CARP

This freshwater fish loves quiet waters, where it usually sits in the mud on the river or lake bed. There are many types of carp, the main differences between them being the number of scales on their body. They can reach up to 1 metre (3 feet) in length and attain quite significant weights.

As Italians are not fond of the muddy-tasting flesh of carp, there are not many recipes suggesting how to cook it. The best suggestion I could give is carp in breadcrumbs, a recipe which comes from Venice where the fish is popular. The fish is also boiled and stewed, often with celery, onion and tomato.

CARPIONE, SEE PAGE 36

CAVIALE, SEE STORIONE

CEFALO, MUGGINE / GREY MULLET

Because of its fine flavour, this is a very popular fish in Italy and is fished around every coast. Grey mullet is fond of estuaries, where it finds the best feeding grounds, so it can taste muddy and the best fish come from clearer waters. There are many varieties, but the most sought-after is the *volpino*, which in season has a rich roe used to make *bottarga* (see page 17). Careful cleaning of the fish helps to get rid of any muddy taste. Mullet is mostly eaten grilled,

ABOVE: VENICE'S WONDERFUL FISH MARKET AT THE RIALTO.

and only the best fish are baked in the oven, with only olive oil, lemon and parsley.

CERNIA / GROUPER
This solitary fish lives in warm seas and reaches huge sizes of up to 1.5 metres. Its tasty firm, white flesh is considered a delicacy in Italy. Due to its size, it is usually fished with harpoons, and when it comes to cooking it is usually cut in slices and either grilled or braised, while other parts of the grouper are used to make a sauce to dress linguine. However, the most interesting way of cooking the fish comes from Sardinia, where the liver is used to produce an excellent sauce to accompany the roasted fish.

CICALA, SEE CANNOCCHIA

CIECHE, SEE ANGUILLA

CODA DI ROSPO, RANA PESCATRICE, ROSPO / ANGLER FISH OR MONKFISH
This ugly fish is becoming more and more sought after by chefs all over the world. Its firm, tasty tail meat is almost completely boneless and, after cooking, it resembles lobster closely enough to be confused with it quite regularly.

With its large mouth, the monkfish is able to take quite large prey and spends much of its life skimming the seabed in search of food. It is therefore fished with a flexible rod which is weighted to reach the seabed. Monkfish grow to quite a large size, but generally only the tail of the fish is used. The large, ugly head is usually discarded in Italy, although in some parts of the world it is used to make fish stock and gelatine, for which it is excellent. The tail is cooked in every way, from grilling and deep-frying to baking and stewing, with simple added flavourings like lemon, garlic, parsley and olive oil.

COLLA DI PESCE / FISH GELATINE
This is a flavourless setting agent obtained from the parts of fish that are normally discarded, and less gluey than ordinary gelatine.

CONCHIGLIA
Conchiglia is the Italian for shell. The term is often used to refer to the scallop as this is sometimes called *conchiglia S. Giacomo*. See Capasanta.

COZZA, MUSCOLO, MITILE, MUSCIOLI / MUSSEL
One of the most common shellfish in the world, the mussel is used abundantly in Italian cuisine, especially in southern Italy and the Venetian lagoon where what they call locally *peoci* are prodigious.

In the clear waters near Chioggia in the Venetian lagoon there is farm after farm where mussels grow on long ropes hanging from wooden frames. The farms are carefully regulated to ensure high standards of hygiene because of the susceptibility of the mussel to pollution.

When bought, mussels must be firmly closed and heavy indicating that they are still alive and so completely fresh. Before cooking, they should be well washed under cold running water, using a knife to scrape off barnacles and the beards. Mussels which come to the surface when submerged in water should be discarded, as should those that do not open after cooking.

At one time, mussels were eaten raw like oysters but today, with the risk of contamination from pollution, it is essential to cook them first. (See Cozze Ripiene, page 30). They are most commonly cooked in a little wine with pepper, parsley, garlic and sometimes chilli, or they may be sprinkled with garlic and breadcrumbs and baked.

CROSTACEI / CRUSTACEAN
The general name for all limbed shellfish armoured with a tough skin, i.e. lobsters, crabs, prawns, etc.

DATTERO DI MARE / SEA DATE
This mollusc, related to the mussel, is so named because it looks like a date. It is oval-shaped, usually reaching 5-10 cm (2-4 inches) in length and is of a dark brown colour. The sea date lives in rocks where, by using acids from its body, it is able to form a niche in the rock which it enlarges as it grows.

The *dattero di mare* is very sought-after and a real delicacy. In

RIGHT: DATTERI DI MARE, VONGOLE AND TARTUFI DI MARE

Puglia and in the Gulf of Spezia, where it grows best, there are special laws to regulate their fishing. To catch them, you literally have to break the rock to which they are attached and the fishing boats need lifting tackle to heft the rocks on board. The practice is likely soon to be made illegal as it is ruining some stretches of coastline.

Provided you know where they come from, you can eat sea dates raw like oysters. Because of their unique habitat, unlike other mussels, they do not contain sand.

DENTICE / SEA BREAM

This very popular Mediterranean fish can reach 1 metre (3 feet) in length. Its flesh is very delicate and can be cooked in any way, from grilling in fillets, baking whole, frying and steaming, with lots of olive oil and parsley, tomato and fennel as added flavourings.

In commercial terms, this fish is as important as the *cernia* or any of the other breams (see Orata and Sarago), all central players on the Italian culinary scene.

DONZELLA

Related to the gurnard and weever, the *donzella* is one of those colourful Mediteranean fish often used in fish soups and stews.

FRUTTI DI MARE / SEAFOOD

This is the generic term used for all seafood, but is most often used to refer to all shellfish, from oysters, mussels, sea dates and sea urchins to crabs, shrimps, prawns and lobsters. *Frutti di mare* can be eaten raw as long as they are extremely fresh, preferably alive, and come from unpolluted waters which can be guaranteed by an excellent fishmonger.

GAMBERO, GAMBERETTO, GAMBERONE, MAZZANCOLLA / PRAWN, SHRIMP

The many varieties of prawn and shrimp belong to the same family as the lobster. Indeed one type of prawn, the *gambero di acqua dolce* (freshwater prawn or crayfish) is an exact miniature copy of the lobster and is almost as popular on the culinary scene. Other types of prawn do not have claws, although their armoured body and head have a very similar look to their larger cousins. Also like the lobster, the many natural colours of prawns, from pale orange and deep red to dark greyish-blue, all turn red when cooked. Prawns and shrimp are well loved and fished all over the world, but Mediterranean prawns have an unmatchable sweet taste and sea fragrance.

Today it is very difficult for most people to get fresh prawns, although there is some farming to supplement the locally caught supply. Huge worldwide demand means that most prawns are caught in large numbers and frozen on board enormous North Atlantic trawlers. The difference between fresh and frozen prawns is great, but the world seems to have accepted the inferior product.

The smallest *gamberetti*, or grey shrimp, are usually eaten dusted in flour and deep-fried until crisp. They are so tender that often one can eat the entire thing without having to shell it. The larger *gamberoni* can be either boiled or grilled with the shells on or sautéed in a pan with just the body shelled so that all the delicious juices contained in their heads can be exuded.

The best recipes originate from the well-supplied coastal regions and include simple recipes such as freshly boiled prawns dipped in dressings or eaten in salads. They are also fried and grilled or baked with olive oil and lemon.

GOREGONE / LAKE FISH

Almost every Italian lake harbours this well-known fish, also called *lavarello*. It usually reaches 30 cm

TOP LEFT: DONZELLE

LEFT: DENTICI

BELOW: GAMBERI

(1 foot) in length and its meat is very delicate. It is especially popular in the northern regions of Italy, where it is used as an alternative to saltwater fish brought in from the coasts.

These very versatile fish can be cooked in many ways: they may be fried and marinated (in *carpione*, see page 36) to make an excellent appetizer, or cut into fillets, dusted with flour, dotted with butter and sprinkled with sage leaves then baked in the oven. Fried, baked or boiled they are equally good however they are cooked.

RIGHT: GRANCIPORRO

GRANCHIO, GRANCIPORRO, GRANSEOLA, GRANCEVOLA, GRANCEOLA / CRAB

The crab family includes a large variety of these extremely tasty crustaceans. In Italy, the smaller variety, such as the *granchio* or sand or common crabs, are eaten in soups. The larger variety, called *granciporro*, is heavy and capable of yielding quite a lot of meat. For the best results these large crabs should be boiled while still alive, like lobsters. They need to be cooked for at least 20 minutes, then left to rest for 15 minutes in their cooking water. Spider crabs (*granseola*, *granceola* or *grancevola*) are prepared in a similar way. The best crabs come from Venice, as do the best recipes.

After cooking, the crab is opened by exerting pressure between the eyes until the back shell lifts off like a lid from a box. After removing the 'dead men's fingers', or gills, the meat from the body and claws is all collected along with the coral and mixed together and served dressed with some salt, lemon juice, parsley and a little olive oil. Larger spider crabs should be grilled or boiled whole, and the flesh added to a good tomato sauce for pasta.

There is a peculiar crab, called *moleca* in Venetian dialect, which is the equivalent of the American soft-shell crab. This is a male crab caught by expert fishermen during the spring and autumn when it discards its old shell and only has a new soft shell which has not hardened. Soft shell or 'naked' crabs can be eaten whole dusted in flour and deep-fried.

GRONGO, SEE MURENA

LANGOSTA, SEE ARAGOSTA

LATTE DI PESCE, SEE UOVA DI PESCE

LATTERINI, SEE ACCIUGA

LAVARELLO, SEE GOREGONE

LUCCIO / PIKE

This freshwater fish can reach a length of 1.5 metres (4½ feet) and up to 4 or 5 kilos (9-11 lb) in weight. It is much sought after, especially in Piedmont, Lombardy and Veneto, for its firm white flesh. It is traditionally cooked *in umido*, i.e. braised with tomatoes, or minced to produce pâtés or fish cakes.

MARMORA, SEE ORATA

MAZZANCOLLE, SEE GAMBERO

MERLUZZO / COD

The mild-flavoured cod is not much eaten as a fresh fish in Italy, only preserved. See Baccalà.

MISSOLTIT / PRESERVED FISH

This is a speciality of the Northern Italian lakes like Maggiore and Como. Fish from the lakes, like *alborella* and *agoni*, are hung to dry in the sun (see the picture on page 12). The dried fish is usually grilled until the skin swells, this is then removed and the fish served with some lemon juice or vinegar.

MITILO, SEE COZZA

MOLECA, SEE GRANCHIO

MOLLUSCO / MOLLUSC

This is the general term for all the soft invertebrate seafood, comprising univalves like limpets, and bivalves like clams, mussels and oysters, as well as squid and cuttlefish.

MORMORA, SEE ORATA

MOSCARDINO, SEE POLPO

MOSCIAME, SEE TONNO

MURENA, GRONGO / MORAY EEL, CONGER EEL

The *murena* or moray eel is the dread of every underwater diver because when defending itself it goes on the attack and its bite is horrible as well as being poisonous. It is a solitary fish that lives in holes in rocks and can reach 1.5 metres (5 feet) in length. The eel's meat was appreciated by the ancient Romans for its fragrance and was widely used in mixed fish soups like *cacciucco*.

The *grongo* or conger eel, unlike the moray, is neither venomous nor dangerous. However great care needs to be taken when preparing it as the raw blood is highly poisonous and it is only after it is cooked that the eel's flesh loses its toxicity. For this reason it is very important that any wound is covered when cleaning the eel.

Both the moray and conger eels are especially good when cut in slices and grilled, although great care must be taken to ensure that it is completely cooked before serving and eating. See Anguilla for more on cooking eel.

MUSCOLO, MUSCIOLI, SEE COZZA

NASELLO / HAKE
Once prepared, this fish is often wrongly identified as cod, but hake does not look like cod at all although it does belong to the same family. It reaches up to 1 metre (3 feet) in length and large fish are sliced into cutlets before being cooked in a variety of ways. Its extremely fragile and delicate flesh is eaten all over Italy and cooked in many different ways according to regional variations. They may simply be brushed with oil and grilled, or fried in oil with tomatoes and garlic.

Nasello al brodetto, poached hake with bread, is a classic recipe in which the fish is briefly cooked in a court-bouillon made from garlic, parsley, a little salt and pepper and some chopped peeled tomatoes. The court-bouillon is simmered for 15 minutes so that it is only just cooked when the fish is added. The liquid must not completely cover the fish, which should also only be cooked for a few minutes in the sauce before being set aside for 10 minutes to rest. The hake should then be served on croutons made with good bread.

NEONATO, SEE ACCIUGA

NERO DI SEPPIA, NERO DI CALAMARO / CUTTLEFISH INK, SQUID INK
Cuttlefish and squid ink come from a sac in the bodies and are mostly used in the making of sauces and *risotti*. They are also used in the making of pasta, where the ink turns the dough black and gives it a distinctive fishy flavour. As well as retrieving the ink sac from any cuttlefish or squid bought fresh and whole from a fishmonger, the ink can be bought separately in sachets.

ORATA, MORMORA, MARMORA / BREAM
All Mediterranean bream are related and, despite the differences in colour, texture, taste and general appearance, are very similar. Both the *mormora* or *marmora* (striped bream) and *pagello* or *pagro* (sea bream) are well loved in Italy. However perhaps the best flavoured is the *orata* or gilthead, known to the French as the *daurade*, and the favoured way of cooking them is to bake them in the oven. They are also often grilled after being brushed with *salmoriglio*, a mixture of lemon juice, olive oil, and chopped parsley and capers.

OSTRICA / OYSTER
It is very curious that this Italian *frutto di mare*, so loved by the Romans that they developed the first oyster farms, is now considered to be the French *fruit de mer* par excellence. In fact it was only after the French (and British) exhausted their own natural fishing grounds that they imported the farming know-how from Italy and made it such a primary industry that it is now France that dictates the rules of hygiene and other regulations for growing oysters.

In Italy the so-called belon or round oyster is still the best loved and is still farmed in the Adriatic Sea around Puglia, especially the town of Taranto. Of the few varieties that exist, Italians prefer the flat *Ostrica piatta* and the round belon which is still eaten raw dressed with just a few drops of lemon juice.

The oyster is easily digestible and eating a dozen as an appetizer is quite normal. I remember once eating 126 small ones, but I certainly could not manage the remaining three courses or the pudding, and the proverbial effect one is said to experience after consumption was noticeable. Raw oysters should only be eaten when the shell is tightly closed, showing that the oyster is still alive. There are not many Italian recipes for eating cooked oysters and an imported recipe *alla Rockerfella*, grilled in the American style.

PAGELLO AND PAGRO, SEE ORATA

PALOMBO / SHARK
This type of shark found in the Adriatic is not much used in the kitchens of Italy any more due to the poor quality of its flesh. At one time, it used to be sliced and grilled like tuna and swordfish, or stewed in tomato sauce like tuna. It still may sometimes be sold in Venice market as *vitello di mare*, or sea veal.

PEOCI, SEE COZZA

PESCE AZZURRO / BLUE FISH
Although members of different families, anchovy, sardine, mackerel, herring, bonito, tuna, and swordfish are all categorized in Italy by the colour of their skins. All are saltwater fish with oily flesh and relatively easy to prepare and cook.

PESCE PERSICO / PERCH
One of the most sought-after freshwater fish, the perch can reach 45 cm (18 in) in length. It is very much at home in the northern rivers and lakes and is usually sold filleted because it is difficult to prepare due to its very delicate flesh and many back fins and bones. The favoured cooking methods are either to dust it with flour and fry it in butter or to dip it in beaten egg, coat it in breadcrumbs and deep-fry in oil. Perch can also be preserved (see *carpione*, page 36) to be eaten as part of *antipasto* or as a snack.

LEFT: PESCE SAN PIETRO

PESCE SAN PIETRO / JOHN DORY OR ST PETER'S FISH
Legend tells of how Saint Peter took the fish from the water with his hands leaving the imprint of his

Right: pesci sciabola

fingers on its skin. He was worried about the payment of a tax but found exactly the right amount of money in the fish's mouth to pay the debt. This is how the fish got its name and is supposed to explain the presence of two black spots on either side of the body.

John Dory has extremely delicate flesh, but it is expensive because only 30-35 per cent of its total weight can be used once it has been filleted, which means that for four people you will need a large fish weighing at least 2 kg (4 lb). The flesh is prized for its firmness and flavour making it very popular with chefs the world over. The fillets are generally grilled, or they may be breaded and fried.

Pesce Sciabola / Sabre Fish

The pesce sciabola really stands out when the fishermen bring their catches on board. Shaped like a large flattened eel and with a bright silver skin, it looks totally different from all other fish. Although quite common, because of its many small bones it is not much sought after for the kitchen. It is mostly used in fish stews and soups, where it is cut into chunks to impart flavour. In parts of the South, it is also stewed with tomatoes, olive oil and garlic in the same way as *baccalà*. Another common way of cooking it is to coat it in flour and fry it in oil, then marinate this in vinegar and red wine, with garlic and mint.

Pesce Spada / Swordfish

Swordfish reach up to 4 metres (12 ft) in length and 200 kg (450 lb) in weight. The fish is readily identified by the long sword or spear on its snout. Many are harpooned by fishermen off the coasts of Calabria and Sicily. It is one of those fish that is generally hung for at least one day before use. The flesh is very similar in texture, colour and taste to that of shark meat and for this reason is cut and cooked in a similar way. It is mostly grilled but more recently it has been served raw as carpaccio and smoked. One of the most interesting ways to cook swordfish is in *involtini di pesce spada*, which is a speciality of Sicily (see page 32). Sicily is one of the largest consumers of swordfish.

Polpo, Moscardino / Octopus

There is a famous stand in the middle of the Vucceria market in Palermo, Sicily where you can eat freshly cooked and locally caught octopus from an old aluminium pot. Into the boiling water goes the fresh, creamy coloured octopus and after a few minutes out it comes, extremely tender and an appetising pinky-red. It is cut up on the stall so that it can be eaten straight away. It does not need to be accompanied by any sauces or spices, nature has already provided all the essential ingredients.

Old fishermen's tales about this creature abound and most concentrate on the power of its eight tentacles, each of which is armed with two rows of suckers for grabbing hold of its prey. The entire length of the octopus can reach anything from 50 cm (20 in) to 3 metres (10 ft). Smaller octopuses, weighing up to 200 g (7 oz), are very tender; anything over this size, and they can reach as much as 25 kg (55 lb) in weight, needs to be tenderized either by beating it with a stick or repeatedly thrashing against rocks to break up the fibres of the flesh.

The octopus can be found easily on all Italian coasts and is very much prized. It has a strong beak in the centre of its oval body which, along with the eyes, has to be discarded when preparing it for cooking. It can be eaten in salads or freshly poached, *affogato*, as in Naples, or by cooking in a covered pot with some oil, garlic, tomatoes, olives, chilli and parsley for about 30 minutes.

Similar to the *polpo* is the smaller *moscardino*, which has only one row of suckers on its tentacles and is not so well appreciated in the kitchen although it is still very good. The same recipes can be used for both,

Right: polpo

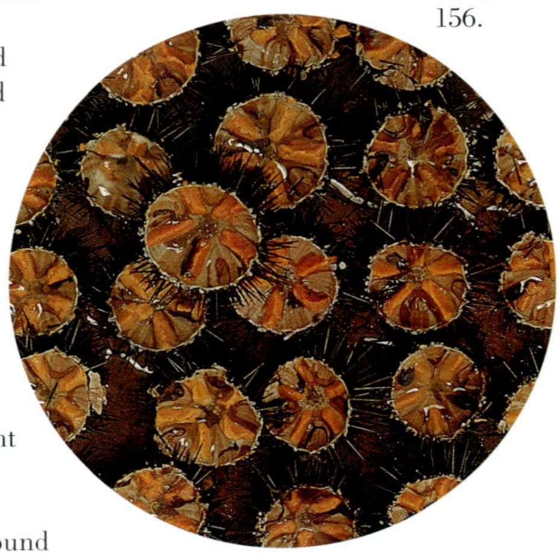

Top left: freshly boiled polpo in Palermo market.

Bottom left: ricci di mare

as long as an adjustment is made in the cooking time for the moscardino's smaller size.

Rana Pescatrice, see Coda di Rospo

Razza, Arzilla / Skate

Skate is similar to monkfish and John Dory in that only a part of this fish is eaten, in this case the wings, or outer fins. The fish is completely flat and lives on the bottom of the seabed where it is perfectly camouflaged under the sand. Skate wings are sold skinned and only the long structural cartilage left in place. It can be enjoyed in a variety of ways in a special fish stew or soup, boiled and eaten with butter or Hollandaise sauce, grilled or deep-fried coated with beaten egg and breadcrumbs. Whichever way it is prepared, though, it is quite delicious and highly recommended, provided you do not mind the cartilage, of course.

Riccio di Mare / Sea-urchin

Holidaymakers in the Mediterranean sometimes have the misfortune to tread on a sea-urchin, whose fragile spines break at exactly the point where they enter the flesh, delivering a painful poison.

Sea-urchins are common around the whole Italian coast, but mostly come from Puglia, Calabria, Sicily and Sardinia, four areas where the water is particularly clean. As well as being enjoyed by the local population, the sea-urchins are distributed to towns and cities all over Italy.

There are many varieties of sea-urchin and the roe of most is edible. The roe is the sea-urchin's egg sac, which reaches maturity in the spring and early autumn. Two varieties of sea-urchin are particularly good, those with violet-to-dark-green spikes and those with shorter spikes of violet with a white spot at the end.

To prepare this most delicate of *frutti di mare*, cut off the bottom half where the mouth lies, using a pair of scissors or a special tool, and clean the inside to remove the black impurities. Leave the star-shaped piles of roe intact and attached to the shell then simply eat with a spoon or, as I prefer, simply lick them out with the tip of your tongue. The salty-sweet taste of the eggs is so delicious that no accompaniment is needed. A superb pasta dish using sea-urchins comes from Puglia, see Linguine con Ricci di Mare, page 156.

Rombo / Turbot and Brill

Belonging to the sole family, these flat fish living partly on the sea bed are both very sought-after for their extremely white and firm flesh with a very delicate flavour.

The two types available in Italy are the *rombo chiodato* (turbot) which can reach 1 metre in length and is recognizable by its dark grey skin covered with small boney humps. The other type, *rombo liscio* (brill) has a paler smooth skin also with a less elongated body.

Both fish are generally cooked and eaten as fillets, either poached and served dressed with olive oil and lemon juice or stewed in a tomato sauce.

Rospo, see Coda di Rospo

Salmone / Salmon

Italians have discovered freshwater salmon in the last few years, probably due to the fact that the farmed variety has only recently become affordable. Until now only a few Italians were familiar with salmon and then only smoked. Although it is not native to Italy, everyone from restaurateurs to private buyers makes the most of this wonderful fish. It is usually grilled or poached and often the flaked flesh is incorporated in creamy sauces for pasta.

Sarago, Sargo / White Bream

The Italians like to fish this much-loved Mediterranean fish all year round; either it is cooked grilled with lemon juice and olive oil, or baked. The best variety is the *Diplodus sargus* which can reach 40 cm (16 in) in length and a weight of 2 kg ($4^1/_2$ lb). White bream prefers rocky seabeds with plenty of vegetation.

Sarda, Sardina, Sardella / Sardine

The name of this fish, actually young pilchard, probably comes from the area where it was mostly fished and known to the Romans around the Island of Sardinia. It is eaten in most of the Mediterranean countries and is almost a staple of all the coastal areas of Italy, where it is not only consumed fresh but also

ABOVE: CANNED SARDINES FROM SICILY.

FAR RIGHT: SCORFANI

BOTTOM RIGHT: SARDINES IN PALERMO MARKET.

preserved in oil and in salt like the anchovy (see page 14). The flesh is relatively fatty and the best way to eat sardines is brushed with a little lemon juice, olive oil, parsley, garlic, salt and pepper and then grilled. They can also be boned and stuffed or dipped in flour, egg and breadcrumbs and deep-fried.

The Sicilians honour the sardine in two special ways; firstly using it as a sauce for *pasta con le sarde* (see recipe, page 166) and secondly as *sardine a beccafico*, which are fillets of sardines rolled and stuffed with breadcrumbs, pine kernels and raisins mixed in olive oil and then baked in the oven and served with a sprinkling of orange juice (see page 33).

SCAMPO / CRUSTACEAN

The *scampo* is similar to a small lobster, and a very close relative of the Dublin Bay Prawn or langoustine, which is mostly fished on the Adriatic sea on the Eastern coast of Italy. Indeed, a great many scampi recipes come from the Venice area. It is a very delightful crustacean with very sweet and tender meat, in my opinion superior to that of lobster.

They are delicious when extremely fresh and simply boiled, then dressed with good olive oil and lemon juice. Many of the *scampi* that come from the North sea arrive frozen and the taste is lost completely. Scampi are used for fish soups, can be grilled and eaten cooked in salads. See also Gambero.

SCORFANO /SCORPION FISH OR RASCASSE

As their name suggests, scorpion fish have poisonous spines that can deliver a nasty sting. They live on rocky seabeds and come in a variety of colours, from reddish-brown to black. They look quite fearsome and are not very friendly if badly handled. However, this ugly fish has an excellent flavour and is very sought after for *cacciucco*, an excellent fish soup (see page 29). Smaller fish are best used in such soups, while the larger varieties (weighing 1 kg / 2 lb or more) are wonderful steamed or poached and eaten with fresh mayonnaise.

SEPPIA, SEPPIETTA / CUTTLEFISH

The cuttlefish has a shorter rounder body than the squid (see Calamaro, page 17) but the same number of tentacles. It has a less chewy texture than the squid, but there is much debate about which has the better flavour.

The cuttlefish also carries ink its body which it ejects to confuse enemies when they are in pursuit. The famous sepia or black colour of its ink was in great use by artists at the time of Leonardo da Vinci and his contemporaries (see Nero di seppia). *Seppiette in nero con polenta* is perhaps one of the most famous dishes made using the ink.

The striped skin is removed when the fish is prepared for cooking. The beak, eyes and innards (including the 'bone') are also removed and the black ink sac in the centre of the tentacles carefully removed and reserved. The ink may also be bought separately in sachets.

Like the squid, cuttlefish are often stuffed and baked or simply grilled or stewed in rich wine and/or tomato sauces.

SGOMBRO / MACKEREL

One of the most common fish in the world, the mackerel is closely related to the tuna and one of the

pesce azzurro or blue fish, because of its unmistakably black-striped, bluish skin. The fatty flesh is very firm and rather delicate but, once caught, it deteriorates quickly so freshness is paramount for the enjoyment of this fish.

However, because the oils in its flesh are healthy and because it is cheap and widely available, it is among the most commonly eaten fish in Italy. There are many recipes for mackerel but the best way to cook them is the simplest, grilled fresh from the sea over charcoal. They are also often stewed with a fresh tomato sauce.

SOGLIOLA / SOLE

Italians coming into my restaurant in London are always impressed by the tastiness of the sole, mainly because they believe Italian sole are the best that can be eaten. I must admit that the Italian dish *fritto misto* (mixed deep-fried fish), when made with a few freshly caught prawns and *sogliolette* (small sole), is one of life's greatest culinary pleasures.

Sole is available around the whole Italian coast, including the islands. There are many types of sole, which can be easily distinguished from other species of flat fish by the fact that both eyes sit on what would have been the right side of the fish. The Dover sole lives on the sandy seabed and is so well camouflaged that it is almost impossible to see. It is fished commercially and is so heavily exploited that it is feared that stocks are seriously depleted.

Whether it is served grilled, fried *à la meunière* or cut into fillets and poached in court-bouillon, the sole is a delicious fish.

SPANOCCHIA, SEE CANNOCCHIA

SPIGOLA, SEE BRANZINO

STOCCAFISSO, SEE BACCALÀ

STORIONE / STURGEON

This large fish, common to the Black and Caspian Seas, used to live in the River Po in Italy. Now, because of pollution however, they have died out there. The sturgeon is valued both for its eggs, which are eaten as caviar, and its fatty but very delicate flesh. In Sicily, farmed sturgeon are delicately smoked. The largest sturgeon is known as beluga in Russia and can reach up to 8 metres (33 ft) in length and about 1,000 kg (1 ton) in weight. Imagine how much caviar it can produce. The flesh of the smaller sturgeon, about 3 kg ($6^1/_2$ lb), is eaten grilled, fried, stewed, baked and steamed accompanied with various sauces.

TARTUFO DI MARE / SEA TRUFFLE

This mollusc is believed by gourmets to be the perfect *frutto di mare*. It is fished with a comb, which drags up all the shells buried in the sandy seabed. Its shell is similar to that of the clam but, unlike that more common mollusc, it is both very meaty and tender. It is usually eaten raw with lemon juice, although some connoisseurs prefer it without. It is also used in a sauce to accompany linguine in a similar way to clams or sautéed with other molluscs, see Sauté Misto di Vongole e Datteri, page 42.

TINCA / TENCH

This small freshwater fish, related to the carp, lives in lake ponds and rivers. Like many such fish, unless caught from clear waters, it can have a distinctly muddy taste. Accordingly it is today not one of the most popular of fish for cooking. It is generally baked, fried or cured in *carpione* (see page 36).

TONNO / TUNA FISH

'*Tonnare*' is the system of nets used by fishermen in Calabria and Sicily to catch tuna. These nets are placed in the sea in such a way as to channel shoals of tuna so that they cannot escape and they are then harpooned. It is a pretty messy way of catching fish, but one trip can produce tons and tons of tuna fish. The canning of tuna fish probably first came into existence as a way to cope with these sudden gluts.

When tinned, tuna fish is eaten in a totally different way to the fresh variety and can be used in sauces and *antipasti*. Fresh tuna, on the other hand, is eaten in a similar way to swordfish, sliced and usually grilled as a steak, or cooked with tomato sauce. Tuna can be eaten raw like *carpaccio*, providing the meat is very fresh, and can also be eaten as *mosciame* – air-dried fillets. *Ventresca* or the belly of the tuna was often salted in barrels or canned as a particular delicacy. When tuna roes are salted and air-dried they are known as *bottarga di tonno* (see page 17).

TOTANO SEPPIA, SEE CALAMARO

TOP LEFT: SEPPIE

BOTTOM: SMALL TUNA FISH

Top right: a tuna head on sale at Palermo market.

Far right: various types of clam.

Triglia / Red Mullet
Probably one of my favourite fish, especially the rock mullet (*Mullus surmuletus*) when it is no more than 15 cm (6 in) long and deep-fried after being dusted in flour. The freshness is the most important aspect of every fish, but for red mullet in particular it is essential. It is very delicate, easily perishable and it offers one of the greatest treats if it is cooked within a day of being caught. It is impossible to freeze or preserve it in other ways.

There are two types of red mullet, one that has a more pronounced head and a pinkish red skin: the other is recognized by its sleek head and its red and yellow skin. The former tastes more muddy.

Red mullet is excellent baked, fried or grilled, or used in fish soups where it should be added at the last minute to avoid over-cooking. Larger fish are often filleted to remove the numerous bones. It can also be eaten in a pasta sauce and the best I have ever tasted was *pasta con le triglie* cooked by Pinuccia of the restaurant S. Giovanni at Casarza in Liguria.

Trota / Trout
The trout is probably the best known and most common freshwater fish in Italy, which with her many lakes and rivers offers it the most wonderful habitats. However, demand still exceeds supply and farming is so common that it is almost impossible to buy wild trout. The two varieties favoured by the trout farmers are the *fario* and the rainbow. Both have wonderful firm flesh, made possible by the high quality of lifestyle reproduced in the farmed conditions.

Trout is as popular on the menus of Italian restaurants as it is with ordinary Italians. The people of the northern regions have an especially strong tradition in cooking this lovely fish. Smaller trout, called *trotelle*, are simply fried in butter, but all types of trout are grilled, baked *al cartoccio* (in a paper bag) and even marinated in *carpione* (page 36) or, as they do exceptionally well in Umbria, served with truffles, *trota al tartufo*.

Uova di Pesce, Latte di Pesce / Fish Eggs, Fish Milt
The eggs and milt of various fishes are delicacies in themselves. Eggs can be found in female fish and milt in male fish when approaching sexual maturity, and these are sold by only the very finest fishmongers.

Especially sought after are salted herring roes which are particularly popular in salads. Fresh herring roe has the same consistency as brains and has to be soaked and thoroughly cleaned before being fried in breadcrumbs.

Carp and mackerel roe is very tasty but the most delicate is that of sea bass. Grey mullet and tuna roe are both salted and air-cured to make *bottarga*.

The most curious fish milt is consumed in Venice and is that of cuttlefish. It is called *latte di seppia* and is simply boiled and eaten with lemon juice and salt. The best place to eat this is, without doubt, the restaurant La Madonna, near the Rialto in Venice.

Ventresca di Tonno / Tuna Belly
This is the juiciest part of the tuna and is usually tinned as a preserve. The *ventresca* is particularly fine because of its fatty and gelatinous texture. It is usually more expensive than other parts of the tuna partly because of its popularity as a preserve. Fresh it is used like normal tuna for all sorts of dishes.

Vongola / Clam
Also known as *arsella* in Liguria and Tuscany, clams are small molluscs which are popularly used to make a sauce for spaghetti or linguine. They are very popular all over Italy, but especially in Naples and along the Amalfi and Adriatic coasts, where special machines are used to comb the sandy sea beds in search of them.

There are two main different types, the *gialla* and the larger

vongola verace or carpet shell clam, the latter much sought-after for its better flavour and occasionally eaten raw like oysters. The *tellina* or wedge shell is said to be the best for soup.

Clams are also very good when eaten cooked on their own. Put some good olive oil, garlic, parsley and a little chilli in a pan with a little water. Heat to a high temperature then add the clams. Cover with a lid and steam for 5-6 minutes, or until all the shells have opened. I like to eat them straight from the shell with some good crusty bread to soak up the delicious juices.

Cacciucco

LIVORNESE FISH SOUP

For 6

- 500 g (1 lb) scorfano (see page 25)
- 500 g (1 lb) monkfish
- 225 g (8 oz) octopus
- 225 g (8 oz) squid
- 225 g (8 oz) clams
- 6 tomatoes, chopped
- salt and pepper
- olive oil for frying

For the stock:

- 1 large onion, chopped
- 1–2 carrots, chopped
- 2 celery stalks, chopped
- chunk of wild fennel, chopped
- 2–3 bay leaves
- 12 black peppercorns

Every town on the coast of Italy claims a fish soup or stew. In Liguria it is called buridda *and in neighbouring Tuscany,* cacciucco, *where it is the speciality of the town of Livorno. They are very similar dishes using the freshest of fish locally caught.*

First clean and prepare the fish and shellfish. Set aside the good pieces. To make the stock, put the fish trimmings, such as heads and tails, in a large pan with the onion, carrots, celery, fennel, bay leaves and peppercorns. Add enough water to cover and then simmer very gently for 20 minutes.

Meanwhile heat a layer of olive oil in a large pan, add the pieces of white fish, octopus and squid and fry gently on each side for about a minute. Add the tomatoes. Strain the fish stock and pour in the pan to cover the fish. Simmer for about 3 minutes, then add the clams and cook for a further 2 minutes, until the shells have opened. Season with salt and pepper and serve immediately.

Insalata di Aringhe, Arance e Pompelmi

SALAD OF SMOKED HERRING, ORANGE AND GRAPEFRUIT

For 4

- 2 pink grapefruit
- 4 oranges
- 1 red onion, cut into thin rings
- 4 smoked herring fillets, thinly sliced
- 4 tbsp extra virgin olive oil
- 2 tsp white wine vinegar
- freshly ground black pepper
- fennel fronds, to decorate

This typically refreshing Sicilian recipe probably came about as a way of using the abundant crops of citrus fruit and the smoked herrings that would have been brought to the island by visiting ships.

Peel the grapefruits and oranges, removing all the white pith, then cut out the segments from between the membranes. Do this over a bowl to catch the juice, then squeeze out any juice from the membranes. Arrange the fruit segments on a plate and scatter over the onion rings, then arrange the herring slices on top.

Add the oil, vinegar and some pepper to the grapefruit and orange juice to make a vinaigrette. Mix well and pour over the salad, then decorate with fennel fronds. Serve with good bread.

Antipasti di Mare

From Pinuccia, owner of the San Giovanni restaurant in Casarza, Liguria, comes this series of fish antipasti. *They are all fun to prepare.*

Acciughe Marinate

MARINATED ANCHOVIES

All dishes serve 4

- 1 garlic clove, cut in half
- juice of 2 lemons
- 500 g (1 lb) extremely fresh anchovies
- 90 ml (3 fl oz) olive oil
- 1 tbsp finely chopped flat-leaf parsley
- salt and pepper

These are treated in a similar way to the lake fish or trout on page 37.

Put the garlic in the lemon juice and leave for about an hour, then discard the garlic when the juice has taken on its aroma. Meanwhile, cut the heads off the anchovies, then slit them down the belly, gut them and open them out flat. Lay them skin-side down on a non-metallic plate.

Whisk together the lemon juice, olive oil, parsley, and salt and pepper to taste. Pour this dressing over the anchovies and leave to marinate for at least a couple of hours before serving.

Insalata di Moscardini

BABY OCTOPUS SALAD

- 500 g (1 lb) moscardini (see polpo, page 23)
- 4 tbsp olive oil
- $1^1/_2$ tbsp lemon juice
- 1 garlic clove, very finely chopped
- 1 tbsp chopped flat-leaf parsley
- salt and pepper

Boil the moscardini in lightly salted water for 12 minutes (the larger they are, the more cooking time is required). Drain and dress with the olive oil, lemon juice, garlic, parsley and salt and pepper.

Cozze Ripiene

STUFFED MUSSELS

- 1 kg ($2^1/_4$ lb) large black mussels
- 1 tbsp olive oil
- 2 garlic cloves, finely chopped
- 1 recipe quantity of filling from sardine ripiene (opposite)
- 1 egg, beaten
- black pepper
- breadcrumbs for coating
- olive oil for deep-frying

Clean the mussels (see page 19) and place them in a large pan with the olive oil and garlic. Cook with a lid on for a few minutes, shaking the pan from time to time to allow the mussels to open. When they have all opened, season with black pepper and leave to cool.

Remove the mussels from their shells and enclose each one in a little of the sardine filling. Put back in the shell and then close the shell, leaving a little filling showing. Dip the mussels in the beaten egg and then in breadcrumbs. Deep-fry in olive oil until golden.

Pesce Spada Carpaccio

SWORDFISH CARPACCIO

- 8 very thin slices of fresh swordfish fillet
- 3 tbsp olive oil
- juice of 1 lemon
- 1 tbsp very finely chopped flat-leaf parsley
- salt and pepper

Raw fish has not traditionally been eaten in Italy but it has recently become fashionable. This dish can easily be mistaken for smoked salmon.

Lay the slices of fish on a non-metallic plate. Mix together all the remaining ingredients, seasoning with lots of pepper. Pour this mixture over the fish and leave to marinate for 30 minutes. Serve as an *antipasto*.

TOTANO RIPIENO

2 LARGE TOTANO SQUID, WEIGHING ABOUT 500 G (1 LB) IN TOTAL
25 G (3/4 OZ) BUTTER
BREADCRUMBS FROM 2 BREAD ROLLS
A LITTLE MILK
1 GARLIC CLOVE, VERY FINELY CHOPPED
25 G (3/4 OZ) PINE NUTS
1 TBSP FINELY CHOPPED FLAT-LEAF PARSLEY
2 EGGS
SALT AND PEPPER

STUFFED TOTANO SQUID

The long body of the totano *makes it ideal for stuffing. It is cut into slices and served cold. Ordinary squid will do, just cut them in half.*

Prepare the squid (see Calamaro, page 17) and cut off the tentacles. Chop the tentacles and fry them in the butter for 6–8 minutes, then set aside.

Soak the breadcrumbs in a little milk to cover, then squeeze out the excess liquid. Mix with the garlic, pine nuts, parsley and salt and pepper to taste. Bind with the eggs and stir in the cooked tentacles. Stuff the squid cavities with this mixture and secure with a toothpick or sew up with a needle and kitchen string.

The squid are best steamed for about 30 minutes but you may also braise them in a pan with lard and a little butter for 20 minutes. When the squid are cooked, leave to cool and then slice.

SARDINE RIPIENE

12 VERY FRESH LARGE SARDINES
1 EGG, BEATEN
BREADCRUMBS FOR COATING
OLIVE OIL FOR DEEP-FRYING

FOR THE FILLING:
BREADCRUMBS FROM 2 BREAD ROLLS
A LITTLE MILK
60 G (2 OZ) EXTREMELY FRESH MORTADELLA, DICED
2 EGGS
55 G (1 3/4 OZ) PARMESAN CHEESE, GRATED
1 GARLIC CLOVE, VERY FINELY CHOPPED
2 TBSP FINELY CHOPPED FLAT-LEAF PARSLEY
SALT AND PEPPER

STUFFED SARDINES

Cut the heads off the sardines and bone them, leaving them attached down the back. Next prepare the filling: soak the breadcrumbs in a little milk to cover, then squeeze out the excess liquid. Mix the breadcrumbs with all the remaining filling ingredients and season to taste. Use to stuff the sardines, then close each sardine like a sandwich. Dip them in the beaten egg and then in breadcrumbs. Deep-fry in olive oil until golden, then serve.

CENTRE: SARDINE RIPIENE; (CLOCKWISE FROM THE TOP) TOTANO RIPIENO, COZZE RIPIENE, PESCE SPADA CARPACCIO, ACCIUGHE MARINATE, INSALATA DI MOSCARDINI

Involtini di Pesce Spada

STUFFED SWORDFISH ROLLS

- 8 SLICES OF SWORDFISH, 1 CM (1/2 INCH) THICK, MORE OR LESS THE SAME SHAPE
- 3 TBSP FRESH BREADCRUMBS
- 8 BLACK OLIVES, STONED AND FINELY CHOPPED
- PINCH OF FRESH OR DRIED OREGANO
- 3 TBSP COARSELY CHOPPED FLAT-LEAF PARSLEY
- 4 TBSP OLIVE OIL
- 600 G (1 LB 5 OZ) TOMATO PULP (SEE PAGE 118)
- SALT AND PEPPER

This recipe is typical of Sicily, where swordfish is regarded as a speciality. Almost every family has its own filling but the result is always extremely tasty.

Put the slices of swordfish on top of each other and cut off the pieces sticking out to obtain equal-shaped slices. Finely chop the trimmings.

Make the filling by mixing the breadcrumbs with the olives, oregano, parsley, swordfish trimmings and some salt and pepper. Place the mixture in the centre of each swordfish slice, roll up and secure with a toothpick. Heat the olive oil in a pan, add the swordfish rolls and fry gently for 5 minutes on each side until cooked through. Remove the swordfish from the pan and set aside.

Put the tomatoes in the same pan and simmer for 5 minutes. Add salt to taste, return the fish to the pan and warm through. Remove the toothpicks and serve.

Acciughe Farcite al Forno

STUFFED BAKED ANCHOVIES

- 24 VERY FRESH ANCHOVIES, BONED AND OPENED BUTTERFLY FASHION
- 6 TBSP OLIVE OIL
- 2 GARLIC CLOVES, VERY FINELY CHOPPED
- 4 TBSP FINELY CHOPPED FRESH PARSLEY
- 1 TBSP FINELY CHOPPED FRESH BASIL LEAVES
- 5 SAGE LEAVES, FINELY CHOPPED
- 1 SMALL CHILLI, VERY FINELY CHOPPED
- 25 G (3/4 OZ) PINE NUTS
- 30 G (1 OZ) RAISINS
- JUICE OF 1 LEMON
- 30 G (1 OZ) DRY BREADCRUMBS
- SALT AND PEPPER

Nothing can surpass freshly caught anchovies, which are good eaten raw with just a few drops of lemon juice. This typical Sicilian recipe, with its raisins and pine nuts, has echoes of its Arabic origin.

Preheat the oven to 220°C/425°F/gas7 and grease a baking sheet with some of the olive oil.

In a bowl, mix the garlic, herbs, chilli, pine nuts and raisins with salt and pepper to taste. Add 1 tablespoon of the olive oil and a few drops of lemon juice and mix well.

Lay 12 of the anchovies skin side down next to each other on the prepared baking sheet. Distribute the mixture on top of them, sprinkle with a few drops of lemon juice and sandwich with the remaining anchovies skin side up. Sprinkle with the breadcrumbs and drizzle over the remaining olive oil. Bake for 10-12 minutes, until just starting to brown. Serve hot, sprinkled with the remaining lemon juice, or cold arranged on lemon slices.

SARDINE ALLA BECCAFICO

ROLLED BAKED SARDINES

- 2 TBSP EXTRA-VIRGIN OLIVE OIL
- 125 G ($4^1/_2$ OZ) DRY BREADCRUMBS
- 2 TBSP SOFT RAISINS (SOAKED BEFOREHAND IF NECESSARY)
- 2 TBSP PINE NUTS
- JUICE OF 2 LARGE ORANGES
- SALT AND PEPPER
- 16 VERY FRESH SARDINES, HEADS REMOVED, BUTTERFLIED OPEN AND BACKBONE REMOVED
- 18 FRESH BAY LEAVES

This celebrated Sicilian recipe is called beccafico *because the rolled sardines resemble the little birds 'fig peckers' of which Italians are – or were – very fond.*

In a frying pan, heat the olive oil and fry the breadcrumbs gently, stirring with a wooden spoon, until toasted and brown. Allow to cool.

Preheat the oven to 200°C/400°F/gas6. Add the raisins, pine nuts, the juice of 1 of the oranges, salt and abundant pepper to the fried breadcrumbs. Mix well. Wash the sardines and pat dry with kitchen towel. Arrange them skin side down. Place a spoonful of the filling on each of the sardines and roll them up. Arrange tightly together on a baking tray, placing bay leaves between them, and bake for 20 minutes.

As soon as the sardines come out of the oven, sprinkle them with the juice of the remaining orange.

BAGNA CAÔDA

FOR 6

- 125 G ($4^1/_2$ OZ) BUTTER
- 6 GARLIC CLOVES, CRUSHED
- 300 G ($10^1/_2$ OZ) ANCHOVY FILLETS (BEST IF TAKEN FROM SALTED ANCHOVIES)
- 200 ML (7 FL OZ) EXTRA-VIRGIN OLIVE OIL
- MIXED RAW VEGETABLES, TO SERVE (SEE RIGHT)

There are many versions of this hot Piedmontese dip, which is served with raw vegetables. Because of the amount of garlic it is probably better to eat it at the weekend to avoid antisocial effects. It is usually enjoyed with friends, sharing a common terracotta pot which is kept warm over a candle. Special pots for individual portions are also available.

The vegetables must be extremely fresh and tender, all cut into strips. Choose from cardoons (see Cardo, page 105), Jerusalem artichokes (cleaned and cut into thin slices), red and yellow peppers, raw cauliflower florets, celery stalks, artichoke hearts, spring onions, or whatever else is available. Abundant bread! Abundant wine to drink!

Put the butter and garlic in a terracotta pot over a very gentle flame and leave, stirring occasionally, until the garlic has dissolved in the hot, but not boiling, butter. Add the anchovy fillets and the oil and continue to cook extremely gently until the mixture becomes creamy. The bagna caôda is now ready to be enjoyed by dipping the vegetables in it.

LEFT (CLOCKWISE FROM THE TOP) ACCIUGHE IN SALSA VERDE (PAGE 224), SARDINE ALLA BECCAFICO, ACCIUGHE FARCITE ALL FORNO

INSALATA DI NEONATO

SALAD OF BABY ANCHOVIES

FOR 4

600 G ($1^1/_4$ LB) NEONATI (SEE ACCIUGA, PAGE 14)

3 TBSP EXTRA-VIRGIN OLIVE OIL

JUICE OF 1 LEMON

SALT AND PEPPER

This very simple dish is a speciality of both Liguria and Sicily. The ingredients need only the minimum of cooking, thanks to their combination of quality and flavour. Baby elvers could be substituted for the anchovies.

Wash the fish and cut out any impurities. Bring a large pan of water to the boil, add the fish and cook for $1^1/_2$–2 minutes. Drain and dress with the olive oil, lemon juice, salt if desired and lots of freshly ground black pepper. Delicious eaten as an *antipasto*.

ANGUILLA ALLA LUCIANA

EEL BAKED WITH BAY LEAVES

FOR 6-8

1 LARGE EEL, WEIGHING ABOUT 1.25 KG (2½ LB), OR 2 WEIGHING 800 G (1¾ LB) EACH
FRESHLY PICKED LARGE BAY LEAVES
COARSE SALT

Luciana Florio, a remarkable gentile donna *from Naples, gave us an enormous amount of patient help and this wonderful recipe. The brilliant results belie the simplicity of the preparation. Needless to say the eel has to be alive, or freshly killed by the fishmonger if you cannot do it.*

Preheat the oven to 200°C/400°F/gas6. Kill and skin the eel if your fishmonger has not already done so. Gut the eel and rub with a cloth to remove some of the shine. Cut into 7.5 cm (3 inch) chunks and layer in a terracotta pot, adding some bay leaves and coarse salt between each layer. Bake, uncovered, for 30–40 minutes, depending on the size of the eel – test with a skewer to see if it is done.

BRANZINO ALL'ACQUA DI MARE

SEA BASS COOKED IN SEA WATER

FOR 4

2 SEA BASS, WEIGHING ABOUT 500 G (1 LB) EACH, CLEANED
EQUAL QUANTITIES OF SEAWATER, DRY WHITE WINE AND EXTRA VIRGIN OLIVE OIL (ENOUGH TO REACH THE BELLY OF THE FISH IN THE PAN)
JUICE OF 1 LEMON
1 TBSP PARSLEY LEAVES
1 TBSP OREGANO LEAVES
BLACK PEPPER

This is a very curious recipe from Sicily, in which seawater functions as an ingredient; naturally it should be unpolluted if you manage to find it. Otherwise, use ordinary water and salt.

Put the fish in a large pan with all the remaining ingredients. Cover the pan and bring to the boil. Remove the lid, reduce the heat and simmer for 10 minutes. Turn the fish over and simmer for a further 12 minutes or until cooked through. Serve with boiled potatoes and a spoonful of the cooking liquid.

Sardine in Carpione

MARINATED SWEET-AND-SOUR SARDINES

For 4

12 LARGE FRESH SARDINES, CLEANED
FLOUR FOR DUSTING
OLIVE OIL FOR FRYING

For the marinade:

90 ML (3 FL OZ) OLIVE OIL
1 LARGE RED ONION, THINLY SLICED
1 CARROT, CUT INTO VERY SMALL CUBES
2 BAY LEAVES
2 TBSP RAISINS
1 TBSP PINE NUTS
1 SMALL CHILLI
5 TBSP WHITE WINE VINEGAR
1 SMALL GLASS OF DRY WHITE WINE
1 TSP SUGAR

This is a delightful summer dish which can be served as an antipasto. *Perch, trout and lake fish are all suitable alternatives for marinating* in carpione. *The most important thing is that the fish should be very fresh.*

Dust the sardines in flour, then shallow-fry them in olive oil until crisp on both sides. Arrange them in a single layer in a shallow dish.

To make the marinade, heat the olive oil in a separate pan and fry the onion, carrot, bay leaves, raisins, pine nuts and chilli until the vegetables are soft. Add the vinegar, wine and sugar, mix well and then pour the marinade over the warm fish. Leave to marinate for a few hours before serving.

Capasante al Burro e Limone

SCALLOPS WITH BUTTER AND LEMON

For 4

12 LARGE SCALLOPS, WITH THE CORALS ATTACHED
55 G ($1^3/_4$ OZ) BUTTER
JUICE OF $^1/_2$ LEMON
ABOUT 2 TBSP FISH STOCK
1 TBSP FINELY CHOPPED FLAT-LEAF PARSLEY
SALT AND PEPPER
FLOUR FOR DUSTING

Scallops are one of the most delicate of shellfish. They should be cooked briefly, either by frying or poaching.

Dust the scallops with flour. Heat the butter in a pan, add the scallops and fry for 2 minutes on each side. Remove from the pan and set aside. Add the lemon juice and stock to the pan, stirring to scrape up the sediment from the bottom. If necessary add a little more stock. Stir in the parsley and some salt and pepper. Return the scallops to the pan, heat through briefly and serve.

Lavarello e Trota Marinate

MARINATED LAKE FISH OR TROUT

For 4

4 TBSP EXTRA-VIRGIN OLIVE OIL
JUICE OF 2 LEMONS
FINELY GRATED ZEST OF 1/2 LEMON
1 TSP SUGAR
1 TBSP FINELY GRATED HORSERADISH
600 G (1 1/4 LB) LAKE BREAM OR TROUT FILLET CUT FROM A LARGE FISH, VERY THINLY SLICED
2 TBSP VERY FINELY CHOPPED FLAT-LEAF PARSLEY
SALT AND PEPPER

Only extremely fresh fish are suitable for this uncooked dish. The fillets are 'cooked' by the acid of the lemon juice in the marinade. This modern way of serving fish in Italy is generally known as carpaccio. *Tuna and swordfish can also be prepared like this and, if you omit the horseradish, so can fresh boned anchovies.*

To make the marinade, beat together the oil, lemon juice and zest, sugar, horseradish and salt and pepper to taste. Lay the slices of fish on a non-metallic plate. Spread the marinade over the fish and leave for a couple of hours, then turn the fish over and cover with the marinade that has not been absorbed. Sprinkle with the parsley and serve with bread or grissini as an *antipasto.*

TIRRENIA

Insalata di Mare

SEAFOOD SALAD

For 4

- 2 garlic cloves, cut in half
- Juice of 2 lemons
- 600 g ($1\frac{1}{4}$ lb) mixed seafood, such as prawns, mussels, small octopus, small squid (or large ones cut into rings), clams, or whatever you find at the fishmonger's, cleaned
- 90 ml (3 fl oz) olive oil
- 2 tbsp finely chopped flat-leaf parsley
- Salt and pepper

As with most Italian dishes, the taste of this salad depends on the freshness of the fish rather than on herbs and spices.

Put the garlic in the lemon juice and leave for about an hour, then discard the garlic when the juice has taken on its aroma. Meanwhile, cook the shellfish in a little water in a covered pan for a few minutes until the shells open. Remove and discard all the shells. Simmer all the other fish in a large pan of water until just cooked and then drain.

Mix the lemon juice with the olive oil, parsley, and salt and pepper to taste. Mix this dressing with the fish, then leave to rest and cool.

Mix again, then serve as an *antipasto* with bread or *grissini*.

Spiedino di Grandi Pesci

SKEWERS OF FISH

For 4

- 1 kg ($2\frac{1}{4}$ lb) mixed fish fillets (see right), cut into large cubes

For the marinade:

- Juice of 1 lemon
- 1 small glass of white wine
- 1 tbsp balsamic vinegar
- 3 tbsp extra virgin olive oil
- 1 tbsp finely chopped parsley
- 1 tbsp finely chopped sage
- 1 tbsp finely chopped mint
- Salt and pepper

Cooking on a skewer works well if you choose chunks of large fish such as tuna, swordfish, large trout, salmon, turbot, halibut or monkfish. A mixture of these is even better.

Make the marinade by mixing all the ingredients together. Put the fish in a bowl and pour over the marinade. Leave for a few hours.

Thread chunks of alternate types of fish on to 4 long skewers and grill for 3-5 minutes, depending on the size of the chunks, on each side over a charcoal grill, on a ridged cast iron pan or under a domestic grill. Baste with the marinade during cooking. Serve with a rocket salad.

INSALATA DI MARE

Seppie al Nero

CUTTLEFISH IN ITS OWN SAUCE

For 4

- 700–800 G (1½ – 1¾ LB) FRESH CUTTLEFISH
- 90 ML (3 FL OZ) OLIVE OIL
- 1 SMALL ONION, VERY FINELY CHOPPED
- 1 SMALL GARLIC CLOVE, VERY FINELY CHOPPED
- 1 SMALL GLASS OF DRY WHITE WINE
- SALT AND PEPPER

You must use cuttlefish for this recipe in order to have enough black ink. Squid and octopus also contain ink, but in less quantity. Serve with boiled rice or with polenta and bread.

Clean the cuttlefish very thoroughly (see Seppia, page 25), detaching the small, silver-coloured ink sac and setting it aside. Cut off the tentacles and wash them.

Heat the oil in a large pan, add the onion and garlic and cook for a few minutes. Add the white wine and bubble for a few minutes to evaporate the alcohol, then add the cuttlefish and tentacles, cover the pan and cook gently for 20 minutes. Now add the black ink and dilute with a little water to make it liquid. Season with salt and pepper and cook for another 10 minutes or until the cuttlefish is tender.

Stocco alla Genovese

STOCKFISH STEW

For 4

- 1 KG (2¼ LB) STOCKFISH (SEE BACCALÀ, PAGE 16)
- 90 ML (3 FL OZ) EXTRA-VIRGIN OLIVE OIL
- 1 LARGE ONION, FINELY CHOPPED
- ABOUT 15 TASTY BLACK OLIVES, IDEALLY LIGURIAN TAGGIASCA
- 2 GARLIC CLOVES, COARSELY CHOPPED
- 4 ANCHOVY FILLETS
- 2 TBSP COARSELY CHOPPED FLAT-LEAF PARSLEY
- BLACK PEPPER

Of the many stockfish recipes from all over Italy, this one is the simplest but also the tastiest. In Liguria they use light local olive oil and the delicious Taggiasca olives, which impart a wonderful flavour to the dish.

Soak the stockfish in cold water overnight, then drain, cover with fresh water and bring to the boil. Reduce the heat and simmer for 2–2½ hours, until tender. Drain and remove the flesh from the bones.

Heat the olive oil in a pan and fry the onion in it until soft. Add the olives, garlic and anchovies and cook for 5 minutes. Stir in the fish and parsley and cook for a further 5 minutes, then season to taste with black pepper. Serve with polenta (see page 173).

Triglie alle Olive

RED MULLET WITH OLIVES

For 4

- 8 whole fresh red mullet, each weighing about 125 g ($4^1/2$ oz), or 4 weighing about 250 g (9 oz), cleaned and scaled
- 3 tbsp extra-virgin olive oil
- 1 garlic clove, finely chopped
- 3 tbsp finely chopped parsley
- 85 g (3 oz) small tasty black olives, ideally Ligurian Taggiasca
- 4 anchovy fillets, coarsely chopped
- 4 tbsp passata
- 200 g (7 oz) tomatoes, peeled, deseeded and cubed
- salt and pepper

In Liguria it is still possible for those with a very good relationship with their local fishmonger to obtain wonderful fresh red mullet. Combine this with the local olive oil, olives and some herbs and you have a superb dish. For those who dislike the many bones in small fish, you can use fillets from larger-sized fish.

Heat the olive oil in a pan and fry the fish for 4 minutes on each side if small or 6-8 minutes if larger. Remove from the pan with a slotted spoon and set aside.

Add the garlic, parsley and olives to the pan and cook gently for 2 or 3 minutes, then add the anchovies. Stir until the anchovies dissolve to a purée.

Add the passata, followed by the tomatoes. Bring to a simmer and return the fish to the pan. Cook for 5 minutes each side. Season to taste and serve warm.

Top: Stocco alla Genovese; bottom: Triglie alle Olive

SAUTÉ MISTO DI VONGOLE E DATTERI

MIXED SAUTÉ OF CLAMS AND SEA DATES

FOR 4

- 1 KG ($2^1/_4$ LB) CARPET SHELL CLAMS
- 1 KG ($2^1/_4$ LB) TELLINE (WEDGE SHELL) CLAMS
- 500 G (1 LB) SEA DATES OR SEA TRUFFLES (SEE DATTERO, PAGE 19, AND TARTUFO DI MARE, PAGE 26)
- 4 TBSP EXTRA-VIRGIN OLIVE OIL
- 1 GARLIC CLOVE, FINELY CHOPPED
- 2 TBSP CHOPPED FLAT-LEAF PARSLEY
- BLACK PEPPER

Everyone in the South likes to eat this speciality made with various types of clams and sea dates. We were very lucky to find sea dates – in my opinion one of the best shellfish – because fishing for them has now been restricted. You could use one just type of clam if that is all you can get but the flavour won't be as interesting.

Thoroughly clean the shellfish under cold running water, discarding any that are open or that do not look very healthy.

Heat the olive oil in a large pan and briefly fry the garlic, ensuring that it does not change colour. Put all the shellfish in the pan and cook with the lid on. After a few minutes the shells will open up. Keeping the lid on, shake the pan so that all the shells cook evenly. Check that all the shells have opened, then stir in the parsley and abundant freshly ground black pepper.

Serve on a plate with the lovely sea water sauce that comes from the seafood, which should be mopped up by very good bread. It is customary to eat this dish with your fingers, sucking out the meat from the shells. Provide finger bowls!

Calamaretti in Umido

SMALL BRAISED SQUID

For 4

- BREADCRUMBS FROM 1 FRESH BREAD ROLL
- A LITTLE MILK
- 600 G (1¼ LB) SMALL SQUID, CLEANED (SEE CALAMARO, PAGE 17)
- 1 GARLIC CLOVE, VERY FINELY CHOPPED
- 3 TBSP VERY FINELY CHOPPED FLAT-LEAF PARSLEY
- 4 TBSP EXTRA-VIRGIN OLIVE OIL
- 2 LARGE RIPE TOMATOES, PEELED, DESEEDED AND CHOPPED
- SALT AND PEPPER

When I bought the fish for this recipe in Pozzuoli, I was given a handful of seaweed, which I dipped in an extremely light batter and then fried very briefly to serve with the squid.

Soak the breadcrumbs in a little milk to cover, then squeeze out the excess liquid. Cut off the tentacles from the squid. Chop the tentacles and mix them with the breadcrumbs, garlic, parsley and some salt and pepper. Stuff this mixture into the cavities of the squid, filling them about three-quarters full.

Heat the oil in a large pan and briefly fry the squid until they become slightly pinkish in colour. Add the chopped tomatoes and cook for about 15 minutes, until you obtain a lovely sauce.

Eggs, Poultry & Game

POLLAME E SELVAGGINA

During the past fifty years, the poultry business has undergone a kind of industrial revolution and vast numbers of birds are now kept in huge sheds, often in terrible conditions. This has meant that free-range chickens are once again in demand, although both they and their eggs naturally cost more to buy.

In many areas of Piedmont, Lombardy, Veneto and Emilia-Romagna – and here and there all over the South – there are still, however, free-range farms producing the tastiest corn-fed chickens. The poor quality of mass-produced poultry also means that any Italian who can afford it still usually keeps domestic animals of their own. When I was growing up in Borgofranco D'Ivrea, this was then quite common and my family was able to keep a few chickens, some ducks, some rabbits and a goat, so that we had milk every day, a couple of eggs and, from time to time, the meat of one of the animals or fowl.

Duck and geese are also favourites for Italians, although they are more popular in some regions than others. In Emilia-Romagna, geese are raised for their meat and the production of *fegato grasso*, the equivalent of the French delicacy *foie gras*, the enlarged livers of force-fed birds; while in the province of Vercelli in Lomellina, traditional and delicious *salame d'oca* or goose salami is made, although production is so small that there is only enough for local consumption so there is none left for export.

Rabbit is also popular in Italy, often eaten as a replacement for wild hare or used as an alternative to chicken because of its white meat. Rabbit is most frequently cooked in a sauce to make a *ragù* as the meat, especially that of the farmed variety, does not have a very developed flavour. One of the best ways to enjoy rabbit is cooked with mushrooms and accompanied by polenta to make *coniglio alla cacciatora*, rabbit the hunter's way.

It is well known that Italians particularly love to eat small wild songbirds and, while I have eaten *passeri* (sparrows) in Bergamo where they prepare them best, I do not consider them a curiosity that I could become passionate about because they simply do not have enough flesh on them. Something bigger is preferable, and wild quail, pigeon and partridge remain my favourites. Tuscany, Piedmont, Liguria, Lombardy, Trentino, Veneto and Calabria are the great game regions and in these areas game is

prepared in so many ways that recipes differ from village to village and sometimes from family to family.

In the past, hunting game was a natural way of getting meat on the table. Today, the average Italian still eats game two or three times a year, which is very much part of a long culinary tradition. The whole range of game is eaten, from the smallest wild birds to the largest furred game such as deer. Nowadays, with growing concern for the preservation of wildlife, hunting is carefully controlled so that people can satisfy their rights without compromising the balance of nature. A fine example of this is at the Sagra del Tordo or festival of thrushes in Montalcino, which still takes place each year, but using farm-raised quails instead.

Sardinia has an incredible tradition of hunting and cooking game and the Sardinians cook most of their game on the spit, marinated and basted with unique natural ingredients and herbs that exist only on the island. Small *cinghiali*, or wild boar, are cooked in ovens made of hollows dug out of the earth. The prepared boar is cooked with *mirto*, a local wild bush like rosemary, and other herbs, all of which impart the most delicious flavours to the meat.

Larger game, like deer, chamois and wild goat inhabit the Aosta Valley and other Alpine valleys, and are used to make the unique recipes of the area, particularly *mucetta*, a kind of air-dried fillet of deer which is a great delicacy.

Tuscany is another region that has enjoyed a long history of hunting and cooking game. Of the many products and recipes it has created, its delicious wild boar sausages are particularly noteworthy. The locals also have a wonderful way of cooking wild fowl on skewers, each bird being separated by pieces of bread to absorb the cooking juices.

Eggs are no less valued than poultry or game in Italy, and when I was a child during the war, my grandmother used to make me suck the contents of a newly laid raw egg through the shell, presenting me with the first culinary challenge to my taste buds. I didn't much enjoy the experience, but I swallowed the thing down in the name of good health. Eggs have always been full of symbolism, evoking the very essence of the perpetuation of life. They are also probably one of the most popular and complete foods, the yolk alone containing most of the necessary vitamins, proteins and trace elements.

It is possible to make a meal with a whole egg, especially if you shave some truffle on top, but the egg can also be used to thicken sauces, make pastries or mayonnaise, or it can be beaten with sugar to make a heavenly frothy dessert that can be flavoured with marsala wine or strong coffee. The whites, on the other hand can be beaten to make a stiff foam that is used to lighten sauces and mousses, as well as being cooked with sugar to make meringue. They are also mixed with flour to make egg pasta, giving it a greater nutritional value and a special delicacy and flavour.

Eggs are particularly significant at Easter, representing new life. In Italy a special pastry called *casatello* or *casatiello* is made for the festival. Whole raw eggs in their shells are embedded on the surface of the pastry and baked with it. Along with other Easter pastries, the *casatello* is given to friends and family to signify peace and prosperity, all indicated by the quantity of eggs used to make them.

LEFT: A GAME BUTCHER PROUDLY DISPLAYS A RANGE OF WILD BOAR SPECIALITIES.

RIGHT: TYPICAL UMBRIAN GAME COUNTRY.

A-Z of Poultry & Game

ALLODOLA / SKYLARK
This small bird can be found only in central and southern Italy, where it is in abundant supply during the months of October to November and March to April when it is migrating. It could easily be mistaken for a sparrow but, unlike the sparrow, it builds its nest on the ground and mainly feeds on grains, giving it an exquisite flavour. It is just a pity that it yields such a small amount of meat. Hunting of the bird is now very restricted and is soon to be made totally illegal.

Because of its size it is often cooked with other, larger birds and is used to give flavour to *ragùs*. In Tuscany, skylarks are wrapped in pancetta and loaded on long skewers between chunks of bread and bay leaves, then spit-roasted or grilled and basted with virgin olive oil, salt and pepper.

ANATRA, ANITRA / DUCK
Under these names are grouped all types of domestic or wild ducks. Whatever form it takes, however, duck is very much loved by Italians and it is much used in their cuisine, especially in the winter. Duck flesh is quite dark and gamy, and quite fatty. Always buy fresh duck as the frozen variety loses much of the quality of the meat.

The most popular variety of farmed duck is the *anatra muta*, because of its free-range lifestyle (its wings are clipped so it can't fly away, but it is left free to forage for food in ponds and the like). The main farming areas for duck in Italy are Piedmont, Lombardy, Emilia-Romagna and the Veneto. In Piedmont and Emilia-Romagna, duck are force-fed to enlarge the liver to make *fegato grasso* (foie gras), more for export to other countries where this speciality is much more appreciated.

There is also an incredible variety of wild duck, *anitra selvatica*, which is usually hunted in the autumn. It is very different to farmed duck, not only in look and taste, but also in the tenderness of its meat. Italians do not hang wild birds for very long and in some cases, as with pheasant, they tend to cook them straightaway, mostly baked or grilled. Surprisingly for such a fatty bird, duck for roasting are often barded with strips of Parma ham, but this does give an incomparable flavour.

BECCACCIA / WOODCOCK
The woodcock is not native to Italy, but it does fly over when migrating in spring and autumn. It has a long flat beak with brownish plumage to camouflage it in its natural woodland habitat. Its flesh has a wonderful flavour and it is one of the best-loved wild birds. Because it cannot be farmed, it is in short supply and as a result has been over-hunted to the extent that in some parts of Italy the shooting or netting of this bird is forbidden.

Once caught, the woodcock should be hung for at least 5 days. It should only be plucked immediately before cooking. When plucking the feathers great care needs to be taken not to tear the skin,

LEFT: BECCACCIA

and it is also important not to wash the woodcock after plucking to retain flavour. Instead the bird should be singed over a flame to burn off any feather stubs. A small minority of purists prefer the woodcock undrawn for better flavour.

The bird is delicious oven-roasted for about 10 minutes only and served on a circle of toasted bread to collect its juices. Very young birds may also be grilled, basted with olive oil and the cooking juices; older birds are often casseroled with mushrooms. One bird is plenty for one person. The woodcock may also be stuffed with a thrush as they do in Tuscany.

BECCACCINO / SNIPE
Snipe enjoys a similar gastronomic reputation as the *beccaccia* or woodcock. As with the woodcock, it cannot be raised commercially, which might in part contribute to its popularity. The snipe can be found in estuaries and lakes, where it rests while on its migration in spring and autumn. It is particularly sought-after in the autumn, when it is good and fat after a summer of feeding. The dimensions of this bird are similar to that of the woodcock and, as with its cousin, one bird provides a good meal for one person. It is prepared and cooked in a similar way to the woodcock.

BECCAFICO / FIG PECKER OR BLACKCAP
Various small birds belong to this family, which takes its name from their habit of eating figs, grapes and other juicy berries. Their meat is especially flavoursome when they feed on figs, of which they are particularly fond. They are quite rare birds and because of this their hunting is usually illegal. The majority of those sold in specialist shops come from abroad so that the consciences of the Italians who enjoy them are not troubled. The birds are prepared and cooked in the same way as sparrows. In Sicily, the name of this bird has been given to a recipe for sardines, *sardine alla beccafico* (see page 33), which probably indicates that the fish should be cooked in the same way as the bird.

CAMOSCIO / CHAMOIS, WILD GOAT
This wild and very sprightly goat is an inhabitant of the northern Alps and Abruzzo. Its dark and very

Right: cervo

gamy flesh is treated very much as a delicacy in Italy and is particularly popular in the Aosta Valley and the Dolomites, where it lives above the tree-line high up on the hills at altitudes of 1,500-3,000 metres.

In Italy the hunting of chamois is limited because of its short supply, but frozen chamois can be bought from other countries. Although the frozen variety tends to be more tender it does not, however, have the wonderful flavour of the real thing. Incidentally, chamois leather is a by-product of this animal.

Mucetta is a special air-dried fillet of chamois which is served thinly sliced as an *antipasto*. This tradition-al method of preserving meat was a necessity for inhabitants of that part of the world as provision for the long winter months. Today, how-ever, it is a delicacy sold at very high prices.

Another way of preparing chamois meat is to stew it with wine, carrots, onions and celery, or in a spicy mix flavoured with cinnamon and nutmeg, to be served with polenta.

CAPPONE / CAPON

The production of capon (a castrated cockerel) is almost exclusively limited to the Christmas period, when this bird is the centrepiece of the celebrations. The main regions where capons are farmed are Veneto, Emilia-Romagna, Lombardy and Piedmont.

Once castrated, it takes just six or seven months for the young cockerel to grow to an impressive 3-5 kg (6-11 lb), with extremely tender and juicy flesh. It is prepared and cooked just like a normal chicken. A particularly good way is boiling, as is done in various parts of Piedmont and Emilia-Romagna. This cooking method produces the most wonderful stock, which is used to cook tortellini. The bird itself gives a generous amount of meat that can be eaten as a part of *bollito misto* (page 92), popular all over northern Italy with *cugna* (see Cotogna, page 265) or with *mostarda di cremona* (page 269).

CAPRIOLO / ROE BUCK OR ROE DEER

The male of the deer family can be easily recognised by its antlers. It is a medium-sized deer with a red-brown coat that changes to grey-brown in winter. It lives in hilly woodland areas and so cannot be found in Sicily or Sardinia, but is abundant in the rest of Italy, especially in the Alps and Apennines.

I once tried *capriolo carpaccio* made with the fillet of the roe deer, which was sublime – especially as it was garnished with a few slices of truffle. The meat can also be used to make a delicious *ragù di capriolo*, with rosemary, juniper berries, nutmeg, cinnamon, anchovy and wine, which goes wonderfully well with polenta and pasta in *pappardelle al sugo di capriolo*. It can also be cut into medallions and cooked with chanterelle mushrooms. These are, however, just a few suggestions for this highly prized meat.

CERVO / RED DEER

This most majestic of all deer is almost extinct in the wild in Italy. There are a few herds in national parks, such as Gran Paradiso in Piedmont, to remind people what Italian fauna used to be like. In addi-tion to the attractions of its meat, known as venison, the deer's massive antlers have a multitude of uses and can be carved into many things, from knife handles to buttons.

Almost all the venison now eaten in Italy comes from Eastern Europe or from Scandinavia, where it is farmed. The deer can grow up to a weight of 350 kg (7 cwt) and its meat is one of the best and healthiest, as it is low in fat and cholesterol. Because it tends to be dry, the meat is usually first marinated in wine and olive oil. It is excellent in stews, *ragùs* and in pot roasts, for which the saddle is especially good. Usual added flavourings include wine, garlic and lemon. Finally, venison can also be roasted in the traditional British style.

CHIOCCIOLA, SEE LUMACA

CIBREO / GIBLET STEW

There are various way of using the *rigaglie* or giblets of chicken or other poultry in Italian cuisine, but the two most popular recipes are *finanziera* from Piedmont and *cibreo* from Tuscany, see Cibreo di Rigaglie, page 58.

It is not certain who created the dish of *cibreo*, but it must have been a *gourmand* or gourmet of the Renaissance period and someone who could not bear to throw anything away! Ingredients include the cockscomb and the testicles, the hen's unborn eggs, the liver, heart and even the sliced gizzards – all in a simple butter sauce enriched with egg yolks and lemon juice.

Whichever bird is used, the result

is stunning and extremely tasty, usually accompanied by rice or polenta. However, you should only eat this dish in places that are well known for using only the freshest of the ingredients.

CINGHIALE / WILD BOAR
Given that Italians love pork of any description, either cooked or preserved, it is not surprising that the wild version, wild boar, excites them so much. Sometimes considered a pest, boar live in the hilly woods of Tuscany, Umbria, Abruzzo, and any other area where there is thick, inaccessible undergrowth in which it can hide and feed on juicy, tender shoots and berries.

Hunting wild boar can be dangerous because this animal, when under pressure, will attack humans. Boar-hunting is, however, a major sport in the regions of Sardinia, Sicily and Calabria, and a successful hunt is accompanied by enthusiastic celebrations.

In Tuscany, wild boar is used to produce many foods, including hams, salamis and *salamini*. While fresh it is wonderful in stews and *ragùs*, such as Ciriole al Ragù di Cinghiale (page 61) and almost every Tuscan and Umbrian family keeps frozen wild boar to make a *ragù* to serve with the famous pinci pasta, hand-made giant spaghetti. Due to big demand for wild boar, many half-wild boar are farmed in enclosed woody areas leading a semi-wild life, producing a less gamy meat.

LEFT: A WILD BOAR IN UMBRIA, HUNTED BY CARLO MONTANI.

CIVÉ, SEE SALMI

COLOMBACCIO, SEE PALOMBACCIO

COLOMBO, PICCIONE / PIGEON
This is the domestic version of *colombaccio* (wood pigeon) and is farmed almost everywhere because of the increasing demand. The common pigeon can be found everywhere, from San Marco in Venice to Piazza del Duomo in Milan, not to mention London's Trafalgar Square, and is a bird that has adapted itself to every situation. Obviously the polluted city pigeon is not really suitable for human consumption, but it is a pity considering they are magnificently fed with grains by the multitude of tourists trying to play Saint Francis of Assisi, their meat could otherwise be particularly good.

Farmed pigeon are not only safe to eat but tasty too, even if they are not as good as the wild variety – the advantage for some is that there is no need to disguise the gamy flavour and they don't require as lengthy cooking as wood pigeon.

Pigeons are sold cleaned and ready for cooking and are used in famous dishes such as *piccione alle olive*, pigeon with olives, and in casseroles. You can tell the age of pigeon by the beak; the younger it is the more elastic the beak.

CONIGLIO / RABBIT
After pork and chicken, rabbit is one of the most popular meats in Italy. Wild rabbit, *coniglio selvatico*, is rare as the animal is almost totally extinct from the countryside. However, the

ABOVE: CONIGLIO

lepre or hare (opposite) is still likely to be the trophy of the Italian hunter.

A small number of rabbits are kept in Italy by anyone who has the space and facilities, but most rabbit is farmed. *Coniglio alla cacciatora*, with mushrooms, is the best-known rabbit recipe, but rabbit *ragù*, made with tomatoes and served with polenta, is also a classic dish. In Liguria, the rabbit is also very much in demand, see Coniglio Affogato alla Ligure, page 62.

CRESTE DI GALLO, SEE POLLO

DAINO / FALLOW DEER
The fallow deer reaches an adult weight of about 100 kg (16 stones), has a coat that varies from darker red-brown in the summer to pale brown in the winter and the male can be identified by the flat horns on its head. Fallow deer live in Sardinia and in some national parks in northern Italy.

The meat of fallow deer is similar to that of other venison and cooks in the same way, although it does need marinating for some time in red wine to tenderize it. I also add some grapefruit juice to the marinade to take away the excessive gamy flavour. The best and most tender cuts are the saddle and the leg. See also Cervo.

DINDO, SEE TACCHINO

FAGIANO / PHEASANT
The noble pheasant was introduced to Europe from Asia during the Middle Ages. It was particularly popular in Tuscany, where its feathers were used to decorate the

tables and the serving dishes whenever it appeared on the menu. The male bird is famous for his beautiful and ornate feathers, while the female looks a little drab. The male is also larger in size than his female counterpart, a fact which is important when buying a brace, a pair of birds of which one is male and the other female.

Italians do not like wild pheasant to be hung for too long and the farmed variety are not hung at all because they are so tender. Pheasant is popular in the north and centre of Italy, especially in Tuscany and Umbria, which have a culinary history in the preparation of these birds. Pheasant has a lovely gamy taste and fragrance, and the rather dark meat contains only a small quantity of fat. It is a fairly versatile bird and is often cooked in a casserole with wild berries to complement its flavour, or simply roasted in the oven after it has been rubbed with olive oil, salt and pepper, or occasionally flavoured with truffles.

FARAONA, GALLINA FARAONA / GUINEA FOWL

It is believed that this bird, well-known to the Greeks and Romans, was introduced from the Gulf of Guinea into Europe by Portuguese sea adventurers around the fifteenth century.

In taste, the guinea fowl has a flavour somewhere between that of the chicken and the pheasant. This bird lives wild in its country of origin, but in Italy and most of the rest of Europe it is mainly raised on farms. Its plumage is typically white spotted with grey, making it one of the most elegant and beautiful of birds.

It is equally good roasted, casseroled or braised and its tender and delicate meat represents a welcome, tasty and sophisticated alternative to chicken.

FEGATINO DI POLLO / CHICKEN LIVER

One of the most underrated parts of the chicken, the liver is something which makes the hearts of offal lovers beat faster. This is an extremely versatile ingredient, which can be transformed into many lovely dishes. It is particularly good for making pâtés, as well as the foundation for various sauces for pasta and risotto. Chicken livers are also an ingredient in the famous dishes of Cibreo (page 58) and *finanziera*. See also Pollo and Rigaglie.

FEGATO GRASSO, SEE ANATRA AND OCA

FOLAGA / COOT

The coot is a bird which lives on and around river estuaries. Because of its fishy taste it used to be eaten in Italy on Fridays as an acceptable alternative to fish. This distinguishing factor is exactly the reason that it is not much eaten in Italy today and in this it has much in common with the rare yellow- and red-beaked bird *gallinella d'acqua* or moorhen.

FROLLATURA

This is the term for the hanging of game and other meat to allow the flesh to become more tender. *Frollare sotto pelle* means the animal is killed and drawn and left to hang with the skin or plumage on for anything up to 7 days.

GALLETTO, GALLINA, SEE POLLO

GALLINELLA D'ACQUA, SEE FOLAGA

GALLO, SEE POLLO

GALLO CEDRONE / GROUSE

In my opinion this is the best of the game birds. Grouse is quite rare in Italy and is a protected species, so I am especially grateful to live in Britain where I can get Scottish grouse, although it is increasingly scarce here too. In Scotland, grouse nest on open moorlands, while in Italy they prefer the habitat of pine forests. Its diet of berries and insects imparts an irresistible flavour to its very dark and fleshy breast. It needs to be hung, unplucked, for at least 3 or 4 days. When in season it has prime position on my restaurant menu, when I like to serve it lightly roasted, so it is still pink, then served with chanterelle mushrooms.

LEPRE / HARE

The most coveted game of the Italian hunters is the hare. Belonging to the same family as the *coniglio* or rabbit, the hare reaches the greater weight of up to 7 kg (16 lb). It differs from the wild rabbit, with which it is often confused, in that it has longer hind legs than forelegs and its meat is dark red in colour. The astuteness and speed of the hare are legendary and hunters who seek this prey without the help of a dog are rarely successful in catching it.

As the blood of the hare is a key ingredient for the marinating and cooking of the animal, it is especially important when buying hare that you check it is very fresh and properly butchered. Frozen, farm-raised hare lack this vital ingredient and, as a result, dishes cooked using them cannot match the flavour of those using their freshly butchered, wild cousins. The hanging process, especially of heavier, older animals, takes place in

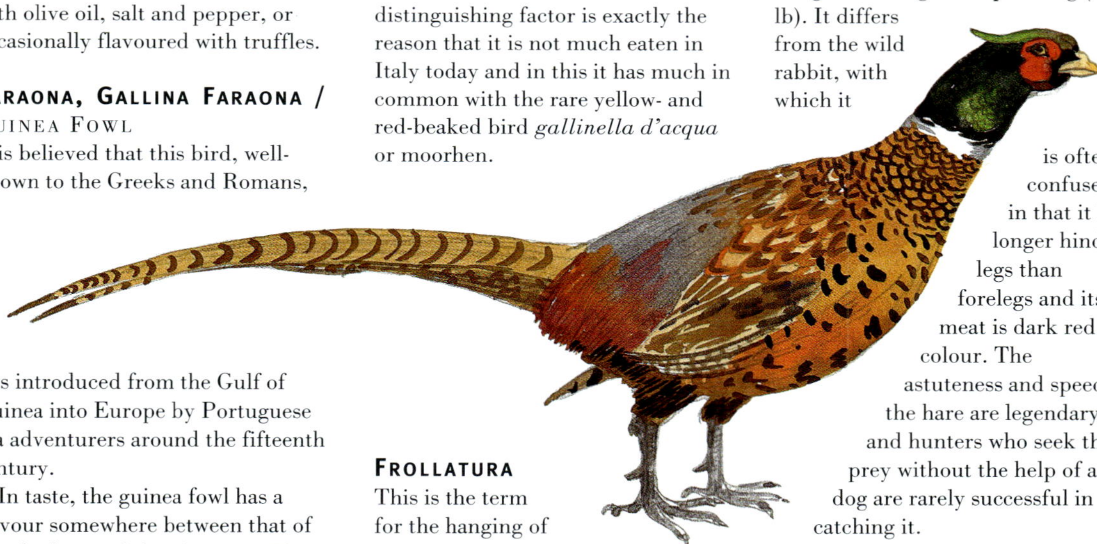

RIGHT: FAGIANO

Top left: lumache di terra

Bottom left: lumachine, small Roman snails

a marinade of blood, wine and spices (see Lepre in Salmi, page 63) and can take at least two days.

Hare is usually stewed to produce a delicious *ragù* that can either be served with polenta or with pasta to form the famous *pappardelle al sugo di lepre*. It is often cooked with spices, such as nutmeg and cloves, and even flavoured with cocoa powder. Whichever way it is cooked, it should be on the menu of every serious restaurant in Italy.

Lumaca di Terra, Bovolo, Marruzelle / Snail

Snails are not easy to categorize as, although they are wild, they are totally different to any other game. Freshly collected snails need to be cleaned or deslimed (*spurgare*) by allowing them to feed on rusk, fresh nettle leaves and salt for a couple of days. They can then be washed and cooked in salted water. When they are done, pull the snail out of its shell, discard the black tail and wash the shell. The snails can then be used according to the recipe you are using. I cannot understand why anyone bothers with tinned snails which have been cooked then stuffed back into their shell, although frozen ones are acceptable.

You can cook snails at home and one of the best ways is Lumachine al Sugo (see page 63), although the larger snails are also good eaten briefly blanched then stuffed with plenty of butter, garlic and parsley and baked in a hot oven. The memory of eating *marruzzelle*, as they call them locally, on street corners in Naples is now dim, but I did see them recently being cooked and sold in a street market in Milan. In Naples, *marruzzelle al sugo* was made with snails harvested from plants growing near the sea and then cooked in a hot tomato sauce so they could be simply sucked out of their shells. They were delicious.

While freshly cooked snails are a true pleasure, the recent trend of eating snails' eggs or snail caviar is just a commercially generated fad. Although the eggs resemble fish caviar in appearance, unlike the sturgeon snails produce very few eggs and those they do are extremely difficult to collect.

Mucetta, see Camoscio

Oca / Goose

There are two types of domesticated goose raised in Italy. The first, the smaller of the two and with grey plumage, is only kept for its meat and comes mainly from Piedmont,

Emilia-Romagna and Padua. The second is the Toulouse type, which can reach a weight of 10 kg (22 lb) and is especially raised for the production of *foie gras* (*fegato grasso*). In Italy, the goose used to have a similar status to the pig because, like the pig, the whole bird had a use, whether it was the meat and fat or the fattened liver and feathers.

Geese are only raised for *foie gras* in Lomellina, a small area between Lombardy and Piedmont. In this part of Italy, goose is also made into a delicious triangular salami called *salame d'oca*. The meat and fat are minced then stuffed into the skin of the long neck and then sewn up tightly. The obvious benefit is that, because it does not include pork, the salami can be eaten by those whose religious belief makes it impossible to eat pork.

Fegato grasso, the liver of force-fed geese, is also a very important product of the bird. The delicious liver can be sliced and fried or made into delicate and expensive pâtés. The French are well known for being particularly fond of their *foie gras*, but the Romans also had much appreciation for it and only now has it seen a revival in modern Italian cooking.

Goose is very similar in appearance and taste to duck, the only real culinary difference being that duck can be slightly undercooked, so that it is pink, and can be eaten cold. The fat content of goose means that it is probably only palatable when cooked all the way through and eaten warm. As with duck, goose benefits from being served or cooked with a slightly acidic sauce, in order to counterbalance this fattiness. Various fruits, such as cherries, blueberries, raspberries and oranges can be used, although balsamic vinegar will give the same contrasting tartness. A series of *asprettos*, vinegars made from fruit (see Aceto di Frutta, page 208) are now available to produce the most flavoursome sauces.

In Italy, goose is mainly eaten at Christmas, like turkey and capon. It is roasted or chopped into portions

ABOVE: OCA

the ordinary variety and one bird makes a fine meal for one person. They are cooked much like ordinary pigeons, as long as you bear in mind that the flesh is better slightly undercooked, to make the most of its juiciness. One curious way of preparing the bird is the Tuscan practice of puréeing the cooked flesh to a paste and spreading this on *crostini*, see Palombacci sui Crostini, see page 60.

and cooked in a sort of casserole. If you roast a goose, make sure you collect the fat from the roasting tray after it has been cooked because, once cold, it solidifies and is delicious served on toast or used for adding flavour to other dishes, such as roast potatoes.

PALOMBACCIO, COLOMBACCIO / WOOD PIGEON

Wood pigeon has a much higher reputation in Italy than the common pigeon. The flavour of the wood pigeon's very dark gamy meat is loved by gourmets, who enjoy this bird with equal enthusiasm whether roasted or used in sauces for dressing pasta.

Colombacci sometimes mix with their city cousins when on migration, but they generally prefer to live in the woods and countryside. Farmers in some parts of the country hang up terracotta pots on their outside walls where the birds can nest. Of course, this simply makes them easier prey for their landlords. The diet of the wood pigeon consists mostly of corn and this gives their meat a particularly fine wild taste.

Wood pigeon need to be hung for a few days, so they can ripen. After this they are sold unplucked, with their giblets still intact. They need to be plucked carefully and thoroughly cleaned. The liver is especially good and so it is worth saving when the bird is drawn. The wood pigeon is generally larger than

PERNICE / PARTRIDGE

There are three varieties of partridge in Italy. The most sought-after is the red-legged (*pernice rossa*), because it has the most delicate flesh and is the only variety which is still completely wild, and available from specialist suppliers only. The grey-legged (*pernice grigia* or *starna*) is less flavoursome and it is mostly raised on farms and sold commercially. The third type, the yellow-leg, can only be found in Sardinia, is similar to the red-legged variety and is equally delicious.

Wild partridges should be hung, drawn but unplucked, for 2-3 days at least to allow the meat to tenderize. The best way to cook partridge is to pan-fry the birds briefly to seal the juices, then to roast them in a very hot oven for no more than 20 minutes. The heart and livers are also very tasty and are delicious when sautéed, reduced to a course paste and smeared on toasted bread, with the roasted birds served on top.

PICCIONE, SEE COLOMBO

POLLO, POLLASTRELLO, POLLASTRINA / CHICKEN

The chicken is the most common source of meat in the world; the reason being that it is extremely easy and economical to raise, as it is cheap to feed and quick to grow. The hen also produces eggs as well as meat. The term *pollo*, like 'chicken', is used for both the hen and cock birds and *gallo* is the name for a fully grown male or cock. Try not to think the Italians barbarians because they eat the pride of a cock, his comb. The delicious *creste di gallo* are sought by a few gourmets.

A young male cock is called *pollastrello*. *Cappone* or capon is a castrated cockerel, which grows to maturity at about between 6 and 8 months, and is sought-after for its delicate meat (see page 49). *Galletto*, or poussin, is a very young cockerel which has reached the lowest possible slaughter weight of 500 g (1 lb). Due to its tender age, it has very delicate flesh and is usually cooked spatchcocked, that is opened out and weighted to keep it flat – also known in Italy as *'al mattone'* (with a brick). I personally do not think the *galletto* worth eating because of its lack of flavour. Older male birds are, however, best boiled because they are particularly tough.

The *gallina*, or hen, is the chicken in a farm that produces eggs. After a couple of years of egg-laying, the hen is destined to end up in a pot as the basis for a good stock. In Italy, there is a saying that old chicken makes good broth (*gallina vecchia fa buon brodo*). Chicken stock, made with a 2- to 3-year-old egg-producing hen bird, is widely used in Italian cooking, but the same type of bird boiled whole makes a wonderful *brodo di gallina*, a soup which can be eaten with tagliolini or tortellini. My memory of chicken will always be strongest in its liquid form as the *brodo* that my mother used to keep hot on the stove when I returned home from long journeys. It was so soothing and invigorating that fatigue was instantly banished.

To prepare *brodo*, just put a well-blessed hen in a large pan and cover with cold water, add some carrots, celery and onion and then simmer over a gentle heat for 2 hours, taking care to skim off the scum as it cooks. Allow to cool then store in the refrigerator or freeze for future use. The meat, although a little tough, can be eaten separately, and – if from a completely free-range bird – will have lots of flavour.

The best chickens are free-range and fed with maize or other grains, imparting a full wonderful flavour to the meat, which is not pale white but pinkish – with a yellow skin. In Italy there are special shops just dedicated to *pollame* (poultry). The butchers are very inventive, and in their refrigerated counters you may find oven-ready stuffed breast of chicken, lovely rolled breast filled with ham, garlic, rosemary and parsley. Other parts are also skilfully prepared for cooking: *spezzatino di pollo*, cubed chicken meat ready to be cooked with tomatoes and peppers; *scaloppine* or *cotolette di pollo*, ready breadcrumbed for frying, a favourite of Lombardy; or *galantina di pollo*, boned chicken stuffed with egg, breadcrumbs, spices and herbs; or *pollo alla cacciatora*, ready to be cooked with wine and mushrooms as in Tuscany. Above all there is usually *pollo arrosto*, chicken stuffed with lemon and rosemary ready for roasting, as they do on the Amalfi coast. See the recipe for Petti di Pollo alla Pizzaiola on page 57.

QUAGLIA / QUAIL

This small, well-camouflaged, beige-brown bird lives wild in fields and woods and is one of the most frequently cooked of the game birds hunted in Italy. As it is easy to raise quail on farms, however, Italians do not rely on wild quail, even if they are bigger and have a natural gamy flavour. The quail has a special place in Italian gastronomy and is much appreciated for its delicate meat and its eggs (see Uova) which are also used to make delicious dishes.

Farm-raised quail are sold cleaned and fresh, without being hung, ready for cooking. If using such a bird, at least a couple are needed per person and, unless it is boned and stuffed, you can eat it with your fingers. Quail can be roasted, stewed, grilled or even boiled.

RANA / FROG

Italians living in the regions of Piedmont, Lombardy, Veneto and Emilia-Romagna are well acquainted with this animal, which is difficult to categorize as either game, meat or fish. Frogs live in any area where water is abundant and in Italy the rice fields of the Po Valley are the perfect place for them. Only the muscular back legs are eaten and these *coscette di rane* are sold pre-cleaned and ready for cooking.

LEFT: QUAGLIA

Frogs' legs have a very delicate flavour and so they are not well suited for cooking with a lot of herbs and spices. They are wonderful simply dipped in beaten egg and breadcrumbs and then deep-fried or '*in umido*', casseroled in olive oil, with a little garlic, parsley and tomatoes. In the rice region, they also make wonderful risottos.

RIGAGLIE, FRATTAGLIE / GIBLETS

Rigaglie di pollo include the usual *fegatini* (liver), *cuore* (heart), *rognoni* (kidneys), *stomaco* (gizzards), as well as the *uova* (unborn eggs of the hen) and *granelli* or *testicoli* (testicles) and the cock's combs or crests. All these bits are particularly loved by Tuscans and Piedmontese, and used in the making of Cibreo di Rigaglie (page 58) and *finanziera*. Chicken livers are also cooked with wine, herbs and spices, then chopped and spread on *crostini*.

SALMI, CIVÉ / COOKING METHOD

Basically *salmi* and *civé* both come from the French and describe ways of preparing game – especially hare, rabbit and venison – either by marinating it in its own blood or adding blood to thicken the sauce at the end of the cooking process. The terms are used confusingly differently from region to region. The principle is the same, however, and generally for Lepre in Salmi, see page 63, the hare is marinated for two days in the blood mixed with good red wine, garlic, thyme, rosemary, squashed juniper berries, crushed peppercorns, cinnamon, sage leaves and bay leaves, before being braised. The sauce is then strained, reduced and served with the tender meat, usually accompanied by polenta.

STARNA, SEE PERNICE

TACCHINO, DINDO, PITO / TURKEY

The turkey is specially raised for the celebration of Christmas in Europe and Thanksgiving in America. This bird was introduced into Europe from the West Indies at the beginning of the sixteenth century, hence its other Italian name, *dindo*, meaning 'from the Indies'. Turkeys are huge and have an incredible breast, which can either be carved from the bird or removed and cooked separately like a veal roast.

Most turkeys eaten are intensively farmed and can be obtained the entire year round, while the more flavoursome free-range variety can only be enjoyed at the Thanksgiving and Christmas period, when they are offered at a higher price. It takes about two months for a free-range turkey to grow to the ideal weight of 4-4.5 kg (9-10 lb) for the female and 6-7 kg (13-16 lb) for the male, when its meat is at its most tender and tasty.

In Italy, turkey breast is mostly eaten sliced and prepared like veal,

RIGHT: FREE-RANGE TURKEYS, CHICKEN AND GUINEA FOWL

i.e. as *scaloppine*, *involtini* or simply *alla milanese* (bread-crumbed and fried). It is only in Lombardy that the whole bird is boned, then stuffed with fruit, minced pork, minced giblets and chestnuts for roasting.

TORDO / THRUSH

There has been a big outcry abroad about Italians eating this wonderful migrating bird. In a time when everyone is concerned about the preservation of wildlife, Italy has now joined in the banning of the hunting of these birds. In Montalcino, where a festival celebrating the birds used to take place, the thrushes are now replaced with quails, although it is still called the Sagra del Tordo.

UOVA / EGGS

Eggs are very versatile in the kitchen as they can be boiled, baked, scrambled, fried and poached, made into omelettes (see Frittata di Carciofi, page 128) as well as being used in cakes, pasta, custards, ice-cream and mayonnaise, scrambled in soups or even used to thicken sauces. Perhaps the most remarkable dish they are used for is zabaglione (see page 65), where the yolks are beaten in a bain-marie with sugar and marsala, sherry or Moscato to make one of the most desirable desserts. Italians use eggs a lot but, curiously, seldom at breakfast. At Easter-time, eggs feature prominently as symbols of new life.

Uova di anatra, ducks' eggs, with their distinctive pale blue colour, can be easily distinguished from other eggs. They have a very rich pale yellow yolk with an intense flavour. Ducks' eggs can be used in place of hens' eggs but the stronger taste gives a more powerful result.

Uova di gabbiano, gulls' eggs, are only available seasonally as they are from wild birds. They were very highly esteemed by the Romans for their purifying qualities and because, unlike other seabird eggs, they do not taste of fish. Gulls' eggs are used in a similar way to quails' eggs. They also have a speckled shell, although they are larger. Their flavour is very delicate and they are used in making *antipasti* or simply eaten hard-boiled with salt.

Uova d'oca, geese's eggs, are among the most sought-after by gourmets, who appreciate the large size and the intense, almost oily, taste. The colour of the shell is dirty white and the eggs are quite large, almost three times the size of the average hens' egg. The culinary use of the goose egg is a little limited because of its intense flavour and they do have to be used when still very fresh.

Uova di quaglia, quails' eggs, are the only other type of bird's egg to be commercially produced. The tiny egg is appreciated both for its flavour and its decorative qualities. When boiled, it cooks solid in about 2½ minutes, and I particularly like to use it with recipes that include truffle dishes (see page 65).

Uova di tacchino, turkeys' eggs, are a similar size to ducks' eggs, but with white shells finely speckled with brown. They are mostly used like hens' eggs, but are difficult to find unless you know a very friendly farmer who can supply them.

Eggs have to be fresh to be good and those laid by free-range chickens, fed on maize or corn, are the best. The way to judge the freshness of an egg is to place it in half a litre (1 pint) of water with 60 g (2 ounces) of salt dissolved in it. If the egg sinks to the bottom of the bowl it is very fresh, probably only a day or two old. If it sinks a little way below the surface it means it is 5 or 6 days old, and if it floats on the surface it could be 10 or more days old. If its bigger end floats to the surface first, it is very old indeed and I would not use it.

As the shells of eggs are porous an egg can absorb strong scents and flavours, including that of the truffle. If you store the two together the egg will have the delicate flavour of the truffle, a great delicacy.

RIGHT (LEFT TO RIGHT): UOVA DI TACCHINO, UOVA DI QUAGLIA, UOVA DI ANATRA

Quaglie allo Spiedo

QUAILS ON A SKEWER

For 4

8 MEATY QUAILS
10 PIECES OF PANE DI CAMPAGNA (COUNTRY-STYLE WHITE BREAD), ABOUT 4 CM ($1\frac{1}{2}$ INCH) SQUARE AND 1 CM ($\frac{1}{2}$ INCH) THICK
10 THIN SLICES OF PANCETTA, THE SAME SHAPE AS THE BREAD SQUARES

For the basting liquid:

4 TBSP OLIVE OIL
JUICE OF 1 LEMON
1 TBSP FINELY CHOPPED FLAT-LEAF PARSLEY
2 TBSP DRY MARSALA
1 TSP HONEY
1 GARLIC CLOVE, EXTREMELY FINELY CHOPPED
SALT AND PEPPER

This Tuscan dish used to be made with a variety of birds. Nowadays the hunting of many birds is restricted but good-quality raised quail make a fine substitute.

Preheat the oven to 250°C/475°F/gas9. Clean the quails and remove and discard the livers if necessary. Roast the birds for 15 minutes. Remove from the oven and thread them on long 2 skewers, alternating them with the bread and pancetta.

Mix together all the ingredients for the basting liquid, adding lots of salt and pepper. Cook the quails over a wood-fired or charcoal grill for 10–15 minutes, basting their breasts regularly with the liquid and turning the skewers often to prevent the quails burning. When they are golden brown, serve with the bread croûtes, which will have collected some of the juices from the birds, and with polenta (see page 173).

Anatra Arrosto al Prosciutto

ROAST DUCK WITH PARMA HAM

For 4

- 1 meaty free-range duck, weighing about 2 kg (4½ lb)
- 4 slices of Parma ham, with lots of fat
- 1 garlic clove, chopped
- small sprig of rosemary
- pinch of freshly grated nutmeg
- salt and pepper
- a little olive oil

This is a speciality of Emilia-Romagna, where both ducks and Parma ham are local produce.

Preheat the oven to 200°C/400°F/gas6. Singe the duck over an open flame to remove the down, if necessary. Mince together the ham, garlic and rosemary to make a paste, then season with the nutmeg and lots of freshly ground black pepper. Rub the duck with a little oil and sprinkle with salt. Spread the paste over the breast and put the duck in a roasting tin. Cover with foil and roast for 1 hour, then remove the foil and cook for another 30 minutes to give a golden finish.

When carving, distribute a little of the crunchy topping on to each plate.

Petti di Pollo alla Pizzaiola

BREAST OF CHICKEN IN PIZZAIOLA SAUCE

For 4

- 4 skinless boneless chicken breasts
- 4 tbsp extra-virgin olive oil
- 2 garlic cloves, finely chopped
- 1 tbsp salted capers, soaked in water for 10 minutes, then drained
- 1 tsp chopped flat-leaf parsley
- 2 anchovy fillets, chopped
- 500 g (1 lb) tomato pulp (see page 118)
- 1 tbsp oregano leaves
- salt and pepper

Pizzaiola sauce originally came from Naples and contains more or less the same ingredients as pizza topping, hence the name.

Fry the chicken breasts in the olive oil for about 8–10 minutes on each side, until brown and cooked through. Add the garlic, capers, parsley and anchovies to the pan and fry briefly, then stir in the tomatoes, oregano and salt and pepper. Simmer for 5 minutes and then serve.

Cibreo di Rigaglie

GIBLET STEW

For 4

- 4 large cocks' combs (see rigaglie, page 54)
- giblets of 6 chickens – livers, hearts, gizzards and, if available, granelli (testicles)
- 60 g (2 oz) butter
- about 250 ml (9 fl oz) chicken stock
- 2 egg yolks
- 1 tbsp flour
- juice of 1 lemon
- salt and pepper

This very delicate dish uses the offal of chicken and something that is rather difficult to come by now – the cock's comb. You may be lucky enough to find some in Chinese food shops, as Chinese cooks commonly use every part of the chicken. A similar dish is made in Piedmont, where it is called finanziera di pollo.

Clean the cocks' combs and put them in a saucepan of cold water. Bring to the boil, then drain the combs and peel them, discarding the tough coarse skin. Cut them into chunks. Remove all the impurities from the livers, hearts and gizzards and cut them into smaller chunks.

Heat the butter in a pan and cook the combs and the hearts until tender, adding some stock from time to time to prevent the mixture becoming too dry. Check with the point of a small knife to see if the meat is done, then add the livers, hearts, gizzards and *granelli*, if using, and cook for another 10 minutes.

Mix the egg yolks with the flour, lemon juice and some salt and pepper. Stir in a little of the stock from the pan, then pour this mixture on to the *rigaglie*. Mix well and serve immediately.

Fegato Grasso al Balsamico

FOIE GRAS WITH BALSAMIC SAUCE

For 4

- 500 ml (18 fl oz) strong red wine
- 1 tbsp sugar
- 1 tbsp balsamic vinegar (not too old)
- 8 fresh foie gras slices without the skin, weighing 55 g (1¾ oz) each
- 25 g (¾ oz) butter
- salt and pepper
- flour for dusting

From the Lomellina, between Lombardy and Piedmont, comes this recipe made with local fresh foie gras. *Although* foie gras *is highly valued by the French, it plays only a minor part in Italian gastronomy. However, gourmets adore this dish, which I modified and adapted a little after seeing the enthusiasm with which the customers in my restaurant ate it.*

Boil the wine with the sugar until it has reduced to a third of its original volume and is beginning to thicken. Add the balsamic vinegar and some salt and pepper and mix in well; the sauce should be thick and dark.

Dust the slices of *foie gras* with flour and fry briefly in the butter until brown on each side. Place the *foie gras* on serving plates and pour the sauce next to it.

FAGIANO AL TARTUFO DI NORCIA

PHEASANT WITH TRUFFLE NORCIA-STYLE

FOR 4

2 PHEASANTS
55 G ($1^3/_4$ OZ) BUTTER
1 SMALL GLASS OF DRY WHITE WINE
ABOUT 85 G (3 OZ) BLACK SUMMER TRUFFLE
SALT AND PEPPER

A noble treatment for a noble bird, this remarkably simple combination of ingredients makes a superior dish that is hard to beat.

Preheat the oven to 180°C/350°F/gas4. Roast the pheasants for 30 minutes; they should not be completely cooked. Cut off the breasts and thighs and set aside. (The rest of the pheasant can be used to make stock, if liked.)

Melt the butter in a large pan, then add the wine and some salt and pepper. Put the pheasant breasts and thighs in the pan and heat through for 1–2 minutes, just to finish the cooking. Grate the truffle over the meat and serve straight away.

Palombacci sui Crostini

WOOD PIGEON ON TOAST

Now famous throughout the world, crostini *are a type of canapé and consist of slices of toasted bread which serve as a base for all sorts of spreads. They are very popular topped with liver, but here is a special Tuscan version made with wood pigeon.*

MAKES 12 CROSTINI

3 WOOD PIGEON, READY CLEANED, WITH LIVERS
12 SLICES OF PANE DI CAMPAGNA (COUNTRY-STYLE WHITE BREAD)
12 CAPERS, TO DECORATE

FOR THE MARINADE:
2 GLASSES OF RED WINE
4 TBSP OLIVE OIL
A FEW SAGE LEAVES
1 TBSP SALTED CAPERS, SOAKED IN WATER FOR 10 MINUTES, THEN DRAINED
1 GARLIC CLOVE
3 ANCHOVY FILLETS
SALT AND PEPPER

Blend all the ingredients for the marinade in a liquidizer and pour into a bowl. Add the pigeons and leave to marinate for a few hours. Preheat the oven to 220°F/425°F/gas7.

Remove the birds from the marinade and roast for 30 minutes. Leave to cool and then remove all the flesh and the livers from the birds and discard the bones. Put the marinade in a saucepan, add the meat and livers and cook for 10 minutes, stirring from time to time. Transfer to a liquidizer and blend to a paste, then leave to cool.

Toast the bread, spread with the paste and decorate each piece with a caper.

Ciriole al Ragù di Cinghiale

CIRIOLE PASTA WITH WILD BOAR SAUCE

For 4

3 TBSP VIRGIN OLIVE OIL
1 ONION, CHOPPED
1 GARLIC CLOVE, CRUSHED
10 JUNIPER BERRIES
PINCH OF FRESHLY GRATED NUTMEG
PINCH OF GROUND CINNAMON
4 BAY LEAVES
2 TBSP TOMATO PASTE
675 G ($1^1/_2$ LB) MINCED WILD BOAR
250 ML (9 FL OZ) RED WINE
150 ML ($^1/_4$ PINT) CHICKEN STOCK
500 G (1 LB) CIRIOLE PASTA (SEE BIGOLI, PAGE 144)
SALT AND PEPPER
FRESHLY GRATED PECORINO CHEESE, TO SERVE (OPTIONAL)

This wonderful dish is from Umbria, where wild boar are at home (until the hunters get hold of them). It is a really delightful combination of strongly flavoured ragù *and robust pasta. Wild boar sounds exotic but it is now available from specialist butchers and some supermarkets.*

Heat the oil in a large pan, add the onion, garlic, spices and bay leaves and fry gently until the onion is softened. Add the tomato paste, meat, wine and stock and simmer gently for about $1^1/_2$ hours. Season to taste. Cook the pasta in boiling salted water until *al dente*, then drain. Add to the sauce, mix well and serve, sprinkled with some pecorino cheese if desired.

Coniglio Affogato alla Ligure

RABBIT STEW LIGURIAN-STYLE

For 4

- 1 RABBIT, WEIGHING ABOUT 1.5 KG ($3^1/_4$ LB), CUT INTO CHUNKS
- 125 ML (4 FL OZ) LIGURIAN EXTRA-VIRGIN OLIVE OIL
- 1 LARGE ONION, THINLY SLICED
- 1 GARLIC CLOVE, COARSELY CHOPPED
- SPRIG OF ROSEMARY
- A FEW SAGE LEAVES
- SMALL SPRIG OF THYME
- 100 G ($3^1/_2$ OZ) TASTY BLACK OLIVES, PREFERABLY TAGGIASCA
- 2 GLASSES OF DRY WHITE WINE
- 8 TBSP TOMATO PULP (SEE PAGE 118)
- SALT AND PEPPER
- FLOUR FOR DUSTING
- A LITTLE STOCK IF NECESSARY

Rabbit is very much loved all over Italy and, as usual, each region has its own recipes. The Ligurian version sees the use of local herbs and, naturally, lots of olive oil.

Wash and pat dry the chunks of rabbit, them dust them with flour. Heat the oil in a large casserole and brown the rabbit on all sides. Add the onion, garlic, herbs and olives, reduce the heat and cook until softened. Stir in the wine and bubble to allow some of the alcohol to evaporate, then add the tomato pulp and some seasoning and cook over a moderate heat for $1^1/_2$ hours, until the rabbit is tender. Add a little stock if the mixture becomes too dry. Adjust the seasoning to taste and then serve. Delicious accompanied with polenta.

Lepre in Salmi

JUGGED HARE

For 6

- 1 large hare, weighing about 3 kg (6½ lb), including the blood
- 55 g (1¾ oz) plain flour
- 100 g (3½ oz) butter
- 1 onion, very finely chopped
- 100 g (3½ oz) pancetta, cut into small pieces
- 200 g (7 oz) calves' liver, cut into small strips
- 3 tbsp brandy
- 55 g (1¾ oz) bitter chocolate
- salt and pepper

For the marinade:

- 1 bottle of strong red wine, such as Barolo
- 1 carrot, finely diced
- 1 onion, finely chopped
- 4 celery stalks, finely diced
- 1 garlic clove, smashed
- a few sprigs of thyme
- a few sprigs of marjoram
- a few sage leaves
- a few bay leaves
- 10 juniper berries
- 1 tsp black peppercorns, lightly crushed

A classic of Northern cuisine, this is usually served with polenta while the sauce is served separately with pappardelle.

Mix together all the ingredients for the marinade. Cut the hare into large chunks, add to the marinade, then cover and leave in the refrigerator for 24 hours.

Remove the chunks of hare from the marinade and pat dry, then dust them in some of the flour. Heat the butter in a large cast iron pan and fry the pieces of meat, a few at a time, until browned all over. Remove from the pan and set aside. Reduce the heat, add the onion and pancetta to the pan and fry until the onion begins to colour. Return the meat to the pan together with the blood, calves' liver and the marinade. Cover and cook gently for 2 hours or until the meat is tender.

Remove the pieces of hare and liver from the pan. Strain the sauce through a fine sieve and discard the solids. Mix together the brandy and just enough of the remaining flour to make a paste. Put the meat and the strained liquid back in the pan and bring to the boil. Whisk in the flour and brandy paste a little at a time to thicken. Let it boil for a minute or two, then add the chocolate, allow it to dissolve and season with salt and pepper to taste.

Serve the hare with polenta and the sauce with pappardelle. Hare cooked like this can be kept for a couple of days.

Lumachine al Sugo

SNAILS IN TOMATO SAUCE

For 4

- 1 kg (2¼ lb) small snails, possibly still dormant or closed
- 4 tbsp olive oil
- 1 garlic clove, finely chopped
- 1 chilli, finely chopped
- 1 tbsp coarsely chopped flat-leaf parsley
- 400 g (14 oz) tomato pulp (see Pomodoro, page 118)
- 2 basil leaves
- salt and pepper

The small snails collected in southern Italy in autumn are best for this dish. They are a real gastronomical amusement. If you manage to get small snails, they will not need purging and cleaning.

Wash the snails thoroughly. Heat the oil in a pan, add the garlic, chilli and parsley and fry for a few minutes. Add the tomatoes, basil leaves and snails, then cover and cook gently for 40 minutes. Season with salt and pepper to taste and serve with a pin to remove the snails from their shells.

Filetto di Capriolo al Barolo

FILLET OF VENISON IN BAROLO WINE

For 6

800 g ($1^3/_4$ lb) venison fillet from a large deer
55 g ($1^3/_4$ oz) butter
a few slices of white truffle, to serve (optional)
flour for dusting

For the marinade:

1 bottle of good Barolo wine
4 tbsp extra-virgin olive oil
a few juniper berries
a few bay leaves
small sprig of rosemary
1 onion, thinly sliced
3–4 cloves
pinch of freshly grated nutmeg
salt and pepper

This is a typical recipe from northern Italy, where it is possible to find venison in specialist shops.

Mix together all the ingredients for the marinade. Trim the meat of gristle and skin, then add it to the marinade, cover and leave to marinate for at least 12 hours.

Remove the meat and pat dry, then cut it into medallions 2 cm ($^3/_4$ inch) thick. Put the marinade in a pan and bring to the boil, then lower the heat and boil until reduced to a third of its original volume. Pass through a fine sieve and keep warm.

Dust the medallions with flour and fry in the butter for 3 minutes on each side; they should be rare and tender. Serve very hot with the sauce, together with polenta sprinkled with a few slices of white truffle if desired.

Rane alla Ghiottona

FROGS' LEGS IN TARRAGON CREAM SAUCE

For 4

1 kg ($2^1/_4$ lb) frogs' legs, ready cleaned
100 g ($3^1/_2$ oz) butter
juice of 1 lemon
90 ml (3 fl oz) dry white wine
1 tsp tomato paste
4 tbsp double cream
1 tbsp very finely chopped tarragon
salt and pepper
flour for dusting

Frogs are served with risotto, with pasta, in soup, and all of this mostly in one area of Italy where these animals are abundant: Vercelli, Novara, Pavia, Milan, Padua and all the other cities lined up along the Pianura Padana, the Po flatlands where the rice fields are.

Dust the frogs' legs with flour. Heat the butter in a large pan and fry the frogs' legs for 10 minutes, until brown on each side. Add the lemon juice, white wine, tomato paste and some salt and pepper and bring to the boil, stirring to loosen the sticky particles on the bottom of the pan. Add the double cream and tarragon and cook for a further 4 minutes, then serve with rice.

Uova al Tartufo

TRUFFLED EGGS

For 4

- 8 eggs
- 8 tbsp double cream
- about 45 g ($1^1/_2$ oz) white truffle (more if you can afford it)
- salt
- butter for greasing

This is one of the most elegant and refined of Piedmontese dishes, which can be served as a first course at the most elegant of dinner parties but, because of its simplicity, is equally suitable for a lesser occasion.

Preheat the oven to 180°C/350°F/gas4. Grease 4 large ramekins with butter. Break 2 eggs into each one and pour over the double cream. Season with salt and then place in the oven. Start checking after 5 minutes to see if the whites have set. Cut the white truffle into slivers and scatter over the eggs. Serve immediately, with bread.

Zabaglione Gelato

ZABAGLIONE ICE-CREAM

For 6–8

- 16–18 free-range egg yolks
- 300 g ($10^1/_2$ oz) caster sugar
- 200 ml (7 fl oz) Moscato Passito di Pantelleria or Marsala (see pages 312-3)
- 500 ml (18 fl oz) whipping cream

Eggs are a complete food and this recipe in their honour is always a success.

Put the egg yolks and sugar in a large bowl and whisk with a hand-held electric beater or a whisk until foamy and doubled in volume. Put the bowl over a saucepan of gently simmering water, making sure the water does not touch the base of the bowl. Continue to whisk until the mixture is very thick and has a homogeneous, creamy but not crumbly texture. It is crucial not to let it overheat or you will end up with scrambled eggs.

Leave to cool, then fold in the Moscato Passito di Pantelleria or Marsala. Whip the cream until it forms soft peaks and then fold it into the mixture. Place in an ice-cream maker and freeze. If you do not have an ice-cream maker, transfer the mixture to a shallow bowl and place in the freezer for about 1 hour, until it is beginning to solidify around the edges. Whisk it well with a fork, then remove from the freezer. Repeat this process 3 times and then freeze until firm.

Fresh & Cured Meats

CARNI E SALUMI

Italians eat 70 kg of meat per person per annum, and more than a third of that is eaten in the form of pork. This is, of course, balanced by a large quantity of fresh vegetables and fruit. As is to be expected from the heartland of the Mediterranean diet, the average Italian meal, divided into anything from three to five courses, rarely includes large lumps of meat. A notable exception is the famous *bistecca alla fiorentina*, a huge T-bone steak that weighs at least 500 g per portion. The beef used for this dish comes from special beef cattle raised in a valley near Florence, the Val di Chiana. The steak is so tender that it is usually grilled and eaten rare, an exception for Italians who prefer their meat to be slightly more thoroughly cooked.

In Piedmont, cattle are raised to make other local specialities like *bollito misto* (mixed boiled meats), *brasato al barolo* (topside braised in red wine), *insalata di carne cruda* (a special salad of raw beef) and *carne all'Albese*, a raw meat salad served with white truffle from Alba. The cattle used to provide meat for these dishes are known as *sanato* or *vitellone*, which although more mature and developed than veal calves are still fairly young, with very tender flesh.

The rearing practices for some animals, especially that of veal calves, cause much controversy. I must say that, while I agree that humans have to be fed, I think it is possible to be more scrupulous about the manner in which the rearing is done. Veal has always been popular with chefs for its short cooking time and blandness, qualities that allow the meat to act as a backdrop to the flavours cooked with it. Personally, I prefer a firmer meat with a more pronounced taste.

In Italy there is no indication that veal, which is an appreciably pale meat while still milk-fed, is kept in narrow crates to avoid exercise. Veal is still kept with the mothers in the majority of cases. The 'industrialization' of meat production is avoided, if possible, because Italians like good meat – even if it is a little more expensive. The best beef animals are fed with hay or with a mixture of grains and corn-based fodder in winter, and in summer on fresh grass.

Pigs are a different matter as, unfortunately, to fatten them up they are raised in barns. They are, however, fed on a mixture of whey (a by-product of Parmesan cheese) and a mixture of grains. In Emilia-Romagna, some of the best pigs are fed on acorns to achieve particularly flavoured meat that distinguishes Parma ham from others.

Many Italians still keep animals if they can and the pig is the most popular, both for its taste and because the whole animal can be used – either for fresh meat and sausages, for salamis or for lard. When I was a boy, during the War, my family were given two suckling pigs. We housed the piglets in a specially made hut at the end of a disused railway line and when they were fully grown and fattened my father called in the local *norcino* or pork butcher. One of the pigs had to be offered to everyone in the village, a rule made by all the villagers when war broke out. With the remaining pig, my mother made salamis, lard and hams.

From Bolzano in Alto Adige, where speck is produced in the Austrian tradition, to Sicily where a dessert is made with pork blood, every region has its customs and recipes for pork. Pigs are usually slaughtered in winter, with much local celebrating.

One region that has made pork famous is Emilia-Romagna where Parma ham and many other preserved meats are made, including salamis, mortadella and *culatello di zibello*. These products, especially *mortadella di Bologna*, *pancetta* and *zampone* (stuffed pigs' trotters) are enjoyed all over Italy. Calabria also has some specialities, including

TOP LEFT: HARVESTING HAY TO FEED THE CATTLE AT PRATOROTONDO.

BOTTOM LEFT: CATTLEMAN NOE BOVO IN THE AOSTA VALLEY.

Above: a herd of pezzatanera cattle grazing the spring grass in the Aosta Valley.

salsiccie piccanti (spicy sausages), while Piedmont has *salam d'la duja*, salami preserved in a terracotta pot covered in lard. Another speciality is *porchetta* (stuffed piglet), a dish much loved by the Romans – ancient and modern.

As well as pork, beef and veal, Italians also eat lamb and goat and, sometimes, horse and donkey meat. Lamb and goat are most popular in Southern Italy, where it easy to raise them. Some people believe that horse meat is particularly healthy and that the best mortadella is made with donkey meat. Only a few specialist shops now sell equine meat and these are very strictly controlled.

Choosing fresh meat is a special skill, but one that should be developed by anyone who wants to eat just a little of the very best meat. I remember being sent to buy meat when I was a child. I returned home with it proudly, only to be sent straight back to the butcher as it was not a good enough cut. I learnt an important lesson then, not only to be sure of what I was being given, but also to know what constitutes a good cut. It is worth finding a good butcher to help you. Pay more and eat less, that is my recommendation.

A - Z of Fresh & Cured Meats

Abbacchio, see Agnello

Affettato / Sliced Meats
This term covers all preserved meats, but is mostly used for pork products like prosciutto and salami. However, items as varied as *bresaola*, *mucetta* and wild boar may be included in the *antipasto* of *affettato misto* so beloved of many Italians.

Agnello, Agnellone, Abbacchio / Lamb, Mutton
Lamb is a very Italian meat, which has been eaten there through the ages. The tradition of raising lamb has been kept alive in the central and southern regions and the islands, where the pastures give the meat a particularly good flavour. Because of the hard work involved, however, the farming of sheep for their meat has declined in the last generation.

Agnello da latte (called *abbacchio* by the Romans) are milk-fed lambs slaughtered at 3 or 4 weeks old, when their meat is very pale and tender. *Agnello* are slightly older lambs, between 9 and 12 weeks old, weighing up to 15 kg (30 lb). They are both milk-fed and reared on pasture and their flesh is both tender and flavoursome. Lambs of this size are often cooked whole on a spit. *Agnellone* are killed at about 6 months old and have very tasty meat which is mostly used in stews and *ragùs*.

Castrato or *montone*, the meat of a castrated ewe, is more popular in Southern Italy where they love a stronger taste of lamb. The meat is of an intense red colour and not so lean. It is ideal for stews but is also roasted if the animal is not too old, or even grilled with rosemary and basted with olive oil and lemon juice. *Pecora*, meat from the adult ewe, is used in the same way, but will be a little tougher. Mutton has a good flavour, but is only eaten in the south where many recipes were developed for its use in stews.

Abbacchio is also the name given to a dish traditional in Rome at Easter. The lamb is cut into pieces and cooked in a sort of egg-and-lemon sauce, probably based on the Greek recipe *avgolemono*. One of my favourite lamb recipes, *agnello ripieno* (stuffed breast of lamb, see page 93), comes from Campania. The most popular flavourings with lamb in Italy are garlic, of course, thyme, rosemary and mint.

Little baby lamb cutlets, called *bistecchine* or *costolette*, are often grilled, when they are called *scottadito* ('finger burn') because they are usually eaten with the hands.

Animelle / Sweetbreads
Sweetbreads are the thymus glands, and only those of young calves and lambs are normally cooked. They are used all over Italy, either sautéed, deep-fried in a breadcrumb coating or incorporated in *ragùs* such as Bolognese. They are also popular as stuffings for various items, including ravioli, and as part of *fritto misto*. The mild taste of sweetbreads is usually paired with lemon juice and, sometimes, sage leaves.

To prepare sweetbreads, they must first be soaked in cold water for several hours, changing the water fairly often to eliminate any blood and impurities. They are then blanched for a few minutes in boiling water so that the nerves and veins can be easily trimmed off and discarded.

Arista / Pork Loin
This Tuscan pork speciality consists of oven-roasted loin on the bone which has been larded with rosemary, fennel seeds and garlic. it has become popular all over Italy. There is a version of the joint without the bone, for slicing by machine in good delicatessens.

Asino, see Cavallo

Battuto / Meat Sauce Base
Battuto, meaning beaten, consists of lard, pancetta or ham mixed with flavourings like rosemary, garlic, onion and chilli until it resembles a fine creamy paste. It is used as a base for soup, stews or sauces or smeared on top of roasts to give extra flavour.

Bistecca, Bistecchine / Beef Steaks and Cutlets
A *bistecca* is a slice of tender meat – with or without bones, depending on where you are in Italy – suitable either for frying or grilling. The most famous and succulent of all Italian steaks is the *bistecca alla fiorentina* (Steak Florentine-style), a T-bone cut from the Chiana cow, raised in the Val di Chiana near Florence. This steak is much larger than the sirloin and fillet, weighing at least 1kg (2 lb) and about 4-5 cm ($1^1/_2$-2 inches) thick. Brushed with olive oil and sprinkled with salt, it is grilled over charcoal for only a few minutes each side to allow the flavour and tenderness of the meat to come through. *Bistecchine* are cutlets from young calves and other smaller animals such as lambs, goats and pigs.

Bocconcino / Veal Pieces
From the diminutive of *boccone*, literally 'mouthful', *bocconcini* can

Left: A Piedmontese antipasto, consisting of coppa, prosciutto and mortadella, with sweet-and-sour onions, preserved wild mushrooms and artichoke hearts.

be of many things. *Bocconcini di vitello*, for instance, are small escalopes of veal containing various fillings like cheese, prosciutto, eggs and herbs and braised in a sauce (see Involtini). *Bocconcini* are also tiny Mozzarella cheeses (see page 238).

BOLLITO MISTO / MIXED BOILED MEATS

This is one of the grandest dishes of Northern Italian gastronomy, native to the regions that traditionally raise beef, veal, chicken and pork. Piedmont, Lombardy, Emilia-Romagna and the Veneto are all famous for this dish and in some regions it is sometimes called simply *bollito* or *lesso* (from *lessare*, meaning to boil). The mixture should contain at least four different types of meat, including some sausages that are cooked separately (see recipe on page 92).

Typical meats used include brisket of beef, veal cheek and breast, capon or chicken, tongue, pork belly and stuffed or plain pigs' trotters. When everything is cooked, the meats are sliced and served with some of the flavouring vegetables and some sauces. In Piedmont, *salsa verde* or green sauce (page 224), is served with the *bollito*, while in Lombardy and Emilia-Romagna a *salsa rossa* or red sauce , based on onions, tomato and chilli, and some *mostarda di Cremona* (page 269), accompany the dish.

The town of Carrú in Piedmont is famous for the celebration of Bue Grasso every December. As the climax of a festival to find the finest beef animals, the prize awarded is a big pot of *bollito* and this is said to be the best in the region.

BOVINO / COW

Pezzata Nera (Black Dappled), the Italian Frisona and the Bruna Alpina are the main cattle varieties used for Italian beef, although such herds are also raised for their milk. The Piemontese, Chiana, Marchigiana and Romagnola are, however, raised exclusively for their meat.

Vitelli are young calves fed on milk and, as a result, they have a very pale meat. *Vitellone* is the meat of a calf 1 year to 2 years old, that has not borne its first calf. *Manzo* is a three-year-old castrated bullock or heifer that has not borne its first calf. Once it has gone over 4 years of age the *manzo* is called *bue*, equivalent to ox. *Toro* and *vacca* are the terms for the adult bull and cow.

RIGHT: A TUSCAN CHIANA BULL IN UMBRIA.

All of these types of meat are used in a different way in the kitchen. Regionally, there are also huge differences, not only in the types of meat but also in the cuts. There are national guidelines to beef cuts which nobody observes because they are very happy with naming the cuts in their own dialect, and the same piece of meat is often known by quite different names in different parts of the country.

BRACIOLE, BRACIOLINE, BRACIOLETTE / MEAT CUTS

This name describes a different cut or dish depending on which part of Italy you are in. In the northern regions *braciole* is used to describe a cut of meat similar to the cutlet, which can be grilled over charcoal or stewed. In the south, the same term is used to describe slices of meat such as beef or pork used rolled around fillings then usually braised in a tomato sauce. See Involtino and Bocconcino.

BRASATO, BRACIATO / BRAISED BEEF

These terms are used to describe casseroles of beef slowly braised in wine with carrots, onions, celery and spices. *Brasato*, typical of Northern Italy (especially Piedmont and Lombardy), is usually made with *manzo* (mature beef), and takes about 2 hours to cook. It is normally eaten in slices accompanied by vegetables.

BRESAOLA / AIR-DRIED BEEF

The Valtellina Valley in Lombardy has a long tradition of curing and air-drying beef which is then thinly cut and sprinkled with lemon juice and oil at the last minute for serving as an *antipasto*. Round in shape and only lightly salted, *bresaola* is not dissimilar to the Swiss *Bündnerfleisch*. It may have been invented to provide a source of protein when fresh meat was scarce.

BRODO DI CARNE / BEEF CONSOMMÉ

To make beef consommé, the beef has to be boiled until the liquid is greatly reduced and it is this that gives it its name – consommé, French for consumed or reduced. *Brodo* is a very popular Italian soup, but it can also be used as stock in any type of cooking. To make it, take some beef and mince it to make it easier to extract all the juices and flavours from it. Place the minced beef in cold water with a bay leaf, some celery leaves, finely chopped carrots and onions, and some whole peppercorns. Bring to the boil and simmer for 2 to 3 hours until the *brodo* has reduced. The broth is the strained and can be clarified.

For clarification it is first passed through a fine sieve, then it is brought to the boil again and some beaten egg white thrown into it. The solidifying egg white collects all the impurities, leaving a very clear liquid. Seasoned as necessary the *brodo* is ready.

BUDELLO / INTESTINE

Intestines are mostly used as skins and containers for salami. The gut of cows, lambs and pigs are those most frequently used by butchers, but the intestines of very young lambs are also popular because, as the animals have only been fed on milk, their guts are relatively clean. A part of veal intestines produces tripe, one of the most loved offals in Italy and for which there are many recipes (see Trippa, page 85).

In Sicily, a special dish called *stigghiole* is prepared with the intestines of milk-fed lambs. They are flavoured with spices then threaded on wooden skewers and grilled over charcoal. I bought some from a roadside vendor in Sicily and my wife Priscilla, usually a little reserved about such foods, agreed that it was delicious. Similar specialities can also be found in Puglia, Calabria and Sardinia.

Bue, see Bovino

Büsecca, see Trippa

Cacciatori, Cacciatorini / Salami

Every Italian loves freshly cut salami and *cacciatore*, weighing about 200 g (7 oz), or smaller *cacciatorini*, about 85g (3 oz), are the ideal salamis for picnics. Traditionally these come from Piedmont and Lombardy and are made from coarsely minced pure pork and cured for at least 3 months. Their name means 'hunter', as the salami was a traditional and handy breakfast for those in the field.

Capicollo, Capocollo, Ossocollo / Preserved Neck of Pork

This is neck of pork cured so that, after about a year, it can be thinly cut and eaten as a part of an *antipasto* or alone with bread. It is a speciality of the south, where it is made using different spices and cured in different ways, according to the region: in some regions it is even smoked. When made from the meat of free-range pigs, *capicollo* is especially delicious. In the north *coppa* (opposite), a similar cut, is air-cured, but it is not as exciting as its southern counterpart.

Cappello del Prete / Salami

Two wonderful charcuterie products come from the area near Busseto, where Giuseppe Verdi lived: the first is the ham *culatello* and the other is *cappello del prete*, a salami made from the leftovers from the ingredients used to make *culatello*. The name means 'the priest's hat', because of its triangular shape. The meat is minced and stuffed in the skin from the upper part of the leg of the pig. When sewn together it takes on its characteristic shape. It needs to be boiled for at least 2 hours and is traditionally served with lentils, cabbage and potatoes.

Capra, Capretto / Goat, Kid

I myself was a shepherd when I was 13 or 14 years old. Just after the War, my father decided to buy a goat and keep it in a railway shed near the station. I was in charge of feeding the animal, which each day gave a couple of litres of milk – enough for the whole family. I certainly never wanted to eat Sisina (as she was called) and she was eventually sold when we couldn't keep her any more. Although it was not the custom to keep goats in the North, my family always had them because my parents originally came from the South, where it was quite customary.

Some goats are only good for milk, but *capretto* (kid) can also be eaten. The meat is different from that of lamb, with more of a wild taste. We usually had kid for Easter, and I had to assist with the preparation of the meat, a job which – despite my tendencies as a gourmet even then – I was always reluctant to witness. The butcher cut the kid's head into two halves and I had to help with the salting and oiling of it before it was baked in the oven.

Above: a 'trullo' with roaming goats in Apulia.

Carbonata / Beef Stew

In the Aosta Valley, where this recipe is mostly found in Italy, this dish is known as *carbonnade* because the local dialect is more French than Italian. It is, in fact, a beef stew cooked for at least 2 or 3 hours in a butter, onion and red wine sauce. It is usually served with boiled potatoes or polenta.

Carpaccio / Sliced Raw Beef Fillet

This dish of very thin slices of raw beef, dressed with a sauce based on mustard, ketchup and other spices, was made for the first time in the legendary Harry's Bar in Venice. The term *carpaccio* is now used all over the culinary world to indicate very thinly cut food – meat, fish or even vegetables – dressed with a marinating sauce, usually based on lemon juice or vinegar, oil and spices. See also Fesa and Carne all'Albese (page 86).

Castrato, see Agnello

Cavallo / Horse

Meat from both horses and donkeys (*asini*) was eaten during the War, when meat was scarce and prices high. Some Italians still have a taste for them, partly because they believe the deep red colour of the meat means it is very good for you.

Few butchers still sell horse or donkey, with no more than one or two places in the major Italian cities supplying the demand of those nostalgic gourmets.

In Puglia, however, horse meat is very much in demand during the summer, especially because it is thought that the meat keeps better than that of pigs or sheep. In Puglia there exist many shops, called *equina*, where it is obvious you can only get horse meat. In Alberobello in Puglia I also discovered a dish made of escalopes of donkey meat formed into rolls and then stewed for several hours in a tenderizing sauce. It was a piece of bravado which did not really meet with my approval.

In Turin, the famous *insalata di carne cruda* (raw beef salad) is still sometimes made with fillet of horse. The very lean meat is minced and dressed with olive oil, lemon juice, garlic and parsley and left to cure for several hours. It has rather a rich flavour. Salami and sausages are also still made with horse meat.

CERVELLA / BRAINS

Brains are believed to be particularly nutritious, which is why they are given to people who need extra nourishment. In fact, brains contain a very high level of cholesterol and have less protein than the rest of the animal. It is only calves' and lambs' brains that are generally used in the kitchen.

The easiest thing is to ask your butcher to prepare the brains for you, but if this is not possible, you start by washing them in very cold water then removing all the veins and blood vessels on the surface with a small sharp knife. Next, soak the brains in water acidulated with a little lemon juice for a couple of hours, changing the water frequently. Remove the remaining membrane and any more veins before blanching them in boiling water for a few minutes. Allow the brains to cool before cooking as desired.

Brains are a must for *fritto misto alla piemontese* (see page 89), but are also dipped in flour, beaten eggs and breadcrumbs, then fried in butter until golden and served with lemon juice. Another popular dish, leaning to the French, is brains with black butter: the brains are sliced and fried in very hot butter with the addition of chopped capers, the butter is then further heated until it goes a nut-brown in colour and poured over the brains, and more whole capers and chopped parsley are scattered over the top.

CICCIOLI, CICOLI, SFRIZOLI / PORK SCRAPS

When pork or goose fat is melted to make lard, the cubes of fat still contain some meat which, when pressed after cooking to extract all the lard, can be salted and kept to be eaten with bread. This is an interesting and very tasty *amuse-gueule* which is quite different from Anglo-Saxon pork crackling.

My mother used to make lard and we would eat the *ciccioli* with some bread while they were still hot and juicy. My mother took special care not to squeeze the cubes of meat and lard too hard and the result compared to those made by local butchers was like the difference between day and night. In some parts of Italy they include the *ciccioli* in the dough when making bread, producing a very appetising loaf called *pane coi cicoli* .

CODA ALLA VACCINARA / OXTAIL VACCINARA-STYLE

Probably one of the best-known recipes of Roman cuisine, the lengthy preparation required for this dish – about 4 or 5 hours – make it difficult to cook, but it is a real treat! The oxtail and part of the cheek of the ox are first soaked in fresh water for 4 hours, then cut into chunks and browned in lard with onion, carrots, celery and parsley. This is then braised over a low heat until the herbs and vegetables are soft. White wine is then added, and slowly cooked off. The braise is then covered with tomato *polpa* and allowed to finish cooking gently for 3 to 4 hours, replenishing the liquid from time to time with some stock as needed. Finally sultanas, pine nuts and bitter cocoa powder are added and the dish cooked on until the sauce becomes thick and succulent.

COPPA / NECK END OF PORK

Fresh neck of pork is very juicy if braised or slowly roasted. The neck of pork is, however, often cured in salt brine, stuffed in a gut casing, bound and set to air-dry for at least 6 months to make the cured meat known as *coppa*. Due to its composition of large pieces of fat and lean meat, *coppa* looks much like a very fatty sausage. However, it is in fact only 40 per cent fat, less than other meat preserves. It is eaten thinly sliced as *antipasto*. See also Capicollo.

CORATA, CORATELLA / LAMB PLUCK

If everyone tasted the *coratella* produced in Umbria and Lazio just

RIGHT: COPPA AND PANCETTA AIR-DRYING IN EMILIA-ROMAGNA.

once, the demand for and price of this lamb and kid pluck would leap. In most parts of Italy the offal of young lambs, including the liver, lungs and heart, are discarded and given to animals. In Umbria and Lazio, however, there is a revival of their use in traditional dishes, usually soupy stews flavoured with sage, rosemary, garlic, chilli and thyme. These are so excellent that I have put my version on the menu of my restaurant in London and it has already found many fans. A similar speciality called *soffritto di maiale* is prepared in Campania using the pluck of pork and it is equally delicious.

COSTA, COSTATA, COSTOLA / CUTLET, STEAK, CHOP
A great deal of confusion is caused in Italy by the different names given to the same cuts of meat. The confusion exists at the highest level, so that discussions between chefs from different regions are needed before they can understand each other. Cutlets are usually taken from the rib and neck. The *costola* (rib) is very tasty and popular because the meat, when attached to bone, has a great deal of flavour and is ideal for cutlets. *Costa* is a term that is only used for beef cuts. It refers to the rib to which the sirloin and the fillet are both attached and, because of its shape, is called the T-bone steak. The most famous of the T-bone steaks is *costata alla Fiorentina*. (See also Bistecca.)

COSTOLETTA / VEAL CHOP
This term is generally used to indicate a beaten-out veal escalope cooked *alla milanese*, that is dipped in egg and breadcrumbs and then shallow-fried.

COTECHINO / PORK SAUSAGE
This sausage is made from *cotica* or pork rind mixed with lean pork meat, fat and spices and some parts, like ears, which when properly boiled for a long time give it incomparable juiciness. The pork rind turns gelatinous and is essential to the taste of the sausage. *Cotechino* is usually served with lentils, cabbage and sauerkraut. It is also an essential ingredient in a good *bollito misto* (see page 92). It can also be eaten in the same way as *zampone*, stuffed pigs' trotters. In Puglia they make a type of *cotechino* which is cooked and eaten cold instead of hot. The difference being an incredible amount of *peperoncino* (chilli) added to it to ensure it is washed down with lots of wine!

COTENNA, COTICA / PORK SKIN OR RIND
Slightly fatty pork skin is very gelatinous and strong and is usually used for making the skins of certain types of sausage. It is also minced and used to make *zampone* or *cotechino*. In some parts of Italy, such as Piedmont, most of the fat is removed from the skin and it is then richly spiced with pepper, salt, nutmeg and parsley, rolled up, bound with string and boiled for a couple of hours until it is soft. It is usually eaten with stewed beans and a little mustard. The gelatinous taste is delicious. In Piedmont, they use it in the famous speciality called Tofeja, see page 95. Today, the *cotenna* is sold ready-prepared by butchers. Ham rind is also used to impart flavour to any bean or vegetable soup. Once it has been used, however, it is usually so hard that it has to be discarded.

COTICA, SEE COTENNA

COTOLETTA ALLA MILANESE / VEAL CUTLET
The name of this dish derives from *costoletta*. In Milan, the cutlet with the bone in is cooked in exactly the same way. With or without the bone, the dish is very popular throughout Italy. (See also Costoletta.)

CRESPONE / PURE PORK SALAMI
This fairly large salami is made only with pork. It is mostly available in the north of Italy and takes its name from the skin of the intestine of the pig. It is usually eaten sliced as part of an *antipasto*. See Salame.

LEFT: COTECHINI

CULATELLO / HAM
Zibello, a town near Modena, is the centre for the manufacture of this famous Emilia-Romagna ham. *Culatello* is the heart of the ham, the most tender part, cut in a round, cured in brine and enclosed in a gut-like skin before being left to air-dry for a long time. It tastes very sweet and, if correctly prepared, melts in the mouth. To enhance the taste of this delicacy further, the air-dried ham can be stripped of its skin then soaked in red wine to moisten it and add flavour. Soaked or unsoaked, this very special ham is usually served thinly sliced as part of an *antipasto* or by itself.

CUORE / HEART
You can find lovers of heart all over Italy, although they are concentrated in the south, where offal is generally more popular. The largest heart eaten in Italy is that of the ox, although it is only used in stews because it is quite tough, while the smaller and more tender veal heart is popular cut in slices then

BELOW: CULATELLO DI ZIBELO

fried or grilled. It is, however, probably the heart of the pig that is the most often used in the Italian kitchen, especially in the south where it is prepared with other offal and used in *ragùs*. Lamb's heart, especially that of very young animals, is usually eaten as part of *coratella* (see previous page), but it can also be fried or stewed in wine with the addition of rosemary, garlic and sage.

EQUINO, SEE CAVALLO

FARSUMAGRU /
BEEF OR VEAL DISH

Probably the most celebrated meat dish from Sicily, the reason this is called *farsumagru*, meaning 'false lean', is because a huge slice of beef or veal, 3.5 cm (1.5 inch) thick, is stuffed with all sorts of goodies then rolled and tied with string and braised or baked in a tomato sauce. The filling generally consists of prosciutto, Caciocavallo cheese, sausage meat, eggs, mortadella, garlic, onion, minced veal and even fresh peas. These ingredients are cut into square batons and placed lengthwise in the middle of the roll so that when it is cooked and cut in slices, a nice multicoloured section is revealed.

FEGATO / LIVER

Liver is the best-known and most popular offal in all of Italy. It contains the important vitamins A and D, and some of the B vitamins, as well as quite a lot of iron. The livers of all domesticated animals are sought after and in some cases are quite expensive. Naturally, like most offal, liver must be very fresh. Whichever liver you use, you must first remove and discard the fat and membrane surrounding it before cooking, as these make the liver bitter and inedible.

Ox liver is large, dark and tough. It is usually sliced and braised in wine. Calves' liver is the most frequently used in Italy and is popular for its tenderness and fine flavour. It is smaller than ox liver, although it still weighs about 2-3 kg ($4^{1}/_{2}$-$6^{1}/_{2}$ lb). As well as being simply fried or grilled, calves' liver is also the foundation of many recipes, including *fegato alla veneziana* in which it is stewed with onions, and as the basis for pâtés. Pigs' liver is also popular in Italian cooking: like ox liver it is very dark in colour, but is much smaller and has an excellent flavour. It can be cooked in various ways, including as part of the *fritto misto* (page 89) or to make *fegatelli*, little parcels of chopped liver enveloped in caul fat and baked or fried in lard. My mother used to pin the caul around the liver using pieces of a bay tree branch, to give it even more flavour.

Many regions, including Puglia, Calabria and Sicily, have recipes for specialities using liver. Popular flavourings include wine, sage, parsley, garlic and balsamic vinegar. *Coratella* (previous page) from Puglia uses both lambs' and goats' liver, while recipes from other regions include tying the liver in bundles with pieces of lung and other meat and then grilling it (see the Involtini recipe on page 92).

RIGHT: FINOCCHIONA

FESA / RUMP OF VEAL

This veal cut taken from the back leg is extremely tender and is usually grilled or fried. Sliced extremely thinly and drizzled with olive oil and lemon juice and perhaps dotted with a few shavings of truffle, it becomes *carne all'Albese* (see page 86). It is also the best cut for *carpaccio*.

FETTINE / VEAL ESCALOPES

Fettine are little veal escalopes which, as they are among the easiest cuts of meat to cook, have been adopted by many busy cooks. They can be fried in breadcrumbs or simply sautéed in butter with Marsala, lemon juice or vinegar added to flavour the rather bland meat. *Fettine* are used to make the well-known *piccata milanese* (see page 87).

FILONE, SEE MIDOLLO

FINOCCHIONA / FENNEL SAUSAGE

This sausage is mostly found in a typical Tuscan antipasto. It takes its name from *finocchio*, or wild fennel, the seeds of which were traditionally used to spice the finely ground pork fat. This savoury salami is huge, reaching 25 cm (10 inches) in diameter. The meat is aged in pigs' intestines for up to one year. Salted Tuscan bread is the ideal foil for balancing the spiciness of this salami. Fennel is also used to spice various other types of salami and sausages, especially those from Campania, Calabria, Puglia and Sicily.

GALANTINA DI CARNE / MEAT GALANTINE

Although the best-known galantines are made with chicken, there is also a version made with a mixture of meats, including large pieces of pork, veal and chicken. The meat is first boiled, then mixed with pistachio nuts, truffle and vegetables, put into a mould and covered with aspic. Cut in slices and served with a little oil and vinegar, the finished galantine may be included in an *antipasto* and makes a lovely snack.

GIAMBONE, SEE PROSCIUTTO COTTO

GIRELLO / ROUND TOPSIDE OR EYE

This round cut of beef is distinctively Italian. Taken from a rather coarse-grained muscle, it is therefore not suitable for grilling or frying, although the meat looks as good as fillet. It is usually minced, to break down the fibre in the meat, and used for raw beef salads or steak tartare. After being boiled it can also be eaten in thin slices with tuna fish sauce (see Vitello Tonnato, page 87).

GRANELLI / TESTICLES
I was once asked to test some unusual foreign foods for a London daily paper and one of the things I tried were rams' testicles, a speciality of Iceland. I was reassured that it was not only the Italians who love to eat these private parts. Although not exactly a common food, the testicles of veal, lamb, mutton and bulls are eaten everywhere in Italy, but are mostly enjoyed in the north. In the south, however, they eat lambs' testicles as part of an *involtino*. Otherwise they are usually thinly sliced and either grilled or fried. You need to ask the butcher to prepare them for you.

GRASSO / FAT
In the plural, *grassi* refers to all cooking fats, animal or vegetable. The fats used in different regions of Italy are dictated by the availability of local products. The northern custom is to cook with butter or lard. With modern nutritional awareness, however, today olive oil from the south has been widely adopted. Animal fats, like lard, are still used in the north, not only for reasons of economy, but also for their flavour. Certain recipes do not work with oil and need the original butter or lard to create the right texture or flavour. (See Lardo.)

GRIGLIATA MISTA / MIXED GRILL
This much-loved speciality is enjoyed all over Italy. Different cuts from of a variety of meats are brushed with olive oil and lemon juice, salted then grilled over charcoal. Many restaurants have this dish on their menu, but nothing can beat a *grigliata* eaten *al fresco* in the company of good friends. A decent mixed grill should contain slices of liver, heart, testicles, sausages, tender lamb and kid chops, and pieces of chicken or turkey. Naturally, if there are also some wild birds, like thrushes or sparrows, then all the better. Italians do not serve sauces with barbecued meat, just lemon juice.

Left: gnemeridde on skewers for grilling in Palermo.

GUANCIALE / PORK CHEEKS
This speciality of Lazio consists of pork cheeks cured in salt then air-dried for a few months. *Guanciale* is the main ingredient for genuine *carbonara* and *amatriciana* sauces. Pancetta is a good substitute, but it is not as tasty.

INSACCATO, SEE SALAME

INTESTINO, SEE BUDELLO

INTINGOLO / MEAT SAUCE
This term basically describes what would be scraped and deglazed from a pan after frying or roasting meat. The resulting sauce can be either served with bread or used as a gravy or even to dress pasta dishes. Today *intingolo* is synonymous with a thick meat *ragù*.

Left: pigs' heads

INVOLTINO / MEAT OLIVE PARCEL
Involtini consist of thin slices of meat wrapped around fillings of various ingredients, such as prosciutto, Parmesan cheese, mortadella, olives, parsley, garlic, sultanas, etc. They are then braised in a tomato sauce or baked. Beef is usually used because it has stronger texture, allowing it to cook slowly without breaking and leaking the filling. When very small, the rolls are also called *bocconcini*.

Involtini in regions such as Puglia or Calabria are mostly of lamb offal, including the heart, liver, lung and even testicles, tied together with a piece of gut, salted and spiced with pepper, chilli and parsley and then grilled over charcoal or baked in the oven. In Puglia these parcels are called *gnemeridde*; in Calabria, *ghunerieddi* or *ghunerielli*; and in Sicily *stigghiole*. For Neapolitans, *involtini di carne* are a festive must, usually on Sundays, and they cook them for a long time in a tomato sauce to be then eaten with pasta, usually penne or rigatoni (see the recipe on page 92).

LARDELLARE OR LARDARE / LARDING
This terms denotes the practice of threading strips of lard or other fatty ingredients into lean meats, like veal, with a special needle to give flavour and moisture while roasting.

LARDO / LARD
Fresh lard is taken from the fatty sides of the pig when the meat is butchered. It is then soaked in brine and hung for a few months and used for cooking. The lard is cut as required during the year and used as the base for sauces (see Battuto, page 70).

Lardo di Arnad, famous for its preserving qualities, is produced in a small town in the Aosta Valley.

This lard comes from particularly fat pigs, in whom the thickness of the fat can reach 10 cm (4 inches). It is cured with salt, pepper and rosemary, and then left to dry. In Piedmont and the Langhe area (Alba and Bra Cuneo), lard is thinly cut and eaten sprinkled with freshly ground black pepper. It has lots of flavour and gives a wonderful sensation in the mouth as it melts.

In an effort to preserve as much of the pig as possible for the following year, the fat may be cut into cubes and melted in a saucepan with bay leaves. This is cooked until the meat and bay leaves end up swimming in the liquid fat. Two precious products are made from this: *sugna*, or pork fat, which is used for frying and *ciccioli*. A Piedmontese speciality with *sugna* is to use it while still liquid and warm to cover freshly made pure pork sausages in terracotta pots. When the fat solidifies it keeps the sausages perfectly preserved so that they are fresh and tender up to a year later. This is called *salam d'la duja*.

Lesso, see Bollito Misto

Lingua / Tongue

Tongue is popular all over Italy. Veal tongue is the most tender and is usually boiled and served sliced with an acidic sauce, tuna fish sauce or *salsa verde* (see page 224). Tongue is an important ingredient in a classic *bollito misto* (see page 92). To achieve the vivid red colour characteristic of the meat it needs to be pickled in a salt solution for several hours and then boiled until tender. When buying tongue, make sure it is already pickled.

Lombo, Lombata, Lombatina, Lonza / Loin

These are the terms used to describe loin of beef, the tender and succulent cut of meat taken from the area around the lower part of the rib cage. Pork sirloin is called *lombo di maiale*, while in central Italy *lombatina* is the name given to describe *costoletta* or veal sirloin. One of the best ways of cooking loin is to grill it or to bind it with string and roast it for a short time in the oven like beef (allow 30 minutes per kilo / $2^1/_4$ lb). *Lonza* in certain parts of Southern Italy is called the *capocollo* or *coppa*.

Luganiga, Luganega, Luganeca, Lucanica / Fresh Pork Sausages

These long thin fresh pork sausages were probably the ancestors of the hot dog. They are made with relatively coarsely minced pork and have a 40 per cent fat content. The minced meat is stuffed into a single piece of gut and sold by the metre, divided into long sausage segments. Such sausages are very common in Italy, especially in the Northern and Central regions where, in winter, they are eaten cooked in a tomato sauce accompanied with polenta. They can also be grilled, fried or braised. The meat can also be extracted from the gut, crumbled and fried as part of the base for a pasta sauce or a risotto. I particularly like them fried with peppers or as in Polenta con Salsiccia, page 96.

Right: lardo

Macelleria / Butcher's shop

In the old days the shop-keeper used to butcher the animals himself on the premises. The *macelleria* of today is more likely to be just a retail shop selling meat, but sometimes also selling meat products, such as salami, etc.

Maiale, Maialino, Porco, Porcello, Porcellino, Porceddu, Suino / Pig, Pork, Piglet

Italians have always loved pork, not only because it is so easy to raise, but because every scrap of the animal can be used. When I was a boy, almost anyone who could kept a pig, feeding it on leftovers and scraps. Today their feed is more rationalized, mixing polenta with other high-energy grains. The industry, however, feeds pigs on other less valuable grains, obtaining larger production but of a less flavoursome meat. Better quality pork is, however, still sometimes obtained from herds partly fed on the whey by-products of cheese-making, and pigs lucky enough to graze in the wild and consume foods like acorns are said to give much of the flavour to better *prosciutto*.

As well as for their meat, pigs were also needed for their fat. Of the 200-plus kilo yield from the average pig, at least a quarter was fat and this was turned into solid and liquid lard. Today, with more information about the dangers of eating too much saturated animal fat, the pig is raised mainly for its meat and the commercially farmed pig – now available all year round – reaches an average weight of 160 kg (3 cwt).

When a pig was raised individually, it would be slaughtered in December or January so that its meat could be processed during cool weather to be preserved for use all year round. After the butcher slaughtered the pig, hams and sausages were made with the fresh meat while the perishable offal and other parts that could not be preserved were cooked for specially invited friends to celebrate the occasion. Nothing was wasted. Even the bones, once stripped of their meat to make salami, were boiled with cabbage, potatoes and beans to make a tasty soup. The blood, which was drained from the pig to keep its meat pale, would have been used either cooked with onion or mixed with pork fat to make black pudding or *marzapane*, or even to make a

LEFT: A BAS-RELIEF NEAR MODENA OF SAINT ANTONIO ABBATE, THE PATRON SAINT OF ANIMALS.

dessert, *sanguinaccio*, with milk, raisins, sugar and spices. Some people still keep pigs today, but the products so loved by Italians are now usually made commercially, not from the pig in the back yard.

Italians are very fond of eating suckling pigs (*maialino*, *porcello* or *porcellino*) that are slaughtered at anything from 8 to 12 weeks of age, and sometimes younger. The meat is regarded as a delicacy. In Sardinia, suckling pig is called *porceddu* and is traditionally roasted on a spit made of *corbezzolo*, the branches of a strawberry tree (see page 264), for at least 2 hours and brushed with lard from time to time. The wood fire is made of the branches of aromatic trees such as olive, juniper and myrtle to give extra flavour to the meat. Suckling pigs are also baked whole in a wood-fired oven. Moreover, *porchetto* or *porcetto*, stuffed roast whole adult pig, is also prepared when local festivals or weddings are celebrated. (See also Porchetta.)

Pork is eaten with equal avidity all over Italy; perhaps the North makes better use of it, because it is eaten during all the seasons. The South, for reasons of climate, tends to consume it only in winter. A great deal of pork is eaten by all Italians in preserved form, as hams, salamis or sausages of any type. The Northern style with these is boiled and accompanied by beans or *crauti* (sauerkraut); whereas from Central to Southern Italy they are preferred roasted, grilled or stewed.

MANZO / BEEF
Manzo is the general Italian term for mature beef, see Bovino.

MARZAPANE / PIGS BLOOD SPECIALITY
Not be confused with the almond paste marzipan, *marzapane* is pigs' blood mixed with pepper, nutmeg, salt, cubes of lard, breadcrumbs and garlic, and marinated in red wine. The mixture is either roasted or cooked in a bain-marie. When it is solid, it is cut into slices and then either fried with onions or, as in Novara, dipped in beaten egg then fried.

MEDAGLIONE / MEDALLIONS
Medaglioni are pieces of beef, veal, lamb or pork fillet cut at least a couple of centimetres ($^3/_4$ inch) thick and 5-10 cm (2-4 inches) in diameter to resemble large medals. Because the meat is usually very tender, *medaglioni* are either briefly pan-fried or grilled and then served with a suitable sauce.

MIDOLLO, SCHIENALE / MARROW, BONE MARROW
One of the attractions of *ossobuco alla milanese*, shin of beef cooked in a tomato sauce, is the marrow. It is pure fat and tastes heavenly. Bone marrow is also used to flavour *risotto alla milanese*. When my mother cooked beef stock she used shin of beef and I would amuse myself by extracting the marrow from the cooked bone, put it on toast and season it with salt and pepper for a real treat. The round marrow that fills the length of the spinal cord is known as *midollo spinale*, *schienale* or *filone* and is considered to be quite a delicacy. It is cut into short sections and fried as part of *fritto misto* (see page 89).

BOTTOM LEFT: PIGS BEING READIED FOR MARKET IN EMILIA-ROMAGNA.

MILZA / SPLEEN
The spleen is one offal that is not often used, as it does not have a very high culinary value. The only place I have seen it being cooked and eaten was in Sicily, in the extremely interesting market of Vucceria, in the centre of Palermo. At around midday, a few stands were preparing the typically Palermitan snack of *guastedde*. Pork spleen is grilled over charcoal, sliced very thinly and then fried in olive oil with chilli, salt and pepper and served between two pieces of bread like a hot dog. Judging by the long queues, it must have been very good.

MONTONE, SEE AGNELLO

MORTADELLA / SAUSAGE
Probably the best known Italian sausage, mortadella is made of pork, but sometimes includes some beef, veal, or even horse and donkey meat. Traditional in Bologna, this is the largest of the Italian sausages, weighing between 5 and 15 kg (11 and $32^1/_2$ lb). Giant mortadellas made for exhibitions can reach up to 150 kg (3 cwt) in weight.

ABOVE: MORTADELLA

Mortadella is 60 per cent pork meat and 40 per cent fat. The pork is finely minced and the fat takes the form of long, square-cut strips of lard. The mixture is seasoned with spices, and sometimes contains pistachio nuts and coriander seeds. Today, the sausage meat is forced into a synthetic gut, but in the past pig's bowel was used. The sausage is then steamed or poached in special ovens.

The best mortadella is made of pure pork and is called *puro suino*, with the letter 'S' stamped on the

Above: offal on sale from a Neapolitan street vendor.

Right: a norcino of Norcia.

skin so that it can be identified. The branding 'SB' means *suino/bovino*, to indicate that it is made with beef and pork or lamb and pork. A less well-known mortadella from Lago d'Orta, called *mortadella di fegato*, is made with pigs' liver.

Mortadella must be sliced very thinly to bring out the flavour and can therefore only be cut by a machine. It is mostly eaten with bread, especially *focaccia*, but it is also used as part of a meat stuffing. In war-time, when meat was hard to come by, my mother would bring home very thickly sliced mortadella which she dipped in beaten eggs and breadcrumbs then fried like a cutlet. Served with salad, it made a perfect lunch.

Musetto / Sausage
This sausage, made with flesh from the pig's snout (*muso*), is a speciality of Friuli and the area of Trenito Alto Adige, in the north-west of Italy. The pork meat is very finely minced with some fat and put in a gut with part of the snout and sometimes the pig's skin. It is served and cooked like *cotechino*, but in the north is accompanied by either sauerkraut or red cabbage stewed with vinegar and wine.

Nervetti / Tendons and Gristle
Nervetti is veal and pork cartilage, mainly from the foot, boiled until tender, then sliced very thinly and seasoned with olive oil, vinegar and raw onions. In Venice, *nervetti* thinly cut and spiced with oil, vinegar, salt and pepper are eaten as snacks or with an aperitif. In Naples it is sold extensively from colourful little roadside stands that also sell cooked veal heads (*'o musso*) and tripe dressed with lemon juice and olive oil.

Nodino / Cutlet
Nodino di vitello is a veal cutlet with the bone in and not too thickly cut. *Nodini* are mostly fried slowly with butter and sage or rosemary (see the recipe for Nodino di Vitello al Rosmarino on page 88).

Norcineria / Pork Butchers
In the town of Norcia in Umbria, the local speciality is based on pork and wild boar. The local butchers, called *norcini*, are very famous for their skill and have given their name to the art of pork and boar butchering. Their shops are called *norcineria*, the equivalent of *macelleria*.

Omento, see Rete di Maiale

Orecchio / Pork Ears
Only the ears of pigs and veal calves are generally eaten. They are cooked for about 2 hours and then thickly sliced and served in a similar way to *nervetti*. Pork ears are also minced and added to *cotechino* or *zampone* (see the recipe on page 97).

Ossobuco / Shin of Veal
Osso meaning bone and *buco* meaning hole, this is taken from the part of the leg where the muscle is particularly thick, giving a cut of meat about 8.5 cm ($3^1/_2$ inches) across cut into 2.5 cm (1 inch) thick sections with the bone and marrow in place. The dish of *ossobuco alla milanese* (see page 95), in which the shin pieces are stewed in a tomato sauce, has been made popular all over the world by Italian restaurants. It is usually served with a *gremolada* and accompanied by saffron risotto (see page 178).

Ossocollo, see Capicollo

Pagliata / Offal Dish
This Roman offal dish is better sampled in restaurants, because of the very particular principal ingredient – which needs to be very fresh – and the elaborate and lengthy preparation required. The offal used is part of the intestines, normally of milk-fed calves, complete with their creamy contents. It is normally lightly flavoured with parsley and then grilled. Although veal offal is most often used, *pagliata* can be made from beef, lamb or even goat offal. The tripe taste is very intense.

Pancetta / Streaky Bacon
A very important ingredient in the preparation of many Italian dishes, pancetta is bacon cured from belly of pork, or *pancia*. Pancetta is usually fried as a base for sauces, the best known of which is *carbonara*, a sauce for pasta based on small cubes of fried pancetta – or *guanciale* as the purist requires – with the addition of raw egg at the end. Fresh pancetta can be used to make minestrone and soups. *Pancetta curata*, salt-cured, air-dried or even *arrotolata*, rolled pancetta, is used thinly sliced as part of an *antipasto*. Today you can also find *pancetta affumicata*, smoked pancetta, which is used in many northern Italian dishes influenced by the cuisine of neighbouring Austria. Tuscany also produces *rigatino pancetta* 'streaky bacon', a very thin

bacon that has the same uses as other pancettas.

PECORA, SEE AGNELLO

PETTO / BREAST

This cut is also called *punta* and can be of veal (*punta di vitello*) or of other animals. In the north of Italy, breast is a cheap way of making a little meat go a long way. A big pocket is cut into the breast between the layers of meat and fat; this is stuffed and sewn up and the breast is then roasted. The best-known version is *cima alla genovese*, a very long-cooked boned and rolled breast of veal.

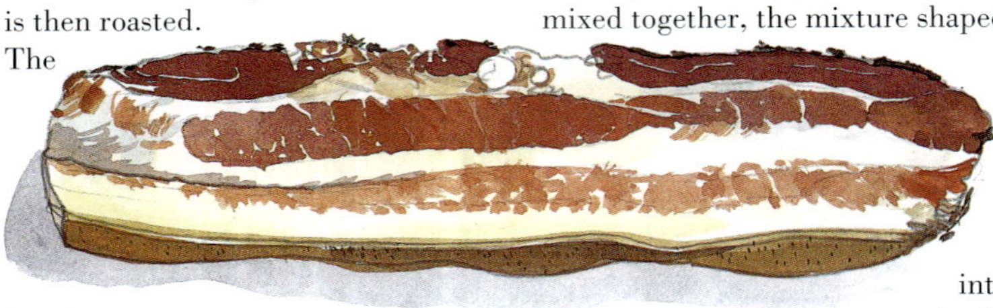

LEFT: PANCETTA

The southern version, made in Campania and all the regions to the south, is made with lamb breast. The filling is made of breadcrumbs, eggs, Parmesan, parsley and garlic. After the pocket has been sewn up, it is cooked for a long time in a *ragù*. The sauce is used to dress a first course of pasta and the meat is sliced and eaten accompanied by spinach.

PICCATA, SEE SCALOPPINA

PIEDINO, SEE ZAMPI

POLMONE / LUNG

Only pork and lamb lung is used in Italian cuisine and this use is mainly concentrated in the south. Lung is part of the pluck and is used finely chopped in Umbrian *coratella*, a mixture of finely cut offal which is fried in olive oil with onions, chilli and wine (see page 73) and *soffritto alla napoletana*, in which finely chopped pork offal is cooked in lard with chilli, bay leaves, tomato purée, onions and wine. *Soffritto* and *coratella* are both winter dishes, generally eaten a little at a time diluted with stock and reheated, then put on slices of toasted bread like soup.

POLPETTE, POLPETTINE, RISSOLE / MEATBALLS

Polpette and rissole, made from minced meat (*polpa*), are cooked all over Italy and are considered to be the most economical and tasty way of using minced meat. Different meats can be minced to vary the flavour. The classic recipe for *polpette* is minced beef or veal mixed with beaten egg, crushed garlic, grated Parmesan cheese, chopped parsley, salt and pepper. The ingredients are thoroughly mixed together, the mixture shaped into rissoles or balls and deep-fried until crispy. They can either be eaten as they are or cooked and served in sauces to dress pasta as they do in Southern Italy, especially in Puglia. *Polpettine* are tiny meatballs crisply fried and used as fillings for pasta timbales (see Timbalo di Ziti, page 161).

POLPETTONE / MEATLOAF

Meatloaf used to be eaten by the poor as a substitute for a large piece of meat. Made from either minced beef or pork, it was traditionally braised for several hours in a rich tomato sauce. The sauce would be used to dress a first course of pasta and the meat was eaten as part of the main course. Today, however, *polpettone* is extremely popular all over Italy, particularly with the Neapolitans.

The recipe for meatloaf is similar to that for meatballs. Mix the minced meat with fresh breadcrumbs, parsley, coarsely chopped onion, beaten eggs, Parmesan cheese, nutmeg, salt and pepper. Form this into a single meatloaf and, in a large pan, carefully brown it on each side in olive oil. Take care when turning the meatloaf not to break it. Add more chopped onions to the pan when the *polpettone* has almost been browned all over. When the onion is translucent, add the tomato sauce and cook slowly for a couple of hours. The sauce will be flavoured with the juices from the meatloaf and can be used to dress pasta. You can also roast meatloaf without any sauce, like any other piece of roast meat. In this case the mixture is kept juicier by reducing the breadcrumbs.

PORCEDDU, PORCELLO, PORCELLINO, SEE MAIALE

PORCHETTA / STUFFED PIG

Porchetta, which originated in Umbria but is now more strongly associated with Lazio and more especially Rome, is one of the most spectacular of the Italian pork specialities. This rather special dish consists of a whole boned pig, weighing 30-40 kg (65-90 lb) which is stuffed with its own offal, like the liver, heart and lungs, which have been sliced and sautéed in oil and seasoned with garlic and herbs like bay and rosemary. The pig is then roasted on a spit over a wood fire or baked in a wood-fired oven for 4 to 5 hours, or until the skin is a red-brown and wonderfully crispy. It often forms the centrepiece of local festivities and slices of it are sold from little roadside stands.

PORCO, SEE MAIALE

PROSCIUTTO / CURED HAM

In the past, meat had to be preserved so that it kept for a long time without the benefit of refrigeration. This need gave birth to a vast industry given over to the production of hams enjoyed as specialities in their own right rather than simply as preserved meat. Prosciutto, probably from the Latin *perexutus* meaning dried, is among the most renowned and is probably one of the best-loved foods from Italy worldwide. *Prosciutto crudo* is the essential ingredient in an Italian *antipasto*. It is eaten accompanied by either melon or figs and with *grissini* or good bread. It can also

How Prosciutto is Prepared

Prosciutto is made from the cured hind leg of the pig. It is cut so that one end is rounded. To preserve it, the meat is massaged with salt daily for a whole month until the salt has penetrated right through to the centre of the flesh. The hams are

then hung in special well-ventilated rooms to mature. This takes from 12 to 16 months and during this time the ham loses at least 30 per cent of its weight.

The curing process gives the meat and fat the wonderful taste that is characteristic of Italian hams. To avoid the loss of weight that occurs naturally during the curing process, some unscrupulous producers release their hams after only nine months. Although such hams look fully cured, they still taste of raw flesh after only this short curing time.

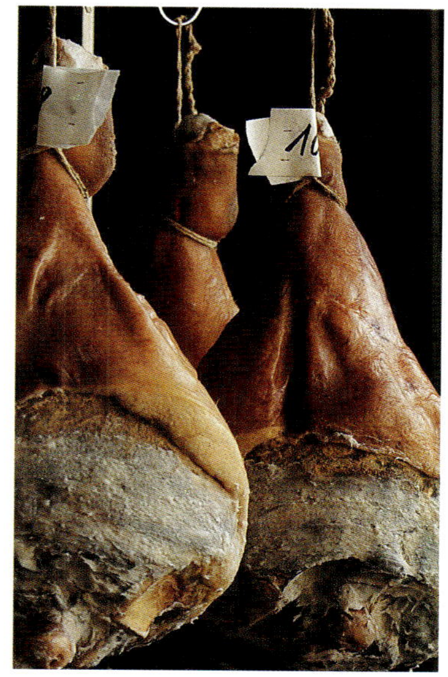

form part of a main course, served for example with buttered asparagus and boiled potatoes.

Parma ham, just one of the types of prosciutto produced in Italy, is so well-known that any Italian ham is almost exclusively associated with it, although many other regions produce their own local hams. Parma ham is made from pigs raised in Emilia-Romagna or Lombardy, where the raw weight of the ham has to be at least 10-11 kg (22-24 lb). The production of Parma ham is controlled by the local producers' association and guarantees that the ham is locally cured and dried in the traditional way. It is also a guarantee that the pigs from which the hams are made are raised traditionally, and fed on the whey used to make Parmigiano Reggiano cheese, maize and other natural food so that the meat is tender and full of flavour. Other good local hams include the slightly smaller but very sweet-flavoured San Daniele from Friuli.

Other regions which produce good hams are Tuscany, Veneto, Campania, in the towns of Langhirano and San Leo (where, it is said, the pigs are partly fed on acorns). The best hams are cured for anything from 16 to 18 and up to 24 months. Those are cured on the bone and cut as thinly as possible by hand.

To make hams suitable for slicing by machine the bone is removed from an aged ham with a special tool by a specially trained *norcino*. The ham is then pressed in a mould to reshape it and vacuum-packed in heavy plastic film once it is turned out. However, the best ham is sold freshly sliced, as those sold ready-packed have little resemblance to the real thing.

According to the Association of Parma Ham Producers, during the curing process, much of the saturated fat in the ham turns into unsaturated, so that prosciutto is actually a much healthier food than it might at first seem, with its perfect balance of proteins, fats, low cholesterol and an abundance of vitamins and trace elements.

Prosciutto Cotto / Cooked Ham

This is a variation on *prosciutto crudo* using the same cut of meat. The seasoned meat is pickled and pressed in a square-shaped mould before being steam-baked in special ovens. Like cured ham, *prosciutto cotto* is eaten as part of an *antipasto*, as well as being used for flavouring sauces and cooked vegetables or for stuffings. A cheaper version is made from shoulder of pork. In some parts of Northern Italy, *prosciutto cotto* is known as *giambone*.

Punta di Vitello, see Petto

Rene, see Rognone

Rete di Maiale, Omento / Caul Fat

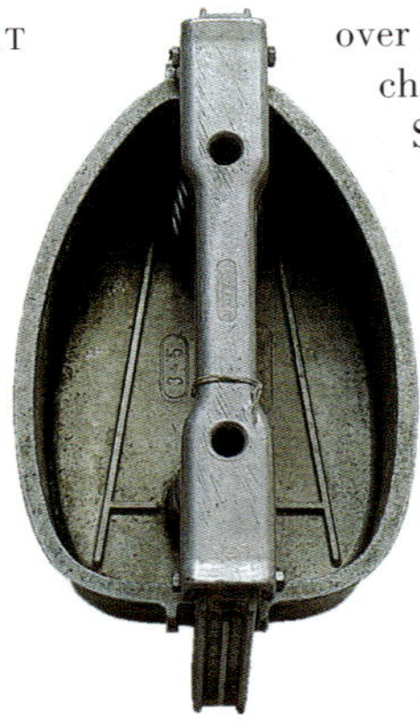

Left: a press for cooked hams.

Caul fat is a lacy membrane of fat lining the stomach of (normally) the pig, used to bard tender pieces of meat or offal before roasting or baking and imparting a wonderful flavour to any meat. After the caul fat is taken from the stomach of the pig, it forms a solid ball. Soaked in lukewarm water this separates into a kind of veiled net; it is then cut into squares for ease of use. Just simply take a piece of pig's liver, season it and wrap in caul fat, then fry for a minute or two on each side.

Rognone, Rognoncini, Rene / Kidney

After liver, kidney is the simplest and most commonly used offal in Italian cuisine. The kidneys of veal calves, lamb and, sometimes, pigs are used in all Italian kitchens. Tender small kidneys from very young animals, called *rognoncini*, are a particular speciality. To get rid of any residual unpleasant tastes or smells, kidneys should be cut into slices and doused in salt or soaked in milk for an hour to draw out the impurities. They must then be thoroughly washed before being cooked.

Veal kidneys are characterized by a series of lobes, connected by fatty strands which need to be cut out and discarded before cooking. Kidneys are embedded in a large lump of suet, which is sometimes melted and used for cooking. However, it is also possible to bake the entire kidney still embedded in that lump of fat for a long time.

Lambs' kidneys, shaped like large kidney beans, are much smaller than veal and pigs' kidneys. They should be prepared in a similar way to veal kidneys and need to be cut open with a knife in order to discard the fatty core inside.

The classic dish for kidneys all over Italy is *trifolati*. Gently fry a chopped garlic clove in butter. Slice the kidneys thinly and toss them in flour. When the garlic is slightly browned, add the kidneys to the pan and fry for 1-2 minutes. Pour in a little dry white wine or Marsala, then add some chopped parsley and fry for another 3-4 minutes, but no longer or the kidneys will be tough. Season with salt and pepper before serving.

Rostida, Rustida, Rosticiada, Rosticiana / Meat Dish

This is a *ragù* made of a mixture of meat cuts, mainly pork, which is cooked in wine until tender. In a separate pan, a large amount of chopped onion is sautéed in olive oil. When both are ready, they are mixed together with some chilli and tomato *polpa*. This dish, a speciality from Lombardy and the region's equivalent of *soffritto di maiale* or Umbrian *coratella*, is then eaten with polenta.

Rumine, see Trippa

Salama, Salama da Sugo, Salamina / Cured Sausage

This is an ancient speciality of the city of Ferrara. Both its contents and the way it is cooked contribute to its special status and make it impossible to reproduce on a commercial basis. You can only buy it locally or find it on the menu of local restaurants.

It is traditionally made using the bladder of the pig as a container and weighs between 600 g (1¹/₄ lb) and 1 kg (2¹/₄ lb). This classic *salame* is made entirely of pork tongue and liver and is spiced with salt, pepper, cloves and cinnamon, with perhaps Marsala, Cognac or even rum added for more flavour. Every kitchen in the town has its own particular recipe and spice mixture, which they guard jealously. This mixture forms the centre of the *salama* and is then wrapped in minced pork taken from the neck and from the head. Once the bladder has been completely stuffed it is bound and hung to dry for at least six months, much like Scottish haggis.

Before eating it is very carefully cooked for about 5 hours, with the bladder tied to a stick so that it does not touch the bottom of the pot of simmering water. The cooked *salama* is cut open and eaten with a traditional accompaniment of potato purée. It smells and tastes absolutely delicious.

Salame / Cured Sausage

Like many preserved meats, *salame* is known as *insaccato* or 'bagged goods'. Over many years, various methods have been developed for preserving meat, including air- or sun-drying, or using salt, sugar, honey, vinegar or alcohol. Preserving meat, especially that of the annually butchered pig, has given rise to specialities like ham and sausages as well as a variety of other commodities which Italians have incorporated into their diet. As well as having an exquisite flavour, compared to a slice of plain cooked meat good salami is highly nutritious and has the benefit of being ready to eat at any time. It is therefore not surprising that Italians have dedicated so many of their natural resources to the creation of such a unique food, and today many salamis are made using the traditional methods.

After being properly cleaned, the intestines of various animals can be preserved over a long period as the minced meat contains certain agents which, along with preservatives, allow the meat to age without deteriorating. The meat for salami is usually seasoned

Below: salame di testa di maiale (pig's head salami) and coppa.

Right: salame varzi

with spices which also help to preserve the meat, and it is then forced into the skins and carefully cured.

Salami is made up of about 40 per cent fat in the form of lard or hard fat cut into cubes of different sizes, as softer fat has a tendency to turn rancid. This fat starts out highly saturated, but during the curing process much of this turns into unsaturated fat.

The meat used for salami is predominantly pork, although some salamis contain a mixture of pork and beef – or sometimes even horse meat – and the label always indicates whether it contains pure pork (*puro suino*) or pork and beef (*suino e bovino*) etc. The meat is minced to different textures and fineness depending on the type of salami being made. Additional flavourings of garlic, salt, peppercorns, chilli, fennel seed, wine, Marsala and even brandy are added to the mixture. After it has been forced into the gut and moulded to the traditional shape, it is tied with string and hung in specially constructed curing rooms where the sausages are left for at least 2 to 4 months to cure under carefully controlled conditions of air-flow and temperature. When the *salumi* are sold they are fully matured and will have lost at least 35 per cent of their initial weight as they dry.

In every town in every region there is a salami specialist and each one has its own local variation. Some of these salamis are now made on a large scale and sold throughout the world. The following are just a few of the many that can be found in Italy. The first group use finely minced meat, and are sometimes referred to generically as '*milano*' or '*ungherese*'.

Salame milano, also called *crespone*, is made with very finely minced pork spiced with salt, saltpetre, coarsely milled black pepper and, in some cases, crushed garlic marinated in red wine. The minced meat is forced into a natural gut to make a sausage with a diameter of about 8 cm (3¼ inches). Once bound, it is aged for at least 3 months, during which time it loses 30 per cent of it initial 2 kg (4½ lb) weight. It is served very thinly cut.

Salame ungherese, or Hungarian salami, has been adopted by Italians who enjoy its smoky flavour. The finely minced meat is made up of equal parts pork, beef and pork fat. It is aged for at least three months and weighs around 1.5 kg (3¼ lb) when cured. It has a diameter of 6-7 cm (2½-2¾ inches) and is served very thinly sliced.

Cacciatori, or hunter's salami, is small, weighing only about 100 g (3½ oz) and only needs to be aged for a short period. It gets its name from its size, which made it convenient for hunters to carry with them. Today it makes an ideal addition to any picnic basket.

The meat of the following salami is of a medium coarseness so that little chunks of meat and fat can be clearly distinguished. They are called *nostrani*.

Salame varzi, from the area of Pavia in Lombardy, is an excellent pure pork salami with 30 per cent fat. Only salt, saltpetre, whole black peppercorns and wine are added. It is about 6-7 cm (2½-2¾ inches) in diameter and is aged for 3-4 months. Only about 25 per cent of its weight is lost during the curing process.

Salame di Felino comes from a little town near Parma and is probably one of the best Italian salamis. It is traditionally very sweet in taste and the meat used includes trimmings from the leg of pork used in making Parma ham as well as some shoulder meat. The spices added are salt, whole black peppercorns, saltpetre and perhaps some garlic and wine. Because of the type of gut used as a casing, it has a long and irregular shape, with a smaller diameter at the top than at the bottom. It takes at least three months to cure.

Salame fabriano, *salame genovese* and *salame veronese* are all very similar to the *salame di felino*, containing only a few different spices and a slightly different ratio of meat to fat.

Salame toscano or *finocchiona* or *sbriciolona*, unlike the previous salamis, contains equal amounts of pork and fat. It is also much larger than the others, with a diameter of about 15 cm (6 inches) and tends to crumble when cut, which is why it is called *sbriciolona* (meaning 'crumbly'). The name *finocchiona* was given to it because, as well as the usual flavourings, fennel is also added.

Salame napoli is a very popular salami made up of equal parts pork, pork fat and beef. It also contains garlic, pepper, wine, salt, saltpetre, paprika and chopped chilli, making it ideal for those who prefer a stronger, spicier flavour. Similar salamis include the *campagnolo*, *salame all'aglio*, *salame abruzzese*, *ascolano bellunese*, *cadorino* and *ventricina*.

Other spicy or hot salamis include the excellent *salsiccie* made in Calabria (*salsiccia calabrese* and *napoletana*). Both are made in the same way, with the meat being pressed into a small round gut and tied into a circle. They are easily distinguished from other *salsiccie* by their hot spices, including chilli, paprika and whole peppercorns.

The *soppressata* is a sort of pressed salami available all over Italy. The Venetian one, called *soppressa*, is made with pork and has a fat content of 30 per cent. It is cured for 10-15 months. The Calabrian *soppressata* is probably the most sought-after and is made up of three-quarters pork and one-quarter pork fat. The meat and fat are cut quite coarsely with a knife and mixed with garlic, pepper, blood, paprika, wine, salt, pepper and chilli. It is forced into a short gut and then placed under a wooden board and weighted down so that it achieves the traditional flat shape. It is then smoked and cured for 3-4 months.

SALAME COTTO / COOKED SALAMI
This is mostly eaten in the north of Italy, where the temperatures allow an unpreserved sausage to be kept for longer period of time. It is made in the same way as Cotechino, but is boiled in water and sold cooked and ready to eat as part of a *bollito misto* (see page 92) or minced to make meat stuffings or fillings for ravioli.

SALAM D'LA DUJA, SEE LARDO
SALSICCIA, SALSICCIOTTO, SALSICCINE, SEE LUGANICA

SALTIMBOCCA / VEAL DISH
Literally translated as 'jump in the mouth', this Roman speciality is based on small scaloppine of veal covered with sage leaves and topped with slices of prosciutto and fried in a pan. These morsels are now made of other ingredients, such as in *saltimbocca d'animelle*, where the veal is replaced by sweetbreads.

SALUMERIA / PORK PRODUCTS
Salumi is the generic term for preserved meat products, mostly pork, and a *salumeria* is a shop specializing in such fare. There are two basic types of preserved meats, the whole cured hams and other meats like prosciutto, and the sausages made of minced meat and fat, like salami.

SANGUE / BLOOD
The only blood that is used in the Italian kitchen is pigs' blood. It has to be stored very carefully and beaten so that it does not coagulate. It is used to make black pudding, or a very tasty tart called *sanguinaccio* (see Maiale on page 77).

SCALOPPINA, PICCATA / VEAL PIECES
Silverside of veal is a tender cut and small thin slices of it are known as scaloppine. They are usually dusted with flour and fried in hot butter for one minute on each side. With the addition of some stock, white wine, Marsala or lemon juice and a little garlic and parsley, the scaloppine can be then ready in few minutes. See also Fettine.

SCHIENALE, SEE MIDOLLO

SFRIZOLI, SEE CICCIOLI

SPECK / SMOKED HAM SHOULDER
This Austrian speciality was introduced into Italy fairly recently, previously being known only to those who lived on the Austro-Italian border. Speck is a smoked, salt-cured, air-dried ham. It is extremely delicious on its own, but is widely used in sauces, *ragùs* and stews and to add a distinguished flavour to vegetables. It is similar to, but much cheaper than, Parma ham and many people eat it as an alternative as part of their *antipasto*. To me they seem so different that it is impossible to compare them.

Left: salam d'la duja on sale in Piedmont.

Above: old shop front in Cocconato.

SPEZZATINO / BEEF STEW
Anyone who was in the military service in Italy will remember *spezzatino* for the rest of his life. It is a very economical meat dish, as any cut of beef can be used to make it. Other ingredients include tomatoes, onion and puréed olives. The sauce was used to dress pasta and the meat eaten with vegetables.

STINCO / VEAL SHIN
A typical Lombardian dish, *stinco di vitello* is whole shin of veal cooked slowly in stock, wine and perhaps a little lemon juice for at least two hours, or until tender. Once cooked, the meat is served off the bone. Similarly, shin of pork can be roasted with herbs, such as rosemary and sage as well as a little wine.

STRACOTTO / BRAISED MEAT
This term, from the word for overcooked, describes a beef stew cooked for at least 3 hours in a slow oven until the meat is very tender. The other ingredients include red wine, celery, carrots, onion and a few tomatoes (see page 88).

STUFATO / STEW
From *stufa* meaning 'stove', *stufati* are meat stews cooked slowly in the oven, sometimes for up to twelve hours.

SUINO, SEE MAIALE

SUGNA, SEE LARDO

TESTA, TESTINA / HEAD
Testa is the head of pork and *testina* the head of veal. Pork head

is used mainly in the south to make *cotechino* or *salame cotto*, while veal head is mainly used in the north of Italy as part of *bollito misto*. *Testina* also refers to the head of a sheep or goat and is popular in central and southern Italy, where it is baked in the oven. The head is usually sold cut in half so that it can be spiced and eaten more easily.

TESTICOLI, SEE GRANELLI

TRIPPA, TRIPE, BÜSECCA / TRIPE

Tripe is part of the stomach of ruminants such as calves. It is a dish that, if properly prepared, is delicious. Today, this is a national dish in Italy and people in every region and every town, whether poor or rich, eat tripe prepared in many different ways according to their own regional traditions.

Only perfect fresh tripe is worth eating, so it is important to start with the right cut of a high quality. Tripe is made from the four parts of a ruminant's stomach. The *ricciolino* or *riccia* is the first section and looks like a curly gut full of glands and has a rich flavour. The second part is the *rumine*, or blanket, and the third is the *reticolo* or honeycomb. The fourth is for me the best of all and is the *millefoglie*, so called because of its many membranes, which look like leaves or the pages of a book.

Tripe should be bought cleaned but uncooked. It is, however, quite difficult to get it like this unless you know a butcher who will sell it in this state. I find that outside Italy, the only place in which tripe is sold uncooked is in Chinese shops.

For all the various regional recipes, at least one per region, there is a basic preparation which blanches the uncooked tripe for 30 minutes. After it is cooled, the tripes are rubbed together like cloths being washed, and rinsed to get rid of impurities. It is then cut into bite-sized pieces, ready to be cooked for up to 3 or 4 hours, depending upon its initial tenderness.

Usually onion, celery, carrots, pepper and bay leaves are the basic flavourings for tripe. After these, the tripe can be eaten with oil, lemon juice and parsley as they do in Naples. However, ingredients like rosemary, pancetta, cinnamon, tomatoes, chilli and sage are among the favourite flavourings in other regions. Fried in lard, butter and oil and then topped with stock, tripe is also made into a moist stew, which in some cases is topped with grated Parmesan cheese before serving.

VIOLINO DI CHIAVENNA / CHIAVENNA VIOLIN

This curious ham takes its name from the town of Chiavenna in Veltellina. It is made from the leg of a lamb or goat, seasoned with garlic, spiced with juniper berries and washed in red wine, then air-dried for a few months. It is called *violino* because in order to cut it the ham must be slung over the shoulder as if playing the violin.

VITELLO / VEAL

After pork, the veal from milk-fed calves is the most important meat in Italian cooking.

All the cuts are used to produce the most varied dishes: cubed in stews with a little white sauce it becomes a *spezzatino*, similar to French *blanquette de veau*. The most popular cut is the *paillard*, a large thin slice of veal, which is seared on the griddle for a minute on each side or dipped in beaten egg and breadcrumbs and then fried as *cotoletta alla milanese*. *Saltimbocca* is a speciality of Rome, with the veal slices covered with just a slice of ham and some sage leaves and fried. Rolled and stuffed with pancetta, they become *uccelli scappati* ('flown-away birds'), a speciality of Reggio Emilia. Of course, we must not forget *scaloppine al limone*, with Marsala and lemon juice, and Ossobuco alla Milanese (page 95), just to mention a few of the regional dishes made with veal. See also Bovino, Fettine, and Scaloppina.

ZAMPI, ZAMPETTI, ZAMPONE, PIEDINO / TROTTERS

Only veal and pork trotters are used in Italian cooking. The foreleg trotters are favoured because they have more meat than the back. Veal trotters develop a wonderfully tender gelatinous quality after they have been cooked for a long time and they make a perfect thickener for stock. Otherwise veal trotters can be eaten sliced and dressed with olive oil and lemon juice or vinegar, either warm or cold.

As they need to be thoroughly cleaned, I suggest that you let your butcher take care of the preparation of pigs' trotters. Once you have got them home, however, they need to be boiled for at least an hour. They can then be tossed in breadcrumbs and shallow-fried in butter. When the skin is crispy and the flesh very soft, they can be served with lemon juice. Alternatively, once they have been blanched they can also be slowly braised in tomato sauce for a couple of hours. Another popular recipe is to stuff the skin around the shin with a mixture of minced pork meat, the meat on the shin itself and the ears, to make *zampone*.

RIGHT: ZAMPI AND TRIPPA IN THE FLORENCE MARKET.

CARNE ALL'ALBESE

ALBA-STYLE RAW BEEF WITH PARMESAN AND WHITE TRUFFLE

FOR 4

- 400 G (14 OZ) BEEF FILLET, CUT INTO VERY THIN SLICES
- 4 TBSP EXTRA-VIRGIN OLIVE OIL
- JUICE OF 1 LEMON
- 12 FRESH ASPARAGUS TIPS, COOKED UNTIL JUST AL DENTE
- 4 CELERY STALKS, THINLY SLICED
- 85 G (3 OZ) PARMESAN CHEESE, THINLY SLICED
- 45 G (1½ OZ) WHITE TRUFFLE, CUT INTO THIN SHAVINGS
- SALT AND PEPPER

The attraction of this sophisticated dish from Piedmont lies in its simplicity and, naturally, in the unbeatable combination of the meat with truffles. Locally in Alba, not only rich people enjoy this dish. The truffle-hunters themselves are very fond of it.

Put the slices of beef between 2 sheets of heavy-duty cling film and beat gently with a meat mallet or the end of a rolling pin until very thin. It should be about 1–2 mm (1/16 inch) thick. Spread the meat over 4 large serving plates without letting the slices overlap. Season with salt and pepper, then brush with the olive oil and lemon juice. Distribute the slices of celery, asparagus tips, Parmesan and white truffle over the meat and serve with *grissini*.

VITELLO TONNATO

VEAL IN TUNA SAUCE

FOR 6

1 LITRE ($1^3/_4$ PINTS) DRY WHITE WINE
2 CELERY STALKS, CHOPPED
1 CARROT, CHOPPED
1 ONION, CHOPPED
1 GARLIC CLOVE, CHOPPED
A FEW BAY LEAVES
1 KG ($2^1/_4$ LB) VEAL TOPSIDE OR EYE OF SILVERSIDE, TIED WITH KITCHEN STRING TO MAKE A LARGE, LONGISH SAUSAGE
SALT AND PEPPER
PARSLEY LEAVES AND CAPERS, TO DECORATE

FOR THE SAUCE:

350 G (12 OZ) MAYONNAISE
45 G ($1^1/_2$ OZ) SALTED CAPERS, SOAKED IN WATER FOR 10 MINUTES, THEN DRAINED AND VERY FINELY CHOPPED
60 G (2 OZ) PICKLED GHERKINS, VERY FINELY CHOPPED
250 G (9 OZ) TUNA FISH IN OIL, DRAINED
2 TBSP FINELY CHOPPED FLAT-LEAF PARSLEY

Fish and meat are very seldom combined, but in this famous recipe they make a perfect and delicate antipasto.

Put the wine, celery, carrot, onion, garlic and bay leaves in a large pan with the meat and add enough water to cover. Season with salt and pepper, bring to the boil, then reduce the heat and simmer for $1^1/_2$ hours, until the meat is tender. Meanwhile, mix together all the ingredients for the sauce and purée in a blender or food processor. Season to taste with salt and pepper if necessary.

Remove the meat from the pan, take off the string and cut the meat into very thin slices. Spread them over a large serving place and cover with the sauce. Decorate with parsley leaves and capers.

PICCATA MILANESE

VEAL WITH PARMA HAM MILANESE-STYLE

FOR 4

4 THIN SLICES OF VEAL, WEIGHING ABOUT 125 G ($4^1/_2$ OZ) EACH
65 G ($2^1/_4$ OZ) BUTTER
55 G ($1^3/_4$ OZ) SPECK (SEE PAGE 84) OR PARMA HAM, CUT INTO SMALL STRIPS
4 TBSP STOCK
1 TBSP FINELY CHOPPED FLAT-LEAF PARSLEY
JUICE OF 1 LEMON
SALT AND PEPPER
FLOUR FOR DUSTING

You can use chicken or turkey breast here instead of veal if you prefer. What these meats have in common is that they cook very quickly and absorb the flavouring, which can also be wine (see Scaloppina on page 84).

Trim the slices of veal to a uniform shape. Heat 45 g ($1^1/_2$ oz) of the butter in a large pan and fry the speck or Parma ham for a few minutes. Season the veal and dust with flour, then fry in the same pan until golden on each side. Remove from the pan and keep warm.

Add the rest of the butter to the pan, then stir in the stock to loosen the bits on the base of the pan. Add the parsley and lemon juice, bring to the boil, then pour over the meat and serve immediately.

Nodino di Vitello al Rosmarino

VEAL CUTLETS WITH ROSEMARY

For 4

- 4 tenderloin veal chops, weighing about 250 g (9 oz) each
- 85 g (3 oz) butter
- 4 small sprigs of rosemary
- 1 glass of dry white wine
- 25 g (3/4 oz) salted capers, soaked in water for 10 minutes, then drained and finely chopped
- zest of 1 lemon
- 1 tbsp finely chopped flat-leaf parsley
- salt and pepper
- flour for dusting

Nodino is a cutlet taken from the ribs. This is one of many ways of cooking it, typical of the North where this kind of meat is mostly consumed.

Dust the chops with flour on both sides. Heat the butter in a frying pan and gently fry the chops, 2 at a time if necessary, for 15 minutes on each side, until well browned. Remove from the pan, add the leaves from the rosemary sprigs and pour in the wine. Bring to the boil, stirring to scrape up the sediment from the base of the pan, then add the capers, lemon zest and parsley. Reduce the heat and mix well. Return the chops to the pan and cook gently for 10 minutes. Season with salt and pepper to taste, then serve.

Stracotto

BRAISED BEEF

For 6

- 4 tbsp olive oil
- a nice piece of beef such as rump or brisket, with a little fat, weighing about 1.5 kg (3 1/4 lb)
- 2 carrots, cut into very small cubes
- 1 large onion, finely chopped
- 3 celery stalks, cut into small cubes
- 10 juniper berries
- 20 peppercorns
- a few bay leaves
- 100 g (3 1/2 oz) fatty Parma ham, cut into thin strips
- 1 litre (1 3/4 pints) dry white wine
- 1 litre (1 3/4 pints) beef stock
- 45 g (1 1/2 oz) butter
- salt

Literally translated this means 'overcooked', which reflects the way this dish is cooked very slowly and for a long time.

Heat the olive oil in a large, preferably cast iron, pan, add the beef and brown on each side, then remove from the pan and set aside. Add the carrots, onion, celery, juniper berries, peppercorns, bay leaves and Parma ham and fry until the vegetables are soft. Return the meat to the pan and add the wine, stock and a little salt. Bring to the boil, then reduce the heat, cover and cook slowly until the meat is very tender, about 2 hours. Pierce the meat with a skewer to check if it is well cooked; if necessary, cook for a little longer. By the end of the cooking time most of the liquid should have evaporated.

Remove the meat from the pan, whisk in the butter and add a little more stock or wine – enough to bring it to a velvety consistency. Pass the sauce through a fine conical sieve. Serve the meat thinly sliced, accompanied by the sauce.

Stinco di Vitello

SLOW-ROASTED SHIN OF VEAL

For 8–10

- 1 whole shin of veal, weighing 2–3 kg (4½–6½ lb)
- 2 tbsp olive oil
- 125 ml (4 fl oz) white wine
- about 1 litre (1¾ pints) veal or beef stock
- small bunch each of sage, rosemary and thyme
- juice of 3 lemons
- 55 g (1¾ oz) butter, rolled in a little flour
- salt and pepper

This dish originated from both the Veneto and Lombardy and has now spread all over northern Italy. Shin of veal has to be cooked whole and can serve quite a few people.

Preheat the oven to 160°C/325°F/gas3. Wash and pat dry the shin of veal, then place it in a large roasting tin and rub with the olive oil and some salt and pepper. Pour the wine into the tin, plus enough of the stock to make a layer 1 cm (½ inch) deep. Add the herbs and cover with foil.

Cook in the oven for 1½ hours, checking from time to time that it has not dried out and adding more stock if necessary.

Remove the foil, increase the oven temperature to 200°C/400°F/gas6 and cook for another 30–40 minutes, basting the meat regularly with the liquid. Remove the meat from the tin and leave to rest for 10 minutes before serving. Meanwhile, put the roasting tin on the hob and add the lemon juice and enough stock to the meat juices to make a sauce consistency. Bring to the boil, stirring to scrape up the bits from the bottom of the tin, then whisk in the butter rolled in flour. Strain through a fine sieve. Thinly slice the veal lengthwise and serve with the sauce.

Fritto Misto alla Piemontese

PIEDMONTESE MIXED FRIED SURPRISE

For 6

- 6 lamb cutlets
- 200 g (7 oz) calves' liver, thinly sliced
- 200 g (7 oz) chicken breast in thin escalopes, sliced
- 200 g (7 oz) beef fillet in thin escalopes, sliced
- 2 artichoke hearts, (see Carciofo, page 105), thinly sliced
- 1 aubergine, thinly sliced
- 1 cardoon (see Cardo, page 105), peeled, lightly blanched and thinly sliced (optional)
- 2 crisp eating apples, peeled, cored and thickly sliced
- 12 amaretti biscuits
- 4 eggs, beaten
- seasoned flour for dusting
- olive oil for frying
- lemon wedges, to serve

It is said that this very typical Piedmontese dish should consist of at least 13 different ingredients, but its true afficionados prefer at least 17 or 18 meats of all types, vegetables, even biscuits and fruit.

Leave the lamb cutlets on the bone but beat out the meat until thin. Dust all the meat and vegetables, the apples and amaretti biscuits with flour and then coat them in the beaten egg. Heat a good layer of olive oil in a large frying pan and shallow-fry everything until golden brown, starting with the vegetables, then the apples and biscuits and finally the meat. Serve straight away, with lemon wedges.

Arrosto di Vitello al Latte

MILK-ROAST VEAL

For 6–8

- 55 g ($1^3/_4$ oz) butter
- 1.5 kg ($3^1/_4$ lb) lean silverside or topside of veal
- 100 g ($3^1/_2$ oz) Parma ham, cut into small strips
- 2 litres ($3^1/_2$ pints) milk
- pinch of freshly grated nutmeg
- salt and pepper

This is a very delicate dish, which should be served in thin slices with green beans, Swiss chard or spinach.

Melt the butter in a large pan into which the veal will just fit snugly. Add the meat and brown on all sides. Add the Parma ham strips, grate over the nutmeg and season with salt and pepper. Then pour in just enough of the milk to cover the meat by two-thirds. Cover and simmer gently for about 2–2½ hours, until tender, topping up with more milk from time to time to prevent the meat becoming dry.

TRIPPA ALLA MILANESE

TRIPE MILANESE-STYLE

FOR 6

150 G (5 OZ) LARGE WHITE BEANS
1.25 KG (2 LB 10 OZ) MIXED TRIPE, CLEANED AND BLANCHED (SEE TRIPPA, PAGE 85)
1 ONION, FINELY CHOPPED
1 LARGE CARROT, THINLY SLICED
2–3 CELERY STALKS, THINLY SLICED
55 G ($1^3/_4$ OZ) PANCETTA, CHOPPED
60 G (2 OZ) BUTTER
2 TBSP OLIVE OIL
500 G (1 LB) TOMATOES, PEELED, DESEEDED AND CHOPPED
A FEW BAY LEAVES
A FEW SAGE LEAVES
A LITTLE STOCK IF NECESSARY
100 G ($3^1/_2$ OZ) PARMESAN CHEESE, GRATED
SALT AND PEPPER

Of the many ways of preparing tripe, the busecca, *as they call it in Milan, is the one that probably pleases most palates.*

Soak the beans in plenty of cold water overnight and then drain.

Cut the prepared tripe into strips. Fry the onion, carrot, celery and pancetta in the butter and oil until soft. Add the tripe and cook until the moisture has evaporated, stirring often to prevent sticking. Add the tomatoes, bay leaves, sage leaves, salt and plenty of black pepper, then cover and cook gently for 2 hours. If the mixture becomes too dry, add a little stock.

Put the beans in a separate pan, cover with water and bring to the boil. Cook for an hour or so, until tender, then drain and add to the tripe. Cook for a further 15–20 minutes or until everything is tender. Add more stock if necessary. The result should be neither soupy nor dry.

Serve sprinkled with the Parmesan cheese and a few sage leaves.

GRAN RAGÙ NAPOLETANO

MEAT STEWED IN NEAPOLITAN RAGÙ

FOR 6

90 ML (3 FL OZ) OLIVE OIL
1 LARGE ONION, FINELY CHOPPED
1 KG (2 LB 3 OZ) BEEF BRISKET
500 G (1 LB) PORK SHOULDER ON THE BONE
500 G (1 LB) LAMB SPARERIBS
1 GLASS OF DRY RED WINE
2 KG ($2^1/_4$ LB) VERY RIPE TOMATOES, PEELED, DESEEDED AND CHOPPED
2 TBSP ESTRATTO DI POMODORO (SEE PAGE 118) OR 6 TBSP TOMATO PASTE
500 G ($1^1/_4$ LB) RIGATONI
90 G ($3^1/_4$ OZ) PARMESAN CHEESE, GRATED
SALT AND PEPPER

Not a Sunday goes by for most Neapolitans without a piece of meat cooked in a tomato sauce. The sauce is used to dress large pasta and the sliced meat is then served separately with some vegetables. The little lamb spareribs in this recipe, known in dialect as spullicarielli, *give a meaty flavour to the sauce and, when cooked, have a little meat left on them, which you can have some fun eating with your fingers. Sometimes the various cuts of meat are replaced by Polpettone (see page 80), a meatloaf large enough to feed many people.*

Heat the olive oil in a large pan or casserole and fry the onion and pieces of meat until the meat is browned on all sides and the onion is soft. Add the wine and allow to evaporate a little, then stir in the tomatoes and tomato paste, cover and simmer on a low heat for $1^1/_2$–2 hours, adding salt and pepper about half way through the cooking time.

Cook the pasta in boiling salted water until *al dente*, then drain. Dress with the sauce and serve sprinkled with the Parmesan cheese. The meat is then eaten with some vegetables as a main course.

Bollito Misto

For 10–12

- 4 celery stalks, cut into chunks
- 3 carrots, cut into chunks
- 1 large onion, peeled and spiked with 4–5 cloves
- A few peppercorns
- 1.5 kg (3¼ lb) beef brisket
- 1 veal tongue, weighing 600–800 g (1¼ – 1¾ lb)
- 1 boiling chicken, weighing 2 kg (4½ lb)
- 1 kg (2¼ lb) veal brisket
- Piece of veal cheek, weighing 500 g (1 lb)
- 2 cotechino sausages (see page 74), weighing about 300 g (10½ oz) each
- Salsa verde (see page 224) and mostarda di Cremona (see page 269), to serve

Piedmont and Lombardy both claim to be the birthplace of this gargantuan dish. Boiled meats have always been eaten everywhere in Italy after being used to make soup. For Bollito Misto the different types of meat are cooked specifically to produce something really succulent. Don't be put off by the enormous piece of meat in the picture. The butcher was a little too enthusiastic, and after the picture had been taken a local restaurant sold that piece to literally hundreds of customers. However, this dish is only worth doing for lots of people on special occasions.

Put the vegetables and peppercorns in a very large pot of lightly salted water and bring to the boil. Add the beef and cook gently for 30 minutes. Then add the tongue, chicken, veal brisket and cheek and simmer for 2 hours, skimming regularly to remove any scum from the surface. (If you don't have a large enough pot for all the meat, divide the vegetables and meat between 2 pans.) Top up with boiling water if necessary to make sure the meat is always covered.

Prick the skin of the cotechino sausages with a needle, put them in a separate pan and cover with cold water. Bring to the boil and cook gently for 1–1½ hours.

When all the meats are cooked and tender, remove them from the water. Peel and trim the tongue. Slice the meats and arrange them on a large serving plate. Serve hot, accompanied by the sauces, vegetables and a little stock.

Involtini di Agnello e Maiale

BUNDLES OF PORK AND LAMB

For 4

- 200 g (7 oz) very fresh lambs' liver
- 200 g (7 oz) pigs' liver
- 200 g (7 oz) pigs' heart
- 3 tbsp extra-virgin olive oil
- Juice of 1 lemon
- 1 piece of caul fat (see rete di maiale, page 82)
- 2 lambs' testicles (see granelli, page 76), cut into quarters
- Salt and pepper
- Cayenne pepper

This is an Apulian speciality. I ate it in Alberobello and it was exquisite. It may be difficult to find all the ingredients but if you know a good butcher he should be able to obtain them for you.

Cut the liver and heart into longish strips the size of a finger. Sprinkle with salt and pepper, cayenne pepper and the olive oil and lemon juice. Soften the caul fat in lukewarm water to obtain a type of lacy net. Cut it into 8 long strips and wrap the mixed meats in them, including the testicles. Place on a very hot charcoal grill and cook for 5–6 minutes on each side. They should be crisp on the outside and succulent inside.

Punta di Petto d'Agnello Ripieno

STUFFED BREAST OF LAMB

For 4–6

- 1 piece of punta di petto of lamb (see right), weighing 1 kg (2¼ lb)
- 3 eggs, beaten
- 8 tbsp soft fresh breadcrumbs
- 1 tbsp raisins
- 1 garlic clove, finely chopped
- 1 tbsp pine nuts
- 60 g (2 oz) Parmesan cheese, finely chopped
- 1 tbsp finely chopped parsley
- salt and pepper
- a little oil

This specific cut, more often used for veal, is the extreme soft part of the breast of lamb, underneath the cutlets. The various layers of meat and fat are ideal for making a pocket, which is filled, sewn together and cooked. Naturally the younger the animal, the more tender will be the final dish, which resembles a small cushion.

Preheat the oven to 180°C/350°F/gas4. Slit open the breast of lamb along one side and made a pocket among the layers. Mix together the eggs, breadcrumbs, raisins, garlic, pine nuts, Parmesan, parsley and some salt and pepper. Stuff the pocket with this mixture and then sew it up with a needle and kitchen string. Brush with a little olive oil and bake in the oven for 1¼ hours.

TOFEJA DEL CANAVESE

PORK AND BEANS

FOR 8–10

400 G (14 OZ) DRIED BORLOTTI BEANS
1 KG (2 LB 3 OZ) PIGS' TROTTERS, TAIL, EARS, SPARERIBS AND SMALL COTECHINOS
500 G (1 LB) FRESH PORK SKIN (SEE COTENNA, PAGE 74)
SMALL SPRIG OF ROSEMARY, FINELY CHOPPED
2 GARLIC CLOVES, FINELY CHOPPED
A FEW SAGE LEAVES
2 CELERY STALKS, FINELY CHOPPED
1 CARROT, FINELY CHOPPED
1 ONION, FINELY CHOPPED
5 TBSP OLIVE OIL
1 CHILLI, FINELY CHOPPED
PINCH OF FRESHLY GRATED NUTMEG
A FEW BAY LEAVES
SALT AND PEPPER

Tofeja *is the name of the lidded terracotta pot specifically designed for cooking this very rich, but exceptionally succulent peasant dish. Canavese is the northern part of Piedmont, bordering with the Aosta Valley where I grew up. We used to eat this dish at* carnevale *(carnival time). All the gelatinous parts of the pig are included.*

Soak the borlotti beans in plenty of cold water overnight and then drain.

Preheat the oven to 160°C/325°F/gas3. Singe the tail and ears to remove any hairs; they should be immaculately clean. Cut the pork skin into rectangles about 7.5 x 12.5 cm (3 x 5 inches) and season with salt and pepper. Mix together the rosemary and 1 chopped garlic clove and place a pinch of this mixture and a whole sage leaf in the middle of each piece of pork skin. Roll up and tie with kitchen string.

Put the drained borlotti beans in a large casserole. Lay the vegetables on top, then sprinkle with the oil, chilli, nutmeg and some salt and pepper. Top this with all the meats and the pork skin rolls and cover with cold water. Scatter over the bay leaves and the remaining chopped garlic clove. Put the lid on and bake in the oven without touching or stirring for 3–3½ hours, then serve.

OSSOBUCO ALLA MILANESE

FOR 4

1.25 KG (2½ LB) SHIN OF VEAL, CUT INTO 4 CM (1½ IN) LENGTHS, WITH THE MARROW BONE IN THE CENTRE
ABOUT 4 TBSP OLIVE OIL
1 ONION, DICED
2 CELERY STALKS, DICED
1 CARROT, DICED
2 GLASSES OF DRY WHITE WINE
ABOUT 300 ML (½ PINT) VEAL STOCK
SALT AND PEPPER
SEASONED FLOUR FOR DUSTING

Dust the veal with seasoned flour. Heat the olive oil in a large pan, add the meat and fry until browned on all sides. Remove from the pan and set aside. Add more oil if necessary, then gently fry the onion, celery and carrot in the same pan until lightly browned. Return the meat to the pan, pour in the wine and stock and bring gently to the boil. Cover and cook for about 1½ hours, until the meat is tender, removing the lid towards the end of cooking. Check from time to time and add a little more stock if the mixture is getting too dry. Adjust the seasoning and serve with Risotto allo Zafferano (see page 178) and *gremolada*, a mixture of finely chopped lemon rind, garlic and parsley.

Fegato alla Veneziana

SAUTÉED LIVER WITH ONIONS

For 4

45 g ($1^1/_2$ oz) butter
1 large onion, thinly sliced
500 g (1 lb) calves' liver, very thinly sliced
salt and pepper
finely chopped flat-leaf parsley (optional)

This is another classic of Italian cuisine, this time representing the Veneto; it differs a little from Venice's version, which contains a shot of vinegar.

Heat the butter in a large frying pan, add the onion and cook until it begins to colour. Add the slices of liver and cook until browned but still moist and pink in the centre – about 3–4 minutes on each side. If you prefer it well done, cook a little longer. Add salt and pepper to taste and serve immediately. Some people add parsley or even a few drops of lemon. It is up to you.

Polenta Concia con Salsiccia

DRESSED POLENTA WITH SAUSAGE

For 6–8 (or even more)

25 g ($^3/_4$ oz) dried porcini mushrooms
400 g (14 oz) luganiga sausage (see page 77), cut into 10 cm (4 inch) chunks
4 tbsp olive oil
2 garlic cloves, coarsely chopped
1 small onion, thinly sliced
sprig of rosemary
1 small chilli, finely chopped
3 tbsp dry red wine
600 g ($1^1/_4$ lb) tomato pulp (see page 118)
salt

For the polenta concia:
2 litres ($3^1/_2$ pints) water
25 g ($^3/_4$ oz) salt
500 g (1 lb) coarse polenta
100 g ($3^1/_2$ oz) unsalted butter
100 g ($3^1/_2$ oz) Parmesan cheese, grated
150 g (5 oz) fontina cheese, preferably from the Aosta Valley, cut into small cubes

One of the most warming dishes you can get high up in the mountains, especially of the Aosta Valley, is polenta concia (see page 174), which sustains even the strongest worker. It is usually accompanied by a stew of chicken or venison. With pork sausages, however, it blends to a perfect marriage.

I like to use traditional polenta but if you use quick-cook polenta instead the cooking time is only 5 minutes. The Bramata polenta is by far the tastiest.

Soak the porcini mushrooms in lukewarm water for about 30 minutes. Put the *luganiga* in a large pan with the oil and fry until brown on all sides. Now add the garlic, onion, rosemary and chilli and fry for 5 minutes. Drain the *porcini* and squeeze out the excess water, then cut them up roughly and add to the pan. Pour in the wine and bubble to evaporate, then add the tomatoes and some salt and simmer for 20 minutes. Keep warm while you prepare the polenta.

To make the polenta, bring the water to the boil with the salt. Gradually add the polenta, stirring constantly with a long wooden spoon until all the flour has been incorporated into the water and is lump-free. At this stage you must be careful that you do not splash hot polenta on to your hands. Stir the polenta constantly over not too fierce a heat for about 30 minutes, by which time it should be pulling away from the side of the pan. Add the butter, Parmesan and fontina cheese and stir well until everything has amalgamated.

There are two ways of serving this: either by the spoonful on a plate or, as they traditionally do, by pouring the polenta on to large wooden board and leaving it to cool a little, then slicing it with a steel wire and putting it on the plate with the sausage stew.

ZAMPONE E LENTICCHIE

ZAMPONE AND LENTILS

FOR 4–6

1 PRECOOKED ZAMPONE, WEIGHING AT LEAST 1 KG (2¼ LB), OR 2 SMALLER ONES
300 G (10½ OZ) CASTELLUCCIO LENTILS (SEE LENTICCHIA, PAGE 113)
4–5 SAGE LEAVES
SMALL SPRIG OF ROSEMARY
A FEW CELERY LEAVES
2 GARLIC CLOVES, PEELED
2 SUN-DRIED TOMATOES, HALVED
A LITTLE PEPERONCINO (CHILLI)
3 TBSP EXTRA-VIRGIN OLIVE OIL
SALT AND PEPPER

A truly Emilian dish where, thanks to the abundance of local Parma hams, zampone, *or stuffed pigs' trotters, are freshly available. The skin of the trotter, including the toes, is filled with a mixture of gelatinous parts of the pig, plus meat and spices. It takes a long time to cook (3 or 4 hours' simmering) and tastes deliciously porky. The alternative to fresh* zampone *is to buy ready-made ones packed tightly in foil, which just require simmering for 20 minutes. It is best to use Castelluccio lentils for this recipe; they do not need presoaking and are ready in 20 minutes.*

Put the *zampone* in a pan of cold water and bring to the boil, then reduce the heat and simmer for 20 minutes, or according to the instructions on the packet. Meanwhile, put the lentils in a pan of cold water with the herbs, garlic cloves, sun-dried tomatoes and chilli. Bring to the boil and simmer for 20 minutes or until tender. Discard the herbs and the whole garlic cloves, then add the olive oil and some salt and pepper to taste. Slice the *zampone* and serve with the lentils.

POLENTA CONCIA CON SALSICCIA (TOP LEFT AND RIGHT); ZAMPONE E LENTICCHIE (BOTTOM)

VEGETABLES & PULSES

VERDURE E LEGUMI

One of the things about Italian food that makes me very proud is the way we prepare and cook vegetables, which are generally eaten instead of meat rather than as adjuncts to it. Especially in the summer, we eat and enjoy vegetables without even thinking of missing meat. This may be due to the fact that the geography and climate suit Italy much more to the growing of produce than the rearing of animals.

Every Italian region has locally grown vegetables which, in season, are the best you can use for the preparation of the excellent traditional dishes which have grown up around them in that area. Due to the Mediterranean climate and their mild winters, Sicily, Calabria, Campania and Puglia are the major regions for the cultivation of vegetables of all types. The extremely fertile soil is also a factor, not forgetting the intelligent and hard-working farmers of the regions. All combine to produce good and tasty vegetables.

Italians very much look forward to the seasons of certain produce, such as asparagus, tomatoes and artichokes, so they can enjoy those particular tastes that can only be obtained when vegetables are cultivated organically and in the open fields. Favourite vegetables of the Italians include asparagus, aubergines, tomatoes and artichokes, and the best recipes combine these with pasta, polenta, rice – or just bread – to make simple but delicious meals. This way of eating vegetables has been passed down through the centuries by farmers and peasants and is still one of the healthiest ways to eat. *La cucina povera* or 'poor food' used to consist of the less romantic and cheaper vegetables like potatoes, beans and cabbage. Today, though, many specialities are produced with these ingredients and often by top chefs who charge a great deal of money for them.

It is really a fantastic sight to see Italian markets, where all the vegetables are exhibited in such an inviting way it is impossible not to be tempted to buy a lot more than you intended. The piling up of very fresh fennel bulbs when just cut and sprinkled with droplets of water, or the display of ten different types of field herbs already cleaned and just waiting to be used, is an irresistible invitation.

I still remember vividly the market in Venice, near the Rialto Bridge, where the market stall-holders sell ready-peeled onions and ready-cleaned artichoke hearts to save you doing such chores at home. This super-service obviously costs a little more, but is highly valued by the customers. Food handled in this way, with such care and knowledge, produces excellent dishes. In the way in which the produce is exhibited in the markets you already have the feeling that the vendor cares for his merchandise, as well as wishing to attract and keep his customers. Quite often you will hear a conversation between the customer and the shopkeeper or stall-holder about the best way to cook or prepare certain special vegetables – a common enough occurrence in most shops in Italy.

When I was a child, my family had a small garden where we grew vegetables. I often walked with my father through row after row of tomatoes and, when I brushed against one of those magnificent plants, the intense scent of the tomato was released, even the leaves of the plant emanated very definite smells which I still remember today. This scent – and the strong flavour of all Italian vegetables – probably comes from the abundance of sun imparting a very special taste.

Italians do not believe in having all fruit and vegetables all year round, the produce has to be seasonal and, if possible, field-grown. Only then can proper ripeness and maturity, the right taste and the vitamin content be guaranteed. It is quite rare to find a domestic freezer in Italy used to stock pre-cooked or convenience foods. I only keep large quantities of *porcini* mushrooms in mine. On the other hand, there is a long tradition of preserving all sorts of vegetables in many different ways – from drying to preserving in vinegar, salt or oil – and for many different purposes.

For instance, no family in Italy would be without a jar of at least one type of vegetable pickles for their *antipasto*, the vinegar's acidity essential to stimulate the gastric juices and balance the fattiness of the meats. More recently, preserves have begun to be valued as foods in their own right and the number of dishes prepared with them is endless.

A good example is the traditional sun-dried tomatoes of Italy which have, in recent years, become one of the fashionable innovations in international cuisine. This is an extraordinary phenomenon to us Italians, as the drying of tomatoes in Southern Italy goes back many centuries. The discovery of the unique taste of concentrated tomatoes has spawned a great array of other similar specialities, like dried peppers, aubergines – even courgettes, which have a certain appeal and taste.

Legumes have a longer history of being dried, although they are also eaten fresh with equal enthusiasm. They are also almost as nutritious when dried. Prepared in many ways, each reflecting regional habits, pulses still have a peasant image that has recently become very fashionable. Any well-balanced diet should include pulses, whether fresh or dried, for their vitamins,

LEFT: CORN GROWING IN EMILIA-ROMAGNA.

BOTTOM LEFT: CASTELLUCCIO IN THE WONDERFUL UMBRIAN VALLEY OF MONTE SIBILLINI, HOME OF THE FABLED LENTILS.

BELOW: ADELVIO AND BEDULLIA, AN UMBRIAN COUPLE, HARVESTING THEIR VEGETABLES.

proteins and trace minerals. They can also have a wonderful flavour, most famously exploited in *pasta e fagioli*, a complete meal containing a perfect balance of carbohydrate, protein and fibre. Other pulse recipes include *insalata di fagioli*, a Tuscan salad of boiled cannellini beans dressed with a little virgin olive oil, salt and pepper, which is a simple but healthy delicacy. Pulses also make excellent soups that are so thick and tasty that they make meals in themselves. The best bean soups are based on dried broad beans, chickpeas and lentils, all of which are available in every region and in every possible guise.

Castelluccio lentils from Umbria are famous not only for their high iron content and for being extremely easy to cook but also because they are not prone to disease and parasites. Above all though, it is their unique flavour which distinguishes them from other lentils. On the way from Umbria to the Marche one has to drive through the plateau of Castelluccio and, as you drive along, you often see farmers with their tractors parked on the verges near the village, selling their lentils directly to customers who stop on their journey. The lentils are always in high demand because they are only grown organically, which makes them expensive. Anyone who is familiar with the flavour, though, always seems prepared to pay three or four times the price of ordinary lentils to get them.

A-Z of Vegetables & Pulses

Acetosa / Sorrel

This sharp-tasting plant, also known as *erba brusca* or 'sour grass', is not as much used by the Italians as it is by the French, which is why it is not widely cultivated in Italy, although it can be found growing wild in May and June. It is used in soups and salads for its pungent flavour and I find it irresistible as a base for risotto.

Aglio, Aglietto / Garlic

Garlic has been cultivated in Italy for many centuries and 70 percent of its entire production is now exported. The major areas of cultivation are Campania, Emilia-Romagna, Veneto, Puglia and Sicily, and it is an important ingredient in the cooking of all these areas.

There are many varieties of garlic, including the white Bianco Napoletano and Bianco Piacentino, and the pink Rosso Napoletano, Rosso di Sulmona and Rosso di Agrigento. Sometimes during the spring you can find *aglio selvatico* or wild garlic, but instead of eating the bulb eat only the dark-green heavily scented leaves (see right).

Left: aglio

I was once given an elephantine garlic, ten times bigger than the normal variety, but it lacked flavour and aroma: so remember that, when it comes to choosing garlic, small is beautiful. To spot a good quality garlic bulb, look for one with a diameter of at least 4.5 cm (1¾ inches) with compact, firm cloves. Avoid any with green shoots sprouting from the top as these are past their best and will be very strong, producing an antisocial aftertaste.

If carefully trimmed and kept whole, garlic will keep for up to a year, although in Italy it is so abundant and cheap that no one needs to store it, unless they have grown their own. To peel it, press on each clove with the palm of your hand until the skin breaks and comes away easily. If you want to get rid of the smell of garlic on your hands, rub them with salt before washing with soap as usual.

Garlic is used in many Italian recipes as a flavouring to enhance a recipe rather than dominate it. There are, however, a few notable exceptions, including the famous recipes for Bagna Caôda (see page 33) and Pesto (see page 228), in which garlic is the predominant flavour. Another less well-known garlic recipe is *agliata*, a pungent Ligurian sauce served with boiled meat and made with garlic crushed in a mortar with breadcrumbs that have been soaked in vinegar then squeezed dry, with olive oil added at the end. My wife likes to cook garlic with roast chicken, roasting whole unpeeled cloves in the same pan as the chicken towards the end of the cooking time, so that they are wonderfully creamy and sweet. It is also delicious in salads and soups. In Piedmont, they make *aja* or *agliata*, a paste made of garlic pounded in a mortar along with walnuts and olive oil which is absolutely delicious spread on bread. Garlic is also used on *bruschetta*, where a raw clove is brushed over the surface of the toasted bread before it is eaten. It may be antisocial, but it is wonderful.

To reduce the strength of flavour of garlic, soak it in cold milk for a few hours before use. This is something they do in Piedmont when making a less powerful version of *bagna caôda*; the garlic is even cooked in milk to control its powerful aroma. If you want only a hint of garlic in your dish, try rubbing a cut clove over the surface of the pan you are going to cook in or around the bowl in which you are going to make a salad. Try coarsely chopping a little garlic, adding it to a bottle of vinegar or oil and leaving it to infuse for a day or two. The strained oil or vinegar can then be used to dress salads and other dishes where only a hint of garlic is required. *Aglietto*, a younger and less powerful garlic, is also ideal for more delicate dishes and salads.

As well as its culinary value, garlic also has many healing properties and was often used as an antiseptic before the discovery of antibiotics. During the War, it used to be placed on wounds to disinfect them and to keep bacteria at bay. Today, it is valued as a means of reducing blood cholesterol levels, as well as warding off vampires, of course!

Aglio Selvatico / Wild Garlic

The best part of wild garlic (*Allium ursinum*) is the tender leaves, which are delicious in salads, soups or as an ingredient in wild garlic butter. Wild garlic is plentiful in the spring, when you can literally smell it in the air on country walks. The bulbs of wild garlic are tough, so leave them to grow.

Asparago / Asparagus

A vegetable much loved by Italians, asparagus is generally only eaten in season so that its natural wild flavour can be enjoyed. Asparagus is a shoot which, if allowed to grow to maturity, blooms into a wonderful delicate lace-like head that can be used in floral arrangements. When

Below: asparagus in Turin market.

the tip of the shoot emerges from the earth, it is cut at its base with special long knife, leaving about 15 cm (6 inches) of tender edible shoot attached.

The regions where asparagus is mostly cultivated are Emilia-Romagna, the Veneto and Piedmont, but there are some smaller areas around Vesuvio in Campania. There are three main types of asparagus grown and enjoyed in Italy, the white, the purple and the green. The white variety, Bianco di Bassano, is derived from the German tradition and grows in the Veneto. Every year the restaurants in the pretty town of Bassano del Grappa on the Piave River compete to present the most original recipe, with the public as the jury. Purple asparagus is called *argenteuil* and is cultivated in Campania, from which it also takes its Italian name of Napoletano, while the green variety is grown in Piedmont and Emilia-Romagna. This is especially tasty and tender and has a dark green tip fading to white at the base.

Asparagus needs to be prepared and cooked with special care and, to my mind, the best way to cook it is by steaming, so that the delicate tip stays intact after cooking and retains its flavour. To be eaten at its best, asparagus should be very fresh, the finest being those with firm heads with tightly closed tips. To prepare them, peel away the tough and stringy skin at the base. If you boil the asparagus, stand it in a tall, narrow pan, keeping the tender tips out of the water so that they do not overcook. Do not cover the pan with a lid, otherwise the heat of the steam cooks the tips faster than the stems.

In Italy, the most popular way of cooking asparagus is boiling it for serving with melted butter and a sprinkling of Parmesan cheese or perhaps, as they do it in Milan, with a fried egg on top. They are good *pasticciati*, that is mixed in chunks with onion and scrambled eggs. In springtime, asparagus is delicious eaten with freshly boiled new potatoes, dressed with a little melted butter and accompanied with a few slices of thinly cut Parma ham. Asparagus risotto is a must and

Right: borlotti beans in the pod.

young tender asparagus spears can even be eaten raw with Bagna Caôda (see page 33).

There are only small quantities of wild asparagus (*Asparagus selvatico*), which is slightly bitter but has a very intense scent. Once, when I was in Sardinia in wild asparagus season it was possible to find it on sale at the roadside, freshly cut by the locals. The spears were thin, did not need peeling and were delicious in an omelette (*frittata con asparagi*).

BARBABIETOLA / Beetroot

This root is from the same family as sugar beet and is much loved as a cooked (or sometimes raw) root for salads. It is also the principal ingredient of soups like the traditional Russian *borscht*. The leaves of fresh beetroot can also be eaten.

To cook beetroot, first cut off the top leaves without damaging the skin and boil the roots for about two hours, depending on the size. They can also be baked in a moderate oven, covered with their own leaves and with water around them, for about 1-1½ hours. Once cool, cooked beetroot may be peeled and cut in slices to add to mixed salads. However, I prefer them in a salad of their own, with just fresh coriander, spring onions, salt, virgin olive oil and some good wine vinegar.

BARBA DI BECCO, BARBA DI FRATE, BARBA DI CAPPUCCINO / Salad Green

This salad plant is similarly to chives and, like the herb, has long, narrow green leaves with a slightly sour taste. It is hardly cultivated commercially, but grows wild all over Italy and, in the springtime, can be picked to make a welcome contribution to salads.

Right below: shelled borlotti beans.

BORLOTTO / Borlotti Bean

One of the best-known and most popular beans in central and northern Italy, whether in its fresh or dried form the borlotti bean distinguishes itself from others by the startling patterns formed by its green and white skin colours. The pod (*baccello*) of the fresh bean is yellowish in colour, with bright red and green speckles while the bean itself is white with red speckles. There are many varieties of borlotti bean, including the British-developed Taylor's Horticultural which is much used in Italy.

The borlotti is harvested when the pods are completely dry and the beans have taken on a darker colour. It is mostly used in its dry form and, like the fresh beans, these are used in soups – especially minestrone – as well as being simply boiled for about 30 minutes and dressed with extra-virgin olive oil, oregano or rosemary and a little vinegar. Salt is only added at the end of the cooking time otherwise the skins of the beans become tough and hard.

Borlotti are widely used in the

LEFT: BROCCOLI

famous northern Italian soup, Pasta e Fagioli (page 157), which has become very popular all over Italy. In the north, however, it is prepared differently, in that half the beans are mashed to give a creamy and velvety texture to the soup. Borlotti are also good married with rice in the thick soup Panissa (page 178). The Piedmontese town of Saluggia is also renowned for its borlotti dishes, which consist of borlotti bean soups cooked with *cotenna* (pork skin).

BORRAGINE, BORRANA / BORAGE

This robust flowering herb always makes me think of Liguria, where it is widely used in *preboggion*, a mixture of wild herbs (see page 167), and it is also used in Campania to make a delicious soup. With its large hair-covered leaves, borage is better cooked and eaten as a fresh vegetable dressed with a little virgin olive oil and a squeeze of lemon juice. It also makes a wonderful filling for ravioli (see Pansôti, page 149). The extremely pretty pale blue flowers are edible and can be used as a decoration for salads or for making little fritters to go with drinks.

BROCCOLO, BROCCOLETTO / BROCCOLI, CALABRESE

Broccoli belongs to the same family as cabbage and cauliflower and comes in many different varieties. It is formed by thousands of buds of the flower at the top of the plant. If the buds flower the broccoli becomes yellow and that is why the freshness of broccoli is measured by the tightness and the intensity of the deep green-blue colour of the buds.

Broccolo is mostly known as calabrese, because it grows best in Calabria, in Sicily (where, incidentally, *broccolo* means cauliflower). The most common variety, Piccolo di Verona, is pale green and ready for eating in the early spring, while Grosso Romano or Violetto di Sicilia, as it is also known in Italy, has very pretty conical florets and a distinctive purple colour that turns green during cooking.

Italians eat a great deal of broccoli and there are many recipes for cooking it. These include a purée that is eaten as an accompaniment to veal or chicken or as a sauce for Pugliese pastas such as orecchiette. Blanched broccoli is also good dipped in egg and deep-fried.

Broccoletti are little branches or florets of broccoli. Like Brussels sprouts, they grow on the main stem after the head (main flower) has been cut. They can be cooked for about 5 minutes until just tender or for 8-9 minutes, until slightly softer, then stir-fried for a few seconds in olive oil with a few slices of garlic and half a chilli. Another popular way of serving lightly boiled broccoli is just to drizzle it with a little extra-virgin olive oil and a few drops of lemon juice.

BROCCOLO DI RAPA / TURNIP SHOOT

The little shoots of turnip look like little spears with heads of flower which turn yellow when they open. The shoots should only be used, however, while they are still green. *Broccolo di rapa* are very popular in the south, where they are called *friarielli*. They can be blanched before any other cooking to moderate their very strong flavour. The most popular way of cooking turnip shoots is braising them in a tightly covered pan with olive oil, garlic and chilli until tender. These are wonderful served with polenta cake.

BRUSCANDOLI, BRUSCANSI / HOP SHOOT

The hop is a climbing plant with small thorns on its stems and only the tops of tender young shoots are used in cooking. This plant grows wild all over Italy, but is a speciality of the Veneto, where it is cooked in risottos. In springtime, little bunches of hop shoots can be found in the vegetable market of the Rialto. In the south, they are used in omelettes or simply boiled then sautéed with garlic. I eat them like asparagus, boiled with a little melted butter or, even better, with some hollandaise sauce.

CANNELLINO / CANNELLINI BEAN

A favourite with all Italians, especially in central Italy, cannellini beans have spread from the kitchens of Tuscany all over Italy. The popularity of the bean is due to its flavour, perfect creamy-white colour and ease of use in the kitchen. It is the most canned and bottled bean in Italian gastronomy.

The beans are difficult to harvest when ripe and are thus harvested in autumn, when the pod is completely dry. As a result, the beans are rarely eaten fresh. To prepare the dry beans, they need to be soaked overnight. To cook them, place them in a pan, cover them with unsalted water and bring to the boil. Reduce the heat, then simmer gently for 2 hours without stirring.

Cannellini are used in minestrone soup and in the famous Pasta e Fagioli (page 157), especially in Campania, where the bean is heavily cultivated. There is a curious recipe in Tuscany called *fagioli al fiasco*, which involves cooking the beans in a Chianti flask with water, oil, garlic and sage. The flask is placed in the embers of a fire to cook the beans very slowly until they have swelled to the point where they can only just slip down the very narrow neck of the bottle. Cannellini are also wonderful simply cooked and

RIGHT: CLEANED ARTICHOKE HEARTS.

seasoned with extra-virgin olive oil, salt, pepper, garlic and rosemary, and eaten with bread.

CAPONATA, SEE SEDANO AND THE RECIPE ON PAGE 135.

CARCIOFO / GLOBE ARTICHOKE

Artichokes belong to the thistle family. The edible parts of the plant are the tender parts of the flower bud and the adjacent stalk. In fact, if you put the stem of an artichoke in water, it may flower, with the choke turning a wonderful purple colour. Artichokes grow best in the Mediterranean region, where the climate and the well-drained soil are perfect. The major areas of production in Italy are Campania, Sicily, Puglia and Lazio, but they are grown in most regions for local use. About 98 per cent of the Italian crop is exported, but Italians adore them too, so a huge number are grown; in fact, Italy is the world's biggest producer of this vegetable.

Artichokes come in a wide variety of colours, from purple to green, as

BELOW: ARTICHOKES ON SALE IN PALERMO.

well as in a range of shapes – both with and without thorns. There are basically three sizes of artichoke, the biggest and first to appear being *La Mamma*, which is usually boiled and eaten leaf by leaf until the fleshy heart is reached, with the hairy choke being discarded. Secondary, smaller plants, called *figli* (children) grow later just below the main head and are wonderfully tender. Finally, even smaller artichokes, called *nipoti* (nephews) grow last further down the plant and these are usually preserved in vinegar and oil as pickles for *antipasto*.

The main varieties are the Romanesco, a large purple globe artichoke without thorns. A smaller artichoke, the Violetto Toscano is also purple in colour and, as its name implies, is cultivated in Tuscany. It is very tender and used mainly in Pinzimonio (see the recipe on page 223), a traditional Tuscan version of crudités. Finally, there is a violet artichoke from Sicily called Spinoso di Palermo, which has a prickly flower that needs to be handled with great care. It has a fantastic flavour and is particularly delicious in *frittella*, a dish of fresh broad beans, artichokes and onion as in the recipe from Palermo (see page 133). Finally, there are two Venetian artichokes: the first, called Precoce di Chioggia – being the largest – is harvested around October or November and is grown with the much smaller Castraure della Laguna.

To prepare artichokes, first cut off the top third of each vegetable and discard the tough outer leaves until you reach the tender heart. As only a small part of the stem of very young and tender artichokes is edible, it will need to be peeled, while the beard or white choke should be discarded. This is done by cutting the artichoke in half and scraping it away with the sharp end of a pointed knife, leaving the tender heart intact. Alternatively, especially if you want to stuff them, the artichokes may be left whole and the chokes scooped out with a sharp spoon. Once prepared, artichokes should be kept in acidulated water to prevent them discolouring.

Artichokes are full of protein, vitamins and fibre, as well as containing phosphorus, calcium, potassium, sodium, iron, copper and zinc. In Italy, they are eaten raw in salads or in Pinzimonio and bagna caôda (see page 33), but they may also be blanched, quartered, dipped in flour and beaten egg and then deep-fried. They are also cooked *in umido* with tomatoes and olive oil. I like them slowly braised in plenty of extra-virgin olive oil, with onions, capers and parsley.

One of the most delicious ways of cooking artichokes is as they do in Sicily. The leaves are loosened from the top with the fingers and coarse sea salt scattered over the centre. Extra-virgin olive oil is then sprinkled on top and the artichoke placed on a bed of charcoal embers and cooked slowly until the outer leaves are charred, but the heart is deliciously tender and with a smoky flavour.

CAROTA, PASTINACA, PASTANACHE / CARROT

This root vegetable is available all year round and grows mostly in temperate climates, with Sicily and Abruzzo being the main areas of production in Italy. The carrot ranges in colour from pale yellow to deep purple and has a strong aroma and taste. It can be boiled and sautéed in butter with garlic or reduced to a purée and served as a side dish. Finely chopped and added to minestrone, meat stews and *ragùs*, it gives a particularly sweet flavour. Raw carrots are eaten in Southern Italy, where they are very tender and sweet and called *pastinaca* or *pastanache* in the local dialect. I enjoy raw carrots coarsely grated and dressed with fresh mint, coriander and a little olive oil, lemon juice, salt and pepper. Carrots are also an important ingredient of Giardiniera (see page 112).

CARDO / CARDOON

The cardoon is related to the thistle and – like its other close relative, the artichoke – it has long leaves. Unlike

LEFT: CARDO

the artichoke, however, it is the stem of the cardoon and not the flower that is eaten. To make it tender enough to eat, the cardoon is specially cultivated, as in Piedmont, where from around September to October the long stems and leaves are bent over (each region bends the stem in a different way) and covered with earth to protect them from the harsh winter weather. Over the following months they become perfectly white and extremely tender. Because of this peculiar way of blanching them they take on a permanently curved shape and are commonly called *gobbi* (hunchbacks).

Cardoons can be eaten raw in the famous dish, Bagna Caôda (see page 33) or *alla parmigiana*. To prepare cardoons, simply discard the stringy outer fibres by peeling them off with a knife, like a celery stalk, then cut the stalk into 1 cm (½ inch) chunks. Place these in water acidulated with lemon juice so they do not turn black, cook them until tender, then drain and lay in a buttered ovenproof dish, dot with more butter and bake in a fairly hot oven for 20 minutes.

CATALOGNA, SEE CICORIA

CAVOLFIORE / CAULIFLOWER

There are many varieties of *palla di neve* (snowball), the technical name given to this king of the cabbage family. In principle, it is the same as broccoli, except that the immaculate white florets which make up the head are extremely compact and heavy and surrounded by a few leaves whose freshness indicates the quality of the cauliflower. The most tender of the pale green leaves are also edible.

Cauliflowers are grown all over Italy, with the major growing regions being in Campania, the Marche, Puglia and Sicily. There are also many varieties, including Precoce Toscano, Gigante di Napoli and Tardivo di Fano. The cauliflower has a very long growing season and is available from October until the end of May.

Italian cuisine makes good use of the cauliflower in a range of dishes from *minestrone* to the famous regional dish of *pasta e cavolfiore* from Campania. It is also wonderful puréed with butter and Parmesan cheese, served in a cheese sauce, *au gratin* (or *gratinato*, as the Italians say), made into simple salads cut into thin slices and dressed with oil and vinegar or dipped into mayonnaise, and freshly boiled and dressed with extra-virgin olive oil, garlic and lemon juice. Cauliflower is also a major component of Giardiniera, the Italian pickle of garden vegetables, and Insalata di Rinforzo (see page 136).

One of my favourite ways of cooking cauliflower is as fritters, where parboiled florets are coated in a batter of beaten egg, breadcrumbs and a little Parmesan cheese, then deep-fried. They can also be dipped in a batter of beaten eggs mixed with a few tablespoons of plain flour and a pinch of salt, then shallow-fried in olive oil until golden. Both versions make wonderful party snacks.

LEFT: GREEN, WHITE AND PURPLE CAULIFLOWERS.

CAVOLINO DI BRUXELLES / BRUSSELS SPROUT

This sprout, which takes the form of a kind of mini cabbage, has only recently been adopted in Italy, despite the fact that Romans are said to have taken them to Belgium in the first place. The sprouts grow on the long stems of this member of the cabbage family up to 1 metre (1 yard) in height. They are harvested in late autumn through to winter and make an interesting change to other types of cabbage.

To cook Brussels sprouts, first discard any damaged exterior leaves, trim the stalk and make an incision in its base to ensure even cooking. Blanch in boiling salted water for 7-8 minutes before using in other recipes, or cook for 10-15 minutes, until just tender, to be eaten as a side dish. In Italy, Brussels sprouts are mostly blanched and baked in the oven covered with a béchamel sauce or, as they do in Parma, boiled and then served dotted with butter and Parmesan cheese.

CAVOLO / CABBAGE

An old Italian saying 'come il cavolo a merenda' translates 'as cabbage for tea', meaning something completely out of place or without sense. I would be very offended if I were a cabbage, because this underrated vegetable is one of the foundations of modern Italian cuisine and is as popular in the south as the north.

My childhood memories take

My childhood memories take me back to Borgofranco during the war, when – at the age of 15 – my friends and I were constantly hungry. I would often create improvised afternoon teas at around five o'clock. We used to pass a field of cabbages on our way home from school and when they were ready for eating, we 'allowed ourselves' to take one from the fields. Each of us brought the other ingredients from home, like olive oil, salt, pepper, vinegar, bread and a big bowl. With a large knife and a chopping board, we were making a cabbage salad out in the open countryside. The white and crunchy internal leaves were very thinly sliced then placed in the bowl and seasoned with the rest of the ingredients. Sometimes a little garlic was crushed and marinated in vinegar before being added. Sitting around the bowl, we then proceeded to eat this intermediary meal that would carry us through to dinner. A mad but wonderfully innocent time.

The cabbage helped us to get through the War and I remember eating it disguised in many ways by my mother who was keen to give us satisfying and nutritious food. She cooked it in many ways, using various types of cabbage, allowing us to appreciate her unforgettable cooking, which has been such a great inspiration in my professional life.

There are four basic types of cabbage cultivated in Italy, with the precious summer variety being grown in the north and the autumn and winter varieties being grown in the warmer climes of the south.

Cavolo cappuccio (flat cabbage)
This flat compact, football-sized cabbage has greeny-blue leaves on the outside and very white leaves on the inside. These internal leaves are very tender and are used to make *crauti*, the Italian equivalent of sauerkraut (see page 110). This type of cabbage is also used to make soups, like minestrone and bean soups, and in rice dishes such as *riso e cavoli*.

Cavolo verza (Savoy cabbage)
Piedmont, Lombardy and the Veneto make particular use of this type of cabbage. It is distinguished from the other varieties by its wrinkled and curly leaves. The deep green, almost blue, outer leaves are often wrapped around a meat stuffing, tied into a parcel and braised (see Caponnet on page 130). The paler internal leaves are very tender and make a wonderful salad if their thick ribs are removed. The leaves are then finely shredded and dressed with a vinaigrette of olive oil, vinegar, a few puréed anchovy fillets and a little mild mustard. Another wonderful way of using Savoy cabbage is in a recipe created by my old friend Nina from the Aosta Valley (see page 234). She boils the shredded cabbage until tender, layers it in a pot with chunks of stale bread, cubes of Fontina cheese and Parmesan, covers all this with chicken stock and finishes with a generous layer of melted butter. She leaves this to rest to allow the bread to absorb all the flavours and then mixes everything together. This is called *zuppa valpellinense* and reminds me of a similar, if more calorific, dish my mother used to prepare.

Right: cavolo nero

Cavolo nero (black cabbage)
This is an unusual variety of cabbage, not just because the leaves are dark green, almost black, but because they are also quite long and curled. It is mostly cultivated in the south and in Tuscany, where it forms an essential part of the famous *ribollita* soup in which it is teamed with beans. The soup is always made a day or two in advance and then re-boiled, hence its name. In the south *cavolo nero* is mostly braised with garlic, a little lard, some *peperoncino* and water then reduced until soft. My wife cooks it in a similar way with a few slices of smoked bacon which imparts an interesting flavour to the dish.

Cavolo cappuccio rosso (red cabbage) This very compact cabbage is a deep red in colour with leaves that grow so tightly together that each cabbage can weigh around $1^{1}/_{2}$ kilos (3 lbs). It is often used in north-east Italy in recipes similar to those used by the Austrians. I usually cut it very finely and place it in a pan with lard or, if possible, goose fat, with a finely chopped onion, a few peppercorns, some juniper berries, 2-3 peeled and thinly sliced Cox's orange pippin apples, lots of apple juice and 1 or 2 chicken stock cubes. Bring this to the boil, then braise the cabbage for about 2 hours until it forms a soft, jam-like consistency with the apples. It is wonderful with pork or game of any description.

Cavolo Rapa / Kohlrabi

Although this vegetable belongs to the cabbage family, it is the root and not the leaves that are eaten. The root can grow as large as a grapefruit, while its spindly stalks and leaves emerge from the top in a rather haphazard manner. It has a pale green skin and an even paler flesh. When young it is extremely tender, with only a hint of cabbage flavour. To prepare it, peel and discard the tough, woody skin. Cut the peeled head into quarters and boil them in salted water for about 15 minutes, or until soft, then drain and dress with butter or Mascarpone and season with salt and pepper. In Puglia the boiled root is cut into slices and dressed with olive oil and vinegar for a salad.

Cazzimperio, see Crudita

Left: cicerchie

Cece / Chickpea

Popular all around the Mediterranean, this legume or pulse has been adopted by every Italian region. For climatic reasons the chickpea, with its unmistakable round shape and cream colour, is cultivated only in the warmer south. It is probably the only legume that maintains a similar quality whether fresh or dry, which is why large quantities are sold commercially canned and bottled, ready for use. Dried chickpeas need to be soaked in water for 8 to 24 hours, depending on their age. They can then be boiled for at least 3 hours (or half that time in a pressure cooker). It is worth remembering that chickpeas double in volume and weight during cooking.

Pasta e ceci is a dish of chickpeas and pasta enjoyed in Puglia, Piedmont and Lombardy. Chickpeas can also be reduced to a purée and dressed with crisply fried slivers of speck. Dried chickpeas can also be ground to a flour and, in Italy, this is mainly used in Liguria to make *farinata* or *faina*, a sort of flat bread.

Cetriolo, Cetriolini / Cucumber, Gherkins

The *cetriolo*, or cucumber, epitomizes summer for me – a salad without cucumber just isn't a salad. It is a pity that its year-round availability has caused it to become so underrated. The Italian cucumber is shorter than its English counterpart, as Italians prefer varieties like Marketer or Carosello which are not cylindrical, but rounder like their squash relatives. Great care has to be taken when choosing cucumbers, they should not be too big and should be quite hard to the touch. Peeling off the cucumber skin makes it more digestible, as does removing the seeds of larger varieties.

Italians are also very fond of *cetriolini*, gherkins or immature cucumbers, which are specially grown for pickling in vinegar to be eaten as a part of an *antipasto*. I have developed a salad which includes peeled and very finely sliced fresh gherkins with salt, olive oil, a few tablespoons of milk, a few drops of lemon juice and plenty of finely chopped dill.

Cicerchia / Pulse

This type of dried bean, closely resembling the chickpea in both appearance and flavour, is widely used throughout Italy. They are most often incorporated in soups, like the Apulian *ciceria e tria*, in which they are cooked with short-cut tagliatelle, and with potatoes in *minestra di cicerchie e patate*.

Cicoria, Cicorietta, Catalogna / Chicory

A great variety of salad and vegetable plants are included under this name. They have a common characteristic in that they are all bitter because they descend from the wild plant *Cicoria selvatica*, a close relation of the *dente di leone* (dandelion).

Catalogna is a cultivated relative of wild chicory, which is similar in shape to the dandelion but is much larger, growing up to 50 cm (1²/₃ ft) high. Its dense leaves grow from a root which, along with the tender white part of the stems, can be braised in a similar way to the wild dandelion. It can also be simply boiled and dressed with extra-virgin olive oil and lemon juice or used to fill vegetable tarts mixed with ricotta, cheese, eggs and spices. *Catalogna puntarelle* (little tips) is a bushy variety of the same plant, with 20-30 tender juicy little shoots attached to the root. It can be eaten cooked and dressed with extra-virgin olive oil and lemon juice.

Cicoria di Bruxelles (chicory or Belgian endive) was discovered by a Belgian horticulturist in the middle of the last century and has since been successfully cultivated all over the world. One of the main appeals of chicory is its tightly packed 15 cm (6 inch) long creamy white leaves which, as well as being delicious braised and grilled, give wonderful variety in salads. My own favourite salad is made up of 2-cm (³/₄-inch) chunks of chicory dressed with a mixture of extra-virgin olive oil, a few drops of truffle oil, some lemon juice, salt and pepper. It is then scattered with slices of fresh black truffle. An older and simpler way of preparing it is to cut the chicory head in half, lay it in a pan with garlic, olive oil, capers and salt, cover with a lid and braise it.

Radicchio is a salad leaf belonging to the chicory family that is widely used for its slightly bitter

Left: radicchio di Treviso

ABOVE: FLAT PIATTA DI BASSANO ONIONS

taste and its deep red-mauve colour. There are two principal varieties of radicchio. The first, Rossa di Verona, is a round and tightly formed ball of leaves, similar to a small red cabbage. It is mostly cultivated in Veneto, especially around Chioggia. The second is the famous Radicchio di Treviso, so-called because it is mainly cultivated in that province. While Rossa di Verona is available all the year round, treviso only makes its appearance in winter, where it ripens from a reddish-green colour to a wonderful deep red. The leaves are long and pointed and it is usually sold with the edible fleshy root attached.

Radicchio di Treviso undergoes quite lengthy preparation before being sold or eaten. After it is pulled from the earth, in order to tenderize it and remove the bitterness, it is bundled with willow branches for 2 or 3 days with its roots sitting in running rainwater. It is then cleaned, leaving only the immaculate leaves in the centre. In Treviso, the traditional way of cooking radicchio is to grill the entire head. As well as adding the leaves to salads, it is also used in risottos or pasta sauces with speck. There is even a recipe for using radicchio to make grappa.

Ceriolo verde and *ceriolo rosso* are two pretty salad leaves from the chicory family. They are both formed like a rose, one with green leaves and the other with red. Both have the typically bitter chicory taste. *Cicorietta da taglio* is another, quite tiny, salad leaf which grows quite quickly. The little plants are tightly sown so that they form a delicate green carpet and are cut at the base so that only the small tender leaves are used. It then grows back after being cut.

Scarola (Batavia) grows in the form of a bushy head of deep green with robust outer leaves, but only the pale cream and yellow centre of this plant is used in salads because the outer leaves are a little tough to eat. It has a slightly bitter taste, characteristic of the family. The entire head can be cooked like a vegetable, usually braised with olive oil, garlic, tomatoes and capers.

Indivia (curly endive or frisée) is a curious salad leaf which is from the same branch of the family as *scarola* and has many similarities with it, having tough outer leaves and a very tender centre – the part of the head used in salads.

CIME DI RAPA / TURNIP TOPS

Cime di rapa, also called *broccoletti di rapa*, is the leafy top of the turnip. The leaves are used in much the same way as broccoli, usually boiled then sautéed in olive oil with garlic and chilli. The taste is definitely stronger than broccoli and slightly bitter, and is very much loved by the Romans and Neapolitans, who call them *friarielli*. See also Brocollo di Rapa (page 104).

CIPOLLA, CIPOLLOTTO, CIPOLLINE / ONION

The onion has been used for thousands of years in Italy. Introduced by the Egyptians then taken up by the Romans, it has been put to use in all sort of ways, including being fermented to make an alcoholic drink. In the Italian kitchen it is widely used in ragùs, soups and risottos. The main areas of cultivation are Sicily, Puglia, Campania and Emilia-Romagna.

The onion has been cultivated through the centuries to produce thousands of varieties, with all manner of shapes, colours and strengths. Most are named after cities, such as Ramata di Milano and Rossa Piatta di Bassano, but there are far too many to list here.

The pink-and-golden-coloured onions have the most intense flavour, while the white and red are usually milder. The best red onions are those from Tropea in Calabria, celebrated for their sweetness.

There is a basic difference between onions for cooking and onion used for pickling or eaten raw in salads, and that is size. Cooking onions are larger and the very large ones are as likely to be eaten stuffed and baked as chopped for use as an aromatic flavouring. Some of the traditional Italian dishes that make the best use of onion are *fegato alla Veneziana* (liver Venice-style) and *zuppa di cipolla* (onion soup). Onions are also good in omelettes, or deep-fried in rings in a coating of beaten eggs and breadcrumbs.

Smaller onions are used raw in dishes such as *tonno e fagioli* (bean and tuna salad). My father used to scoop this salad up with a leaf of a spring onion, which he would eat along with the salad itself. The *cipollotto* (salad onion) is a special variety of onion that is harvested in the spring when it is still small and tender. It is especially important in Pinzimonio (page 223) and in salads. The *cipollina* (spring onion) is another small white onion that can be round or flat. The round variety is usually pickled to be eaten as part of *antipasti*, while the flat one is used to make *cipolline in agro dolce*. The peeled onions are blanched, then fried in olive oil with added vinegar and sugar until tender.

I have two tips to help overcome the worst effects of onions when preparing them: first to stop them from making you cry, soak them in water for 30 minutes before handling them and breathe through your mouth rather than your nose when you cut them; secondly, to get rid of the smell of onions on your fingers, rub them with salt.

RIGHT: TROPEA RED ONIONS

Char-grilling Vegetables

Char-grilling is most effective when done over real charcoal, because of the woody smoky flavour it gives to the food. It is a very healthy way of cooking vegetables and also gives them a more interesting flavour than just plain boiling. Although radicchio was one of the first vegetables to be grilled, vegetables such as courgettes, aubergines, peppers, onions and artichokes are also good for the grill. Just after they have been removed from the grill, the skins of certain vegetables, like peppers and tomatoes, can be peeled off with ease. Harder vegetables like fennel and celeriac need to be blanched first, then cut into slices before being put on the grill.

To prevent the vegetables from getting too charred and to give them even more flavour, brush them with a marinade of olive oil, lemon, crushed garlic, salt and pepper. Char-grilled vegetables can be eaten on their own as a starter, or served as a side dish with grilled meat or fish.

Cocozza, see Zucca

Concentrato di Pomodoro, see Pomodoro

Contorno / Vegetable Side Dish

An important part of any meal is the *contorno* or vegetable side dish to accompany the main course. The term is most often used of the vegetable most suited to the main dish. A *contorno* can consist of potatoes and one other vegetable.

Coste / Swiss Chard

Similar in flavour to spinach, chard is called *erbette* in Emilia-Romagna – the name used to refer to parsley in Rome. Chard leaves are the basis of an Emilian flan called *erbazzone*, which is basically an omelette made with Swiss chard leaves gently cooked and then puréed, before being mixed with breadcrumbs, a little flour, a couple of beaten eggs, a handful of grated Parmesan, salt, pepper and some nutmeg, then fried in lard or butter as you would an omelette.

As well as cooking the leaves of chard in the same way as spinach, the white ribs of the long leaves can be cut in chunks and braised until tender to make a good accompaniment to meat dishes.

Crauti / Sauerkraut

This piece of Germanic culinary culture has infiltrated the Northern border regions of Alto Adige, Friuli, and the Veneto, and has been adopted because it perfectly suits the local pork dishes, which are also in all likelihood echoes of Austrian invasions. A platter of boiled mixed pork delicacies like smoked loin, belly, sausages and *cotechino*, accompanied by *crauti* makes a wonderful peasant dish.

There are a few good brands of ready-made *crauti* in jars, but if you like making it yourself, as many families do, here is how. Trim a flat white cabbage of the tougher outer leaves, then shred the rest very finely. Layer the shredded cabbage with salt in a wooden or ceramic container and put a large weight on top. After a few days, the cabbage will start to ferment, a process which will take about 4 weeks, after which the *crauti* is ready to use. Before use, rinse the *crauti* with fresh water and cook with the addition of some juniper berries, caraway seeds, a little white wine and some lard. After an hour or so the *crauti* is ready.

Left: char-grilled aubergines.

Crudita / Crudité

Crudités are simply raw vegetables eaten with dips or in salads. There are two important speciality *crudite*, one from Piedmont and the other from Tuscany. The first is the famous *bagna caôda*, meaning 'hot dip' in Piedmontese, which is based on a sauce of anchovies, garlic and butter, all dissolved together and kept warm in special terracotta containers heated by candles. Into this aromatic mixture, one dips selected tender autumn or winter vegetables, the whole accompanied by bread and washed down by plenty of Barbera wine. The classic vegetables for *bagna caôda* are Jerusalem artichoke, cardoon, celery, peppers, artichoke and carrot, but any tender raw vegetable will do. Because of the amount of garlic used it can be a rather antisocial meal; however, if the garlic is softened in milk first, it is far less pungent. See the recipe on page 33.

The other well-known crudité is the Tuscan *pinzimonio* (see the recipe on page 223), which is known as *cazzimperio* in other parts of southern Italy. This is nothing more than seasoned extra-virgin olive oil in a little bowl into which you dip spring vegetables like asparagus, artichokes, carrots, cucumbers, fennel, spring onions, celery, artichokes and any other tender tasty vegetable you can find. It is usually served in Tuscan trattorias as a starter.

Below: catalogna puntarelle (little tips) chicory and dandelion leaves.

Dente di Leone / Dandelion

Also known as *pissialetto* because of their diuretic quality, wild dandelion leaves can be used in salad in spring, when new growth makes them very tender. Toss the leaves with hard-boiled eggs, anchovy fillets and a vinaigrette of extra-virgin olive oil and wine vinegar. Larger leaves are wonderful braised slowly until tender with garlic, olive oil, chilli pepper and a little stock.

ERBA BRUSCA, SEE ACETOSA

ESTRATTO DI POMODORO, SEE POMODORO

FAGIOLINO / GREEN BEAN

Italians use *fagiolini* frequently, especially in summer when, as well as making a delicious summer vegetable, they are ideal as an ingredient in salads. This much appreciated vegetable comes in a widely varying number of varieties. Most green beans are collected when they are still young and not quite mature, so that they are tender and full of flavour. The smallest and most slender bean is Contender, although the slightly larger Bobis (Italian for Bobby) has a little more substance and, when fresh and picked very young, in my opinion tastes much better. Re dei bleu, (King of the Blues) is much longer than either of these, being about 15 cm (6 inches) in length and with a good flavour.

Two other varieties of *fagiolini* are a creamy white colour rather than green. One is Burro di Roquencourt, which possibly originated from France and is the same size as the Bobby bean. The other is Meraviglia di Venezia or Venice Wonder, a fairly large but very tender bean if picked young and resembling the mange-tout pea in size. An exceptionally long bean is the Stringa (string bean) which can reach up to 50 cm (20 inches) in length and is a green to greeny-red colour.

Almost all beans, and especially the older ones, need to be topped and tailed so that the tough ends of the bean are removed, along with any stringy fibres. One of the most evocative sights in Italy is to see the women gathered at the back of a country trattoria preparing beans. This is a fine indicator of the freshness of the products, most of which are locally grown without chemicals and are wonderfully fresh, tender and very tasty. Only the youngest and freshest beans do not need to be topped and tailed. To check the freshness of a bean, break it in half. If it snaps easily and is moist on the inside it is fresh.

The traditional way of cooking beans is to boil them in salted water for 7-12 minutes, depending on the size and freshness of the bean. Another way is to blanch them in a large pan of salted boiling water for 2-3 minutes or until *al dente* then to finish the cooking by sautéing them in butter or dressing them with vinaigrette. My own special way of serving them is dressed while still warm with slices of garlic, extra-virgin olive oil, wine vinegar, salt and abundant fresh mint leaves. They are also extremely delicious cold in *fagiolini in umido*, which is made by braising uncooked beans in a pan with olive oil, garlic and tomatoes. A few minutes before the end of the cooking time, salt and basil are added for flavouring. My mother used to add new potatoes to the dish to make a main course which we would eat with bread.

RIGHT: FAGIOLI, LARGE WHITE BEANS

FAGIOLO / BEAN

Known from antiquity, beans have been eaten through the ages by peasants because they were easy to cultivate and preserve. Today dried beans have become an increasingly important part of our diet and they are valued for their high protein, vitamin and mineral content as well as for their fibre. Every region in Italy can name at least one bean or pulse dish. See also Borlotto, Cannellino.

FAVA / BROAD BEAN

These beans have only one thing in common with green beans and that is the colour of the pod. Unlike their cousins, however, they need to be podded before being eaten. This is a very pleasant exercise because as the finger enters the pod it touches the soft velvety, almost woolly, padding inside in which the beans are embedded.

Broad bean plants grow up to a metre high, first producing a wonderfully white flower and then the fruit – the pod with the beans inside. Broad beans are a very old food indeed, taken up by the Romans after they were introduced to them by the Egyptians. For a long time they were the only beans eaten in Italy, and then mostly by peasants. Now the broad bean is eaten and cultivated with much enthusiasm all over Italy, although the main area of growth is in the warmer south.

Broad beans are only eaten raw in springtime, when they are young and tender. One of the best ways to enjoy them is in the Tuscan style with fresh Pecorino cheese. Otherwise both fresh and dry beans can be cooked. The fresh variety, if tender, takes only 10 minutes to cook and if you discard the tough outer skin, less. If you use dry beans, then they have to be soaked in water for 18 to 24 hours before being cooked in boiling water for at least 2 hours, but check by tasting during the cooking time to make sure they do not get too soft.

When buying fresh broad beans, check that the pod is shiny and firm and that the beans inside are firm and tightly packed. One major tip when buying broad beans is to allow for the fact that three-quarters of the weight will have to be discarded, so if you need 500 g (1 lb) of shelled beans then you will need to buy 2 kg (4 lb).

I like broad beans cooked with onions and speck or Parma ham cut into little cubes. They are also good reduced to a purée and eaten with pork. They can also be used as part of a larger dish, as in the case of the Sicilian speciality Frittella (see the recipe on page 133).

FINOCCHIO / BULB FENNEL
Fennel has such a sweet taste and pleasant aroma that it was often served at the end of a meal as a dessert in Italy. It is delicious in every form, raw or cooked and is an indispensable ingredient in *pinzimonio* (page 223), when the curved leaves can be used as a spoon to scoop up the olive oil. Fennel grows from spring through to October, depending on the area in which it is grown and which of the many varieties is cultivated.

It is used all over Italy, thinly sliced in salads, baked in the oven with butter and Parmesan cheese and blanched, quartered, dipped in an egg batter and deep-fried. One of the main signs of summer for me is a fennel salad where the bulb is thinly sliced then dressed with extra-virgin olive oil, salt, pepper and a few drops of lemon juice.

LEFT: FINOCCHIO

FIORE DI ZUCCA/ZUCCHINA, SEE ZUCCA/ZUCCHINA

FRIARIELLI, SEE BROCCOLI DI RAPA, CIME DI RAPA

FRITTELLA, SEE CARCIOFO AND PAGE 133

GIARDINIERA / MIXED VEGETABLE PICKLE
An *antipasto* is not complete without a *giardiniera* or *vegetali alla giardiniera*, meaning 'garden vegetables'. This wonderfully crunchy and very appetising pickle is made up of a mixture of vegetables, such as carrots, beans, onions, cucumbers, courgettes, cauliflower, kohlrabi and anything else that is in season, cut into small pieces and cooked in wine vinegar until tender (see the recipe on page 134). When the pickle is eaten with slices of salami or prosciutto as part of an *antipasto*, the acidity of the vinegar helps stimulate the appetite.

Giardiniera is usually made at home in the summer, when the ingredients are fresh and abundant, and it can then be stored in jars for the winter. Over time, the its commercial production has grown into a huge industry because it is such an intrinsic part of *antipasto*.

INDIVIA, SEE CICORIA

INSALATA / SALAD
The word *insalata* comes from the old Italian verb *insalare* meaning 'to add salt' and is now the general term used for vegetables, green salad leaves and all manner of other ingredients combined together then dressed with olive oil, vinegar or lemon juice, salt and pepper. Italians eat salad with the main course as an accompaniment to meat, especially when grilled.

Insalata used only to refer to a collection of edible green leaves with lettuce as its foundation, but today there are literally hundreds of varieties of salad leaves, including chicory, radicchio, lamb's lettuce, etc. A salad made up of green leaves with herbs, like rocket or mint or dandelion, is called an *insalata verde* (green salad), whereas a salad made of a mixture of salad ingredients including tomatoes and cucumber is called *insalata mista* (mixed salad). Salads can also be made with raw and shredded root vegetables, such as fennel, celeriac, carrots, Jerusalem artichokes, radishes or with diced cooked vegetable like green beans, carrots, fennel, courgettes, cauliflower. Salads are so flexible that almost any combination of ingredients or even a single ingredient can be called a salad, for example pasta salads and, say, *insalata di carciofi* (artichoke salad).

LAMPASCIONE, LAMPAGIONE, LAMPASCIUOLO / MUSCARI
This bulb of the *muscari* or wild hyacinth plant is much used in Puglia and southern Italy and is now cultivated as a vegetable to meet growing demand. Looking like a shallot, it is slightly bitter and is mostly eaten when it ripens in the summer. *Lampascione* can be pickled, like onions, without losing its bitter taste. It is also good boiled in water then dressed with olive oil and vinegar.

LATTUGA / LETTUCE
The Italians are very fond of lettuce. A salad almost invariably contains one or two of the very different varieties grown in all seasons all over Italy. *Romana*, or Cos, is the most universally popular for its crispness and flavour. There is also *lattuga d'inverno* or winter lettuce, which is more resistant to cold weather and *insalata primaverile* (springtime lettuce), with its pale but very tender leaves. *Lattuga da taglio* are those lettuce plants producing small bunches of very tender leaves which may be cut at the base every time lettuce is needed and the lettuce will then grow back again.

LEGUMI / LEGUMES

This is the general term for peas, beans and lentils. See also Borlotto, Cannellino, Cece, Fagiolino, Fagiolo, Fava, Lenticchia, Pisello.

BELOW: LENTICCHIE DI CASTELLUCCIO

LENTICCHIA / LENTIL

Probably the pulse most used by mankind, the lentil comes from a small climbing plant never growing more than 50 cm (20 inches) high. Its pods are rectangular and usually contain 4 lentils each. The plant originated in South Asia, but lentils arrived in the Mediterranean region a long time ago and the Romans immediately adopted them as a means of feeding their troops as well as solving the problem of feeding the poor. The name lentil comes from the Latin *lens*, which incidentally gave the name to the optical lens as it has a similar shape.

There are various varieties of lentils, all bearing the name of the area where they are produced. The most known are the *lenticchie di Castelluccio* from Umbria, which are organically grown and are tasty, full of iron and many vitamins, and cook in just 20-30 minutes without being presoaked. Naturally, demand for these lentils is very high and so is their price! Another famous variety are the lentils of Alta Mura in Puglia.

After being cooked until tender, lentils can be prepared in salads, dressed in olive oil, vinegar, salt and pepper and a pinch of oregano. Lentils are deemed lucky in Rome, where they are consumed in large quantities during New Year's celebrations. I prefer them served with *zampone* or *cotechino*, see the recipe on page 97.

MELANZANA / AUBERGINE

This vegetable is common throughout the Mediterranean region and used in an infinite number of recipes. In Italy, it is mainly eaten in the south and is grown in Campania, Puglia, Calabria, Sicily and Sardinia. Aubergines may be long and oval in shape or round like a huge egg. When fresh, they should be quite firm to the touch. They usually have rather tough skins, ranging in colour from dark purple to pale violet and even white (hence the American name eggplant). The pulp is white or slightly green, with a lot of little soft seeds. The aubergine has a slightly bitter taste, especially in the thinner varieties, so prior to cooking these are often sliced and sprinkled with salt, then left to rest while the bitter juices are drawn out.

Aubergines can be used in many ways, including as in the recipe for *melanzane al funghetto*, where they are peeled, cubed and fried in olive oil with garlic, parsley and salt. To avoid the aubergines absorbing too much oil, blanch them prior to cooking. *Parmigiana di melanzane*, often thought to be an Emilia-Romagnan recipe, actually originated in Sicily. In this recipe the aubergine is cut lengthwise and sprinkled with salt to remove any bitterness and excess moisture. It is then dipped in flour and then in beaten egg and fried until golden brown. The aubergine slices are then layered in an ovenproof dish with tomato sauce and Parmesan and Mozzarella or Fontina cheeses, then baked for 30 minutes in a hot oven. It is eaten hot or cold as a main course.

RIGHT: THE VEGETABLE MARKET IN NAPLES.

Another way of preparing aubergines is to slice them lengthwise and fry the slices, then place a mixture of breadcrumbs, anchovies, capers, oil, salt and pepper in the centre and roll up the stuffed slices, securing them with a cocktail stick, and grill them. A wonderful Sicilian recipe uses peeled, cubed and blanched aubergines squeezed of excess water and mixed with breadcrumbs, anchovy paste, beaten egg, crushed garlic, a few capers, lots of chopped parsley, salt, pepper and a little cinnamon powder to make a paste. Teaspoons of the mixture are then gently fried in hot oil until golden.

Perhaps the best-known recipe for aubergine in Italy is an aubergine preserve, *melanzane sott'olio*, in which the aubergine is cut lengthwise into ribbons then cooked in vinegar and salt before being thoroughly drained, put into a jar mixed with dried oregano, very finely chopped garlic and pieces of chilli and covered with good olive oil. Another popular dish is the Sicilian recipe *melanzane alla norma*, in which fried aubergine is mixed to a paste with salted ricotta, then dressed with garlic, basil and a tomato sauce.

Finally from the Amalfi coast comes an aubergine recipe which is eaten as a dessert! Two slices of aubergine are fried in oil, then nuts and various candied peels are placed in the middle of one slice and the slices sandwiched together. The 'sandwich' is then dusted with flour, dipped in beaten egg and deep-fried until golden. While still warm the aubergine 'sandwich' is then dusted with cocoa powder and sugar and left to cool. When cool it is given a final dip in melted chocolate.

MISTICANZA, MESTICANZA / WILD SALAD
This is a Roman expression for a mixture of wild salad leaves, including wild mint, wild rocket, dandelion, wild garlic, wild fennel, wild sorrel, usually mixed with traditional greens like endive or lettuce. It is traditionally dressed with extra-virgin olive oil, wine vinegar, salt and pepper. The same word in Umbria means a mixture of dried beans to make soup.

ORTICA / NETTLE
One of the most annoying of weeds, nettles are nevertheless edible and enjoyable. There are various types, but the edible one is the common stinging nettle with a greenish white flower. It is essential that you wear gloves when you pick the tender spring tips. To stop them from stinging, put them in the refrigerator for a while, then boil them in slightly salted water for 5 minutes or until tender. You can then use them in a soup, or dress them with olive oil and lemon juice to serve as a vegetable. They may also be used in a risotto or instead of spinach as a filling for ravioli, mixed with ricotta, Parmesan and egg.

PANISCIA / BEAN SOUP
From the middle of the rice-producing area of Novara comes this bean soup not dissimilar to a soft risotto. Fresh borlotti beans are cooked slowly together with Savoy cabbage, celery, tomato, onion and a piece of *cotenna* (pork shin) for a couple of hours. In another pan put some butter, lard, a fresh sausage and a finely chopped onion. Cook briefly, then add the rice as for making a risotto. Add a good glass of Barolo wine and then slowly, ladleful by ladleful, the vegetables and the broth. After 18-20 minutes the *paniscia* is ready. There is a similar version of this speciality from neighbouring Vercelli, but this is called *panissa*.

PANNOCCHIA / CORN ON THE COB
Grilled tender young corn cobs are called *pannocchia di granoturco arrostita* and boiled corn on the cob *pannocchia lessa*. In season these are sold at little stands by the roadside, especially in the South.

PAPPA AL POMODORO, SEE POMODORO

LEFT: MISTICANZA

PASTINACA, PASTANACHE, SEE CAROTA

PATATA / POTATO
Although fulfilling the same role in northern Europe as bread in southern Europe, the potato has never been part of the staple diet in Italy. Indeed it was only in the middle of the nineteenth century that the potato started to be widely used as a vegetable in Italy. Originally from South America, the potato is mostly cultivated in the Veneto, Puglia, Campania and Calabria, where the soil is particularly well-suited to them.

Early potatoes, usually known as *patate novelle* (new potatoes), are small, firm and waxy and ideal in potato salads, where cooked potatoes are dressed with olive oil, vinegar, spring onions, salt and pepper. Of the many varieties available, the most important are the floury winter potatoes such as Tonda di Napoli and Bianca di Como, the white flesh of which is used to make purées, gnocchi, croquettes and toppings for savoury pies. They can also be baked whole with their skins on, cut into cubes or sliced with onions. They make a useful thickener for soups such as minestrone and a tasty accompaniment to pasta in *pasta e patate*. Potatoes are probably most popular fried in matchsticks or thin slices called *patatine* (crisps). Those with a firmer more waxy yellow flesh, such as Primura and Sirtema, are ideal for making chips or sautéed potatoes. There is a potato called the Bintje which has been developed in Holland and can be used for every sort of dish.

Potatoes can also be reduced to a flour called *fecola di patate* that is used to make cakes or to thicken sauces and soups. The importance I give to the potato shows in my recipe Insalata di due Tuberi (see page 200).

PEPERONE / CAPSICUM
Along with the aubergine, the sweet pepper is perhaps the vegetable most closely associated with Mediterranean countries. Native to South America, the pepper was introduced to Italy towards the end of the eighteenth century, when it became a popular ingredient in Italian cooking. The cultivation of the pepper, which takes its name from the spicy flavour similar to that of a peppercorn, is widespread throughout Italy.

RIGHT: LUNGO MARCONI PEPPERS

are also an important part of *peperonata*, a sort of ratatouille made with onions, celery and tomatoes to be eaten with polenta.

My mother used to make *peperoni fritti* for me whenever I returned home after a journey. She would cut the peppers into small ribbons, then fry them in good olive oil until soft and slightly burned at the edges before adding some garlic and finally a few spoonfuls of wine vinegar for flavour. I still remember the sublime taste.

Finally, peppers can also be cut in half and stuffed with a variety of mixtures, including one of fresh breadcrumbs moistened with olive oil, tomato juice, garlic, capers, anchovies and parsley, then baked in the oven until the pepper is soft and the filling crispy on top (see the recipe on page 126).

Peppers are now sun-dried and stored like tomatoes, the best of those on offer being the yellow and red varieties. They can be reconstituted at any time with a little vinegar and water and their concentrated intense flavour makes a powerful addition to salads and sauces.

The squarish Quadrato di Asti is grown all over Italy, but most notably near Carmagnola in Piedmont, where it is used in the local dish, Bagna Caôda (see page 33). Of the other varieties, there is the Carnoso di Cuneo, a large meaty pepper of yellow or red and sometimes green. Another variety looks like a tomato, being bright red in colour and square-looking, almost squashed. My mother used to pickle this in vinegar for the winter when she would cook it with chunks of pork. Peppers may also be long and conical in shape like the Lungo Marconi. I think the best peppers are the yellow and red, but the very small green ones are good cooked whole, although it is worth tasting one first to check the flavour. These are called *puparuoli* in Naples.

Although the pepper (*peperone*) should not to be confused with its close relative the *peperoncino* or chilli pepper (see page 219), it can still have a spiciness mingled with its sweet flavour. When cleaning it, discard the internal seeds and membranes and take care to wash your hands after handling them.

As well as frying and preserving, peppers can also be grilled, skinned, cut into ribbons and dressed with olive oil, salt and garlic, before being served either hot or cold with all sorts of meat. They can also be cut into quarters and baked with a little olive oil to form a natural container for a *bagna caôda* sauce to be eaten as an *antipasto*. Peppers

PINZIMONIO, SEE CRUDITA AND PAGE 223

PISELLO / PEA

Peas are grown in almost every region in Italy as the plant can grow in most climates. The best-known varieties are Senatore, Superbo di Luxton, Piccolo Provenzale and Meraviglia d'Italia. When buying peas, the pod should be as fresh a green as the pea itself. If it is yellow or a pale green it means that the peas are old and will be hard. Try to insist on being able to open and sample at least one pod.

Eaten as a vegetable, usually as an accompaniment to meat, they can find wonderful expression on their own. My mother used to use them for *pasta e piselli* – the *piselli* were very sweet, and I always helped to pod them and more than the odd one disappeared into my mouth. For this dish, the pasta my mother made was without egg, just flour and water. For the sauce, a little prosciutto was fried with onion in a pan, and then the peas were added with a little water to cook gently. The dish was finished with a sprinkling of olive oil and pepper on top. The sweetness of the fresh peas still lingers on my taste buds.

Dried peas can also be used to make excellent soups, with potatoes, *salamini* or spare ribs, or smoked ham. They are also puréed to accompany *zamponi* and various other cooked meats.

Also a member of the pea family is the *taccola* or *pisello mangiatutto* (mange-tout pea), a kind of pea where the pod and the barely developed pea inside are eaten as one. They should be cooked only briefly to maintain their colour and crunchiness.

RIGHT: POMODORO

POMODORO / TOMATO

This vegetable fruit is one of the most versatile and important of foods, and forms the backbone of much of Italian cooking. It can be used for salads, sauces and pickles, it can be preserved, dried, reduced to a pulp or paste and even used as a drink or to make jam.

Originally from Mexico, the tomato was brought back by explorers and made its first appearance in Europe in the second half of the 16th century. For a long time it was

SUN-DRIED TOMATOES

The principle of the sun-dried tomato is similar to that of the *estratto*. A tomato – usually the San Marzano – is cut in two, sprinkled with salt and put in the sun to dry. The dehydration and concentration of salt in the dried tomato ensure that it can be kept for a long time. Because it is fairly inedibly salty in this form, however, its use is limited either to stews, where you certainly will not add any salt, or it can be soaked in water for a couple of hours to let it swell and lose some of the salt – then eat it as an *antipasto*. Alternatively, sun-dried tomatoes are first soaked in a solution of 2 parts of wine vinegar and 1 part of water for 4-5 hours, then completely drained and dried and immersed in olive oil – possibly with the addition of flavourings like chilli, small pieces of garlic, basil or oregano. In this way, they keep for a long time and can be eaten as a snack with some good bread. My favourite way of cooking sun-dried tomatoes is to make them into fritters, which are excellent with aperitifs: simply dip the rehydrated tomatoes into a batter of water, salt, fresh yeast, finely chopped garlic and parsley and then deep-fry them until golden brown.

considered to be a curiosity, used more as an ornament rather than in the kitchen. In Italy, the first appearance of the tomato in cooking was recorded in a book by Vincenzo Corrado (1765), *Cuoco Galante* (The Gallant Cook), in which he used tomatoes in sauces, for stuffing and frying. From that moment on, however, the tomato was taken to the Italian heart.

Once it was discovered which regions had the best climate and soil, the tomato became – alongside pasta – among the first industrialized food products to be used all year round. All Italians who had access to a little land cultivated and produced tomatoes for themselves, which they consumed either raw or preserved in bottles. *Estratto*, or concentrated tomato paste, and sun-dried tomatoes were created to extend the use of the tomato, giving each family, even those that bought tomatoes for preservation, the pleasure of capturing the taste of summer.

Emilia-Romagna and Campania became the leading regions for the cultivation and preservation of tomatoes. A new technology was invented to improve an expanding industry. In the Parma area, small engineering companies developed specialist machinery and there are still found the leading producers of state-of-the-art methods of canning and bottling various tomato derivatives. The Italians consume approximately 50 kg (110 lb) of tomatoes per head per year, most of this in the form of sauces and purées.

Among the most famous varieties of tomatoes to be eaten raw in salads are Cuor di Bue (Ox's heart) and Palla di Fuoco (fireball). In

ABOVE: SUN-DRYIN TOMATOES AT THE PLANT OF FIORDELISI, CERIGNOLA IN PUGLIA IN JULY.

FAR LEFT: GRADING AND WASHING TOMATOES BEFORE DRYING.

NEAR LEFT: SALTING THE TOMATOES WITH SEA SALT AS A PRESERVATIVE.

Far right: tomatoes on the vine.

Bottom right: cuor di bue tomatoes

Southern Italy they prefer to eat tomatoes very ripe and they also generally eat a variety of tomato which is usually used in preserving, the San Marzano. In the North, they prefer the tomato to be almost green with a lot of acidity. They use these in salads, not using any vinegar for dressing, just virgin olive oil, salt and pepper.

The San Marzano, Roma, Napoli and Marena are all types of tomatoes preferring a rich potash soil – like the wonderful terrain around the Vesuvius area where material from the volcano has made the soil extremely fertile. These varieties are mostly used for canning or bottling.

These are the bright-red plum-shaped tomatoes that you can find in cans worldwide, not requiring the addition of sugar to make sauces.

The *pomodorino* (cherry tomato or vine tomato) is small and grows in bunches. This type of tomato is mostly found in the South, Puglia, Sicily and Calabria and generally used fresh. It has a tough skin, does not grow bigger than a cherry and can be kept in bunches for the entire winter. It is consumed raw in salads, but is mainly used in the preparation of quick pasta sauces. Of the varieties grown, the *pomodorino di Cerignola* is the most sought-after.

One of the best ways to use tomatoes is in *fresella*, a peasant dish in which slices of Pugliese bread are baked twice until dry and biscuit-like, then they are quickly passed under cold running water allowing excess to drip off and arranged on a plate. The moistened toasts are then covered with freshly chopped ripe tomatoes, drizzled with a little extra-virgin olive oil, sprinkled with salt and topped with freshly chopped basil.

My mother used to produce a sort of *pappa al pomodoro* which used pieces of celery (leaves included), onion, very ripe tomatoes (collecting all the juices), a little fresh oregano, good olive oil and, sometimes, a little garlic. All these ingredients were finely chopped and mixed

LEFT: ESTRATTO DI POMODORO, MADE BY SUN-DRYING PURÉED TOMATOES.

together with some slightly moistened stale bread and left to stand for a couple of hours. It may have looked like chicken food, but it was delicious to eat. In the northern Italian tradition, she also used to make a sweet jam from unripened green tomatoes, finely chopped and slowly cooked with sugar, cinnamon and vanilla.

Various types of *concentrato di pomodoro* or tomato pastes are used in sauces and stews, to enhance the flavour of many dishes. Only in Sicily do they produce the *estratto di pomodoro*, which is a super-concentrate of tomato (in fact 6 times more concentrated than the usual paste); it is tomato pulp where most of the moisture has been removed by drying – a thick paste with a very dark red colour. As it is slightly salted, it will keep for a long time. The typical use of this is epitomized by *Pasta all'anciova* in Sicily, where a sauce for bucatini pasta is made out of olive oil in which some fillets of anchovies have been dissolved. In addition, the *estratto* (or *strattu* as it is called in Sicily) is dissolved in water and brought to a sauce-like consistency with added pine nuts and roasted breadcrumbs sprinkled on top instead of Parmesan. I like to eat *estratto* thinly spread like jam on a piece of toast sprinkled with a little virgin olive oil.

The tomato industry is also developing products such as *passata di pomodoro*, a very finely strained tomato sauce. While it is very convenient and useful, I think it is no more than a thick tomato juice or a thin tomato purée, rather than a product with an intrinsic culinary worth. I prefer *polpa di pomodoro*, which includes chunks of tomato. Using this can save you the work of chopping up peeled tomatoes for fine sauces such as *salsa di pomodoro*, a simple sauce based on olive oil, garlic, onion, tomatoes and basil. This sauce is used as the foundation for all Italian tomato sauces, which are usually called *napoletana*.

However it is used and in whatever form, the tomato deserves the Italian name of *pomodoro* or 'golden apple' (the first tomatoes, used for decoration, were yellow), because no other vegetable is more versatile and it is, without doubt, the most important item in Italian cooking!

PORRO / LEEK

This vegetable is like a cross between garlic and onion – and belongs to same family. It is cultivated all over Italy, but mainly in Liguria, Marche, Abruzzo and Puglia. The varieties have such names as Gigante d'Inverno, Mostruoso di Carentan, Elefante and Porro d'Italia. The Romans took this vegetable with them all over Europe, indeed in Wales the leek is now the symbol of that country.

In Italy, it is eaten in soups and for that purpose you use both the white and green parts. Those cultivated in the summer are more tender and they are usually eaten raw in Pinzimonio (see page 223). Leeks are also eaten with béchamel sauce. I prefer them freshly boiled and eaten as an *antipasto*, dressed with a little olive oil and vinegar.

PORTULACA / PURSLANE

This wild leafy summer plant grows almost anywhere and is characterized by its reddish coloured branches which spread over the ground. It has small thick leaves which, when young, add a special juiciness to salads.

RADICCHIO, SEE CICORIA

RAPA / TURNIP

Belonging to the cabbage family, the turnip is one of the most widely used winter vegetables. It has a delicate flavour akin to that of kohlrabi and is particularly good as an accompaniment to meat or fish. I like turnips freshly boiled and sautéed in butter with a little garlic and parsley. They need to be thoroughly cleaned and as little of the skin as possible removed. Very young turnips can also be eaten raw, shredded in salads. Turnip shoots and tops are also eaten, see Broccolo di Rapa and Cime di Rapa.

RAVANELLO / RADISH

This wonderful vegetable is mainly eaten raw. The little roots come in varying shapes, from round or conical to straight. They are very hot in flavour, but refreshing, and their red and white colouring can enliven many salads and *antipasto* plates.

RIBOLLITA, SEE CAVOLO

BELOW: THE FRUIT AND VEGETABLE MARKET IN FLORENCE.

RUCOLA, RUCHETTA / ROCKET
The longish but small irregularly shaped leaves of *ruchetta* have a sharp taste which is exceptionally good when mixed with other salad leaves, as in Misticanza. Rocket is often used as a tasty garnish for Carpaccio, in a salad with tomatoes and mozzarella and as a flavouring for pasta sauces and sometimes risottos. *Rucola*, the cultivated version of *ruchetta*, has much larger and rounder leaves.

SCALOGNO / SHALLOT
The shallot, which looks like a small onion, is divided into two sections inside. Its flavour falls somewhere between the onion and garlic, but its use is limited to flavouring special sauces cooked with butter and scattering raw and finely chopped on salads. Shallots keep better than onions, and so can be stored for a long time. With the rise in interest in Mediterranean food, they have recently become fashionable again, but in the past they were very much peasant food in the Italian south.

SCAROLA, SEE CICORIA

SCORZONERA / BLACK SALSIFY
This is a very long straight root vegetable that belongs to the lettuce family. It is harvested in autumn and winter and is enjoyed for its delicate but bitter flavour. The root can grow up to 30 cm (1 foot) in length and must be thoroughly scraped with a knife until the white pulp is visible. If it is old, cut it in two and discard the woody centre. If it is very young, though, it can be boiled whole and eaten with melted butter like asparagus. In Italy nowadays there are few enthusiasts of the vegetable, but it makes an interesting change to the usual fare.

SEDANO, SEDANO RAPA / CELERY, CELERIAC
Celery is very versatile plant that is as valuable both as a herb and as a vegetable. There are two basic varieties. One is a plant with a long stem of deep green on the outside and creamy white on the inside. The other variety is *sedano rapa* (turnip-rooted celery or celeriac) which grows mainly underground in a round root. The leaves of this root are usually sold as a herb for salads and soups. They have a strong scent and their skins are quite tough but full of flavour.

Celery is grown almost everywhere in Italy but most notably in Puglia, Calabria and Campania, while Sicily cultivates a small amount of stick celery which has very small stems and larger leaves than flat parsley. It is mostly used in the local speciality called *caponata* which is made with aubergine, celery, onion, capers and pitted green olives, all stewed with the best extra-virgin olive oil, a little sugar and vinegar (see the recipe on page 135).

Celeriac can be peeled, boiled, cut into slices and baked in the oven with butter, nutmeg and pepper and a touch of double cream and it is also good both braised and deep-fried. Finely shredded young celeriac is good raw in salads.

White celery is grown in the shade away from the sun so that it is blanched of its green colouring. It is used cut into small pieces in salads. Green celery can be used in soups, cut into 10-cm (4-inch) chunks and boiled as a vegetable, or served *gratinato* dotted with butter and Parmesan. Naturally, the most tender parts of both varieties of stalk celery can be eaten raw (see Pinzimonio and Bagna Caôda, page 33).

SOTTACETI / PICKLES
Generic name for all vegetables pickled in vinegar and used in *antipasto* or for aperitifs, see Giardiniera.

RIGHT: SPINACI

SPINACI / SPINACH
The Arabs introduced this popular vegetable to Italy around the year AD 1,000 and it is now grown in Northern and Central Italy, where the climate is mild but not hot. Modern cultivation techniques mean that spinach is available all year round rather than just in the autumn and winter as in the past. It grows close to the ground and has substantial deep green leaves. Spinach contains large amounts of vitamins A and C, but is best-known for being rich in iron.

It is used in a multitude of ways, including *alla fiorentina*, a dish of cooked spinach and a firm white sauce flavoured with Parmesan, and it is also good raw in salads as long as the leaves are young and tender. Spinach requires careful cleaning, especially if it has been grown organically. Unfortunately, however, repeated cleaning in cold water strips it of some of its most valuable nutrients.

My favourite way of preparing spinach is cooking it briefly in a very small amount of water, draining it and dressing it with extra-virgin olive oil and lemon juice while it is still warm. It is particularly good mixed with ricotta and Parmesan and used to fill *crespelle* (small pancakes), ravioli or

FAR LEFT: CARDOON AND PUMPKIN.

large pasta shells. My own recipe for *uovo in raviolo* is based on a mixture of spinach and ricotta, which is formed in a ring on a large square of pasta. An egg yolk is placed in the centre of the spinach mixture and another large square of pasta pressed on top. The whole thing is cooked in boiling water and served with melted butter and a few slivers of truffle.

Fresh or frozen spinach can also be liquidized and added to pasta dough to colour it green (see page 142) and it also makes a wonderful soup if cooked in a good stock with a couple of beaten egg yolks quickly stirred in and served sprinkled with Parmesan cheese.

TACCOLA, SEE PISELLO

VALERIANELLA / LAMB'S LETTUCE

One of the most delicate wild salad leaves, this plant is now widely cultivated. It is used largely in modern cuisine to decorate various dishes and is usually eaten raw on its own or as part of a green salad. The little bushy leaves are extremely tender and delicate. I prefer to eat it dressed with extra-virgin olive oil and a little lemon juice. As with all their salads, Italians like to dress *valerianella* at the table, first pouring on the oil to avoid damaging the delicate leaves with the acidity of the lemon or vinegar.

LEFT: VALERIANELLA

ZUCCA / SQUASH, PUMPKIN

One of the most widely used family of vegetables in Italy, all types of squash, pumpkins and the smaller courgettes (see right) are loved for their flavour, varying shapes, and wide range of uses in the kitchen. Only the marrow is not much eaten in Italy, as it is considered to be no more than an overgrown courgette but without the flavour. The family of plants originates from South America, where they were cultivated for decoration, some varieties being cultivated to reach gigantic proportions, the largest being the Mammouth or the Melone Gigante which can reach more than 100 kilos (250 lb) in weight.

Pumpkin and other types of thick-skinned winter squashes will keep for up to a month as long as the skin is not broken. Once cut, however, they will only last for a day or two. For the best flavour, squash and pumpkin should only be picked when fully ripe.

All varieties of squash, including courgettes, grow close to the ground, spreading long tentacles over the ground, then producing the fruit from the flower.

Today, pumpkin is popular in Piedmont, where the whole thing is baked in the oven and the cooked flesh spooned out, in the Veneto where they serve it with pickles, and in Lombardy, where they use it to make risotto. In Campania it is called *cocozza*, and is sliced and lightly boiled then fried. It is also known as *salmone di campagna* or country salmon, because of its orange-red colour. In Emilia-Romagna it is used to make *tortelli di zucca* (see page 160), which uses cooked pumpkin mixed with *mostarda*. Dried pumpkin seeds can also be eaten and are particularly tasty when toasted and scattered over gratins or salads. They are mostly sold and eaten in southern Italy.

NEAR LEFT: PUMPKIN FLESH.

One unusual variety of squash is the spaghetti pumpkin, whose cooked flesh resembles strings, like spaghetti. It is delicious eaten simply with butter and Parmesan. Another curiosity is the Piena di Napoli, also known as the Piena di Chioggia or Piena di Albenga. It grows up to a metre (1 yard) in length and has to be suspended from a pergola so it has room to grow to full size. It can also be picked before it is completely ripe, when it is just 5-6 cm (2-2½ inches) in diameter and can be cooked in the same ways as courgette. In Sicily this type of squash is also cut into long strips and candied for the making of *cassata Siciliana*, a ricotta and marzipan dessert.

Squash and pumpkin flowers are also used in the same way as courgette flowers. Generally slightly smaller than those of the courgette, they do however have a more intense flavour.

RIGHT: COURGETTES DRYING IN THE SUN.

ZUCCHINO / COURGETTE

Like the other larger *zucca*, *zucchini* also grow over the ground but are more bushy than other plants in the family. When buying them, try to get organically grown ones and try to buy them in season when their flavour is at its best. Courgettes are delicious when freshly picked, blanched and served dressed with a little melted butter and salt or extra-virgin olive oil and lemon juice.

Courgettes come in a huge range of shapes, colours and sizes, from the round, dark green Tonda di Nizza to the long, straight dark green Verde di Milano and from the common Striata di Italia or di Napoli to the pale green Bianca Sarda. What they all have in common though, is their flavour, which is almost exactly the same regardless of their outer appearance.

RIGHT: COURGETTES AND COURGETTE FLOWERS.

To get the best courgettes, look for those which are firm to the touch with a shiny skin. Inside they should be white with small edible seeds. They are grown all over Italy and they adapt themselves quite readily to many soil types. They are universally popular for their culinary versatility and their nutritional value.

Like other plants in the family, courgettes have exquisite flowers which are edible. Only the non-fruit-bearing male flower, with its characteristic long thin stem, is usually sold in huge bunches at markets all around Italy. Courgette flowers are at their best when open and are ideal for stuffing with mixtures of spinach, ricotta and Parmesan before being dipped in beaten egg and deep-fried. They are also good simply dipped in a batter of flour, water and salt then deep- or shallow-fried in good olive oil (see the recipe on page 123).

Recently, due to demand for the flowers, courgette plants have been bred expressly for their flowers and only tiny courgettes are produced as a result. These baby courgettes are extremely tender but, like all plants that are not allowed to reach maturity, lack flavour in comparison with the fully grown vegetable.

Courgettes can be served in a huge variety of ways. Tender young courgettes are delicious simply eaten raw grated in salads or, as in my own recipe *marmellata di zucchini*, as a courgette marmalade simply finely shredded with garlic, extra-virgin olive oil and a few drops of lemon juice added after everything has been gently simmered for about 20 minutes.

Courgettes can also be served as a vegetable accompaniment or as a snack with drinks, cut into batons then dipped in a batter of egg and flour and shallow-fried. They are also delicious in the Neapolitan dish *alla scapece*, in which they are cut into thin slices and fried until lightly browned and served dressed with extra-virgin olive oil, vinegar, garlic and mint (see the recipe on page 124). Alternatively, they can be sliced then grilled and served dressed with extra-virgin olive oil and vinegar. They are also delicious cooked *al funghetto*, fried in cubes with garlic, extra-virgin olive oil and parsley. They may also be sliced lengthwise, shallow-fried and used in place of aubergine to make *parmigiana* (see Melanzana) or stuffed with a meat or bread-and-egg filling and baked, or chopped and added to a minestrone soup.

Finally, *tenerume* or tender courgette plant tops can be used at the end of the season to make a *zuppa* with potatoes, tomatoes, garlic and extra-virgin olive oil (see the recipe on page 123).

BOTTOM RIGHT: TENERUME, THE TENDER SHOOTS OF THE COURGETTE PLANT USED FOR SOUPS, ON SALE IN TURIN MARKET.

Zuppa di Verdure (top), Fiori di Zucchini Fritti (below).

ZUPPA DI VERDURE

VEGETABLE SOUP

FOR 4

2 TBSP OLIVE OIL
1 ONION, SLICED
2 GARLIC CLOVES, CHOPPED
3 TOMATOES, FINELY CHOPPED
1 LITRE ($1^3/_4$ PINTS) CHICKEN OR VEGETABLE STOCK
150 G (5 OZ) NEW POTATOES, PEELED AND CUT INTO SLICES 5 MM ($^1/_4$ IN) THICK
1 KG (2 LB 3 OZ) TENERUME (SEE ZUCCHINO, PAGE 121) OR 2–3 COURGETTES, CHOPPED
SALT AND PEPPER

This soup uses tenerume, *the tender shoots at the top of a courgette plant, including the young flower and courgettes still attached.*

Heat the oil in a large pan, add the onion and garlic and fry briefly until softened. Add the tomatoes, stir well together, then pour in the stock and bring to a simmer. Add the potatoes and tenerume or courgettes and cook for about 20 minutes or until the potatoes are tender.

Season to taste and then serve immediately with some good bread.

FIORI DI ZUCCHINI FRITTI

DEEP-FRIED COURGETTE FLOWERS

FOR 4

2 EGGS
150 G (5 OZ) PLAIN FLOUR
4 TBSP BEER
20 COURGETTE FLOWERS, ORANGE-COLOURED BUT STILL CLOSED
SALT AND PEPPER
OLIVE OIL FOR DEEP-FRYING

There are two ways of cooking this curious dish – with the flowers either stuffed (see overleaf) or simply dipped in batter and fried. Both ways are wonderful.

Beat the eggs with some salt and pepper and then add the flour and beer and mix well to obtain a light batter. If the flowers are already open, check for insects inside.

Dip the flowers in the batter one by one and deep-fry in hot oil a few at a time until golden. Use a fairly small pan for frying so the oil level is higher and you will need less.

FINOCCHIO FRITTO

FRIED FENNEL

FOR 4

3 LARGE TENDER FENNEL BULBS
2 EGGS, BEATEN
60 G (2 OZ) BUTTER
SALT AND PEPPER
FLOUR FOR DUSTING

This is a very simple way to prepare fennel, versatile enough to accompany all sorts of delicate meat and fish dishes.

Cook the fennel bulbs in boiling salted water until tender; check by inserting the tip of a knife. Drain and leave to cool, then cut into quarters.

Beat the eggs with some salt and pepper. Dip the fennel segments into the flour and then into the beaten egg to coat them completely. Melt the butter in a pan over a gentle heat and fry the fennel until golden on each side.

Fiori di Zucchini Ripieni

STUFFED COURGETTE FLOWERS

For 4

12 COURGETTE FLOWERS
275 G (10 OZ) RICOTTA CHEESE
PINCH OF FRESHLY GRATED NUTMEG
BUNCH OF CHIVES, CHOPPED
1 EGG, BEATEN
4 TBSP FRESHLY GRATED PARMESAN CHEESE
4 TBSP OLIVE OIL
SALT AND PEPPER

For the batter:
2 EGGS
55 G ($1^3/_4$ OZ) PLAIN FLOUR
4 TBSP COLD WATER

The Italians pay special attention to the flowers of the courgette and pumpkin. They are sold in bunches at the street markets and in good shops, when they are in season.

First make the batter: beat the eggs lightly in a bowl, then stir in the flour evenly. Gradually add the water to make a smooth consistency. Set aside.

Clean the courgette flowers carefully. Gently wash and dry the outside and make sure there are no insects inside. Prepare the filling by mixing together the ricotta, nutmeg, chives, egg, grated Parmesan and some salt and pepper. Fill the flowers with spoonfuls of this mixture.

Heat the oil in a large frying pan. Dip the flowers in the batter and fry them, a few at a time, in the hot oil until golden brown, turning from time to time. Drain on paper towels before serving.

Zucchini alla Scapece

MARINATED COURGETTES

For 4–6

800 G ($1^3/_4$ LB) YOUNG COURGETTES, CUT INTO SLICES 2 MM ($^1/_{12}$ INCH) THICK
2 TBSP MINT LEAVES
1 GARLIC CLOVE, PEELED AND CUT IN HALF
SALT
ABOUT 2 TBSP WHITE WINE VINEGAR
OLIVE OIL FOR FRYING

Scapece *probably comes from the Portuguese word* escabeche, *which means marinated. This is a delightful little accompaniment for grilled lamb or pork or to eat as part of an* antipasto.

Fry the courgette slices in abundant hot oil until browned on both sides (not too dark). The courgettes have to swim freely in the oil; if necessary, fry them in batches. Drain through a sieve to get rid of excess oil and then put them in a porcelain dish.

When all the courgettes have been fried, add the mint leaves and the garlic (which is only to flavour the courgettes and should be discarded before eating). Season with salt to taste and stir in at least 2 tablespoons of vinegar, more if desired. Leave to marinate for at least 2 hours.

Melanzane Fritte

FRIED AUBERGINES

For 4

2 LARGE AUBERGINES, CUT INTO FINGER-SIZED STRIPS
125 ML (4 FL OZ) OLIVE OIL
SALT

In this very simple way of eating aubergines the flavour is provided by good olive oil and the aubergines themselves.

Leave the aubergines in lightly salted cold water for an hour, then drain and squeeze out the excess water. Heat the oil in a large pan, add the aubergines and fry until brown on each side. Season with salt to taste. They can be served hot or cold.

Peperoni e Olive

PEPPERS AND OLIVES

For 4

- 125 ML (4 FL OZ) OLIVE OIL
- 2 EACH YELLOW AND RED PEPPERS, DESEEDED AND CUT INTO LARGE STRIPS
- 2 TBSP FINELY CHOPPED BLACK OLIVES
- 2 GARLIC CLOVES, FINELY CHOPPED
- 2 TBSP WHITE WINE VINEGAR
- 1 TSP SUGAR
- SALT

This is a very welcome southern addition to an antipasto.

Heat the oil in a pan, add the peppers and fry, stirring from time to time, for about 20 minutes, until they are tender. Add the olives and garlic and fry for another couple of minutes. Add the vinegar and stir until it has evaporated, then add the sugar and some salt to taste. Serve hot or cold.

Clockwise from the top left: Zucchini alla Scapece, Peperoni Fritti, Peperoni e Olive, Melanzane Fritte

PEPERONI RIPIENI

STUFFED PEPPERS

FOR 6

- 3 LARGE YELLOW OR RED PEPPERS, OR A MIXTURE OF BOTH
- 300 G ($10^{1}/_{2}$ OZ) FRESH BREADCRUMBS
- 1 TBSP SALTED CAPERS, SOAKED IN WATER FOR 10 MINUTES AND THEN DRAINED
- 1 TBSP FINELY CHOPPED BLACK OLIVES
- 3 LARGE TOMATOES, PEELED, DESEEDED AND FINELY DICED
- 1 GARLIC CLOVE, VERY FINELY CHOPPED
- 2 TBSP COARSELY CHOPPED FLAT-LEAF PARSLEY
- 4 ANCHOVY FILLETS, FINELY CHOPPED
- 125 ML (4 FL OZ) OLIVE OIL
- SALT AND PEPPER

This way of preparing peppers, and also aubergines and courgettes, is typical of the South. With a few variations, this is how they are cooked in Naples.

Preheat the oven to 180°C/350°F/gas4. Cut the peppers in half and discard the seeds.

Soak the breadcrumbs in enough water to cover and then squeeze out the excess liquid. Mix with the capers, olives, tomatoes, garlic, parsley, anchovies, half the olive oil and salt and pepper to taste. Fill the peppers with this mixture and put them on a baking tray. Sprinkle with the rest of the olive oil and bake for 30 minutes, until the peppers are tender and starting to char a little at the edges.

They are excellent hot or cold.

PEPERONI AL POMODORO

PEPPERS AND TOMATOES

FOR 4

- 90 ML (3 FL OZ) OLIVE OIL
- 600 G (1¼ LB) PEPERONCINI DOLCI (SEE PEPERONE, PAGE 114), STEMS TRIMMED
- 1 GARLIC CLOVE, FINELY CHOPPED
- 400 G (14 OZ) RIPE TOMATOES, PEELED, DESEEDED AND CHOPPED (OR THE EQUIVALENT AMOUNT OF POLPA DI POMODORO – SEE PAGE 118)
- 6 BASIL LEAVES
- SALT

In some parts of the South these small sweet peppers are also called friarielli *– confusingly, since* cime di rapa *(see page 109) is given the same name. This is a common way of eating the very small peppers that look like chillies but taste sweet. When buying them you have to be sure to get the real thing.*

Heat the oil in a pan and fry the whole peppers (the little seeds inside are edible) for 10 minutes, stirring constantly. Add the garlic and fry for a minute, then stir in the tomatoes, basil and salt. Cover and cook for about 15–20 minutes, until the peppers are soft.

My mother used to add some new potatoes and serve these as a first course accompanied by bread.

PEPERONI FRITTI

FRIED PEPPERS

FOR 4

- 6 TBSP OLIVE OIL
- 600 G (1¼ LB) WHOLE BABY SWEET PEPPERS
- 2 GARLIC CLOVES
- ½ SMALL CHILLI, DESEEDED AND CHOPPED
- SALT

Heat the olive oil in a heavy-based pan and, when hot, put in the peppers. Fry the peppers for 5 minutes, stirring from time to time so that they fry on all sides. Their skins will begin to blister, and at that point add the garlic and almost immediately afterwards the chilli and salt to taste. Cook for a further 5 minutes.

Serve hot or cold as part of an *antipasto* or as a side dish.

CICORIA BELGA AL TARTUFO NERO

CHICORY WITH BLACK TRUFFLE

FOR 4

- 5 LARGE HEADS OF CHICORY
- 1 TBSP TRUFFLE OIL
- 2 TBSP EXTRA-VIRGIN OLIVE OIL
- 1 TBSP BALSAMIC VINEGAR
- 1 SUMMER TRUFFLE (SEE PAGE 195), WEIGHING ABOUT 55 G (1¾ OZ), THINLY SLICED
- SALT AND PEPPER

This is one of the favourite starters in my restaurant. The simple combination produces an outstanding result.

Cut the chicory into strips 1 cm (½ inch) wide, removing the tough core which is slightly bitter. Put the chicory into a bowl and add the oils, vinegar, salt and pepper. Mix well and serve topped with thin slices of summer truffle.

Carciofi Ripieni

STUFFED ARTICHOKES

For 4

- 1 KG (2¼ LB) VERY FRESH YOUNG ARTICHOKES
- 300 G (10½ OZ) FRESH BREADCRUMBS
- SMALL SPRIG OF MINT, ROUGHLY CHOPPED
- ZEST OF ½ LEMON
- 3 ANCHOVY FILLETS, FINELY CHOPPED
- 1 SMALL GARLIC CLOVE, VERY FINELY CHOPPED
- 2 TBSP CHOPPED FLAT-LEAF PARSLEY
- 25 G (¾ OZ) SALTED CAPERS, SOAKED IN WATER FOR 10 MINUTES, THEN DRAINED AND ROUGHLY CHOPPED
- 3 TBSP EXTRA-VIRGIN OLIVE OIL
- SALT AND PEPPER
- OLIVE OIL

It's essential to use very fresh and tender artichokes for this recipe.

Discard the tough outer leaves of the artichokes until you reach the tender leaves, then slice off the top. Cut off the stems so they will stand upright. Remove the choke from the centre with the help of a melon baller, leaving a cavity (see page 105).

Soak the breadcrumbs in a little water to cover, then squeeze out the excess moisture. Mix the breadcrumbs with the mint, lemon zest, anchovies, garlic, parsley and capers. Stir in the extra virgin olive oil, then add a little salt and plenty of pepper.

Fill the cavity of the artichokes with this mixture and put the artichokes in a large pan, making sure they stay upright. Add enough water to come half way up the artichokes and then pour in enough olive oil to increase the level of the liquid by about 1 cm (½ inch). Bring to a simmer, cover with the lid and braise over a very gentle heat for 30 minutes.

Frittata di Carciofi

ARTICHOKE OMELETTE

For 4

- 8 YOUNG AND FRESH MEDIUM ARTICHOKES
- 4 TBSP OLIVE OIL
- 1 LARGE ONION, THINLY SLICED
- 6 FREE-RANGE EGGS
- 2 TBSP COARSELY CHOPPED FLAT-LEAF PARSLEY
- 45 G (1½ OZ) PARMESAN CHEESE, GRATED
- SALT AND PEPPER

Artichokes combine extremely well with eggs. This frittata isn't turned during cooking; it is cooked on one side only, until the eggs are set.

Discard the tough outer leaves of the artichokes until you reach the tender leaves, then slice off the top. If the artichokes are young and tender, simply trim the stems, leaving about 5 cm (2 inches) still attached, then peel them. Cut them into quarters and remove the choke with a knife. Put the artichokes in a frying pan with the olive oil, onion and about 6 tablespoons of water. Cover and cook gently until they are tender and all the liquid has evaporated.

Beat the eggs with the parsley, Parmesan cheese and some salt and pepper. Pour the egg mixture on to the artichokes and leave to set over a moderate heat without stirring. After a little while the eggs will have solidified and the frittata is ready. Serve cut into wedges.

Carciofi in Agrodolce

SWEET-AND-SOUR ARTICHOKES

For 4

- 12 young and fresh medium artichokes
- 3 tbsp white wine vinegar
- 1 tbsp caster sugar
- 3 tbsp coarsely chopped flat-leaf parsley
- 3 tbsp extra-virgin olive oil
- salt

A very appetizing and unusual way to prepare artichokes, which can be eaten as an antipasto.

Discard the tough outer leaves of the artichokes until you reach the tender leaves, then slice off the top. Trim the stems, leaving about 5 cm (2 inches) still attached; if you peel this it will be edible and very tender. Cut the artichokes into quarters and remove the choke with a knife. Boil the artichokes in lightly salted water for about 15 minutes or until tender; check by piercing with the tip of a knife. Drain and set aside.

Heat the vinegar and sugar in a small pan until the sugar has dissolved. Leave to cool, then mix with the parsley, olive oil and a pinch of salt. Pour over the artichoke quarters and leave to absorb the flavours for an hour or so before serving.

Clockwise from the top left: Frittata di Carciofi, Carciofi in Agrodolce, Carciofi Ripieni

CAPONNET

SAVOY CABBAGE PARCELS

FOR 4

8 SAVOY CABBAGE LEAVES (SEE RIGHT)
100 G ($3^1/_2$ OZ) LUGANIGA SAUSAGE (SEE PAGE 77)
200 G (7 OZ) LEFT-OVER ROAST MEAT
2 EGGS, BEATEN
2 TBSP DRIED BREADCRUMBS
1 GARLIC CLOVE, VERY FINELY CHOPPED
A PINCH OF FRESHLY GRATED NUTMEG
55 G ($1^3/_4$ OZ) PARMESAN CHEESE, GRATED
25 G ($^3/_4$ OZ) BUTTER
SALT AND PEPPER

In Canavese, and especially in Ivrea, this dish is a must at winter parties and celebrations. It is served as part of a very varied antipasto. *The leaves for making the parcels must be from a Savoy cabbage. Choose the second layer of leaves because the outer layer will be too tough. Finely minced left-over roast meat and some sausagemeat are used in the stuffing but if you don't have any left-over roast meat, use minced beef that has been briefly browned.*

Preheat the oven to 160°C/325°F/gas3. Boil the cabbage leaves in lightly salted water for 5 minutes, until they are flexible. Drain and pat dry on a cloth. Cut out the central stalk if it is tough.

Take the sausagemeat out of its skin and crumble it. Mix with the roast meat, eggs, breadcrumbs, garlic, nutmeg and 45 g ($1^1/_2$ oz) of the Parmesan cheese, adding salt and pepper to taste. Place the mixture in the centre of the cabbage leaves and fold them up to make parcels, securing with a cocktail stick. Put them on a baking tray, dot with the butter and dust with the remaining Parmesan. Bake for 20 minutes.

Serve hot or cold.

CAPONNET AND CIPOLLE RIPIENE

Cipolle Ripiene

STUFFED ONIONS

For 4

- 8 large onions (the size of a small orange)
- 200 g (7 oz) luganiga sausage (see page 77)
- 1 tbsp olive oil
- 1 tbsp breadcrumbs
- 1 egg, beaten
- 1 tbsp raisins
- 1 tbsp pine nuts
- 2 amaretti biscuits, crumbled
- 1 tbsp Parmesan cheese, grated
- small pinch of freshly grated nutmeg
- pinch of cinnamon
- salt and pepper

Very often in Piedmont baked onions are served with Caponnet (see opposite) and sometimes the same stuffing is used for both. Here the stuffing is different, but it is still Piedmontese despite the inclusion of spices, pine nuts and raisins, which are of Southern origin.

Preheat the oven to 180°C/350°F/gas4. Peel the onions. Cook them in lightly salted boiling water for 10 minutes and then drain.

Take the sausagemeat out of its skin and crumble it. Heat the olive oil in a frying pan, add the sausagemeat and fry until browned. Leave to cool, then mix with the breadcrumbs, beaten egg, raisins, pine nuts, crumbled amaretti biscuits, Parmesan cheese, nutmeg and cinnamon, adding salt and pepper to taste.

Cut the top off each onion and remove the centre with a spoon to make a container. Fill them with the stuffing and bake for 20–25 minutes. They can be served hot or cold.

Salsa di Pomodoro alla Napoletana

NEAPOLITAN TOMATO SAUCE

For 6

- 90 ml (3 fl oz) extra-virgin olive oil
- 2 garlic cloves, crushed
- 1 kg (2¼ lb) ripe tomatoes, peeled, deseeded and chopped (or use 800 g (1¾ lb) polpa di pomodoro – see page 118)
- 6 basil leaves
- salt and pepper

The name given to a dish or sauce usually denotes its place of origin or the place where it is usually cooked. Naples is synonymous with spaghetti, pizza and naturally, therefore, with one of the basic tomato sauces. This sauce is known not only in Italy but also everywhere in the world a Neapolitan immigrant has set up a business. It is indeed a delightful sauce, usually prepared with sunripened tomatoes. During winter, however, tinned or bottled tomato pulp is used. Some people prefer to cook the sauce for only about 5 minutes if the tomatoes are very ripe, while others let it simmer for 20–30 minutes for a more concentrated flavour, even adding a spoonful of tomato paste. I prefer the briefly cooked version. The general Italian basic tomato sauce involves frying onion, carrot, celery and parsley before adding the tomatoes and some basil.

Heat the oil in a pan and gently fry the garlic for a few minutes without allowing it to colour. Add the tomatoes and fry, stirring constantly, for 5 minutes, allowing just the excess liquid to evaporate.

Add the basil and salt and pepper to taste and the sauce is ready to use for the most wonderful plate of spaghetti or many other dishes.

Gattò di Patate

Potato Cake

For 6

- 1 kg (2¼ lb) floury potatoes
- 55 g (1¾ oz) prosciutto cotto, cut into cubes
- 25 g (¾ oz) buffalo mozzarella, cut into small cubes
- 100 g (3½ oz) provola cheese (smoked mozzarella, see page 244), cut into small cubes
- 55 g (1¾ oz) Parmesan cheese, grated
- 4 eggs, beaten
- 2 tbsp finely chopped flat-leaf parsley
- knob of butter
- 4 tbsp dried breadcrumbs
- 4 tbsp olive oil
- salt and pepper

Gattò *is derived from the French* gâteau, *which this resembles in shape when baked. It is very common in Naples, where many French-influenced recipes are cooked even today – a legacy of the Bourbon occupation in the 18th century.*

Preheat the oven to 180°C/350°F/gas4. Boil the potatoes until tender, then drain and peel them. Pass them through a sieve to make a purée. Mix the potato purée with the prosciutto, mozzarella, provola, Parmesan, beaten eggs, parsley and some salt and pepper.

Use the butter to grease a round 25 cm (10 inch) cake tin, and dust with some of the breadcrumbs. Pour the potato mixture into it and press gently with a fork to give some shape. Sprinkle with the remaining breadcrumbs and then trickle over the olive oil. Bake for 30 minutes, until browned on top.

The cake is very good warm but also excellent cold.

FRITTELLA PALERMITANA

ARTICHOKES, PEAS AND BROAD BEANS FROM PALERMO

FOR 2 AS A MAIN COURSE, 4 AS AN ACCOMPANIMENT OR A PASTA SAUCE

4–5 SMALL YOUNG ARTICHOKES
90 ML (3 FL OZ) OLIVE OIL
1 LARGE ONION, THINLY SLICED
150 G (5 OZ) SHELLED FRESH PEAS
150 G (5 OZ) SHELLED FRESH BROAD BEANS
1 TSP SALTED CAPERS, SOAKED IN WATER FOR 10 MINUTES, THEN DRAINED
300 ML (1/2 PINT) WATER
SALT AND PEPPER

Made when the new season's vegetables have just appeared, this dish is the epitome of Sicilian springtime. A speciality of Palermo, it is extremely simple to make. Sometimes a teaspoon of white wine vinegar is added after the vegetables have been cooked. Without the vinegar it can be used as a pasta sauce. It can also be made into a more substantial dish using potatoes. In Sicily they enjoy this dish when the vegetables are overcooked.However, I prefer it cooked my way so that the vegetables remain separate. If you do overcook it, try serving it on pasta with some freshly grated Pecorino cheese.

Prepare the artichokes by removing the stalks and outer leaves (see Carciofo, page 105). Small young artichokes have hardly any choke and should need very little preparation. Cut the artichokes into quarters.

Heat the oil in a saucepan, add the onion and fry briefly, until softened. Add the peas, broad beans, artichokes, capers and some salt and pepper, then pour in the water and stir well. Put the lid on the pan and cook over a moderate heat for about 20 minutes or until the vegetables are tender, stirring from time to time.

ABOVE: FRITTELLA PALERMITANA AND PANELLE DI PALERMO (TOP)

PANELLE DI PALERMO

CHICKPEA FRITTERS

FOR 4–6

1 LITRE (1 3/4 PINTS) WATER
250 G (9 OZ) CHICKPEA FLOUR
1 TBSP FINELY CHOPPED FLAT-LEAF PARSLEY
SALT AND PEPPER
OLIVE OIL FOR FRYING

These are traditionally served with Frittella Palermitana (above). Like many Sicilian dishes, it has a strong Arab influence.

Bring the water almost to the boil in a large pan, then take off the heat and gradually add the chickpea flour, mixing very well in order to prevent lumps forming. When all the flour has been added, put the pan back on the heat and cook for about 30 minutes, stirring all the time. Add the parsley and season with salt. Pour the mixture on to a wet marble surface or baking sheet and flatten with a spatula to about 1 cm (1/2 in) thick. When cool, cut into squares with a knife or into rounds with a pastry cutter. Shallow-fry in olive oil until golden brown on both sides. Serve hot, with a sprinkling of freshly ground black pepper.

GIARDINIERA

MIXED GARDEN PICKLE

MAKES ENOUGH TO FILL A 2.5 LITRE (4½ PINT) JAR

- 2 KG (1¼ LB) MIXED VEGETABLES SUCH AS PICKLING ONIONS, GHERKINS, CAULIFLOWER, CARROTS, CELERIAC AND PUMPKIN
- 2 LITRES (3½ PINTS) WHITE WINE VINEGAR
- 1 LITRE (1¾ PINTS) WATER
- 55 G (1¾ OZ) SALT
- 30 G (1 OZ) SUGAR
- SMALL HANDFUL OF BAY LEAVES
- SMALL HANDFUL OF CLOVES
- CHILLI, TO TASTE (OPTIONAL)
- A FEW JUNIPER BERRIES (OPTIONAL)

Few people prepare their own Giardiniera nowadays because commercial versions are readily available. However, the home-made variety is by far the best and can be kept for a long time in the brine. I encountered this particular recipe in Emilia-Romagna, where they love it served as an antipasto, *dressed with olive oil. The vegetables, especially root vegetables such as carrots, celeriac, etc, can be cut with a serrated knife to give an attractive pattern. Red and yellow peppers are usually pickled separately, since they require a shorter cooking time and are used on their own in various dishes.*

Peel the vegetables as necessary, then cut them into bite-sized chunks. Put the vinegar and water in a large pan with the salt and sugar and bring to the boil, stirring to dissolve the salt and sugar. Add the vegetables and simmer for 30 minutes, until tender.

Transfer the hot pickle to a 2.5 litre (4½ pint) sterilized preserving jar (or several smaller jars), tucking in the bay leaves, cloves, and chilli and juniper berries, if using. Seal the jar and store in a cool place. The pickle can be used straight away.

CREMA DI CANNELLINI

CREAM OF CANNELLINI BEANS

FOR 4

- 200 G (7 OZ) DRIED CANNELLINI BEANS
- 30 G (1 OZ) DRIED PORCINI MUSHROOMS
- 85 G (3 OZ) BUTTER
- 1 LARGE ONION, FINELY SLICED
- 1 CHICKEN STOCK CUBE, CRUMBLED
- 2 SAGE LEAVES
- 4 SLICES OF BREAD, CRUSTS REMOVED, CUT INTO SMALL CUBES
- SALT AND PEPPER

For this very creamy soup, which is served topped with croutons, the ingredients are available all year round and it makes a welcome starter for a delicate meal.

Soak the cannellini beans in plenty of cold water overnight and then drain. Cover them with fresh water, bring to the boil and simmer for at least 1½ hours or until soft. Drain well. Meanwhile, soak the porcini in lukewarm water for 30 minutes, then drain them, reserving a little of the water, and chop finely.

In another pan, melt 60 g (2 oz) of the butter and fry the onion in it until golden. Add the porcini and fry for a couple of minutes, then add the drained beans and enough water to reach about 2 cm (¾ inch) above the level of the beans. Stir in the reserved porcini soaking water, add the stock cube and sage leaves and cook gently for 15–20 minutes. Remove the sage leaves and purée everything in a food processor or liquidizer to obtain a velvety, creamy soup. Reheat and add salt and pepper to taste.

Lightly toast the bread and then fry it in the remaining butter. Serve the soup garnished with the croutons.

Caponata

SICILIAN VEGETABLE STEW

For 6

- 1 LARGE ONION, CHOPPED
- 3–4 CELERY STALKS, INCLUDING LEAVES, CHOPPED
- 5 TBSP OLIVE OIL
- 1 KG (2$^1/_4$ LB) AUBERGINES, CUT INTO 2.5 CM (1 IN) CHUNKS
- 1 TBSP SALTED CAPERS, SOAKED IN WATER FOR 10 MINUTES, THEN DRAINED
- 20 GREEN OLIVES, STONED
- 1 TBSP SUGAR
- 1 TBSP WHITE WINE VINEGAR
- 55 G (1$^3/_4$ OZ) CONCENTRATED TOMATO PASTE
- SALT AND PEPPER

This is a typical Sicilian dish based on vegetables, above all on aubergines. The vegetables are fried and then simmered in a sweet-and-sour sauce. The origins of the word caponata *are unclear, although some say it is Catalan. It could derive from the Latin* caupona, *meaning* osteria *(bar), where you would always find a caponata ready to eat. Whatever its origin, this dish, served cold as an* antipasto, *is now popular all over Italy. It can also be eaten warm as an accompaniment to meat and poultry or used as a pasta sauce.*

Blanch the onion and celery in lightly salted boiling water for a few minutes, then drain.

Heat the oil in a large frying pan, add the aubergine chunks and fry until brown and tender (don't overcrowd the pan; you will probably have to cook them in batches). Add the onion, celery and all the remaining ingredients. Stir well, then cover and cook for about 15 minutes, removing the lid of the pan towards the end of cooking. Should the sauce require extra moisture, add a tablespoon or two of water during cooking. Season to taste with salt and pepper.

Insalata di Rinforzo

REINFORCED SALAD

For 6

- 1 CAULIFLOWER
- 150 G (5 OZ) BLACK OLIVES
- 200 G (7 OZ) PICKLED YELLOW OR RED PEPPERS
- 200 G (7 OZ) GIARDINIERA (SEE PAGE 134)
- 30 G (1 OZ) LARGE SALTED CAPERS, SOAKED IN WATER FOR 10 MINUTES, THEN DRAINED
- 100 G ($3^1/_2$ OZ) ANCHOVY FILLETS
- VIRGIN OLIVE OIL, FOR SPRINKLING
- FINELY CHOPPED CHILLI (OPTIONAL)

A typical Neapolitan dish made at the beginning of the Christmas season, this is called rinforzo *(reinforcement) because it is topped up with fresh ingredients each time any is used. It can be eaten as an* antipasto *or a snack with bread and is very appetizing indeed.*

Cut the cauliflower into florets and cook in lightly salted boiling water until *al dente*, then drain. Put the cauliflower, olives, pickled peppers, Giardiniera and capers in a bowl and sprinkle with olive oil, then transfer to a large screw-top jar. Decorate with a lattice of anchovy fillets, then seal the jar and store in a cool place. The salad should last throughout the festivities.

Insalata di Campo

Wild Salad

For 4

- 300 g ($10^1/_2$ oz) trimmed weight of the following wild leaves, or any combination of them: dandelion, rocket, wild garlic, tender nettle leaves, lamb's lettuce or whatever you fancy
- small bunch of spring onions
- 4 tbsp extra-virgin olive oil
- 30 g (1 oz) anchovy fillets, reduced to a pulp
- 1 garlic clove, very finely chopped
- 2 tbsp balsamic vinegar
- salt and pepper

A popular springtime activity for many people is roaming the fields to collect the first tender leaves of the dandelion and other wild herbs for a hearty salad. With all the pollution nowadays, however, it is necessary to go to remote fields deep in the countryside to be sure of collecting something worth eating.

Thoroughly wash all the leaves and pat or spin them dry. Chop the spring onions into small chunks and arrange on a serving dish mixed with the leaves.

In a small bowl, put the oil, anchovies, garlic and balsamic vinegar with salt and pepper to taste. Mix well and pour over the salad. Toss to mix again and serve.

Mozzarella Caprese

Mozzarella, Tomatoes and Basil, Capri-Style

For 4

- 500 g (1 lb $1^1/_2$ oz) buffalo mozzarella, sliced
- 2 large, ripe tomatoes, sliced
- 10 basil leaves
- 4 tbsp extra-virgin olive oil
- salt and pepper

The best way of serving buffalo mozzarella as a starter is to combine it with ripe tomatoes, good olive oil and fresh basil. This is often called insalata caprese.

Arrange the slices of mozzarella on a plate, alternating them with the slices of tomatoes and basil leaves. Pour over a little stream of olive oil, then season with salt and pepper.

PASTA

PASTA

I think I do have to begin this chapter with an apology to the reader. Pasta is such a rich, complex and diverse subject it really deserves an entire book of this size all on its own. That would allow a proper study of all the more than 600 shapes and regional sub-varieties that exist in the intricate Italian pasta tapestry, as well as the myriad sauces used with them. What I have tried to do in the limited space available here, is provide a fairly comprehensive selection of some of the most important points and types of pasta.

It is frustrating that the exact historical origins of pasta are unknown. For a long time it was thought that Marco Polo brought it back from China, but the recent discrediting of his journals – which are now said to have been written without him ever leaving Venice – means that this theory has been abandoned. Despite this, however, it is known that pasta was eaten in Italy by the Romans long before this time. The noodle they ate was called *laganum*, although it is not clear whether it was boiled, fried or baked.

Pasta is now very much perceived as a staple of Italy in general, but it started its life largely as a southern Italian — or even Sicilian – food. In Sicily, *macaroni* was introduced by the Greeks or Arabs who were frequent visitors to the island. During the Renaissance, pasta flourished as a food mainly due to the fact that southern Italy was invaded by many marauders who pillaged the local people of much of their produce. As a result, the filling flour-based food became a vital staple for feeding hungry families as it was cheap to produce and easy to store. Naples and the surrounding area became, in time, the birthplace of a huge pasta-making industry using the (then) pure water from the hilly hinterland, the locally grown grain and the wonderful Mediterranean climate to dry the pasta.

Over time, pasta has travelled with emigrating Italians all over the world, where it is a central part of many Western diets and valued for its vitamins and as a source of complex carbohydrates as well as for its culinary versatility. Unless you dress pasta with high-fat sauces, it is one of the most balanced foods you can eat being made up of 60% carbohydrates, 25% fat, 15% protein, minerals such as iron, and vitamins B1, B2, and niacin. Being high in complex carbohydrates, it releases energy slowly through the body, making it a good source of energy.

Today, *pasta alimentare*, the flour-and-water dough used to make dried pasta, is produced in factories and dried in special drying rooms over a period of about 12 hours rather than in the sun. The demand for pasta is now so great that factories are in production 24 hours a day and the grain for the flour has to be imported from Russia, Turkey, Canada and America. *Pasta alimentare* can only be made from durum wheat semolina

(*Triticum durum*), which is quite different to *T. vulgare*, the soft grain from which bread is made. Only durum wheat has the structure needed to make pasta strings and shapes. The dough it produces has to be elastic and firm enough not to break up while cooking and absorbent enough to soften on the outside but still remaining *al dente*, or resistant to the bite, on the inside.

The other main type of pasta is *pasta all'uovo* or egg pasta. Unlike *pasta alimentare*, this is usually made by hand and sold fresh, although commercially made versions can be bought in supermarkets and versions made with durum wheat are dried. However, the best fresh pasta is made at home, where the freshness of the ingredients and storage can be carefully controlled to produce the finest pasta – to be dressed with the very best ingredients. Contrary to popular opinion, you do not need a pasta machine to make pasta at home, although if you make it a lot, you might like to indulge in a small machine which rolls the pasta to the required thicknesses and allows you to cut the sheets into a variety of shapes.

The shape of any pasta, whether dried or fresh, is as significant as the dough itself. Many different shapes have been created over the last 300 years since the early *maccheroni* – which literally translated means 'quite expensive' – was first formed. Strings of pasta looking like little worms, hence the name *vermicelli*, came later. It is vital to combine certain sauces with certain shapes, so that the texture of the sauce is complemented by the shape of the pasta itself (see the note on Matching Sauces to Pasta Types at the end of this introduction).

Large pasta companies employ people to test new shapes and the feeling of the pasta on the palate. A pasta manufacturer called Voiello even commissioned the car designer Giugiaro to make a new shape to hold more sauce. The result was an ergonomic and functional shape (see Marille). Nowadays many shapes are cut out of sheets of pasta by machine, although some are purely decorative and miss the point of crafting the shape to suit a sauce.

Pasta can be divided into five main categories, according to the dough used and its culinary function.

1 Pasta di semola di grano duro secca

(dried durum wheat semolina pasta)
This is the basic dried pasta made from a flour-and-water mixture, using durum wheat semolina. The dough is forced through a die to make long pasta shapes, such as spaghetti, which are cut to length and then dried, packaged and sold. It keeps for a long time if stored correctly.

Dried pasta can be further broken down into three categories:

(a) *Pastina* or *pasta corta minuta* (very short pasta): this pasta is often used to make the tiny shapes used in broths and soups. Extra protein is sometimes added to the dough in the form of gluten to make *pastina glutinata* for use in soups for children.

(b) *Pasta corta* or *pasta tagliata* (short pasta): this

THE GRAIN FIELDS OF PUGLIA GROWING HARD DURUM WHEAT FOR THE CELEBRATED PUGLIESE PASTA.

is larger than the type used for broth and includes most of the familiar shaped pasta like farfalle and fusilli. It is usually hollow, so that it cooks more evenly and is dressed with a tomato sauce (most short pasta is eaten with just enough sauce to coat it – this is known as *pasta asciutta*) or baked in timbales, known in Italy as *sformati*, *timpani* and *timballi*.

(c) *Pasta lunga* (long pasta): in the past, pasta like spaghetti and tagliatelle were cut in long strings that were originally sold in traditional blue paper packaging (as were sugar and salt, indeed many modern manufacturers have gone back to this nostalgic look). However, this very long cut of pasta had to be broken when cooked, otherwise it would be too difficult to eat. Good dry pasta should still be flexible when bent and should have a glowing amber colour. Most long dried pasta is eaten as *pasta asciutta*, like short pasta, with just enough sauce to coat each strand, although some very fine varieties like capelli d'angelo (angel's hair) are suitable for broths.

2 Pasta di semola fresca

(fresh durum wheat pasta)

This is made from a dough of fresh semolina and water, and is usually hand-made. It is mostly produced and used in the south of Italy, particularly

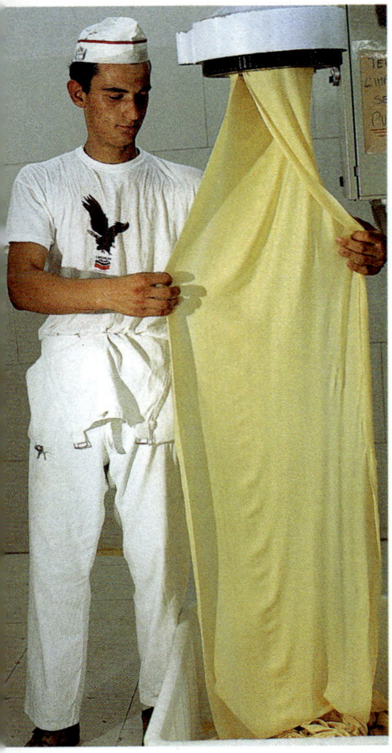

in Puglia. It takes a bit longer to cook than fresh egg pasta. The most frequently used shapes are fusilli, cavatelli, strozzapreti and orecchiette, with Sardinia producing the well-known malloreddus or gnocchi sardi.

3 Pasta all'uovo secca

(dried egg pasta)
The combination of durum wheat semolina and eggs is only produced commercially, as the very firm dough needs to be worked by machine to combine the ingredients sufficiently well. It is usually cut into ribbons of various sizes, which are arranged in nests or *matassa* (plaits), to avoid the strands being damaged. It is dried for 12 hours so that it can be kept. Stuffed pasta like tortellini or ravioli can also be made with this dough but, while commercially produced dried egg tagliatelle is a good standby, industrially produced stuffed pasta is never very appealing.

4 Pasta fresca all'uovo

(fresh egg pasta)
Fresh egg pasta is made using free-range eggs and 00 (*doppio zero*) flour, the same tender wheat used to make cakes, rather than durum semolina. The dough is very malleable and can be formed into many shapes. Emilia-Romagna is the centre of egg pasta production and home to lasagne, tortelli and tortellini.

5 Pasta speciale

(special pasta)
As pasta has become more and more popular, many variations in shape, flavour and colour have been created. Green pasta (*pasta verde*) is made by adding a well-drained spinach purée to the dough; black pasta (*pasta nera*) with the ink of cuttlefish (for use with fish sauces); red pasta (*pasta rossa*) is made with tomato purée and pink pasta (*pasta alla barbabietola*) with beetroot; while brown pasta is made by adding cocoa powder and is eaten as a dessert. Pasta is also flavoured with mushrooms, such as porcini, as well as with truffle and sometimes wine. From Lombardy and Piedmont come other special pastas made from a combination of 00 flour and buckwheat flour (see Pizzoccheri).

LEFT: EXTRUDING A PASTA SHEET FOR THE MAKING OF ORECCHIETTE AT THE PAP FACTORY IN PUGLIA.

HOW TO COOK PASTA

Pasta has to be cooked in plenty of boiling salted water – allow 1 litre ($1^3/_4$ pints) of water and 1 tablespoon of salt for every 100 g ($3^1/_2$ oz) of pasta. Add the salt to the boiling water just before the pasta. It is also important that the pan used is large enough for the water to remain at a good rolling boil to ensure the pasta moves around as it cooks, helping to prevent it from sticking together. Because pasta exudes starch as it cooks, the amount of water used in relation to the pasta is significant. If there is too little water in the pan, it becomes clogged by the starch and the pasta does not cook properly.

Try to let the pasta fall gently out of your hands into the water rather than feeding in clumps which will encourage it to stick together. Gently curl long strands down into the water. Once the pasta has been added to the boiling water, put the lid on the pan to get the temperature of the water back to boiling point as quickly as possible. As soon as it has reached boiling point again, remove the lid and loosen the pasta with a fork. Never add oil to the water, unless you are cooking large sheets of lasagne which may stick together.

Timing is all-important in cooking pasta, a minute more or less can have an enormous influence on the quality of a dish. Fresh egg pasta cooks in a couple of minutes, or even less if it is very fine like capelli d'angelo. When using fresh egg pasta, make sure the sauce is ready before you start to cook the pasta and that your guests are seated at the table and ready to eat. Pasta is cooked when it is *al dente*, that is tender but offering a little resistance and firmness to the bite. Interestingly, Neapolitans like their vermicelli almost undercooked or *fujenni*.

When the pasta is cooked, take the pan off the heat and add a cup of cold water to stop the cooking process, then wait for half a minute before draining it. Do not rinse the pasta under running water or you will strip it of flavour and nutrients. If cooking pasta

BELOW: MACHINERY NOW REPRODUCES THE ORIGINALLY HAND-MADE SHAPE FOR ORECCHIETTE.

RIGHT: PASTIFICIO DEFILIPPIS IS A FAMED SPECIALIST SHOP FOR PASTA IN TURIN.

for use in timbales, then make sure it is slightly undercooked so it does not overcook in the oven. Reserve the drained cooking water as this can be used to adjust the texture of the sauce (just drained pasta continues to absorb moisture, so a sauce which was the right consistency before being added to the pasta can otherwise suddenly seem too thick). When serving pasta it should neither be drowned in sauce nor be too dry.

MATCHING SAUCES TO PASTA TYPES

Although the combinations are almost limitless, the following are some good guidelines on how best to optimize the effect on the palate and the digestion.

• Thin egg ribbons, like tagliolini, are mostly served with truffles, butter and Parmesan, or light fresh tomato sauces.
• Thicker ribbons, like tagliatelle, are good with sauces of tomato, mushroom, cheese, cream, ham and fish, and with Bolognese.
• Long flat dried pasta, like trenette or linguine, best suit pesto and sauces of tomato, meat and fish.
• Long pastas like spaghetti, lasagnette and festoni are best with tomato-based *ragùs* and for use in timbales and *pasticcios*.
• Tubes, both long and short, like rigatoni, are made for long-cooked tomato and other *ragùs*.
• Short shapes of pure semolina pasta, like cavatelli and orechiette, are very good with vegetable sauces like those using broccoli, cauliflower, chicory, artichoke, etc., and seafood sauces.
• Stuffed pastas, like ravioli and tortellini, need only simple sauces like the juices from a roast or butter and sage, or a light tomato sauce.

EATING PASTA

When eating long pasta, as soon as it arrives in front of you, loosen it on the plate to distribute the sauce evenly. Then, lift a few strands and push them to the side of your plate to make some space to turn the fork, then twist the pasta strands around the fork. Put the curled ball of pasta elegantly into your mouth. Never allow strands to hang from your mouth nor cut long strands with your teeth. The use of a spoon with the fork is considered impolite by Italians.

RIGHT: LUCIA PACKING FRESHLY MADE RAVIOLI AT THE PASTIFICIO DEFILIPPIS.

A-Z of Pasta

Agnolini / Stuffed Pasta
Agnolini is a small stuffed egg pasta, similar in shape to cappelletti, which can only be made by hand. Fillings of minced roast meat, eggs and Parmesan are placed in the centre of circles of pasta, which are then folded over the fillings to make semi-circles. The corners of the semi-circle are bent round until they touch, to form little rings. Agnolini come from Lombardy and Emilia-Romagna, and are mostly eaten in a good chicken broth (*in brodo*), but also dressed with sage and butter. Similar filled pastas include agnoli, tortellini and raviolini.

Agnolotti / Stuffed Pasta
A great deal of confusion is caused by the variety of names given to this pasta in different parts of Italy. Agnolotti, very much like ravioli, are little square cushions of stuffed egg pasta. The Piedmontese, who claim them as their own, fill agnolotti with cooked greens, such as spinach, Swiss chard and cabbage, mixed with egg, Parmesan and cooked sausage. The original idea was to use any leftovers of meat and sausage to make a very economical dish.

Agnolotti are usually eaten either with melted butter, sage and Parmesan, with a light tomato sauce or even better with the deglazed juices from a roasted joint. Similar pastas include the Sardinian angiulottus and culingiones, the Tuscan tordelli, the Ligurian ravioli, and tortelli from Emilia-Romagna. The fillings vary from region to region with, for example, the Sardinians using Pecorino cheese, spinach, saffron, nutmeg and eggs as a stuffing, while the famous Emilia-Romagnan tortelli are filled with pumpkin (see the recipe for Tortelli di Zucca on page 160). Rather confusingly, a smaller version of agnolotti is called tortellini, while a larger one is called tortelloni. See also Ravioli.

Left: alphabet pasta for soup.

Alfabeto, Lettere / Alphabet Pasta
This is simply a durum wheat semolina pasta extruded from a special die and cut very short into the shapes of letters of the alphabet. They are used in soups and often made with extra gluten for children.

When I think of alfabeto, I am reminded of when I arranged the wedding meal for my stepson and daughter-in-law. I decided to add their initials and some love hearts to the soup and had to go through hundreds of packets of alphabet pasta to get the letters 'S' and 'G' (Sarah and Granby). The disappointment came when only a few people noticed as they reached the bottom of their bowls of soup.

Alphabet pasta is just one of an endless variety of tiny pasta scribbles for soups and is, naturally, one that is a special favourite with children.

Amatriciana / Pasta Sauce
Pasta *alla amatriciana* is a speciality of the Lazio region, particularly the town of Amatrice after which it is named. The main ingredient of the sauce is *guanciale*, air-dried pork cheeks (see page 76), with a little *polpa di pomodoro* and spiced with some chilli peppers. Versions are often made simply using prosciutto. It is traditionally served on bucatini and dressed with Pecorino cheese.

Anelli, Anellini / Pasta Shape (Rings)
This is a ring-shaped durum wheat semolina pasta which is very popular in Sicily but quite difficult to obtain in other regions. It comes in various sizes, the smallest, anellini, being used in soups. The largest version has a diameter of about 15 mm ($^5/_8$ inch) and is mostly used by the Sicilians to make their traditional *sformato*, a pasta and tomato sauce cake.

Anolini / Stuffed Pasta
This smallest type of tortellini is typical of the cuisine of Parma. Because they are so tiny, they are usually handmade, formed round a woman's little finger. The thinnest possible *sfoglia* or pasta sheets are needed for their manufacture. The stuffing is usually of chicken, mixed with breadcrumbs, Parmesan and a touch of nutmeg.

Bavette, Bavettine, Lingue di Passero / Long and Oval Pasta
Bavette or *lingue di passero* (sparrows' tongues) is a long pasta like a thick flattened spaghetti, with an oval section rather than round, giving a lovely mellow sensation to the palate. Its shape makes it particularly good with pesto and seafood sauces. Smaller sizes are called bavettine, linguettine and linguette, while a Genovese version is called trenette and is almost exclusively eaten with pesto.

Bigoli / Mantuan Noodle
This popular pasta, originally from Mantova in Emilia-Romagna, is a wholewheat egg pasta that looks like a large, fat spaghetti. In the past, the pasta dough would have been handmade and forced through a little machine called

Bottom: cirioline from Umbria (see Bigoli).

ABOVE: CUTTING PASTA BY MACHINE.

a *torchio* or *bigolaro*, but today it is also produced commercially. Among many specialities from the region using bigoli there is the Venetian dish called *bigoli in salsa*, in which it is served with a sauce of onions, olive oil and anchovies.

Similarly shaped handmade pastas include the variously named pinci, ciriole, cirioline and stringozzi or strengozzi, as it is called in Umbria and Tuscany. These pastas are quite large, with a diameter of about 4 mm (1/6 inch). Unlike bigoli, they are made from a dough of durum wheat, water and a little olive oil, and are long and have an irregular shape, obtained by rolling and stretching the dough. In Umbria, strengozzi are served with Norcia truffle, or *ragùs* of wild boar, rabbit, mushroom and, naturally, tomato. Great care has to be taken when cooking it as, being made without eggs, it breaks up readily.

BOCCOLOTTI MEZZANI, SEE ZITE

BUCATINI / HOLLOW NOODLE
Mostly used in Campania, Lazio and Liguria, this long pasta is slightly larger than spaghettoni but has a *buco*, or small hole, through the middle, making it easier to cook. Bucatini is good with both amatriciana and carbonara sauces. In Naples this pasta is eaten with meat *ragù*. Similar pastas include perciatellini and fidelini bucati. Larger versions include perciatelli and ziti.

CANDELE, SEE ZITI

CANNARONI RIGATI / LARGE PASTA TUBE
This is one of the larger pasta shapes that are preferred by the southern Italians. Cannaroni or canneroni can be *lisci* (smooth) or *rigati* (fluted), but always have the same tubular shape and are usually at least 4-5 cm (1½-2 inches) long. They are popular in a number of regions and have many different names, from the larger *cannolicchi* and *denti di cavallo* (horse's tooth) to the smooth *sciviotti* and *occhio di lupo* (wolf's eye). It is used with a variety of sauces, as well as in soups, including the famous minestrone.

CANNELLONI / LARGE STUFFED PASTA TUBES
This archetypal pasta from Emilia-Romagna is universally well-known, as its fame has been spread all over the world via Italian restaurants and trattorias. Today it is not only Italian manufacturers who make this large tubular pasta, it is made in many other countries as well, and is sold fresh, dried and ready-cooked in chilled cabinets and freezers everywhere.

Cannelloni was originally made with a sheet of rectangular pasta that was cooked as usual in boiling water, drained and rolled around a filling of meat, vegetables or even fish, then baked in a tomato sauce and topped with Mozzarella or sometimes with a béchamel sauce and Parmesan. Now pasta manufacturers have developed ready-made tubes about 12.5 cm (5 inches) in length which are easier to fill and can be cooked in the same way.

CANNOLICCHI, SEE CANNARONI RIGATI

CAPELLI D'ANGELO / ANGEL'S HAIR PASTA
Resembling long strands of blond hair, hence the name capelli d'angelo (angel's hair), this long pasta is also known as fidelini or capellini and is the thinnest form of spaghetti you can find. It is a pasta which is at its best with delicate sauces, and with butter and Parmesan cheese, but it is also good in a light broth. It cooks very quickly so you will need to keep a close eye on the cooking time. There is also a black version, coloured with cuttlefish ink, which is mostly used with seafood sauces.

CAPPELLACCI, SEE TORTELLI

CAPPELLETTI, CAPPELLETTINI / LITTLE HAT
Resembling a hat (*cappello*), from which it gets its name, this handmade egg pasta is the trademark of Emilia-Romagna. There is a smaller version called cappellettini. Cappelletti are similar to tortellini but differ mostly in that the filling is made of beef, pork and veal fried in butter, with some cubed Parma ham and Parmesan. In Bologna they are eaten dressed with the juices from a roast or with a tomato sauce. They are also eaten *in brodo*, cooked in chicken broth. The freshly made variety take only about 5-7 minutes to cook, while the inferior mass-produced ones need at least double that time.

RIGHT: SERVING CUSTOMERS THEIR PASTA.

CARBONARA / PASTA SAUCE
Like *amatriciana* sauce, pasta *alla carbonara* is another speciality of the Lazio region, making use of *guanciale*, air-dried pig cheek. The pork (nowadays usually replaced with pancetta) is cubed and fried in oil until crisp. This is then stirred into a seasoned mixture of beaten eggs and grated Pecorino let down with a little of the pasta cooking water. The freshly drained pasta, traditionally bucatini, is then stirred into the sauce so that the egg mixture just coats the pasta but does not cook.

Câsonséi / Stuffed Pasta
Originating in Lombardy, this stuffed pasta is a speciality of the Valcamonica Valley. A rectangle of pasta is folded several times to make a dumpling shaped like a plaited loaf, which is then filled with potatoes, greens, mortadella, pork sausage, Parmesan cheese, eggs, garlic, breadcrumbs and chopped parsley. Once they have dried out, they are cooked for 7-8 minutes and served with melted butter and more grated Parmesan cheese.

The Veneto produces casonziei, a stuffed egg pasta similar to casônséi, but folded into a circular plait rather than a rectangular one. The filling is made of spinach, prosciutto, San Daniele ham, eggs, Parmesan, and a little butter and ground cinnamon. There are many similar types of pasta with the same basic filling but a slightly different shape.

Cavatelli, Cavatieddi, Cavatiddi, Cecatelli / Pugliese Handmade Pasta
This typical southern Italian speciality is made of durum wheat semolina and water. Cavatelli are made of pieces of dough about 2-3 cm (3/4-1 1/4 inch) long which are pressed and pushed with the thumb to make a curved and slightly hollowed oval shape. The name comes from *cavare*, meaning 'to dig', because of the movement needed to make the shape, although it is called *strascinati* in Basilicata.

This pasta shape is now also popular in the north because it is ideal for serving with vegetable sauces like those made with broccoli, rocket, courgette and aubergine. In the southern regions of Puglia and Sicily, cavatelli is served with a rich tomato sauce made with the very best local ingredients. It also goes well with seafood, especially mussels.

Chifferi / Pasta Shape (Elbows)
This manufactured durum wheat semolina pasta is in the shape of a curved tube about 3-4 cm (1 1/4-1 1/2 inches) in length and looks like an elbow. It probably gets its name from the Austrian bread or biscuit called a *Kipferl*, which is curved into a croissant-like shape. There is a smaller version of this shape called mezzi gomiti (half elbows) as well as the similarly shaped gobboni (with a hump), stortoni (curved) and gozzettoni. All these varieties come with both smooth (*lisci*) and fluted (*rigati*) surfaces. In northern and central Italy this pasta is used in soups like minestrone while rigatoni, the comparable version of chifferi used in the south, are served with sauces.

Chiocciole, Lumache, Lumachelle / Pasta Shape (Snails)
Mostly eaten in Campania and Liguria, these are types of pasta in the shape of a snail's shell and can be either smooth or fluted. They come in a range of sizes, the smaller ones being used in soups while the larger variety are eaten with tomato-based sauces.

Chitarra, Manfricoli, Tonnarelli / Square Spaghetti
Called maccheroni alla chitarra in Abruzzo, manfricoli in Umbria and tonnarelli in Lazio, this long pasta is much like spaghetti, except that it has a square rather than round section. It is made by laying a flat sheet of pasta over a special cutter made of many closely spaced steel wires called a *chitarra*. The sheet of pasta is pressed through the wires with a rolling pin. The thickness of the pasta is equal to the distance between the wires so that when it goes through the *chitarra*, it is cut into long square strands.

Ideally it is eaten with a slow-cooked tomato and lamb *ragù*, a light tomato sauce dressed with Pecorino cheese or with a vegetable sauce. I have created a sauce based on *bagna caôda* and roasted peppers which suits it well.

Cialzons / Sweet Stuffed Pasta
This sweet Friulian version of casonziei, made especially in Carnia, is the result of Austrian influences. The filling of spinach, raisins, candied peel, cinnamon and chocolate is contained in a semicircular pocket of pasta. The cialzons are cooked for 7-8 minutes, then served dressed with melted butter, sugar and ground cinnamon.

A savoury version is made with a filling of potatoes, parsley, onion, mint, sugar, breadcrumbs, cinnamon and even a little Grappa and served with melted butter and Parmesan cheese.

Ciriole, see Bigoli

Conchiglie, Conchiglioni, Conchigliette / Pasta Shells
This shell-like pasta shape from Campania has a ribbed surface and thus collects a lots of sauce. Because of its structure, however, it also takes about 14-16 minutes to cook. A larger version of the same shape, called conchiglioni, is often stuffed, usually with spinach and ricotta, and served with a tomato sauce. Conchigliette is a small version of conchiglie used in soups and made with extra gluten for children. See Alfabeto.

Corzetti / Ligurian Handmade Pasta
This Ligurian speciality pasta, typical of the Polcevera valley, uses a dough made with both egg and

Left: machine-made orecchiette being sorted for packing (see Cavatelli).

RIGHT: FARFALLE

water (only 1 egg per 300 g of flour). A small round piece of dough is then pressed with both thumbs to make a figure-of-eight shape about 2 x 5 cm ($^3/_4$ x 2 inches) in size. It is served with a sauce of walnuts, cream, Parmesan and wild marjoram or with a meat *ragù*. There is also a variety of corzetti called stampati, meaning 'pressed', made with a special wooden tool with a carved design etched into it that is transferred on to the pasta.

CULINGIONES / SARDINIAN RAVIOLI

This Sardinian contribution to stuffed pasta is rectangular in shape and filled with fresh Pecorino cheese, Swiss chard, nutmeg, eggs and grated aged Pecorino. In some areas the little pockets are pinched shut in artistic ways. The pasta is served dressed with tomato sauce and more grated Pecorino.

DENTE DI CAVALLO, DENTE DI PECORA, SEE CANNARONI RIGATI AND MACCHERONI

DITALI, DITALINI, DITALONI, TUBETTI / PASTA SHAPES (THIMBLES)

A dried pasta from Campania, ditali is closely associated with Neapolitan cooking. Its name describes its shape, that of a little thimble, and these short pasta tubes come in a variety of sizes.

The smallest, called ditalini, are used in broths; the larger ditali are used in thicker vegetable soups, while the largest, ditaloni, are dressed with a variety of sauces. The smooth variety are used for more delicate sauces while the *rigati* or ridged type are dressed with tomato and chilli sauces.

BELOW: FARFALLINE FOR SOUP.

ELICOIDALE, SEE FUSILLI

FAGIOLINI, SEE MACCHERONI

FARFALLE, FARFALLINE, FARFALLETTE, FARFALLONI / PASTA SHAPE (BUTTERFLIES, LITTLE BOWS)

Shaped like a butterfly, this pasta shape is usually commercially manufactured, although it can easily be made by hand using fresh pasta. To make it, cut long ribbons of pasta 3-4 cm ($1^1/_4$-$1^1/_2$ inch) wide from a sheet of dough and then divide the ribbons into sections about 2-3 cm ($^3/_4$-$1^1/_4$ inch) long. Pinch each rectangle of pasta in the centre, pushing the edges together in the middle to make the butterfly shape. Farfalle is mainly eaten in northern Italy, dressed with light tomato sauce or cream and ham.

A small version, variously called farfalline, canestrini and tripolini and of about 13 mm ($^5/_8$ inch) in length, is used *in brodo* while farfallette, called stricchetti in Bologna, are slightly larger at 3 cm ($1^1/_4$ inch) long and are used in thicker soups. Farfalle and the largest version, farfalloni (about twice as long), are only used dressed with tomato sauces, or butter, ham and peas.

FETTUCCE, FETTUCCINE, SEE TAGLIATELLE

FIDELINI, SEE CAPELLI D'ANGELO

FIDELINI BUCATI, SEE BUCATINI

FORMATO / PASTA SHAPE

From *forma* meaning 'shape', the term *formati* is used to encompass all the varied pasta shapes.

FUSILLI / PASTA SHAPE (SPIRALS)

Fusilli were first made in Campania by hand and were probably the first semolina pasta to have been made with a dough of just semolina and water, like Sicilian maccheroni. The technique has not changed much over the centuries and today it is still made by hand in Campania and Puglia and sold for a high price. The easiest way to buy fusilli nowadays is in dried form. Commercial imitations of fusilli have produced spiral shapes in many colours. Similar pastas to fusilli include elicoidale, spirale and eliche, a southern version of fusilli with a substantial consistency that is dressed with meat and tomato sauces and now used all over Italy.

To make the traditional fusilli, roll a long thin sausage of pasta between your hands or on a board, then twist it around a needle so that it makes a spiral shape. Gently slip the spiral off the needle and leave it to dry. Fusilli are delicious with meat *ragùs* and simple tomato sauces (see the recipe for Salsa di Pomodoro alla Napoletana on page 131).

GARGANELLI / HANDMADE PASTA

This handmade egg pasta can be found only in Emilia-Romagna, where it was created. It is widely used there, either eaten *in brodo* or dressed with a light Bolognese *ragù*. The egg pasta dough is made in the usual way, but with the addition of grated Parmesan cheese and grated nutmeg. To make the garganelli a special gadget is needed which gives the outside of the pasta a ribbed texture. The dough is rolled out, then cut it into 4 cm ($1^1/_2$ inch) squares which are wrapped around a slightly conical tool like a knitting needle and pressed on to a ribbed wooden block, like a butter pat, leaving a fluted hollow pasta shape of about 5 cm (2 inches) in length and 1 cm (1/2 inch) in diameter and with two pointed ends, like a quill.

GIGANTONI, SEE MANICHE

GNOCCHI, GNOCCHETTI / LITTLE DUMPLINGS
It is very difficult to distinguish between gnocchetti and other similar pastas like cavatielli, conchiglie, chiocciole or lumache. All were created in response to the practice of boiling small, shapeless pieces of coloured semolina-and-water dough in water and then serving them with butter and Parmesan.

With the entry of the potato into the culinary world, gnocchi started to be made with flour and potatoes instead of the standard semolina dough, and it is this which distinguishes them, making *gnocchi di patate* one of the first handmade pasta specialities. From this, a whole industry has developed around making short pastas shaped in the form of little curls, snails or shells.

Gnocchetti are round pasta shapes with a cavity, originally made with the thumb (see also Cavatelli). Depending on their size, they are also called conchigliette, coccioline and, if they are very small, margheritine, which are used in soups. The larger ones, about 12 mm (5/8 inch) in diameter are called tofarelle or mezze cocciolette or margherite, and are often served with pesto alla Genovese or light tomato sauces. Conchiglie or arselle are the largest examples and can be up to 35 mm (1 1/2 inches) in diameter; they are mostly used in Campania.

Finally, there are two other types of gnocchi that are very different to those mentioned above. The first is *gnocchi alla Romana*, which is made from cooked semolina, egg, Parmesan and butter and baked in the oven. The other is the exceptionally high-quality gnocchetto, also called malloreddus in Sardinia, which are cooked for at least 15-18 minutes then dressed with a tomato sauce and Pecorino cheese. They come in three or four sizes, ranging from 5-30 mm (1/4-1 1/4 inch) thick and are concave with a ribbed back. They are also made in the shape of huge shells by Sardinian women, who gather to make them for special occasions and celebrations.

GOBBONI, GOZZETTONI, SEE CHIFFERI

GRANDINE / PASTA SHAPE
Grandine, literally meaning 'hailstone', is as its name suggests shaped like a very small round dot. It is made by cutting the thickest freshly make spaghetti into lengths of only a few millimetres. It is used in soups and broths only.

LASAGNE, LAGANE, LAGANELLE / FLAT PASTA SHEETS
In Naples this wide, flat sheet of semolina-and-water pasta is called laganelle, the name used by the Romans, although it is not known whether in ancient times the pasta was fried, baked or boiled. In Campania lasagne is called lagane, in Calabria laganedde and in Basilicata, laane. Whatever the name used to describe it, lasagne is a long sheet of pasta rolled to a thickness of about 1 mm (1/24 inch) and cut in widths of about 3 cm (1 1/4 inches), although laganelle are just 1 cm (1/2 inch) wide. Lagane, like lasagne, is layered with mozzarella, tomato sauce and plenty of freshly grated aged Pecorino or ricotta salata, and sometimes even salami. To help make the layers and produce a lighter and more airy dish, some lasagnes are given a curled or corrugated edge; these are known as lasagna riccia, which are 35 mm (1 1/2 inch) wide, and lasagnetta doppio riccio (half as wide) a smaller curly-edged lasagne.

The widest industrially made lasagne is called lasagnoni and is usually 8-10 cm (3 1/4-4 inches) wide and about 20 cm (8 inches) long. This is the only type of pasta that requires a little oil in the water when cooking to avoid the sheets sticking together. A smaller version of this curly pasta is called arricciata tripolini or signorine and is only 5 mm (1/4 inch) wide, while mafalde or fettuccelle ricce is 12 mm (5/8 inch) wide and manfredi, trinette and mezza lasagna are all 20 mm (3/4 inch) wide. All these pasta are eaten with tomato sauces and *ragùs* of beef, pork, lamb or game. They are also used to make *pasticci*.

Due to its versatility, lasagne has become one of the most popular dishes considered to be 'convenience food', not just in Italy but worldwide. It can be, and is mostly, prepared in large quantities industrially and then distributed in supermarkets either chilled or frozen.

LASAGNETTE / PASTA SHAPE
Also known as festoni, riccioline, reginette and lasagnette ricce, these are long, flat, wide pasta ribbons with curled edges, which prevent the ribbons from sticking together during cooking and make them ideal for collecting more of the sauce. This type of pasta is not cut like tagliatelle but extruded through a die. Lasagnette is mostly eaten in southern Italy with Neapolitan-style *ragùs*, or in Puglia with game sauces or cheeses such as ricotta or Pecorino.

LEFT: FRESH GNOCCHI.

LETTERE, SEE ALFABETO

LINGUE DI PASSERO, LINGUINE, LINGUINETTE, SEE BAVETTE

LISCI / SMOOTH
The term used to describe pasta which is smooth on the surface, i.e. without any ridges.

LUMACHE, LUMACHELLE, SEE CHIOCCIOLE

MACCHERONI, MACCHERONCELLI / MACARONI
Historians cannot agree about where maccheroni originally came from.

Right: the Marille pasta designed by Giorgetto Giugiario for Voiello.

Some think maccheroni was first made in Sicily and is the result of the Arabic influence, while others attribute it to the Ligurians. Indeed, centuries ago Genova had the monopoly in the grain trade in the Mediterranean; hence its long tradition of pasta making.

Irrespective of its exact historical origins, maccheroni is synonymous with Italy. The term indicates a series of short pasta tubes, either smooth or fluted, like maccheroncelli, sedani rigati, maniche and many others. In the south, and especially in Naples, maccheroni is a generic term for all types of pasta. For example, the *frittata di maccheroni*, a pasta omelette so beloved of the Neapolitans, may use any type of pasta, including vermicelli, linguine and bucatini.

Maccherone includes pasta shapes such as cannolicchi medi, cannolicchi grandi, sciviottini, fagiolini, fischiotti, dente di pecora, dente di cavallo and many more. Maccheroni, like penne and ziti, is used for timbales of cooked pasta and other ingredients which are baked in the oven (see the recipe on page 161). Maccheroni alla chitarra (see Chitarra), maccheroni bobbiesi, macčeruna di casa and maccheroni a ferritus (from Sardinia) are all made by turning a fresh egg pasta dough around or through a special iron tool, and are similar to fusilli but not twisted. These are usually eaten with sauces based on meat, sausages and tomatoes.

Malfatti / Dumplings
Literally meaning 'badly made', the name for these little *gnocchi* refers to their irregular shapes. Apart from flour and eggs, they may contain chopped spinach or Swiss chard and either mascarpone or ricotta cheese.

Malloreddus, see Gnocchi

Maltagliati / Pasta Shape
Literally meaning 'badly cut', maltagliati is made by cutting irregular shapes from a thinly rolled sheet of pasta. Mostly found in Emilia-Romagna, small pieces are used in *pasta e fagioli* and larger pieces are dressed with a wide variety of sauces, including a simple tomato sauce and those made with roasted meat juices. See also Taccozze.

Manfredi, see Lasagne

Manfricoli, see Chitarra

Maniche, Gigantoni / Pasta Shape (Large Tubes, Arms)
This is a large, straight hollow pasta tube about 6 cm (2½ inches) in length and 1.5 cm (⅝ inch) in diameter. The outside can be smooth or ribbed, when they resemble rigatoni. In Manica, the tubes are slightly curved. They are especially popular in the south, where large pasta shapes are preferred, and they are eaten with meat sauces or as part of a timbale, (see the recipe on page 161).

Manilli de Sea, see Taccozze

Marille / Pasta Shape
Marille was created by a car designer, Giorgetto Giugiaro, under commission from a pasta company in Campania. The idea was to design a pasta shape that would absorb and retain an abundant amount of sauce, so that each piece of pasta would become a juicy morsel in its own right. The pasta was designed on a drawing board and is made of two tubes joined together. It is ribbed on the inside and smooth on the outside, with an aerodynamic wing attached to the side of one of the tubes. It holds the sauce inside it and is especially delicious dressed with a good tomato sauce and Parmesan.

Marubini / Stuffed Pasta
This is a large, round ravioli-type pasta with a serrated edge. It is a speciality of Cremona and comes with two types of filling. The first consists of walnuts, Parmesan, eggs, breadcrumbs and nutmeg. These are usually cooked in a good chicken broth and either served in it or

drained and dressed with melted butter and Parmesan cheese. The other filling is a meat filling like that used to fill ravioli.

Mezzani, see Ziti

Mezzi Gomiti, see Chifferi

Millerighe, see Rigatoni

Occhio di Lupo, see Cannaroni Rigati

Orecchiette, see Cavatelli, Cavatieddi

Paglia e Fieno, see Tagliatelle

Pansôti / Stuffed Pasta
This stuffed pasta, typical of Liguria, may either take the form of a triangle or be shaped like tortellini. The classic stuffing is *preboggion*, a mixture of wild local greens including borage, with Parmesan. This is traditionally served with *tocco di noce*, a walnut sauce.

Pappardelle, see Tagliatelle

Pasticcio, Pasticciata, Pasta 'ncasciata / Pasta Pie
The origins of the *pasticcio* probably lie with medieval Tuscan chefs mimicking the pies of Elizabethan England; and in those days the *pasticcio* would probably have contained meat. Nowadays, however, most consist of a pastry

shell containing a filling of cooked pasta, like tortellini, layered with cheeses and tomato sauce. Every region now has its own variation, like the *pasta 'ncasciata* of Sicily, which more closely resembles a timbale.

Pastina per Brodo / Pasta for Soup
This very soothing dish is mostly to be found in private homes rather than in restaurants. It is also more a part of life in Northern Italy, where it forms part of supper, accompanied perhaps by some cheese and bread. The *brodo* (broth) can be of chicken, veal, beef, or other meats cooked for some time with some onion, celery and carrot. In this stock are cooked the following types of pasta, which have been specifically designed to cook in a short time: anellini (little rings), avemarie and tubettini (short tubes), conchigliette (small shells), cuoricini (tiny hearts), diavolini (little devils), farfalline (baby butterflies) grandine (hailstones), lumachine (small snails), pepe (peppercorns), pepe bucato (peppercorns with a hole), perline (pearls), puntine (points), quadrettini (squares), stelline (stars), as well as seme d'avena (oat grains), d'orzo (barley), di riso (rice), di mele (apple seed), di melone (melon seeds) and di peperone (pepper seeds) and many, many others. See also Alfabeto.

Penne / Pasta Shape (Quills)
Penne are tubes of pasta cut at an angle so that they have pointed ends, like a quill. After spaghetti, this is arguably the next best-known pasta shape in the world. It comes in two varieties, penne lisce (smooth) and penne rigate (ribbed) and in many different sizes. The smallest are pennettine and pennine and the largest penne di ziti, penne a candela and penne di natale – which has a huge length of 15-18 cm (6-7 inches).

Penne is most popular in Liguria and Campania, where there are many recipes for sauces, including the Campanian sauces based on tomatoes with meat and chilli. The smaller varieties, called pennette, are best served in a much lighter fresh tomato sauce with basil and little cubes of Mozzarella which melt when they come into contact with the hot pasta. Penne are also used for timbales.

Another dish *penne all'arrabbiata* ('angry penne') is penne with a very hot chilli sauce, the anger in the name suggesting the ferocity of the heat, which can, of course, be adapted according to taste. It is perhaps due to the popularity of *penne all'arrabbiata* in both Italy and now abroad, that penne has become so popular throughout the world.

Perciatelli, Perciatellini, see Bucatini

Piccagge, see Tagliatelle

Pinci, See Bigoli

Pizzelle, see Taccozze

Pizzoccheri / Buckwheat Noodle
Pizzoccheri is a long pasta typical of a valley in Lombardy called Valtellina, where the dough is made with one-third 00 (*doppio zero*) flour and two-thirds buckwheat flour. The best way to use pizzoccheri is to let it cook with potato cubes, green beans or cabbage and then to layer it with bitto (a cheese, see page 238), Parmesan, melted butter and garlic and bake it.

Puttanesca / Pasta Sauce
This typically Roman sauce gets its name from the Italian for whore. The spirited combination of extra-virgin olive oil, black olives, chilli, capers, and tomato goes very well with *spaghetti al dente*. Dishes using this sauce are never served with cheese.

Ragù / Rich Pasta Sauce
From the French *ragoût* or meat stew, this term has been adopted for long-cooked rich sauces, especially in Emilia-Romagna for their universally renowned *ragù alla Bolognese* and in Naples for their *ragù alla napoletana* (a sauce of tomatoes, meat, herbs and other flavourings). *Ragù bolognese* is mainly used to savour tagliatelle in the north and the Neapolitans use their *ragù* mostly on large pasta shapes like rigatoni, candele and ziti.

Ravioli / Stuffed Pasta
After spaghetti, ravioli is probably one of the most successful of pastas worldwide. You can find genuine ravioli in almost every respectable restaurant and with every filling you could desire. Raviolini, one of the smallest of the square stuffed pastas, is usually eaten *in brodo* and ravioloni, the largest, is traditionally dressed with melted butter, sage and Parmesan cheese. These little pasta parcels are called ravioli in most regions, with the exception of Piedmont where they are called agnolotti.

My own version of raviolo

Left: fresh filled pansôti (see page 149) from Liguria.

Left: penne

is called Raviolo Aperto (see the recipe on page 160). Two large squares of pasta the size of a plate are cooked in water, one is laid on the bottom of the plate, the filling, which can be of meat, fish or mushrooms, cooked separately, placed in the centre and covered loosely with the other pasta square.

RIGHT: RAVIOLI

RIGATI / RIDGED
The term used to describe pasta which is ridged.

RIGATONI / FLUTED PASTA SHAPE (TUBES)
Rigatoni is a group of large pasta tubes that are ribbed on the outside and served with meat *ragù* or other strong sauces, or baked in the oven. All of the various pasta shapes included in this group are quite large, being about 5-6 cm (2-2½ inch) in length and 1-2 cm (¼ - ¾ inch) in diameter. Rigatoni is only produced commercially as a dried pasta.

Because of its huge size, rigatoni is most popular in southern Italy. There it is eaten mostly on Sunday, dressed with a slow-cooked tomato sauce in which a large piece of beef has also been cooked. The meat is sliced and eaten as part of the second course with vegetables. Rigatoni is also eaten with a simple tomato sauce or baked in the oven to make timbales. Variations include giganti, maniche, schiaffoni, millerighe, tortiglioni and paccheri, meaning 'a slap in the face'. See also Chifferi.

RISTORANTI, SEE SPAGHETTI

ROTOLO / PASTA DISH
A speciality of Emilia-Romagna, rotolo is made from a very large sheet of egg pasta which is usually covered with a mixture of spinach and ricotta cheese, then rolled over like a Swiss roll, wrapped in a cloth and cooked in boiling salted water for at least 30 minutes. It is served cut in slices, with either a very light sauce of fresh tomatoes, basil and Parmesan or with melted butter and Parmesan. The filling can be varied to include spinach and meat, or simply a meat *ragù*.

RUOTE, ROTELLINE / PASTA SHAPE (WHEELS)
Made in the shape of a wheel, this is an example of a pasta which has no special use except that of being pretty. It is mostly served with a tomato sauce, but for me it is a little gimmicky.

SCIVIOTTI, SEE CANNARONI RIGATI AND MACCHERONI

SEDANI / PASTA SHAPE (TUBES)
Literally translated sedani means 'celery' because the shape of this pasta resembles a small stick of celery. Probably from the same group as maccheroni, it is mainly used in southern Italy and is a hollow pasta which can have either a smooth or ribbed surface. The smaller sizes are eaten with a tomato sauce, while a meat *ragù* usually dresses the larger sizes, which are known variously as cannolicchi, fischiotti or dente di pecora (sheep's tooth). (See also Maccheroni.)

SEMI DI... / SEEDS OF...
There are a variety of pastas *per brodo* which are shaped like seeds and grains, such as those of wheat (*semi d'avena*), barley (*semi d'orzo*), melons (*semi di melone*), chicory (*semi di cicoria*) and pepper (*semi di peperone*). They are exclusively used in soups (see Alfabeto and Pasta per Brodo).

SFOGLIA / SHEET OF PASTA DOUGH
Sfoglia is the term used to describe what you have to achieve after working a pasta dough with lots of elbow grease until you have obtained a silky consistency. The dough is then flattened with a rolling pin to an almost transparent sheet. It is from this *sfoglia* that you can then cut out any shape as desired, from lasagne to tagliolini.

SPAGHETTI, SPAGHETTINI, VERMICELLI, VERMICELLINI
The area around Naples has the type of air, climate and water which makes it natural to produce vermicelli, meaning 'little worms' (the term favoured for spaghetti in the south), which can still be found drying in the sun there. The dough for Neapolitan pasta is a mixture of hard durum semolina flour and water. The cooking time varies from 4 to 5 minutes for fine pasta and 8 to 9 minutes for the larger – and even 12 to 13 for the largest. Neapolitans like their pasta quite undercooked and a typical portion there would be 125 g (4½ oz) per person, while in other places 100 g (3½ oz) per person is more usual.

Nowadays spaghetti is made everywhere, in all the regions of Italy and all over the world. The commercial manufacture involves pushing dough through an extrusion system to make the noodles. These can either be smooth (*liscio*) or a brass die can be used which gives a slight roughness to the pasta, enabling more sauce to be caught on it. Capelli d'Angelo is the thinnest spaghetti, closely followed by spaghettini, similar to the vermicellini of Naples, with a diameter of 1.5 mm (1/16 inch). Spaghetti and vermicelli, also called ristoranti, in Naples have a diameter of 1.8-2 mm (1/15-1/12 inch). The largest, spaghettoni or vermicelloni, range from 2 to 2.4 mm (1/12-1/10 inch) in diameter. Anything thicker than this would be difficult to cook well and so the next largest pasta in this group, bucatini or perciatelli, have the slight variation of a hole through the length of each strand.

It is still possible to buy spaghetti at the original length of 40-50 cm (16-20 inches), but it is more common now to find spaghetti at

20-25 cm (8-10 inches) long, about half of its original length, as this is much easier to handle. The longest hand-made spaghetti you can get, a staggering 10 metres (30 feet) in length, comes from Abruzzi. They are locally called strangolapreti or strozzapreti ('priest choker'), borrowing the name from another speciality.

Spaghetti can be eaten with a variety of sauces, from the simple *aglio, olio e peperoncino* (garlic, oil and chilli) to a refined sauce of langoustine or sardines as beloved by the Sicilians. *Spaghettini alle vongole* (with clams) is a sublime dish and even more heavenly is the spaghetti that I cooked in Puglia dressed with fresh roe of sea-urchin (see the recipe on page 156). I would, however, never eat spaghetti with a Bolognese sauce, because this is traditionally better suited to tagliatelle. I have developed a way of frying leftover spaghetti so that the strings at the bottom of the pan stick slightly and produce a lovely crunchy effect. The whole lot can then be turned over to reveal a delicious pasta crust.

SPIRALI, SEE FUSILLI

STELLINE, SEE PASTINA PER BRODO

STORTONI, SEE CHIFFERI

STRANGOLAPRETI, STRANGULAPRIEVETE, STROZZAPRETI / LONG PASTA, DUMPLINGS

Priests in Italy are assumed to eat well and also to possess even more than the normal healthy Italian appetite, hence these names (all meaning 'priest strangler') for various types of pasta, related specialities and dishes in the different regions. In Puglia, the term is used for a type of twisted pasta; in Abruzzi *strozzapreti* for extra-long spaghetti; in Naples and Campania *strangulaprievete* is applied to potato gnocchi; and in the North it mostly describes a type of *canederli* or bread dumpling. See also Spaghetti.

STRASCINATI, SEE CAVATELLI AND BIGOLI

STRINGOZZI OR STRANGOZZI, SEE BIGOLI

TACCOZZE, TACCONI, PIZZELLE, MANILLI DE SEA / PASTA SHEETS

These are all types of flat pasta made by hand from a dough of flour and water which is widely used in many parts of Italy. From Marche, Campania and Umbria comes taccozze or tacconi, which are 4 cm (1½ inch) squares of very thin *sfoglia*. The dressing varies from a meat *ragù* or tomato sauce to the juices from the roasting pan. Very similar but larger 6 x 7 cm (2½ x 2¾ inch) rectangles called pizzelle are found in Puglia. The dough for these is made with salted water and durum semolina.

The largest variety, measuring 12 cm (4¾ inch) square, comes from Liguria and is called manilli de sea (sea meaning 'silk'). Indeed it is so thin and large that it looks like silk cloth. It is eaten dressed with pesto, mushroom or meat sauces. Another, irregularly shaped version of taccozze is maltagliati, which is made with an egg pasta dough.

TAGLIATELLE, TAGLIOLINI, TAGLIARINI, FETTUCCE, FETTUCCINE, PICCAGGE, PAPPARDELLE / FLAT PASTA RIBBONS

These long flat pasta ribbons come in a variety of widths and so go under a number of names depending on the region, but are basically tagliatelle or fettuccine. Fettuccine is associated mainly with central Italy around Rome, while its close relative, tagliatelle (fettuccine is a little narrower and thicker) is northern, with Bologna being its main centre. Generally speaking, the further south you go, the thicker the pasta ribbons.

Tagliare means 'to cut', hence the name for this Emilia-Romagnan pasta, which is cut with a knife from a very thin *sfoglia* of egg dough. Pasta ribbons can easily be made by hand by simply cutting to any width from a single sheet of pasta. To do this, simply roll up a sheet of pasta and cut it to the width desired then unroll each little disc of pasta to reveal the long strands. Most of the tagliatelle eaten today are commercially produced and sold dried and packed in nests to give a homemade feel.

Tagliatelle and similar pasta ribbons, like the thinner tagliolini and tagliarini, can be dressed with *ragùs* of meat, tomato, or seafood (for the smaller varieties), as well as pesto and mushroom sauces. A mixture of green and yellow varieties of tagliolini are used to give the effect of 'straw and hay' described by the name of the traditional dish *paglia e fieno*, which is mostly dressed with a creamy ham and cheese sauce.

Fettuccine is the name given to pasta ribbons 12 mm (⅝ inch) wide and these are generally eaten dressed with meat or mushroom sauces. Smaller fettuccine of just 8 mm (⅜ inch) in width are typical of Lazio, and especially of Rome where they are eaten with tomato sauces and *all'Alfredo*, with a cream and pepper sauce.

The piccagge of Liguria are 10 mm (½ inch) wide ribbons

LEFT: STROZZAPRETI

BELOW: TAGLIATELLE

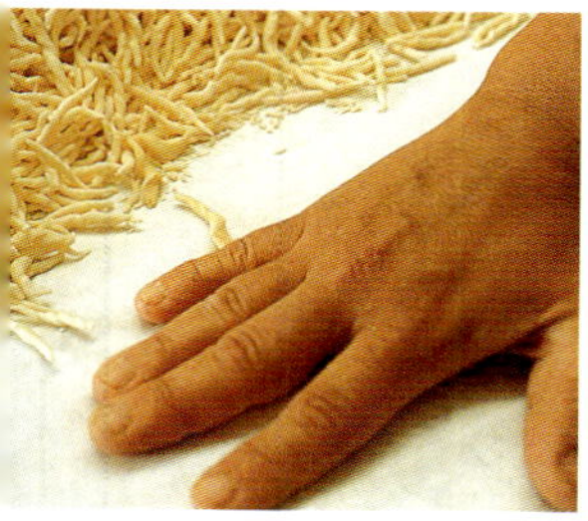

ABOVE: MAKING TROFIE BY HAND IN LIGURIA.

made with egg dough, and often dressed with an artichoke sauce. Another speciality of Liguria is trenette avvantaggiate, which is only 3.5 mm ($^1/_8$ inch) wide and made with a mixture of 00 (*doppio zero*) flour and *farina integrale* (wholemeal flour). This gives the pasta a darker colour and it is usually served dressed with the famous pesto sauce.

The widest pasta ribbons are lasagne piccole, which are 15-18 mm ($^3/_4$ inch) wide and lasagne grandi, 25-30 mm (1-1$^1/_4$ inch) wide, which are popular in Emilia-Romagna and northern Italy. Traditionally baked in layers with meat *ragùs* but also lately with vegetables, the pasta and ragù layers are interleaved with tomato sauce, soft cheese and Parmesan.

Pappardelle are pasta ribbons of various widths used in the Veneto and Tuscany. In Veneto the sauces are based on chicken giblets and tomatoes, while game sauces are favoured in Tuscany, as in Pappardelle al Sugo di Lepre, based on braised hare and sometimes wild boar.

RIGHT: ZITI AND SPAGHETTI

TAJARIN / PASTA RIBBON

This Piedmontese pasta is a local version of tagliolini, which is 2.5 mm ($^1/_8$ inch) wide and probably the smallest type of fresh cut pasta. It is traditionally cut from the *sfoglia* with a knife and is either served *in brodo* or with a sauce of white Alba truffle.

TONNARELLI, SEE CHITARRA

TORTELLI, TORTELLINI, TORTELLONI, TORDELLO, CAPPELLACCI / STUFFED PASTA

Depending on the region, tortelli may be either square or round, and are filled with all sorts of ingredients, like pumpkin, meat, sausage or herbs. The diversity ranges from tordello, a Tuscan half-moon raviolo made from an egg pasta and filled with a mixture of Swiss chard or spinach, ricotta, pecorino, veal, brains and spices, to tortelli di magro (meaning lean, without meat) which are usually filled with ricotta, spinach, eggs and cheese. Tortellini is a smaller version of the same pasta, while tortelloni is the largest. The sweet tortelli di San Giuseppe, filled with ricotta, sugar and spices, are fried in oil.

Cappellacci are a handmade round or triangular version of this type of pasta, originally from Emilia-Romagna. The filling used is generally baked pumpkin and mostarda di Cremona (see page 269), Parmesan, egg, crushed amaretti biscuits and nutmeg, giving an interesting, sweetish savoury taste which is unusual for Italy. Cappellacci are served with melted butter, sage and more Parmesan. There are versions with fillings of ricotta and other vegetables, such as spinach or Swiss chard. See also Agnolini, Agnolotti and Ravioli.

TORTIGLIONI, SEE RIGATONI

TRENETTE / LONG PASTA

Trenette is a flat and long Ligurian pasta, similar to bavette but slightly larger. It is eaten exclusively with Genovese pesto sauce.

TROFIE / PASTA SHAPE (SPIRALS)

Handmade using a dough of 00 (*doppio zero*) flour and water, sometimes with the addition of potato purée, trofie are little pieces of dough twisted to look like little spirals with pointed ends. To make these Ligurian specialities, roll some fresh dough in the palm of your hand until it is long and thin, like spaghetti. Cut it into 4-cm (1$^1/_2$-inch) chunks and roll them again with your fingers to make the spiral shape and the pointed ends. They are eaten mostly with pesto sauce but are also very good with other sauces, called *tocchi* in Liguria, including *tocco di noce*, a walnut sauce, which is also used to savour Pansôti al Preboggion (see page 167). See also Bavette and Fettuccine.

TUBETTI, TUBETTINI / PASTA SHAPE (TUBES)

These small pasta tubes are used in soups such as minestrone and for *pasta e fagioli*. They are available all over Italy and can be either ribbed (*rigati*) or smooth (*lisci*) on the outside. The size varies, with the larger variety being served with tomato sauce. Tubettini are the smallest of the range and are used *in brodo*.

VERMICELLI, SEE SPAGHETTI

ZITE, ZITI, ZITONI / PASTA SHAPE (TUBES)

Today ziti is only made commercially, using durum wheat semolina and water. It is generally more popular in the south than the north, and over the years has somehow become the symbol of the south, and of Naples in particular. It is a long tubular pasta up to 5 cm (2 inches) in length and with a diameter of about 1 cm ($^1/_2$ inch) and a smooth surface. Cut into shorter tubes, it makes ditali, and cut into slightly longer tubes, maccheroni. If the sections are cut obliquely it makes penne.

If the ziti have a large diameter they are called mezze zite or boccolotti mezzani, while the largest are called zitoni or candele. If broken into irregularly shaped pieces they can be cooked and eaten either with a strong meat *ragù* or mixed with strong cheeses like Caciocavallo, Provola, Pecorino or mozzarella, and sometimes sliced aubergines, to make *pasticci*.

LINGUINE CON ARAGOSTA SERVED WITH A GARNISH OF A WHOLE COOKED LOBSTER SHELL ON A RARE OLD PLATTER FROM GROTTAGLIE.

Pasta Fresca all'Uovo

FRESH EGG PASTA

Makes about 500 g (1 lb)

300 g ($10^1/_2$ oz) 00 (doppio zero) flour, plus more for dusting
3 eggs
pinch of salt

This is the basic recipe for hand-made egg pasta.

Sift the flour on to a work surface (marble is ideal), forming it into a volcano-shaped mound with a well in the centre. Break the eggs into this and add the salt.

With your hands, incorporate the eggs into the flour, gradually drawing the flour into the egg until it forms a coarse paste. Add a little more flour if the mixture seems too soft or sticky. With a spatula, scrape together all the dough.

Clean your hands and the work surface. Lightly dust the work surface with flour again and then knead the dough with the palms of your hands, giving it lots of shoulder power. Work the dough for 10-15 minutes, until the consistency is smooth and elastic. Wrap the dough in cling film or foil and leave it to rest for about 30 minutes.

Lightly flour the work surface again and a rolling pin. Gently roll out the rested dough, rotating it by quarter turns, to obtain a round sheet of pasta with a thickness of 2 or 3 mm. Cut the sheets into noodles, or use to make lasagne, ravioli, etc., as described in the other recipes.

Linguine con Aragosta

LINGUINE WITH LOBSTER

For 4

1 live lobster, weighing about 1.25 kg ($2^1/_2$ lb), or 2 lobsters weighing 600 g ($1^1/_4$ lb) each
90 ml (3 fl oz) extra-virgin olive oil
$^1/_2$ garlic clove, finely chopped
1 glass of white wine
700 g ($1^1/_2$ lb) tomatoes, peeled, deseeded and chopped
400 g (14 oz) linguine
1 tbsp coarsely chopped flat-leaf parsley
salt and pepper

You will find this 'posh' pasta dish in most of the coastal regions, cooked in many different ways. This is the simplest.

Bring a large pan of lightly salted water to the boil. Put the lobster in, cover and simmer for 15–25 minutes, depending on size. Remove the lobster and leave to cool, then cut it in half lengthwise and remove the 2 gills (near the head), the dark vein running down the tail and the small stomach sac in the head. Do not discard the green, creamy liver in the head. Take out the tail meat, then crack open the claws and remove the meat. Cut it into small chunks.

Heat the oil in a pan and briefly fry the garlic without letting it brown. Add the wine and bubble for a few minutes to allow the alcohol to evaporate, then stir in the tomatoes and simmer for 10 minutes. Add the lobster meat, plus the liver and the shells, and heat through gently.

Cook the linguine in the water in which the lobster was boiled, then drain. Season the sauce with salt and a generous amount of pepper. Remove and discard the shells and mix the sauce with the linguine. Serve sprinkled with parsley.

Linguine con Ricci di Mare

LINGUINE WITH SEA-URCHINS

For 4

- 40 freshly caught sea-urchins
- 400 g (14 oz) linguine or lingue di passero (see bavette, page 144)
- 4 tbsp extra-virgin olive oil
- 2 garlic cloves, finely chopped
- 1 small chilli, finely chopped
- salt
- 1 tbsp chopped flat-leaf parsley (optional)

It is essential to use sea-urchins that have been fished in immaculately clean waters, so be sure to buy them from a really good fishmonger you can trust. You could always fish for the sea-urchins yourself, of course, as does my friend, Paola Navone, when on holiday!

Open the sea-urchins and remove the roe (see page 24).

Cook the pasta in boiling salted water until *al dente*. Meanwhile, heat the oil in a pan and gently fry the garlic and chilli for a few minutes without letting them brown. Drain the cooked pasta, mix it well with the oil, garlic and chilli, then transfer to a serving dish and top with the sea urchin roe and the parsley if using.

PASTA E FAGIOLI

PASTA AND BEAN SOUP

FOR 4

- 200 G (7 OZ) DRIED CANNELLINI BEANS OR 400 G (14 OZ) FRESH BEANS
- 90 ML (3 FL OZ) EXTRA-VIRGIN OLIVE OIL
- 2 GARLIC CLOVES, FINELY CHOPPED
- 1 SMALL CHILLI, FINELY CHOPPED
- 2 CELERY STALKS WITH LEAVES, FINELY CHOPPED
- 1 CARROT, FINELY CHOPPED
- 2 LARGE TOMATOES, PEELED, DESEEDED AND CHOPPED, OR 1 TBSP TOMATO PASTE
- 1 LITRE ($1^{3}/_{4}$ PINTS) WATER
- 2 BASIL LEAVES, PLUS EXTRA TO DECORATE
- 300 G ($10^{1}/_{2}$ OZ) MIXED PASTA
- SALT AND PEPPER

There are many regional variations on this dish but I like the traditional peasant way best. In fact, I always judge a chef by the way he or she prepares Pasta e Fagioli! It is very easy to make, provided you use the correct ingredients in the correct way. This recipe is the Neapolitan version, where they use cannellini beans instead of borlotti beans. It's a good way of using up odds and ends of different pasta shapes, known as munnezzaglia *in Neapolitan dialect.*

Soak the cannellini beans in water to cover for 12 hours if using the dried variety. Then drain, cover with fresh water and cook for about 2 hours or until tender. If using the fresh variety, simply simmer for 30–40 minutes until cooked. Remove about a quarter of the cooked beans from the pan and purée in a liquidizer, then set aside.

Heat the oil in a pan add the garlic, chilli, celery, carrot and tomato and fry for a few minutes. Add the water with salt to taste, then stir in the whole and puréed beans with the basil leaves. Bring to the boil, then add the pasta and simmer for 8–10 minutes, until *al dente*. Leave to rest for a few minutes, then decorate with a few basil leaves and serve.

ABOVE: VINCISGRASSI; OPPOSITE: VARIOUS STAGES OF PREPARATION OF THE DISH.

VINCISGRASSI

MEAT AND VEGETABLE LASAGNE

This is my version of vincisgrassi, *the classic lasagne from the Marche region. I have adapted it to use more readily available ingredients, substituting a Bolognese ragù for the traditional sauce made with testicles, liver and cockerel giblets. I've also added layers of fried vegetables, which make the whole dish lighter but still interesting. It is worth cooking it for a large number of people for special occasions.*

If you cannot get fresh porcini, substitute chestnut mushrooms.

Wash the spinach, put it in a pan with just the water clinging to its leaves and then cook for a few minutes until wilted. Squeeze out all the excess liquid. Chop roughly and mix with 1 egg, 30 g (1 oz) of the grated Parmesan and nutmeg and salt to taste. Stir in the breadcrumbs to give a binding consistency, then form the mixture into small balls. Heat some olive oil for deep-frying and fry the spinach balls until golden brown. Drain on paper towels and set aside.

Lightly beat together the 2 remaining eggs. Dust the aubergine slices with

For 10

900 G (2 LB) FRESH SPINACH
3 EGGS
150 G (5 OZ) PARMESAN CHEESE, GRATED
ABOUT 1 TBSP BREADCRUMBS
2 LARGE AUBERGINES, CUT INTO SLICES 5 MM (1/4 INCH) THICK
450 G (1 LB) LARGE PORCINI, SLICED
6 SMALL, THIN COURGETTES
1 RECIPE QUANTITY OF BASIC PASTA DOUGH (SEE PAGE 155)
1 RECIPE QUANTITY OF BOLOGNESE RAGÙ (SEE PAGE 163)
400 G (14 OZ) FONTINA CHEESE, THINLY SLICED
SALT AND PEPPER
FRESHLY GRATED NUTMEG
OLIVE OIL FOR FRYING
SEASONED FLOUR, FOR DUSTING

seasoned flour, dip them in the beaten egg and then shallow-fry them in a good layer of olive oil until golden. Drain and set aside. Shallow-fry the porcini in olive oil, too, then season with salt and pepper.

Cook the whole courgettes in boiling salted water until just tender, then drain.

Preheat the oven to 200°C/400°F/gas6. Roll out the pasta dough and cut it into sheets of lasagne. Cook the lasagne in a large pan of boiling salted water for 3–4 minutes or until *al dente* and then put on a tea towel to drain.

Take a deep 20 x 30 cm (8 x 12 inch) baking tray and spread a third of the *ragù* sauce over the bottom. Cover with a layer of lasagne, then a third of the Fontina and Parmesan, then half the fried aubergines and mushrooms. Add more sauce and another layer of lasagne, then arrange the whole boiled courgettes on top lengthwise. Cover with another third of the cheese and the remaining aubergines and mushrooms. Finish with a layer of sauce, then the spinach balls and the remaining cheese. Bake in a hot oven for 30 minutes, until golden brown on top. Remove and leave to set for 10 minutes before cutting into squares to serve.

Gnocchetti Sardi al Ragù

SARDINIAN GNOCCHI WITH SAUCE

For 4

4 TBSP OLIVE OIL
400 G (14 OZ) KNUCKLE OR SHOULDER OF PORK, ON THE BONE
1 ONION, FINELY CHOPPED
1 GLASS OF DRY WHITE WINE
A FEW BAY LEAVES
A FEW JUNIPER BERRIES
700 G (1 1/2 LB) TOMATO PULP (SEE PAGE 118)
1 TBSP TOMATO PASTE
500 G (1 LB 1 1/2 OZ) MALLOREDDUS (SEE GNOCCHI, PAGE 148)
60 G (2 OZ) SARDINIAN HARD PECORINO CHEESE, GRATED
SALT AND PEPPER

In Sardinia these little gnocchi are known as malloreddus.

Heat the oil in a large heavy-based pan, add the meat and brown on all sides. Add the onion and cook gently until soft, then stir in the wine, bay leaves and juniper berries. Simmer until the wine has evaporated, then add the tomato pulp and tomato paste, reduce the heat and cook gently for about 1 1/2 hours. Season with salt and pepper to taste. Remove the meat from the pan and cut it into small strips, discarding the bone. Return the pieces of meat to the sauce.

Cook the pasta in lightly salted boiling water for 12–14 minutes or until *al dente*. Drain and mix with the sauce. Serve with Pecorino cheese.

RAVIOLO APERTO CON FUNGHI SURROUNDED BY TORTELLI DI ZUCCA AND AGNOLOTTI PIEMONTESI AL BURRO E SALVIA (PAGE 164).

RAVIOLO APERTO CON FUNGHI

OPEN RAVIOLO WITH MUSHROOMS

FOR 4

- 600 G ($1^1/_4$ LB) MIXED WILD MUSHROOMS, CLEANED
- 60 G (2 OZ) BUTTER
- 1 GARLIC CLOVE, FINELY CHOPPED
- 1 TBSP TOMATO PASTE
- 1 TBSP CHOPPED FLAT-LEAF PARSLEY
- 1 SMALL GLASS OF WHITE WINE
- 8 SHEETS OF FRESH PASTA DOUGH, 15 CM (6 INCHES) SQUARE (SEE PAGE 155)
- 55 G ($1^3/_4$ OZ) PARMESAN CHEESE, GRATED (OPTIONAL)
- SALT AND PEPPER

This is a modern pasta dish found in very good restaurants. The filling can vary from fish and meat to vegetables and, in this case, mushrooms.

Cut the mushrooms in half if large; otherwise leave them whole. Heat the butter in a pan, add the garlic and fry gently until softened but not browned. Add the mushrooms and stir-fry for 5 minutes, then add the tomato paste, parsley and some salt and pepper. Pour in the wine, bring to the boil and let it bubble for a few minutes.

Cook the sheets of pasta in boiling salted water until *al dente*, then drain. Carefully lay 4 sheets of pasta on 4 hot serving plates. Divide the mushroom mixture between them, reserving some of the sauce. Top the mushrooms with the remaining sheets of pasta and brush the top with the remaining sauce. Sprinkle with the Parmesan cheese if desired and serve immediately.

TORTELLI DI ZUCCA

PUMPKIN RAVIOLI

FOR 6

- 1.75 KG (4 LB) PUMPKIN
- 6 AMARETTI BISCUITS, FINELY CRUMBLED
- 100 G ($3^1/_2$ OZ) PARMESAN CHEESE, GRATED
- 55 G ($1^3/_4$ OZ) MOSTARDA DI CREMONA (SEE PAGE 269), CUT INTO VERY SMALL CUBES
- 60 G (2 OZ) BUTTER
- 12 SAGE LEAVES

The pasta dough here is softer than the basic dough on page 155, making it particularly suitable for these delicate ravioli.

Preheat the oven to 200°C/400°F/gas6. Cut the pumpkin into large slices and bake in the oven for about 40 minutes, until soft. Scrape the flesh off the rind, put it in a colander to drain and then squeeze out most of the moisture. Mix with the amaretti, half the Parmesan cheese and the mostarda di cremona fruits to make a compact paste.

Make the pasta, following the method on page 155, adding enough water to make a soft dough. Roll out into very thin sheets and cut out discs about 6 cm

FOR THE PASTA DOUGH:
600 G (1¼ LB) 00 (DOPPIO ZERO) FLOUR
4 EGGS

(2½ inches) in diameter. Place a little of the filling to one side of each disc, then fold into half-moons, pinching the edges together to seal.

Cook the tortelli in plenty of boiling salted water for 6–7 minutes, until *al dente*, then drain. Put the butter and sage leaves in a large pan and heat until the butter is foaming. Add the cooked tortelli and mix to coat with the butter. Transfer to serving plates and sprinkle with the remaining grated Parmesan cheese.

TIMBALLO DI ZITI

BAKED TIMBALE OF ZITI PASTA

This is a typical dish served at weddings in the province of Caserta in Campania. It is relatively elaborate if you want to make it in the shape shown in the picture but is worth doing for a large number of guests, whether or not it is for a wedding.

FOR 10

1 KG (2¼ LB) LONG ZITI
125 ML (4 FL OZ) VIRGIN OLIVE OIL
700 G (1½ LB) LEAN MINCED PORK
250 G (9 OZ) NEAPOLITAN SALAMI (SEE PAGE 83), CUT INTO SLICES, THEN INTO THIN STRIPS
2 LARGE ONIONS, FINELY CHOPPED
1 GLASS OF DRY WHITE WINE
1.4 KG (3 LB) TOMATO PULP (SEE PAGE 118)
350 G (12 OZ) HARD CACIOCAVALLO OR MATURED PROVOLONE CHEESE, GRATED
8 EGGS, BEATEN
SALT AND PEPPER
FRESHLY GRATED NUTMEG

Cook the pasta in boiling salted water for 4 minutes, until pliable but not too soft, then drain and set aside. Heat the olive oil in a large pan, add the pork and the salami and brown the meat, stirring from time to time to break up the lumps of minced pork. Add the onions and some nutmeg and cook until the onions are tender, then add the wine and boil until evaporated. Stir in the tomato pulp and cook gently for 2 hours. Add salt and pepper to taste and allow to cool a little.

Preheat the oven to 180°C/350°F/gas4. Line a deep baking dish with some of the pasta. Mix the rest of the pasta with the sauce and stir in 300 g (10½ oz) of the grated cheese and the beaten eggs. Fill the baking dish with the mixture, sprinkle the remaining cheese on top and bake in the oven for 40 minutes. Carefully turn it out on to a serving dish and cut into slices to serve.

ORECCHIETTE CON POMODORINI

ORECCHIETTE WITH CHERRY TOMATOES

FOR 4

- 600 G ($1^1/_4$ LB) VERY RIPE FRESH CHERRY TOMATOES OR CHERRY TOMATOES PRESERVED IN BRINE
- 4 TBSP EXTRA-VIRGIN OLIVE OIL
- 1 GARLIC CLOVE, FINELY CHOPPED
- 5 BASIL LEAVES, TORN INTO STRIPS
- 500 G (1 LB) ORECCHIETTE
- 60 G (2 OZ) PECORINO CHEESE, GRATED (OPTIONAL)
- SALT AND PEPPER

Nowadays you can buy pomodorini *preserved in brine from Apulia. The cherry tomatoes taste so sweet and have such an intense colour and flavour that you hardly require any other ingredients.*

If you are using preserved tomatoes, drain off the brine. Squash the cherry tomatoes lightly with the tip of a knife. Heat the oil in a pan, add the garlic and fry gently for a few minutes, then add the tomatoes. Stir-fry for a few minutes, then add the basil and some salt and pepper.

Cook the pasta in boiling salted water until *al dente*, then drain and mix well with the sauce. Sprinkle with Pecorino cheese if desired and serve immediately.

PENNE CON PINOLI E MELANZANE

PENNE WITH PINE NUTS AND AUBERGINE

FOR 4

- 400 G (14 OZ) AUBERGINE, CUT INTO SMALL CUBES
- 90 ML (3 FL OZ) EXTRA-VIRGIN OLIVE OIL
- 1 GARLIC CLOVE, FINELY CHOPPED
- 1 TBSP ESTRATTO DI POMODORO (SEE PAGE 118) OR 3 TBSP TOMATO PASTE
- 25 G (3/4 OZ) PINE NUTS
- 10 LARGE SALTED CAPERS, SOAKED IN WATER FOR 10 MINUTES, THEN DRAINED AND CHOPPED
- 1 SMALL CHILLI, FINELY CHOPPED
- 20 BLACK OLIVES, STONED
- 400 G (14 OZ) PENNE
- 60 G (2 OZ) MATURE PECORINO CHEESE, FRESHLY GRATED

Leave the aubergine cubes in lightly salted water for 1 hour, then drain, squeeze out the water and pat dry on paper towels. Fry them in the oil with the garlic until brown. Add the tomato paste, pine nuts, capers, chilli and olives and fry gently for 10 minutes. Add a little water if the mixture is too dry.

Cook the pasta in boiling salted water until *al dente*, then drain and mix well with the sauce. Serve with the grated Pecorino.

TAGLIATELLE AL RAGÙ BOLOGNESE

TAGLIATELLE WITH BOLOGNESE SAUCE

FOR 4

- 500 G (1 LB) FRESH TAGLIATELLE OR 400 G (14 OZ) DRIED EGG TAGLIATELLE
- 60 G (2 OZ) PARMESAN CHEESE, GRATED

FOR THE RAGÙ:

- 55 G (1 3/4 OZ) BUTTER
- 55 G (1 3/4 OZ) MINCED PROSCIUTTO FAT OR PANCETTA
- 1 LARGE CARROT, FINELY CHOPPED
- 1 CELERY STALK, FINELY CHOPPED
- 1 ONION, FINELY CHOPPED
- 100 G (3 1/2 OZ) MINCED LEAN VEAL OR BEEF
- 100 G (3 1/2 OZ) MINCED LEAN PORK
- 1 GLASS OF DRY RED WINE
- A LITTLE BEEF OR CHICKEN STOCK
- 3 TBSP TOMATO PASTE
- SALT AND PEPPER

This is by far the best-known Bolognese recipe which, to be genuine, has to be made with fresh tagliatelle and not spaghetti.

To make the *ragù*, heat the butter in a large pan, add the prosciutto fat or pancetta, carrot, celery and onion and fry gently for about 10 minutes. Add the minced meats and stir with a wooden spoon to break them up into smaller chunks. Cook for about 15 minutes to brown the meat, then add the wine and bubble for a few minutes to allow the alcohol to evaporate a little. Stir in a little stock to prevent the mixture sticking to the pan. Stir in the tomato paste and dilute with a few tablespoons of stock to give a saucelike consistency. Leave to simmer for 1 1/2 hours, adding more stock if the mixture becomes dry. At the end of the cooking time, add a little more stock to obtain a smooth consistency. Season to taste with salt and pepper.

Cook the tagliatelle in boiling salted water until *al dente*, then drain and mix with the sauce. Serve with the Parmesan cheese.

Orecchiette con Broccoli

ORECCHIETTE WITH BROCCOLI

For 4

500 g (1 lb) broccoli florets
90 ml (3 fl oz) extra-virgin olive oil
2 garlic cloves, finely chopped
1 small chilli, finely chopped
500 g (1 lb) Apulian cavatelli pasta
salt
freshly grated Pecorino cheese (optional)

In Puglia, broccoli and orecchiette are almost synonymous. The combination of pasta and the very strong flavours of local broccoli, tomatoes, olive oil and some chilli makes it a really wonderful dish.

Cook the broccoli in lightly salted boiling water until tender, then drain. Put the oil in a pan over a low heat, then add the garlic and chilli and cook gently for a few minutes until softened. Add the broccoli florets and mix well. Season with salt to taste.

Cook the pasta in boiling salted water for 14–18 minutes, until *al dente*, then drain, mix with the broccoli sauce and serve, accompanied by grated Pecorino cheese if desired.

Agnolotti Piemontesi al Burro e Salvia

PIEDMONTESE RAVIOLI WITH BUTTER AND SAGE

For 6

300 g (10½ oz) spinach or Swiss chard leaves
300 g (10½ oz) brasato (see page 71) or other left-over cooked meat
85 g (3 oz) cooked chicken breast
100 g (3½ oz) cooked sausage, or fresh sausage such as luganiga
2 eggs
85 g (3 oz) Parmesan cheese, grated
1 recipe quantity of basic pasta dough (see page 155)
60 g (2 oz) butter
10 sage leaves
salt and pepper
freshly grated nutmeg

This Piedmontese stuffed pasta dish was created to use up left-over cooked meat. There are many different versions but this one is typical of Ivrea, where I was brought up.

Cook the spinach or Swiss chard leaves in boiling salted water until tender, then drain and squeeze out the excess liquid. Mince or very finely chop all the meat and the spinach or Swiss chard. Put them into a bowl and stir in the eggs and 30 g (1 oz) of the grated Parmesan, plus nutmeg, salt and pepper to taste. Set aside.

Dust a work surface with flour and roll out 2 long thin sheets of pasta. Place teaspoons of the filling at 2.5 cm (1 inch) intervals in rows along one sheet of pasta, then cover with the other sheet and press gently round each pile of filling, making sure the pasta sticks together all around it. Cut into squares with a serrated pastry wheel.

Cook the pasta in plenty of boiling salted water for 6–7 minutes, until *al dente*, then drain. Put the butter and sage leaves in a large pan and heat until the butter is foaming. Add the cooked agnolotti and mix to coat with the butter. Transfer to serving plates and sprinkle with the remaining grated Parmesan cheese.

Strangozzi all'Acciuga e Peperone

STRANGOZZI WITH ANCHOVY AND PEPPERS

For 4

- 2 TBSP EXTRA-VIRGIN OLIVE OIL
- 1 GARLIC CLOVE, FINELY CHOPPED
- 1 SMALL CHILLI, FINELY CHOPPED
- 3 RED PEPPERS, ROASTED, SKINNED AND SLICED
- 8 ANCHOVY FILLETS, FINELY CHOPPED
- 500 G (1 LB) STRANGOZZI OR SIMILAR HARD DURUM WHEAT PASTA SUCH AS PINCI OR BIGOLI
- 1 TBSP COARSELY CHOPPED FLAT-LEAF PARSLEY

Heat the olive oil in a pan, add the garlic, chilli and roasted peppers and fry gently until they are turning slightly brown. Add the anchovies and let them dissolve over a gentle heat.

Cook the pasta in boiling salted water until *al dente*, then drain, reserving a couple of tablespoons of the cooking water to dilute the sauce. Add the pasta and reserved cooking liquid to the sauce and toss well, then mix in the parsley and serve. You may add salt if you wish, but be careful because the anchovies are salty.

PASTA CON LE SARDE

PASTA WITH SARDINES

FOR 6 AS A MAIN DISH, 8 AS A STARTER

- 12 FRESH SARDINES
- 100 G ($3^1/_2$ OZ) WILD FENNEL LEAVES (SEE PAGE 214)
- 1 ONION, FINELY CHOPPED
- 2 TBSP CURRANTS
- 2 TBSP PINE NUTS
- 6 ANCHOVY FILLETS, CHOPPED
- 55 G ($1^3/_4$ OZ) ESTRATTO DI POMODORO (SEE PAGE 118), DISSOLVED IN A CUP OF LUKEWARM WATER
- 1 TSP FRESHLY GRATED NUTMEG
- 500 G (1 LB) MACCHERONCINI OR BUCATINI
- SALT AND PEPPER
- FLOUR FOR COATING
- OLIVE OIL FOR FRYING

Cut the heads and tails off the sardines, gut and bone them, then open them out flat. Coat them lightly in flour. Heat a good amount of olive oil in a large frying pan and fry the sardines until golden brown on each side. If they are very fresh, this should take only a couple of minutes. Lift the fish out of the pan, drain on paper towels and keep warm.

Cook the fennel in boiling water for about 20 minutes or until soft, then drain, reserving the cooking water. Finely chop the fennel. Heat 2 tablespoons of olive oil in a large pan, add the onion and fry gently until softened. Stir in the fennel, currants, pine nuts, anchovy fillets, estratto di pomodoro and a little of the fennel water and mix well. Take 6 of the sardines and break them into the mixture in the pan. Mix well to make a fairly thick sauce and heat through. If the sauce is too thick, add a little more of the fennel water. Season with the nutmeg and some salt and pepper, being careful with the salt as the sardines can be salty.

Cook the pasta in boiling salted water until *al dente*, then drain and mix well into the sauce. Serve in a large dish, decorated with the remaining sardines.

RAGÙ ALLA NAPOLETANA CON PENNE

PENNE WITH NEAPOLITAN RAGÙ

FOR 6

- 6 SLICES OF BEEF TOPSIDE, WEIGHING ABOUT 125 G ($4^1/_2$ OZ) EACH
- 1 GARLIC CLOVE, THINLY SLICED
- BUNCH OF FLAT-LEAF PARSLEY, COARSELY CHOPPED
- 55 G ($1^3/_4$ OZ) PINE NUTS
- 55 G ($1^3/_4$ OZ) SULTANAS
- 60 G (2 OZ) PROVOLA OR PARMESAN CHEESE, GRATED
- 45 G ($1^1/_2$ OZ) LARD
- 25 G ($^3/_4$ OZ) PARMA HAM FAT
- 2 GLASSES OF RED WINE
- 2 TBSP TOMATO PASTE
- 450 G (1 LB) PENNE
- SALT AND PEPPER

For many Neopolitan families Sunday is not Sunday without ragù. *A piece of beef or pork – or even sometimes lamb – is given lengthy cooking in a tomato sauce, at least 2 hours in order to extract all the flavour from the meat and to concentrate the tomato sauce. The result is usually stunning.*

Season the beef with salt and pepper. Mix together the garlic, parsley, pine nuts, sultanas and grated cheese, then divide this mixture between the slices of beef and roll them up. Secure each roll with a wooden cocktail stick.

Heat the lard and Parma ham fat in a heavy-based saucepan, add the beef rolls and brown them all over. Then add the red wine and tomato paste plus enough water to three-quarters cover the meat. Cook slowly for about 2 hours, checking occasionally to make sure it is not getting too dry and adding more water if required. When the meat is tender, adjust the seasoning if necessary.

Cook the pasta in boiling salted water until *al dente*, then drain. Serve the meat and sauce on the pasta.

PANSÔTI AL PREBOGGION

PASTA STUFFED WITH MIXED GREENS

FOR 4

FOR THE SAUCE:

175 G (6 OZ) WALNUTS, BLANCHED AND PEELED
70 G ($2^1/_2$ OZ) PINE NUTS
BREADCRUMBS FROM 1 FRESH BREAD ROLL
1 VERY SMALL GARLIC CLOVE, FINELY CHOPPED
A FEW MARJORAM OR THYME LEAVES
4 TBSP STRAINED GREEK YOGHURT
EXTRA VIRGIN OLIVE OIL, TO DILUTE
SALT AND PEPPER

FOR THE PANSÔTI:

1 KG ($2^1/_4$ LB) MIXED GREENS (SEE RIGHT)
250 G (9 OZ) RICOTTA CHEESE
60 G (2 OZ) PARMESAN CHEESE, GRATED
2 EGGS
1 RECIPE QUANTITY OF BASIC PASTA DOUGH (SEE PAGE 155)

The name pansôti comes from pansa, *a Ligurian dialect word meaning tummy. These small, tummy-shaped ravioli are filled with a typical Ligurian mixture of wild herbs and vegetables such as fresh borage, Swiss chard and dandelion. You can substitute spinach and other greens if you like. It is most unlikely that you will be able to buy these ravioli freshly made, so make them yourself; they are delicious.*

TOP: PANSÔTI AL PREBOGGION; BOTTOM: PESTO ALLA GENOVESE CON TROFIE (PAGE 228).

First make the sauce: blend together the walnuts, pine nuts, breadcrumbs, garlic and herbs with a pestle and mortar until they are reduced to a thick paste. Gradually work in the yoghurt and then enough oil to give a smooth, fairly thick sauce. (Alternatively purée all the ingredients together in a blender.) Season to taste with salt and pepper.

For the pansôti, cook the greens in a little boiling water until tender, then drain and squeeze out the excess water. Chop the greens very finely and combine with the ricotta, Parmesan cheese, eggs and some salt and pepper. Mix well to a fairly stiff paste.

Roll out the pasta into long sheets about 2 mm ($^1/_{12}$ inch) thick. Cut out circles 7.5 cm (3 inches) in diameter, divide the filling between them, then fold them in half to make half-moon shapes, pressing the edges together well to seal. You could also make triangular pansôti by cutting the pasta into 7.5 cm (3 inch) squares.

Lightly warm through the walnut sauce. Cook the pansôti in boiling salted water for 5–6 minutes, until *al dente*, then drain and mix with the sauce. Serve immediately.

RICE & GRAINS

RISO E GRANO

Grains have been known to mankind since the beginning of time and today they are still a basic food that sustains the world's population. In fact, the growth in the importance of grains in the world's diet continues, despite Western developments in agriculture and the production of alternative foods. Although climatic changes and political upheavals threaten to disrupt the lives of half the population of the world, people survive thanks to the cultivation of a few grains. Every society has made the choice of which particular grain to cultivate, depending on what is suited to the local soil, water and farming skills.

All types of grains are important to Italians, but probably the most important is wheat, which is used in the making of bread and that all-important staple Italian food, pasta (to which I have devoted a special chapter all of its own because of its complexity). Rice is also important, however. Piedmont, Lombardy and Veneto are the main areas in which rice is grown and it is from these regions that the most interesting recipes originate.

Rice was brought to Italy about one thousand years ago, although there are many theories about how it came to be introduced to Italy. One theory is that Islamic expeditions in the Mediterranean, as a result of the slave trade with East Africa, led to it being brought to Sicily. The Romans are also believed to have used rice, but it was only in the Middle Ages that it began to be taken seriously. The plague of 1345-52 left widespread devastation throughout Europe and a reliable agricultural food was needed to build the recovery of the population.

Over the next 500 years, rice brought a better diet to the people of Italy, where the ideal conditions for its cultivation were discovered in the Po Valley, which is straddled by four Northern Italian regions. The valley is blessed with an abundance of the vitally important element of water, which is needed to grow the rice plant successfully. It flows through the Valley from the Alps and lakes, and the Po Valley was one of the first places where an irrigation system of canals was used. These systems ensured that the water needed to submerge the plants was constant and abundant.

The film 'Riso Amaro' (Bitter Rice), one of the neo-realist films of the 'fifties, made it perfectly clear how arduous life was for those involved in the cultivation of this crop. The *mondine*, or 'rice women', were at the receiving end of an industry which kept them in conditions of squalor and deprivation. The modern techniques used today in the cultivation of rice no longer require such human sacrifice and the entire process, from planting to harvesting, is now done by machine. Today, the roughly 400,000 hectares used to cultivate rice in Italy produce about 60 per cent of the total European crop.

Another, but by no means less important, grain used in Italian cuisine is corn or maize, or *granoturco* (Turkish grain), so called because it was believed to have come from Turkey. In fact, maize was discovered in America by Christopher Columbus, who got something of a surprise when he arrived there as he believed he had landed in India. Instead of finding rice he found maize, a plant never seen before by Europeans. Impressed by the quantity consumed by the locals, Columbus introduced the grain to Europe, where it was first used for physical adornment. The Spanish were the first to attempt to cultivate maize as a food and their trade connections took it as far as Venice. The Venetians were more than happy to plant a grain which was so well suited to the local agricultural conditions, and it proved to yield a much heavier crop than any other grain planted in the area.

ABOVE: A MONDIN[A] PLANTING RISOTTO RICE IN PIZZAROST[O] NEAR VERCELLI.

small amount of sauce, meat or cheese, however, it was found to make a valuable contribution to a well-balanced diet. The word *polentone* is still used by Southerners as a derogatory term to describe people from the North, because they are such keen consumers of polenta.

In Italy it is now not only very fashionable to eat maize, cooked in many different ways in the form of polenta, but it is also used to feed animals. The yolk of an egg from a corn-fed chicken is bright yellow and tastes wonderful. Pigs fed on maize yield the tastiest meat, which is used in the production of some of the best hams and salamis.

Before the advent of versatile corn, the polenta eaten by the Romans was based on a flour made from *farro* (a type of spelt), probably the longest-surviving grain grown in Italy. Today, however, there is a revival in the popularity of *farro*, especially in Umbria and Lazio, where it is used to make fashionably popular peasant food. In fact it is very much in vogue to rediscover *cucina povera*, the food on which poor people of the past survived, and today local chefs prepare wonderfully tasty soups using *farro*, *miglio* (millet) and *grano saraceno* (buckwheat), which have been the foundation of country cooking for many centuries past.

RIGHT: THE RICE FIELDS NEAR VERCELLI FROM ABOVE.

It came to be used in the making of what was then known as *pollen or puls*, a sort of porridge previously made from other grains such as millet or buckwheat and the ancestor of polenta. For many years polenta made with corn was the staple diet of farmers, who ate it unadorned. However, it was later discovered that a diet too heavily dependent on this porridge alone would bring about the deficiency disease pellagra. If it was eaten with a

A-Z of Rice & Grains

AVENA / OATS
This cereal belongs to the same family as wheat, but has a very different function in Italian cooking. Oats are mainly grown in areas with good rainfall due to the fact that, like rice, it needs a lot of water to grow. In Italy, it is mostly grown in Naples and Puglia, and is mostly used as feed for animals. It is, however, also ground into oatmeal, a popular food for young children, and is used flaked in porridge. Oats are widely recognized as having good health-giving properties.

LEFT: AVENA

CRUSCA / BRAN
Crusca is the outer part of wheat, a sort of brown cuticle. The bran husk used to be separated from the grain by polishing, then given to the animals. However, its high fibre content makes it an important ingredient for a healthy diet. See Integrale.

CUSCUS / COUSCOUS
Couscous was introduced into Italy from North Africa via Sicily and Sardinia. Some people associate the introduction of couscous with the French occupation of Algeria, while others think it was introduced much earlier when the Arabs invaded Europe. Couscous is not actually a grain in its own right, but is made from tiny pellets of semolina. It is traditionally cooked for about two hours in a special pot called a *cuscussièra*. During this rather long cooking time, a spicy *ragù* of lamb, chicken or vegetables can be prepared for serving with it or it can be eaten on its own dressed with a hot chilli sauce. A fish stew is its traditional accompaniment in Sicily, and the *cùscusu* itself is flavoured with saffron.

FARINA / FLOUR
This generic term, probably derived from *farro* (spelt), denotes the product of milling any dry seed, grain or pulse. While the word *farina* on its own is only used to describe wheat flour, other ground grains are described in the same way, hence *farina di mais* (cornflour or polenta), *farina di orzo* (pearl barley flour), etc.
With the addition of liquid and spices, flour was found to be an endlessly versatile ingredient which could be made into pasta, bread, biscuits, or used as a thickening for sauces and soups. Flour is graded by its fineness and its suitability for different types of cooking: farina 00 (*doppio zero*) is used for fresh pasta and cakes; tipo 0 is used for bread. See Grano Duro, Frumento.

FARRO / TYPE OF SPELT
One of the most wholesome grains available, *farro* is a type of the ancient grain spelt, which was used by the Romans for making bread and pasta. Its versatility made it the staple ingredient in the diet of the Roman soldier. *Farro* is now cultivated in Umbria, Tuscany and Lazio, where it is still used to produce traditional dishes that have recently become popular on the broader culinary stage.

One of the best known speciality dishes, *minestra di farro* or *farricello* comes from Lazio, where it is made into a soup. Another way of preparing it is to cook it whole with beans, a method popular in Garfagnana, the mountainous region of Tuscany. Personally, I prefer to use it in a kind of stew flavoured with sun-dried tomatoes, olive oil, parsley and basil, which I serve with vegetables.

FREGOLA / TYPE OF COUSCOUS
This is a type of small-grained *cuscus* from Sardinia, which is made from fragmented toasted hard wheat and is served in soups and *ragùs* of fish or meat.

FRUMENTO / TENDER WHEAT
This cereal belongs to the *Triticum* genus, of which *farro* is also a member. This variety of wheat is a tender grain. It is densely cultivated in the extensive Po Valley, where it is popularly used to make bread.

GERME DI GRANO / WHEATGERM
If you put wheat grains into water for a brief period they will germinate. This sprouted seed is very precious because it contains large amounts of valuable nutrients. It is popularly used in the preparation of wholefoods.

GRANO DURO / HARD WHEAT
This type of wheat, known as hard durum wheat, is ground into a fine semolina before being worked as pasta. In southern Italy, the warm dry climate is ideal for the cultivation of hard durum wheat. See also Semolino.

LEFT: PUBLIC GRAIN MEASURES IN NORCIA.

RIGHT: DRIED CORN FOR ANIMAL FEED.

GRANO SARACENO / BUCKWHEAT

This grain, belonging to a different family from wheat, originated in Mongolia and was brought to Europe by the Moors in the Middle Ages, hence its Italian name. In the sixteenth century it was used to make bread all over Italy, now there are only two small areas where it is grown. One is Valtellina, a valley in Lombardy, where it is used to make a type of pasta called *pizzoccheri* (see page 150), as well as a type of coarse rustic polenta. This *polenta taragna* uses a mixture of maize and buckwheat flours, together with the local cheese Scimud or Bitto. The other buckwheat-growing region is the Veneto, where it is also still used to make polenta.

GRANOTURCO, MAIS / MAIZE

Maize was discovered by Columbus during his voyage to America, but was only popularized some time later by the Spanish conqueror Cortès, who first introduced it into Spain around the year 1500. The northern Italians and French were very impressed with the cereal, which grew abundantly in difficult dry conditions.

While it was originally used to feed animals, it later became popular with the peasant population who found that it could be dried and ground into a flour that could be used to make polenta, bread and biscuits. It was then widely used as a substitute for wheat flour, although the corn itself was also eaten fresh on the cob either boiled or roasted (see Pannocchia, page 114).

RIGHT: GRANOTURCO

INTEGRALE / WHOLE

The word *integrale*, meaning complete or whole, is used to describe a grain or flour where the bran as well as the grain is milled. There are many whole-grain foods, including *pane integrale* (wholewheat bread), *farina integrale* (wholewheat flour), *grissini integrali* (wholewheat breadsticks) and *pasta integrale* (wholewheat pasta).

Although wholewheat products are high in vitamins and have lots of roughage, my opinion is that this is at the cost of taste, as wholewheat foods are not as appetising as those made with ordinary white flour.

MIGLIO / MILLET

This cereal was very popular with the Greeks and Romans, who used it largely for making bread and for thickening soups. Today, millet has been almost entirely replaced by maize as this has a more palatable taste and is much easier to cultivate. Millet is now mainly grown as a fodder for cattle.

Migliàccio, an ancient cake, was originally made with *miglio* and the blood of a freshly slaughtered pig, but is now made without the blood and using other flours. In Emilia-Romagna, *migliàccio* is made with polenta, while in Tuscany it is a sweet *focaccia*, made with raisins, and in Naples it is a baked polenta eaten with stewed vegetables.

ORZO / BARLEY

I can remember when I was a child we had a sort of 'coffee' for breakfast made from barley grains. When roasted and soaked in water or milk, barley produces a brownish liquid that resembles coffee. Another derivative of barley that delighted us as children during the summer was a drink called *orzata*, which was made with germinated barley, and ground almonds preserved in sugar and water. *Orzo perlato*, or pearl barley, is used in soups in the Alto Adige and Friuli regions, where the Austrian influence can still be felt.

RIGHT: FARRO

PASTA, SEE PAGES 138-167

POLENTA / PORRIDGE

In Roman times polenta was a porridge made from the flour of various grains and pulses, such as broad beans, spelt, etc. Today the name usually refers to a porridge of yellow or white maize flour. Polenta can, however, be used to describe any type of porridge as long as the grain or pulse of origin is used to specify what it is made from, i.e. *polenta di fagioli* (bean polenta) etc.

Polenta is best made in a copper pan by cooking the maize flour with water until it achieves a fairly solid consistency. It takes about 40 minutes to cook, depending on the coarseness of the grains, and requires constant energetic stirring to prevent it from sticking to the bottom of the pan. The polenta can then be poured on to a wooden board and served in the middle of the table, where everyone can take as much as they like. It is usually eaten with a meat, mushroom or vegetable *ragù*. Polenta, usually eaten as a substitute for bread, can be eaten cold or hot, or cut in slices and fried. It is also popular layered with cheese and a tomato sauce to make *pasticcio*, a sort of timbale.

An easy-cook variety called *polenta svelta* has been created in order to reduce the cooking time. It is made by pre-cooking ordinary polenta, which is then dried and milled again. The results are not as tasty as the original, but it is fine when butter and cheese are added to make a *polenta concia* (see the recipe on page 96).

The best polenta can be found in northern Italy, where it has been a staple food for a long time. It is traditionally eaten in winter as it is a wonderful comfort food. Vicenza in Veneto is the best place to eat *polenta e baccalà*, which is simply air-dried cod cooked in milk with polenta. The other speciality of Veneto and parts of Lombardy is the controversial *polenta e osei*, polenta with sparrows.

LEFT: COOKED AND GRILLED POLENTA.

POLENTA TARAGNA, SEE GRANO SARACENO

RISO / RICE

The rice eaten by Italians is produced almost entirely in Italy. The variety cultivated by the Italians is ideally suited to making risotto, the most Italian of rice dishes. The main characteristic of risotto rice is that it is able to absorb moisture and swell by to up to three times its initial volume on being cooked, while still retaining a bite in its centre. In other words, it has to be *al dente* like pasta to makes it palatable.

The plant's Latin name is *Oryza sativa*. It is planted in the spring and reaches maturity after about 140 to 180 days. During this time, great care must be taken to keep it steeped in water and to protect it from pests. The rice is harvested between September and October. It is then completely dried and the grains are sorted, washed and separated from their husks before finally being polished to produce a perfect white grain. The polishing is a very delicate operation because only the smallest amount of the surface of the grain should be removed so that the vitamins from the outer skins are not entirely eliminated. Ideally rice should be eaten whole, with the husk on, but this would impair its vital quality of absorbency.

Types of Italian rice can be categorized according to their qualities and use:

Riso comune (common rice) is the lowest quality rice grown in Italy. It is a small round grain which tends to lose a lot of starch when cooked. It is ideal for soups and desserts and only needs 12-13 minutes cooking time. Varieties include balilla, originario, elio, selenio and trio.

Riso semifino (semi-fine rice) has similar characteristics to common rice but has a larger grain. As a result it also needs a slightly longer cooking time (14-15 minutes). The varieties include Italico, lido, alfa, argo, cripto, comellino, Piemonte, monticelli, Maratelli, Padano, Romeo, Rosa Marchetti, rubino, and vialone nano. *Riso semifino* is at its best when used in timbales, *arancini* (rice croquettes, see the recipe on page 179) and dry rice dishes, as well as in soups like minestrone.

Riso fino (fine rice) has a larger grain but is a little more difficult to digest due to its size and the fact that it loses little starch when cooked. It takes 16-17 minutes to cook and is ideal for risottos, rice salads, and other main course dishes. The varieties include Europa, ariete, giara, molo, pierina marchetti, RB, ribe, ringo, riva Smeraldo, veneria, Senit belgioioso and Santi Andrea.

Riso superfino (superfine rice) is the Ferrari of rices and includes varieties such as arborio, baldo, volano gritna, koral, onda, silla, strella, miara, Indio, carnaroli, corallo and Roma. The large grains take around 18-20 minutes to cook and are perfect in risottos and salads as well as special timbales and *arancini* or polenta.

A typical rice dish from the area around Piacenza is *bomba di riso*. It is made with plainly cooked risotto rice, such as vialone nano, mixed with melted butter and Parmesan cheese. One or two pigeons are roasted with sage, butter, white wine and a little tomato purée. The meat is removed from the birds and piled

Making a Risotto

Top right: vialone nano (top) and carnaroli rice.

I have been making risotto for 40 years, so the following tips should help you to cook it perfectly. The best rice for risotto is arborio, baldo, carnaroli, vialone nano or Roma. Anything else will not do. Make sure that you do not wash the rice before cooking it as this removes the valuable starch which makes the risotto creamy. The principle of risotto is to cook the rice slowly by letting it gradually absorb stock or wine that is added little by little until the rice is cooked. It is important to stir risotto continuously to prevent it from sticking to the bottom of the pan.

Before starting the risotto, make the stock. Depending on the recipe, you will need about 1.25 litres (2 pints) of chicken, beef, fish or vegetable stock. Once it is made, keep the stock on the hob so that you can easily transfer the liquid to the risotto pan. It is important to keep the stock at boiling point, so that the rice does not stop cooking when the stock is added.

In a separate large heavy-based pan, sweat a finely chopped onion in butter and olive oil along with any desired spices and herbs and cook until the onion is soft. Stir in the rice and allow it to be coated in the oil and butter. Then start to add the liquid. If you are using wine, then allow it to evaporate/be absorbed completely before adding the stock. Start by adding a ladleful at a time, stirring continuously, for about 15 minutes. When most of the stock has been used, test a grain of rice to check its consistency and add more stock as necessary. The rice is done when it is tender on the outside but has a firm bite in the centre. Be sure to take the rice off the heat just before you think it is ready because it will continue to cook in its own heat. The ideal consistency for risotto is soft and runny (you should be able to pick it up with a fork). Risotto should never be cooked until it is solid.

Finally, add some butter and grated Parmesan cheese and beat the risotto energetically to make sure all the ingredients are thoroughly mixed and the risotto looks creamy and shiny. Serve on warmed plates, offering more Parmesan separately.

in the middle of some of the cooked rice in a mould, then covered completely with more rice. This is cooked for 15-20 minutes in a bain-marie, then uncovered and baked in the oven for a further 20 minutes until golden.

Risotto

This unique dish can be found in good Italian restaurants throughout the world. The appeal of risotto is that it can satisfy any palate, provided, of course, that it is made properly. It is no surprise that it is in the rice-growing regions of Piedmont, Lombardy and Veneto that the classic risotto dishes such as risotto with truffles or risotto with porcini have their origins. Other regions, such as Tuscany, Campania, Sicily – and even Sardinia – have contributed some tasty dishes to the genre, but they cannot equal the great northern dishes.

There are various ways of using up leftover risotto, one *arancini* (see page 179) adds beaten egg to the cold mixture with a little grated Parmesan, some parsley and breadcrumbs. This is mixed well and formed into little balls with the hands. These are then deep-fried until golden, and served hot.

Segale / Rye

This ancient grain is very similar to wheat and flour ground from it is used to make bread, biscuits and *grissini* (see page 293). It has lots of roughage and is full of nutrients. Rye bread is particularly popular in the northern regions of Italy, especially those bordering Austria, where it is often flavoured with cumin or fennel seeds.

Semolino, Semola / Semolina

Ground durum wheat, called *semolino*, is mainly used for making pasta, but is also used to make couscous, soups and gnocchi, dumplings from Rome. *Gnocchi alla romana* are made with semolina which has been mixed with milk and a pinch of nutmeg to form a firm mixture. When it is cool, beaten egg is added. The semolina is then spread out on an oiled surface and patted flat with a spatula. Medallion-sized rounds are then cut from the mixture and placed on a buttered baking tray. More butter and Parmesan are dotted over the top, then the gnocchi are cooked in a very hot oven for 10-15 minutes or until a golden crust has formed on top. Seasoned with freshly ground pepper, the gnocchi are served either as a first course or a side dish with a meat stew.

Right: an old grain sieve in Tuscany.

Pastiera di Grano.

Pastiera di Grano

GRAIN TART

For 10 or more

FOR THE PASTRY:
- 150 g (5 oz) caster sugar
- 150 g (5 oz) butter or cooking fat, plus more for the pan
- yolks of 3 large eggs
- 300 g (10½ oz) flour

FOR THE FILLING:
- 200 g (7 oz) whole wheat, or 500 g (1 lb) canned cooked wheat (called gran pastiera)
- 500 ml (18 fl oz) milk (if using fresh whole wheat)
- grated zest of 1 lemon
- 1 tsp ground cinnamon
- 2 tsp vanilla sugar
- grated zest of ½ orange
- 300 g (10½ oz) ricotta cheese
- 4 large eggs, separated
- 1 small wine glass of orange flower water
- 150 g (5 oz) candied peel, finely chopped
- 225 g (8 oz) caster sugar
- icing sugar for dusting

This recipe will probably appear in every book I write, because it is my mother's and has always been traditional in my family. It is very much an Easter cake, made with grains of wheat – symbol of wealth and prosperity – and in large quantities, as the cakes are given as presents to friends. The Neapolitans drink the locally produced wine, Lacrima Christi, to accompany this delicious tart.

If using fresh grain, two days ahead soak it for 24 hours in several changes of water. Next day simmer the grain in the milk with the zest of half a lemon for 3 or 4 hours on a very low heat. When it is cooked (or if using canned), stir in a pinch of cinnamon, the vanilla sugar and the remaining lemon zest and the orange zest. Leave overnight for the flavours to mingle.

Make the pastry: in a large bowl, work together the sugar, butter and the eggs until smooth, then add the flour and gradually incorporate to make a smooth pastry. Set aside in a cool place for 1 hour or more.

Preheat the oven to 190°C/375°F/gas5. Grease a 35-cm (14-inch) diameter flan pan with butter or fat.

To finish the filling: beat the ricotta with the egg yolks and the orange water. Add the candied peel and the flavoured grain to the mixture. Beat the egg whites with the sugar until stiff and fold them very gently into the mixture.

Roll out two-thirds of the pastry and use to line the flan pan, covering the bottom and sides with an equal thickness. Pour in the filling. Roll out the remaining pastry and cut it into long strips to form a lattice top for the tart. Bake for about 45 minutes until coloured light golden. Allow to cool and then dust with icing sugar.

Risotto con Asparagi

ASPARAGUS RISOTTO

For 4

- 900 g (2 lb) fresh asparagus
- 4 tbsp olive oil
- 85 g (3 oz) butter
- 1 small onion, finely chopped
- 350 g (12 oz) carnaroli or vialone nano rice
- about 1 litre (1¾ pints) vegetable stock
- 55 g (1¾ oz) Parmesan cheese, grated
- salt and pepper

Trim the asparagus and cook it in boiling salted water until tender. Drain, reserving the cooking liquid. Cut the asparagus into 1 cm (½ inch) chunks, leaving the tips whole. Make up the asparagus cooking liquid with stock to 1.75 litres (3 pints). Prepare the risotto in the usual way (see page 175), adding the chopped asparagus, but not the asparagus tips, just before the rice. Decorate with the asparagus tips before serving.

PANISSA

BEANS AND RICE

FOR 6

- 300 G (10½ OZ) DRIED BORLOTTI BEANS
- 4 TBSP OLIVE OIL
- 1 LARGE ONION, FINELY SLICED
- 100 G (3½ OZ) PANCETTA, CUT INTO SMALL CUBES
- 55 G (1¾ OZ) PARMA HAM, CUT INTO SMALL CUBES
- 400 G (14 OZ) RISOTTO RICE SUCH AS CARNAROLI OR ARBORIO
- 100 ML (3½ FL OZ) RED WINE, PREFERABLY NEBBIOLO OR SPANNA
- 2 LITRES (3½ PINTS) CHICKEN STOCK (FROM CUBES IS OK)
- SALT AND PEPPER

Originally from Vercelli, this is a risotto with beans, not to be confused with paniscia, *a similar but much more complicated dish from the town of Novara. Ideally it should be made with fresh borlotti beans but because they are hard to come by, especially outside Italy, you could use the dried ones.*

Soak the beans in plenty of water overnight, then drain. Put them in a saucepan, cover with fresh water and simmer for about 2 hours or until tender. Drain.

Heat the olive oil in a pan, add the onion, pancetta and Parma ham and fry for 5–6 minutes. Add the rice and beans and stir well. Add the red wine and then continue as for making risotto (see page 175). Serve hot, without Parmesan.

RISOTTO ALLO ZAFFERANO

SAFFRON RISOTTO

FOR 4

- 350 G (12 OZ) VIALONE NANO RICE
- 4 TBSP OLIVE OIL
- 85 G (3 OZ) BUTTER
- 1 SMALL ONION, FINELY CHOPPED
- 10 STRANDS OF SAFFRON OR 3 SMALL SACHETS OF SAFFRON POWDER
- 1.75 LITRES (3 PINTS) VEGETABLE STOCK
- SALT AND PEPPER

Make the risotto in the usual way (see page 175), adding the saffron to the stock. This is traditionally served with Ossobuco alla Milanese (see page 95).

RIGHT: RISOTTO CON ASPARIGI (TOP) SEE PAGE 177; OSSOBUCO ALLA MILANESE SERVED WITH RISOTTO ALLO ZAFFERANO (BELOW).

Risotto ai Funghi

MUSHROOM RISOTTO

For 4–6

- 300 g (10½ oz) fresh porcini mushrooms
- 85 g (3 oz) butter
- 1 large onion, finely sliced
- 400 g (14 oz) Carnaroli rice, or Vialone Nano or Arborio
- 1.75 litres (3 pints) chicken stock
- 60 g (2 oz) Parmesan cheese, grated
- salt and pepper

Ideally you should use porcini to make this risotto. However, they have only a limited season and are difficult to buy, especially outside Italy in countries such as Britain and America, where this type of mushroom is known only in its dried form. If you cannot find freshly picked porcini, then the combination of cultivated mushrooms and dried porcini should give a good result, although naturally not to be compared to the real thing.

Carefully clean the mushrooms (see page 185) and then slice them.

Heat half the butter in a pan, add the mushrooms and onion and sauté until soft. Prepare the risotto in the usual way (see page 175). Remove from the heat and leave to rest for 1 minute, then add the remaining butter and the Parmesan cheese and stir vigorously to obtain a very creamy but not too liquid and not too firm risotto. Serve on hot plates, with a little black pepper ground over.

Arancini di Riso alla Palermitana

RICE BALLS PALERMO-STYLE

Makes 20

- 350 g (12 oz) minced beef
- ½ recipe quantity of Salsa di Pomodoro alla Napoletana (see page 131)
- 800 g (1¾ lb) Carnaroli or Arborio rice
- 6 eggs
- 1 tbsp finely chopped flat-leaf parsley
- 100 g (3½ oz) hard Pecorino cheese, grated
- 150 g (5 oz) soft caciocavallo cheese, cut into small cubes
- salt and pepper
- flour for dusting
- dried breadcrumbs for coating
- olive oil for deep-frying

Perhaps the most famous arancini *come from Sicily, where they were given the name because they are the same size as a small orange. As they are so nice to eat, rather like a little ball of risotto,* arancini *have been adopted in all the quick-service bars, where you can have them piping hot at lunchtime. They are ideal for parties or picnics because they can also be eaten cold.*

Cook the minced beef in the tomato sauce for 30 minutes, then add salt and pepper to taste. Cook the rice in 2 litres (3½ pints) of lightly salted boiling water for 12 minutes only and then drain. Spread it out on a work surface and leave to cool. Beat 4 of the eggs with the parsley and Pecorino cheese and mix thoroughly with the rice. Take some of the mixture and thickly cover the palm of your hand with it. Put a tablespoon of the meat sauce and a few cubes of caciocavallo cheese in the centre. Close your hand and seal with a little more rice to make a ball the size of a small orange. Repeat with the remaining mixture.

Beat together the 2 remaining eggs. Roll the balls in flour, then in the beaten egg and finally in the breadcrumbs. Deep-fry them in plenty of olive oil for about 5 minutes, until golden brown. To achieve more crispness, after frying you could bake them for 5 minutes in an oven preheated to 230°C/450°F/gas8. In bars they are just wrapped in a napkin and eaten standing up and with your hands. They are fantastic for picnics.

Polenta e Baccalà

POLENTA AND SALT COD

For 6

- 1.5 kg (3¼ lb) salt cod, taken from the middle part of the fish
- 175 ml (6 fl oz) extra-virgin olive oil
- 1 onion, finely sliced
- 2 garlic cloves, coarsely chopped
- 400 g (14 oz) tin chopped tomatoes, or 3 large ripe tomatoes, peeled and coarsely chopped
- 8 basil leaves
- 3 tbsp coarsely chopped flat-leaf parsley
- 1 glass red wine
- salt and pepper

For the polenta:

- 2 litres (3½ pints) water
- 25 g (¾ oz) salt
- 300 g (10½ oz) coarse polenta

Synonymous with peasant comfort food, this can often be found on winter Fridays in small towns, where there will probably be a street market. Baccalà *is a preserved fish (see page 16) which used to be cheap food eaten in the valleys where supplies of fresh fish were hard to come by. But today it is eaten everywhere because of its remarkable taste, and it is more expensive than fresh cod. The recipe for salt cod I find most suitable for eating with polenta is this one from Livorno. Sometimes you may find salt cod on sale already desalted. Otherwise you will have to soak it in water for 36 hours.*

If necessary, cut the salt cod into smallish pieces; this helps it lose more salt while soaking. Put it to soak in plenty of cold water for 36 hours, changing the water about every 6 hours. Drain and remove the bones and fins, then cut the cod into 4 x 6 cm (1½ x 2½ inch) chunks.

Cook the polenta in a copper pan with a rounded bottom, if possible. Put the water and salt in the pan and bring to the boil. Sift the polenta through your hand, letting it fall into the water a little at a time while stirring constantly to avoid lumps. Cook for 40 minutes, stirring all the time, until the polenta is pulling away from the sides of the pan.

Heat 125 ml (4 fl oz) of the olive oil in a pan, add the onion and garlic and fry until soft. Add the tomatoes, basil and parsley and simmer until the sauce begins to thicken. Heat the remaining oil in a separate pan, add the salt cod and fry for 6–7 minutes on each side. Pour the tomato sauce and the red wine over the fish and season with black pepper and some salt if necessary. Cook gently for 20 minutes, then serve with the polenta.

Polenta Taragna

BUCKWHEAT POLENTA

For 6

- 2.5 litres (4½ pints) water
- 25 g (¾ oz) salt
- 500 g (1 lb) polenta taragna (see right)
- 150 g (5 oz) butter
- 150 g (5 oz) bitto, asiago or fresh toma cheese, very finely sliced

This uses a mixture of two types of flour, maize and buckwheat, which the inhabitants of Valtellina, a valley in Lombardy, prefer to plain polenta. It is very tasty but requires a longer cooking time than standard polenta. If you cannot find the ready-mixed flour you can make it yourself, mixing 45 g (1½ oz) yellow polenta with every 100 g (3½ oz) buckwheat flour.

Put the water and salt in a large heavy-based pan and bring to the boil. Sift the polenta taragna through your hand, letting it fall into the water a little at a time while stirring constantly to avoid lumps. Cook for 1 hour, stirring all the time, until the polenta is pulling away from the sides of the pan. Stir in the butter and then the cheese slices. Either serve immediately, alone or as an accompaniment to stews, or leave to cool, cut into slices and then fry in butter or grill.

PIZZOCCHERI

BUCKWHEAT PASTA WITH POTATOES AND CABBAGE

FOR 6

2 LARGE POTATOES, PEELED AND CUT INTO SMALL CUBES
500 G (1 LB) SAVOY CABBAGE, CUT INTO STRIPS
2 GARLIC CLOVES, SLICED
6 SAGE LEAVES
100 G ($3^1/_2$ OZ) BUTTER
300 G ($10^1/_2$ OZ) BITTO, TOMA OR ASIAGO CHEESE, THINLY SLICED
85 G (3 OZ) PARMESAN CHEESE, GRATED
SALT AND PEPPER

FOR THE PIZZOCCHERI:
250 G (9 OZ) BUCKWHEAT FLOUR
100 G ($3^1/_2$ OZ) 00 (DOPPIO ZERO) FLOUR
2 EGGS
4 TBSP MILK
PINCH OF SALT

Probably the only buckwheat pasta used in Italy, pizzoccheri *comes from the Valtellina, a valley in Lombardy not far from Milan, and is popular in many northern regions. Traditionally served with cabbage, potatoes and cheese, as here, it is quite a rich dish which could be served as a main course. It is, however, especially loved by vegetarians. If you can find ready-made* pizzoccheri *you will need 350 g (12 oz).*

To make the pasta, pile the two flours up into a volcano shape on a work surface and make a well in the centre. Add the eggs, milk, salt and enough water to make a fairly firm dough. Knead for 8–10 minutes, until smooth and elastic, then cover and leave to rest for 20 minutes. Roll out with a rolling pin to 5 mm ($^1/_4$ inch) thick and cut into strips about 6 cm ($2^1/_2$ inches) long by 1 cm ($^1/_2$ inch) wide. Either use straight away or store in the refrigerator for up to 2 days.

If using freshly made pasta, cook the potatoes and cabbage in lightly salted boiling water until almost tender, then add the pizzoccheri for the last 6–8 minutes. If using dried pasta, cook everything together until tender. Meanwhile, fry the garlic and sage very gently in the butter, then remove from the heat. Drain the pizzoccheri and vegetables, arrange a layer of them in a preheated dish and cover with some of the cheese slices. Reheat the butter, garlic and sage until the butter is foaming. Pour a little of the hot butter and garlic over the cheese and sprinkle with some of the Parmesan cheese. Repeat these layers, then pour the remaining butter and garlic over the top. Leave for 1–2 minutes and then mix everything from top to bottom to check that the cheese has melted. Spread the mixture on a warmed plate, season with salt and pepper and serve straight away.

FUNGI

FUNGHI

For most Italians, when you talk about mushrooms their first thought goes immediately to *porcini* (ceps). This mushroom grows only in the wild, from mid-summer through the autumn, is picked by local gatherers and then sent to checking centres so that you may safely buy them in shops and markets. Porcini-hunting usually involves outings in the very early morning (only because you need to be first on the territory), armed with a basket, a knife and possibly a stick.

While in Britain in autumn most people parking their cars near woods are either simply taking the air, walking their dogs or having a picnic, in Italy parked cars in such a vicinity means fungi-hunters are about. Due to the overwhelming popularity of this pastime, the Government has instituted laws which allow people to pick only a limited quantity of mushrooms, with levels varying from area to area but usually not more than 3 kg per person per day, and to specified measurements to prevent the picking of the very small immature mushrooms. Heavy fines are attached to the trespassing of these laws.

The history of gathering fungi in Italy is an old one. The Romans (who else!) were very fond of mushrooms, and one of the most precious to them was the favourite of the Emperor Caesar – which is why it is still today called Caesar's Mushroom (*Amanita cesarea*, see page 186). Fungi grow all over Italy, especially in high valleys. The best areas are, however, the valleys of Piedmont, Lombardy and the Veneto, and more especially Trentino, Liguria, and Emilia-Romagna, with Borgotaro as one of the most famous centres for the best *porcini*. Quantities of mushrooms are also found in Tuscany, Umbria, Basilicata and even Calabria, where the high plains of Sila, being similar to parts of Switzerland, harbour a good quality of *porcini* and other fungi, like the saffron milkcap, and even the white truffles usually only associated with Piedmont, Emilia-Romagna and Umbria. The regions which offer perhaps the biggest variety of fungi are Veneto and Trentino-Alto Adige. In the market of Trento you may find for sale in season up to 60 different kinds of mushroom.

For reasons of safety, all the mushrooms sold in markets and shops are first checked for edibility by the local authorities, to avoid potentially dangerous errors. Despite this, however, every year in Italy fatalities occur, mainly among families picking their own with ignorant confidence. The culprits on these occasions are usually *Amanita phalloides* or *A. virosa*, which are easily mistaken for edible relatives. Unfortunately, there is no antidote for their toxins and often the indications of poisoning come too late for anything to be done.

Fungi and truffles have a very high gastronomic importance in Italian cuisine. In fact fungi are a considerable industry of some economic importance to the nation. Hundreds of companies produce industrially or artisanally dried and

LEFT: UMBRIAN TRUFFLE COUNTRY.

preserved fungi for local demands, but also increasingly for export. In fact, many mushrooms are now imported from Eastern Europe and North Africa to keep this part of the industry supplied with sufficient raw materials.

People often think that mushrooms are complicated to understand and fear eating or collecting poisonous fungi by mistake. However, while some are difficult to identify in the wild and definitely require an expert eye, many are very distinctive and can be picked with confidence. Of course, it is worth having a visual reminder of what you are looking for before you go mushroom hunting, so that you can quickly identify any that you find, but you should be guided by the location and conditions as much as anything.

However, I do firmly recommend that you have a fungi expert go with you for the first few outings and that you prepare by studying some good books on the subject. Under no circumstances should you pick mushrooms at random. Some of them are very beautiful and look very innocent and edible. You may, however, inadvertently pick the one that provides you with your last meal!

Fungi can be divided into three major groups or families: gilled mushrooms, tubular mushrooms and tubers such as truffles, each of which has its own distinctive characteristics and growing habits. Mushrooms have Latin names, like flowers or plants, so that they can be identified internationally. However, the same fungus can have more than one Latin name, depending on how many people claim its discovery. Hopefully, the simple guide that follows will help to make the categories easier to understand.

The gilled mushrooms form the largest family, with literally hundreds of fungi making up the group. The main characteristic of the family, as its name suggests, are the lamellae, the gills beneath the cap. It is in these gills that the fungus develops its spores, minute seeds that are invisible to the naked eye. To see the spores, leave the cap gill-side down on a piece of paper and, after a couple of hours, an imprint will be left from the microscopic spores being released by the fungus. This imprint is unique in form and colour to each individual mushroom and can indicate as distinctively as a fingerprint the mushroom from which it came. The majority of mushrooms fall into this category, but the most widespread is the common field mushroom.

The second type of fungus is no less prolific than the gilled mushroom and is made up of the cep genus, *Boletus*, and closely related genera. Unlike the gilled mushroom, it has closely packed little tubes beneath the cap. These tubes are invisible in the youngest fungi, when the plant is still immature, but they eventually develop with age and it is here that they harbour the spores, allowing the mushroom to reproduce itself. The mushrooms that fall into this group include the famous *porcini* (cep), which together with the *cantarello* (chanterelle) and *spugnola* (morel) represent probably the best edible fungi in the world.

BELOW: GIANNI AND GIOVANNI DISCUSS THE TRUFFLES THEIR DOGS HAVE HELPED THEM FIND.

RIGHT: BLACK TRUFFLES

The third type of fungus is a tuber. Tubers produce their spores on their surface and these are distributed not by the wind or rain but by insects, flies and maggots. The truffle is the most famous member of this group and the very best of the group have a fine and distinctive aroma and flavour and carry very high prices. Truffles look like potatoes and grow underground. They are notoriously difficult to find and so dogs — and, in the past, pigs — were used to sniff them out. Those truffle hunters who used pigs had to be able to present good rewards for their animals' findings, or they were likely to eat the truffles.

The life-span of a mushroom depends on the prevailing weather conditions so it can either be very short or very long, lasting from less than a day to a few days from the time it first appears through to maturity. The best mushrooms are those that are about halfway through their life-cycle. Avoid the smallest, even though they may look tender and very tempting. Conversely, as they mature the flavour deteriorates and the proteins begin to degenerate, they also attract more maggots as they age.

When out collecting mushrooms, make sure you take a knife with you so that you can remove any maggot-infested areas or decayed parts on the spot. This prevents their spread from one mushroom to another. It is best to carry them in a basket so that they are well-ventilated and so that the spores can fall as you walk, allowing the mushrooms to propagate new fungi rather than their being lost in the kitchen. Of course, as you are dealing with the natural environment you should be clean and tidy and treat any suspect or unknown specimens with respect. Do not touch them unless you know what they are, as some mushrooms are even poisonous to the touch.

When preparing mushrooms for cooking, do not wash them but instead wipe them with a clean damp cloth. The only exception is when cleaning chanterelles and morels: with these, sand is sometimes embedded in the gills and they have to be thoroughly cleaned under running water. Some of the flavour will be lost, but you cannot have it both ways. When cleaning mushrooms, great care should be taken to ensure that maggot-infested or decayed parts are cut out. Both fungi collected from the wild and those bought from shops or market stalls should be used straight away, whether they are being used fresh or preserved. They only keep for a short time in the refrigerator.

There a few golden rules to remember when using fungi. First of all make sure that they have been properly identified as being edible by a competent authority. Secondly, never take mushrooms as a present from someone you do not know. Thirdly, remember that some people are allergic to certain edible fungi, so avoid eating too many of any new variety and remember not to drink alcohol with fungi as the two can sometimes react badly with one another. Lastly, mushrooms should be cooked and eaten when they are collected; do not keep leftovers, as the proteins in the mushroom degenerate quickly.

Despite all these caveats, fungi are still a wonderful natural gift, as long as you understand them. My favourite way of cooking them is simply sliced and sautéed in butter or olive oil, with a little garlic, parsley and sometimes some chopped chilli.

A-Z of Fungi

LEFT: AGARICO DELIZIOSO

AGARICO DELIZIOSO / SAFFRON MILKCAP *Lactarius deliciosus*
One of the most beautiful of the Agarico family of mushrooms, the saffron milkcap belongs to the subspecies *Agarico lactarius*, indicating that when cut or broken it exudes a yellowy milky substance, as its name implies. The saffron milkcap reaches about 4-6 cm ($1^1/_4$-$2^1/_2$ inches) in height and has a fairly thick and meaty flat, orange-to-green coloured cap made up of concentric circles, with a depression in the centre. The edges of the cap are turned under, with the gills on the underside quite tight and of the same saffrony colour as the straight hollow stem. In Calabria it is called *sanguinello* or *fungosanguigno* because of the reddish tinge to its milk.

The flesh is utterly delicious, tasting nutty and slightly resinous. Make sure when buying or collecting it that it is free of maggots. To check, just cut the mushroom in half. It needs to be well cooked or it will be indigestible. Although it is not suitable for drying, it can be frozen. However, the best way to enjoy it is cooked in olive oil, with a little garlic, parsley and chilli.

The saffron milkcap is unfortunately often confused with the toxic woolly milkcap (*Lactarius torminosus*), which although similar in shape, has white gills, a white stem and flesh, and exudes a white milk. Its surface is also different, being covered in hairs rather than being smooth. The woolly milkcap grows singly or in small groups near pine trees and grass all over Italy in late summer and early autumn.

AGARICO NUDO / WOOD BLEWIT *Lepista nuda*
A fairly common but beautiful fungus from the Agarico family, the wood blewit can be found from autumn through to early winter in deciduous woods and fields that are adjacent to woods. It usually grows singly, but can sometimes grow in little groups.

The whole of the young fungus is usually violet in colour, turning brown with age. The round flat cap can reach up to 12 cm (5 inches) in diameter, with the irregular edges rolled under. The flesh is quite firm, with a nutty flavour and delicate perfume. It is slightly poisonous when raw but perfectly edible when cooked. Try braising them in butter until the moisture from the mushroom has evaporated, then season with chives, salt and pepper and eat as an accompaniment to meat or fish.

Although the wood blewit cannot be dried, it can be preserved by pickling and freezing.

LEFT: OVOLI

AMANITA
This is the name of the most famous family of funguses, embracing a wide range of mushrooms from the most delicious, the *Amanita Cesarea* (see right), to the most poisonous – including the *A. phalloides*, *A. virosa*, *A. pantherina* and the *A. verna*. All these are deadly mushrooms for which there is no antidote. The family also includes the very beautiful *A. muscaria* (fly agaric), which is red with white spots and is considered to be a hallucinogen, but can possibly cause death.

AMANITA CESAREA, OVOLO, COCCO, FUNGO IMPERIALE / CAESAR'S MUSHROOM *Amanita caesarea*
Named after the Roman emperor Caesar, who was very fond of it, the *Amanita cesarea* is probably one of the most sought after mushrooms in Italy. Probably exceeding the very popular *porcino* (cep) for extreme delicacy of taste and splendid colours, it grows under oak and chestnut trees in very warm, dry areas, especially in the south, but is particularly popular in northern Italy, where it can be bought in specialist shops.

It can grow up to 8.5 cm ($3^1/_2$ inches) in height and has a bright orange cap of up to 20 cm (8 inches) in diameter, with a slightly paler orangey yellow gills and flesh. When mature, a yellow ring or skirt appears on the stem. As it grows, the mushroom resembles a thick white egg out of which the orange 'yolk' of the mushroom breaks, hence its Italian name *ovolo* or *cocco*, meaning 'egg'. When collecting it, be sure to pick the right one because, when small and undeveloped, it is very similar to other very poisonous mushrooms from the same family (see Amanita).

Italians love to eat this mushroom raw, finely sliced in salads with slices of truffle and dressed with extra-virgin olive oil and a few drops of lemon juice.

ARRICCIATA / CAULIFLOWER MUSHROOM *Sparassis crispa*
The cauliflower fungus does not look like a mushroom at all. It grows at the base of old pine trees during the autumn, reaches more than 50 cm (20 inches) in diameter and weighs several kilos. It develops from a single thick, short stem hidden at the base of the tree, into a series of tightly packed branches with little off-white lobes at the end, which makes it look like a huge cauliflower or brain (hence its other English name, 'brain fungus'). It is not a common fungus and cannot be bought easily in Italy, except in local markets such as Trento where, in

autumn, up to 60 different types of mushroom are on sale in any one day.

Great care has to be taken when cleaning the *arricciata* and, depending on their size, it is advisable to cut them into chunks to check for insects, pine needles and small stones. If they have been growing in a sandy area it is also necessary to wash them. Before being cooked they should be briefly blanched in boiling salted water. They can then be fried in butter or cut into small chunks, sautéed with a mixture of other types of mushrooms or dipped in beaten egg and deep-fried. They can also be cut into chunks and skewered along with small pieces of chicken for barbecuing over charcoal.

BOLETO BAIO / BAY BOLETE *Boletus badius, Xerocomus*
Many Italians wrongfully doubt the edibility of this fungus belonging to the Boletus family (beneath the cap it has pores instead of gills) as, when cut, the flesh turns a little blue on coming into contact with the air. Otherwise it looks quite ordinary and is sometimes confused with other boleti, some of which are edible and others poisonous, and it is also sometimes confused with *porcini*. It can, though, be distinguished by the fact that it grows in the northern and central regions of Italy in summer and autumn under beech and pine trees, where there is grass or moss. Its surface looks like brown velvet or leather when dry, although it turns slippery and sticky when wet. It grows in large families so, when you do find them, there are always plenty to take home.

The cap grows up to 15 cm (6 inches) in diameter and is quite firm and meaty when young, turning spongy when fully developed. The undeveloped pores are tight and cream-coloured, gradually turning from pale to deep green as they age. The fairly solid edible stem is pale brown with stripes and can grow up to 12 cm (5 inches) high.

When preparing the fungus, discard any infested by maggots. Only perfect examples should be collected and eaten. They are good dried, but should first be cut into slices. Although it does not have the same intensity of flavour as *porcini*, it is still valuable as a flavouring for sauces and soups, etc. Young boleti freeze well and are good for pickling. They can also be puréed, simply sautéed in butter or oil, or dipped in beaten egg, tossed in breadcrumbs and shallow-fried. Make sure you know the origin of bay boleti before you buy them, as more than any other mushroom, they absorb pollution and nuclear fall-out — especially radioactive strontium.

BOLETO ELEGANTE, LARICINO / LARCH BOLETE *Boletus elegans, Suillus grevilley*
Although it looks similar to other boleti, the *elegante*, as its name suggests, looks much better than it tastes. It is not one of the most sought-after fungi, but it has its merits, not least its abundance. It can mainly be found from summer through to autumn under larch and pine trees, where the ground is free of brambles and other heavy shrubs. This fungus is always a little moist, whatever the weather conditions, but fully developed specimens should not be picked after rain as they can become waterlogged.

The yellow-orange cap reaches up to 15 cm (6 inches) in diameter and the stem up to 12-15 cm (5-6 inches) in height. The ring around the stem is the remainder of a veil, and under the cap are bright yellow pores. Take care not to confuse it with some varieties of the very toxic *cortinarius*, so if you want to collect it yourself make sure you have a professional mycologist with you. The larch bolete grows in the Alps and Apennines, where pastureland borders larch and pine woods. It is common in Calabria on the Sila flatlands.

RIGHT: WINTER CHANTERELLES

In my opinion, most mushrooms should not be cooked for too long, but a recipe of Rosetta, a local forest warden, changed my mind. She peeled them, removed the viscous skin, then chopped and fried them for half an hour in extra-virgin olive oil, with garlic, chilli and parsley, until all the moisture had evaporated. They were delicious. Incidentally salt should always be added at the end of the cooking of mushrooms so that they do not sweat too much.

BOLETO GIALLO, PINAIOLO / SLIPPERY JACK *Boletus luteus, suillus*
Even in dry weather, the cuticle (skin) of this fungus is always viscous and wet. It belongs also to the Boletus family and mainly grows in pine woods during the spring and autumn. It grows freely and can be found in large groups. The wet cuticle is a browny-purple colour and should be removed when the fungus is being prepared. The cap is about 12 cm (5 inches) in diameter, with yellow pores on the underside. The tubular stem is 8-10 cm (3-4 inches) high and whitish in colour. It also has a ring around it from the remains of the veil. It can be used in the same way as the *boleto elegante*, but is also good sautéed and in soups.

BULE, BRISA, SEE PORCINO

CANTARELLO / CHANTERELLE *Cantharellus cibarius*
This mushroom is also known as *galletto, gallinaccio, gialletto, cantarello, finferlo, margherita* and *garitula* in Italy,

and *girolle* in French. The fact that almost every region in Italy has a different name for this fungus shows how popular it is. It is, however, equally highly appreciated all over the world. Like the *porcino*, the chanterelle is available during the summer and autumn from most specialist food shops, although at quite a high price. As well as its subtle flavour, the chanterelle is also popular because of its pretty bright yellow-to-apricot colour, its size, attractive shape and firm, chunky texture. It looks like a funnel with an irregularly shaped cap, its fairly loose gills running down on to the short stem which is just a few centimetres high. It is quite abundant, growing in large groups on mossy ground in dank woodland.

The chanterelle's fragrant yellowy-white flesh is delicious simply fried in butter with a few chopped shallots and chervil or parsley. Some people add cream to this dish, but I think it smothers the delicate flavour. It is also good with scrambled eggs or in an omelette, but can also be used to accompany steamed fish and meat dishes. The chanterelle can be preserved in many ways, including being pickled in vinegar to be eaten as part of an *antipasto*, as well as frozen and dried, although this method is more effective for retaining the shape and colour of the mushroom than the flavour. I have discovered a way to sweet-cure them so they can be used as a decoration for exotic desserts (see the recipe for Finferli al Liquore on page 201).

CARDONCELLO, CARDARELLO, FUNGO DI FÄROLA / TYPE OF OYSTER MUSHROOM *Pleurotus fuscus*

This extremely popular fungus grows wild only in southern Italy and mainly in the Basilicata and Puglia. It can grow at altitudes of up to 2,000 metres (6,000 feet) and prefers to be among the fallen needles of the umbrella pine. It is an irregularly shaped fungus belonging to the Pleurotus family and grows in abundant clumps on thick tree stumps or wood that is decaying beneath the soil. Under its meaty head, which ranges in colour from pale-brown to grey, are its loose off-white gills which run down to the top of the stem.

Like other types of oyster mushroom (see Pleuroto), it is commercially grown in sacks filled with wood chips injected with the spore of the fungus and stored in temperature- and moisture-controlled rooms. This farmed product is not very different from the wild one, as its main characteristics lie in its firm, bulky flesh and crunchy texture rather than its aroma or flavour.

It is this textural quality which makes the *cardoncello* so ideal for preserving. The Pugliese cook it in wine vinegar before grilling it *alla brace* (over charcoal) and then preserving it in jars with Pugliese extra-virgin olive oil and garlic, parsley and chilli. Another popular Pugliese recipe is to bake the mushrooms, sprinkled with fresh breadcrumbs, parsley, salt and pepper, and lots of extra-virgin olive oil, in a fairly hot oven for half an hour.

CEPPATELLO, SEE PORCINO

CHIODINO, FAMIGLIOLA BUONA / HONEY FUNGUS *Armillaria mellea*

In the autumn, this mushroom can be bought for a modest price at every Italian market. As a fungus it is greatly feared by foresters and owners of orchards or fruit trees because of its parasitic habit of feeding on not only decaying wood but the sap of living trees, which threatens their survival.

LEFT: CHIODINI

Its Italian names, *chiodino* and *famigliola*, refer to its shape, *chiodo* meaning 'nail', and pattern of growth as *famigliola* means 'small family', indicating that it grows in tight bunches. Its Latin name, *mellea* means 'honey', hence its English name, although this is a reference to its colour rather than its flavour.

The little fungus heads grow close together on a very long stem and start off being round and honey-coloured with a black top and centre. The gills are initially white, but turn to a creamy brown when the cap opens. The best time to pick them is when they are closed, otherwise they become fragile and break easily.

When you find them, they will be available in abundance. Once it took me and a friend just a couple of hours to collect about 150 kg from the stump of an enormous beech tree which had a surface of only 3 or 4 square metres. However, this mass of mushrooms left a very unpleasant smell in my car. Be sure to avoid picking the very similar – but very poisonous – *Hypholoma fasciculare*, which grows in similar circumstances to the honey fungus, often right next to it, but can be distinguished by its sulphurous yellow colour and green-to-dark-brown gills.

The honey fungus can only be eaten after it has been cooked as it is also poisonous when raw. Despite this, the *chiodino* is an excellent and versatile fungus which is excellent pickled in vinegar or preserved in extra-virgin olive oil along with some spices for flavouring. It can also be frozen, as long as it has been thoroughly cleaned, with only one-third of the stem still being attached to the head.

Before using it, cook the honey fungus in slightly salted water for a few minutes, then throw away the water as the toxins may be left in it.

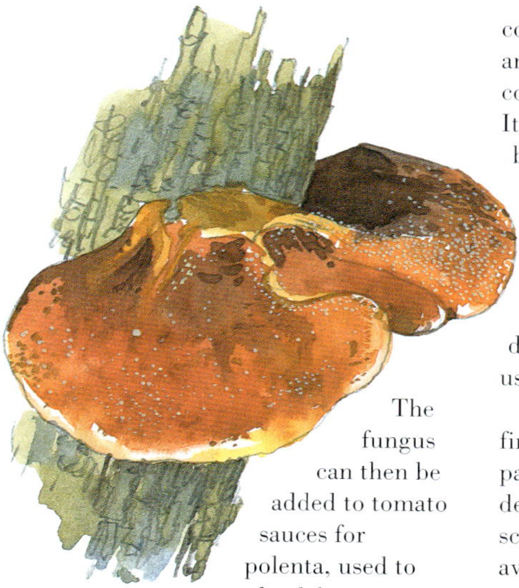

Right: Lingua di bue

The fungus can then be added to tomato sauces for polenta, used to make delicate risottos, or as a flavouring for pasta. My favourite way of eating the blanched mushroom is sautéed in extra-virgin olive oil, with garlic and chilli and then dressed with lemon juice, salt, pepper and parsley as a cold salad.

Colombina Maggiore

Russola verde, R. cyanoxantha

There are literally hundreds of varieties of this particularly pretty fungus. The fungus has an infinite range of colours and it is easily confused with other species, both poisonous and edible. It can be difficult even for experts to distinguish them, so I would advise against collecting them unless you are in the company of a real expert.

It is a delicate mushroom with a cap that is red, yellow, green or even pale blue and purple. It usually appears in deciduous woods during August and September. The field variety is usually white with a straight and hollow stem that can be either white, yellow or a pinkish colour. If you find it in a shop, check that it has been passed by the forestry authority for edibility and prepare as for the *Agarico delizioso*.

Coprino Chiomato / Shaggy Inkcap *Coprinus comatus*

This curious, but fairly common, fungus from the Agarico family grows from spring to autumn in large clusters on rich soil and along country lanes. It has a hollow stem and a shaggy oval cap, which is covered with a rash of brown spots. It is quite delicious, but should only be eaten when closed, as once it is fully open and ripe the gills turn black and the mushroom becomes inedible. In order to avoid the white gills turning black once collected, pull off and discard the stem (which is not very useful anyway).

The shaggy inkcap is difficult to find in markets, but grows on pastures and hills all over Italy. It is delicious stewed in butter with scrambled eggs and parsley, but avoid drinking alcohol when you eat it as this could make you quite ill.

Elata, see Spugnola

Famigliola Buona, see Chiodino

Fungo di Färola, see Cardoncello

Fungo Imperiale, see Amanita Cesarea

Fungo Ostrica, see Pleuroto

Gelone, see Pleuroto

Gialla, see Spugnola

Laricino, see Boleto Elegante

Lepiota Bruna, see Mazza di Tamburo

Lingua di Bue / Beefsteak Fungus

Fistulina hepatica

Each country names this fungus according to its impression of it, hence its Latin name means liver, its Italian name means ox tongue and its English name beefsteak. Indeed, it is generally known as 'the poor man's steak'.

Lingua di bue belongs to the Polypore family, meaning that the underside of the cap is made up of a vast number of pores. Being of the bracket variety of this species, the fungus grows like a shelf on old oak trees and occasionally old chestnut trees. Although the fungus feeds on the tree, in the case of the oak it returns a resinous liquid which turns the wood a reddish colour, making it much sought after by the furniture trade.

It grows from late summer to early autumn and reaches 25-30 cm (10-12 inches) in diameter. Its flesh is dense, moist and very heavy, with some mushrooms weighing around 2 kg (4½ lb). The surface of the cap is sticky and dark red, while the underside is pinkish in colour. When cut, it secretes a blood-like liquid which colours any sauce in which it is cooked.

I think the ideal way of cooking this fungus is to take the young mushroom, clean it thoroughly (it is not usually infested with maggots) and slice it thinly. Rub a pan with half a garlic clove, then add some butter and oil and melt the butter over a moderate heat. Add the beefsteak fungus and fry for 5 minutes, then add a couple of spoonfuls of double cream, some salt and some finely chopped fresh dill.

Loffa, see Vescia Maggiore

Right: Mazze di tamburo

Mazza di Tamburo, Lepiota Bruna / Parasol Mushroom

Lepiota procera

The Italian name for this mushroom means 'drumstick', referring to the way the undeveloped mushroom looks like a ball attached to a long stick.

When ripe, the cap can reach 20 cm (8 inches) in diameter on a thin stem of up to 30 cm (12 inches) in height, hence the English name, parasol.

The *mazza di tamburo* belongs to the Lepiota family and so has very thick gills, which are cream turning pinkish with age. The cap can be oval or round and is borne on a thin brownish stem. As the mushroom grows and the hat opens out, its woolly surface starts to flake from the top, sprinkling the brown skin with white. It is widespread from late summer through to the autumn, growing singly or in very small groups, under pines, in fields near woods and sometimes on large lawns. There is a similar but much smaller mushroom which is poisonous – so take care to pick the right one.

The parasol must be checked carefully for maggots before being sliced and sautéed or cooked in a variety of other ways. One of the best is the method used in Veneto, where this fungus is particularly popular. Beat together an egg, a little chopped parsley and some pepper then detach the open caps from the stems, dip them in the egg mixture and fry them on both sides in a generous amount of olive oil and serve sprinkled with salt and a little lemon juice. An unusual use of the fibrous stems is to dry them, then reduce the dried stems to an aromatic powder.

ORECCHIETTA / JUDAS EARS
Auricularia auricula, A. judae
This mushroom gets its English name from the fact that it usually grows on older elder trees, the tree from which Judas Iscariot hung himself. The Italian name refers to the fact that it is shaped like a human ear. It is brown in colour, with a velvety texture on the surface and shiny inside. It grows in colonies, one above the other throughout the year, even in winter if the weather is mild and humid. It does not have either pores or gills. Instead its spores are produced inside the mushroom and it propagates itself on the bark of the tree when it is wet.

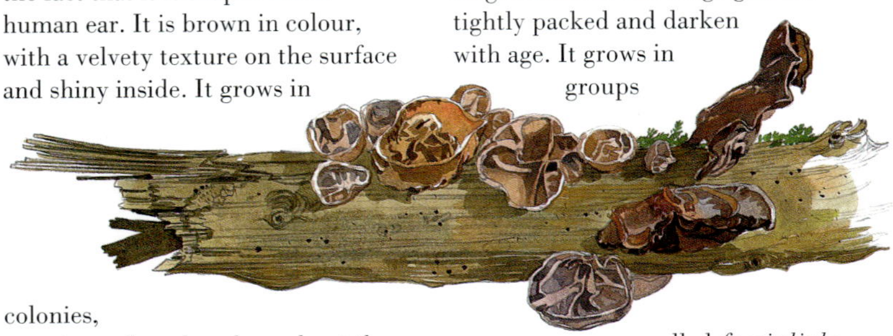

LEFT: ORECCHIETTE

It is much sought after in China, where its gelatinous consistency is an integral ingredient in many stir-fried dishes. In Italy it does not have much use, although it is cooked *trifolato*, that is sautéed in oil or butter with garlic, chilli and parsley. Make sure you cook it over a low heat, though, as a pocket of hot vapour can build up inside the fungus and explode, splattering you with hot fat.

I have cooked it with great success in my restaurant, in tandem with honey fungus, in butter, stock and brandy as a sauce for poached turbot. If you collect a large number, you can dry them and use them later, rehydrating them until they reach their original size. You can also buy them dried in specialist Oriental food shops.

OVOLO, SEE AMANITA CESAREA

PINAIOLO, SEE BOLETO GIALLO

PIOPPARELLO, PIOPPINO
Pholiota aegerita
This is as common as the honey fungus and is enjoyed all over Italy, but especially in the south. It appears in the early spring and late autumn on tree stumps of all types of tree, but especially the poplar and willow. Its flat head changes from brown to beige, but has a little more colouring in the middle. It is carried on a long thin stem with a whitish ring around it. The beige gills are tightly packed and darken with age. It grows in groups called *famigliole* (small families) and so is easy to collect and clean on the spot by cutting off three-quarters of the fibrous stem. The *piopparello* has recently been cultivated, so it can be found on sale all year round. These look very pretty in the market as the little heads are still closed and dark brown, but they lack the flavour of the wild variety.

The *piopparello* has been used in Italian kitchens at least since the time of the Romans and possibly even before. The best way of cooking it, however, remains almost exactly the same. In the South it is combined with tomatoes to make a pasta sauce, as well as cooked *trifolato*, that is sautéed in oil, with garlic, chilli and parsley. It can be also cooked in the same ways as the honey fungus.

BELOW: PLEUROTO

PLEUROTO, GELONE, FUNGO OSTRICA / TYPE OF OYSTER MUSHROOM *Pleurotus ostreatus*
This fungus is now commercially cultivated and can be found all year round on supermarket shelves packed in hygienic plastic trays – far from its natural habitat of decaying fallen trees and tree stumps, which give it a lovely aroma and more powerful flavour.

Like the *cardoncello*, it belongs to the large Pleurotus family, the most common one being the *ostreatus*, so-called because it resembles an oyster. It attaches itself to beech and elm trees – which it has the potential to destroy – forming numerous shelves. Given the right conditions of moisture and warmth, they can grow all year round, even in winter if the weather is mild. They are flat, with a short stem to the side attaching it to the tree. The stem itself is as sought-after as the fungus itself. It varies in colour from dark grey, almost blue, to creamy grey.

There is a variety called *cornucopioide* (cornucopia-like), which is funnel-shaped and pale cream in colour. The gills beneath the flat tongue are slightly grey, tending to yellow or cream.

The *pleuroto* is an excellent mushroom and is delicious dipped in beaten egg and breadcrumbs then deep-fried, brushed with olive oil and then grilled over charcoal, *trifolato* (briefly sautéed in olive oil with garlic, chilli, parsley and lemon juice) then served in a salad. It also responds well to being preserved in numerous ways, from pickling to freezing.

POLIPORO SOLFOROSO, POLLO DEL BOSCO / SULPHUR POLYPORE OR CHICKEN OF THE WOODS *Laetiporus or Polyporus sulphureus*

This magnificent fungus grows out of the bark of oak and willow trees to an astonishing size and weight. It is splendidly coloured, being sulphur-yellow on its underside and an orangey-yellow on top. It is very meaty and grows in shelves in groups of three, with the top one reaching up to 40 cm (16 inches) in diameter and the whole group several kilos in weight.

It belongs to the Polypore family, which indicates that myriad pores cover the underside of the fungus. These pores carry the spores, which form a white stain on the bark of the tree when the fungus is reaching maturity and becoming old and woody.

Some believe the *poliporo* is inedible, but I regularly serve it in my restaurant sautéed with other mushrooms. It is only edible when just picked, preferably still dripping its pale juices. Its slightly acidic but very tasty and tender, chicken-like flesh has gained it the name 'chicken of the woods'. Also belonging to this family are the Giant Polypore and Grifola Frondosa, which are only edible when small and tender.

PORCINELLO GRIGIO, PORCINELLO ROSSO / BIRCH BOLETE *Boletus scaber, B. rufus, Leccinum versipelle*

The *porcinello rosso* (*Boletus rufus* or *Leccinum versipelle*) appears from July to early autumn and belongs to the Boletus family, growing in symbiosis with birch trees, hence its English name. There are a few similar varieties, all of which are edible, although they all have a slightly different colouring and grow from conifers or oak trees. All members of this family are bulky and fibrous, with a white stem covered with blackish-brown tints. The cap is an orange-red colour, with one branch of the family, the *porcinello grigio* (*B. scaber*), tending to a darker grey/brown. The *grigio*, however, is not as firm or as tasty as the *rosso*.

Especially when growing straight from the ground around the roots of a tree, the young *porcinello rosso* has a phallus-like appearance. It has a stem of 5 cm (2 inches) in diameter and a height of up to 20 cm (8 inches), with a white scaly surface surrounded by a round, tight bright red cap. The cap later develops into a rather large and solid round of up to 20 cm (8 inches) in diameter, with very compact dark grey pores that fade in colour with age.

RIGHT: PORCINI

It is sought after for its very firm and solid flesh, which tends to discolour to bluish-pink when cut and turn black while cooking. It is, however, definitely still edible, with a wonderfully crunchy texture. It is much used in Northern Italy, where it is abundant in the woods on the slopes of the Pre-Alp valleys. It is seen as a culinary treat, much like *porcini*, although it cannot be eaten raw.

PORCINO, CEPPATELLO, BULE, BRISA / CEP *Boletus edulis*

Funghi in Italy really means *porcino*, the king of all the edible mushrooms. Its popularity is the result of both its culinary usefulness and its looks. There are a number of varieties of this fungus from the Boletus family, and all but a few are excellent. The first one to avoid is the *Boletus felleus*, which is so bitter it is inedible, and the second is the *B. satanas*, which is both poisonous and ugly. The ones to seek out are the following:

B. reticulatus: appearing from early May to June, then again from August to September, its name comes from *rete*, meaning 'net', because of the typical net-like pattern on its stem.

B. pinicola: in my opinion the best of all the *porcini* because of its dark chocolate-brown colour, its extremely meaty cap and solid stem. It appears from the end of summer through to autumn, in coniferous woods growing on common and red pines.

B. aureus: often confused with the excellent *pinicola*, this is equally delicious. It is most common in the South, the best coming from Calabria, Sardinia and Campania, where the climate is warm and oak trees are abundant. The more intense red-brown colour of its cap differentiates it from other types of boletus.

A common characteristic of these three varieties is that the spores start out as a creamy-white, then turn from pale green to dark green as the mushroom reaches maturity and the cap opens to a diameter of up to 30 cm (12 inches). The stem is bulky, even when the mushroom is small, which is why it has the name *porcino*, meaning 'piglet'.

An entire industry has grown up around this fungus, which sustains both commercial and cottage

Dried Mushrooms

While most fungi and truffles are eaten fresh in season – prepared in any of hundreds of different ways according to ancient and local custom – out of season they are still available preserved. Dried mushrooms are mostly used in sauces, they are also used to boost the flavour of fresh cultivated mushroom dishes. Mushrooms are also preserved in oil and these are traditionally eaten in *antipasto* like a pickle. The most recent means of preserving mushrooms is to freeze them and this conserves a great deal of their flavour, although the texture gets lost in the process. Frozen mushrooms are, however, still very good for sauces, soups and stews.

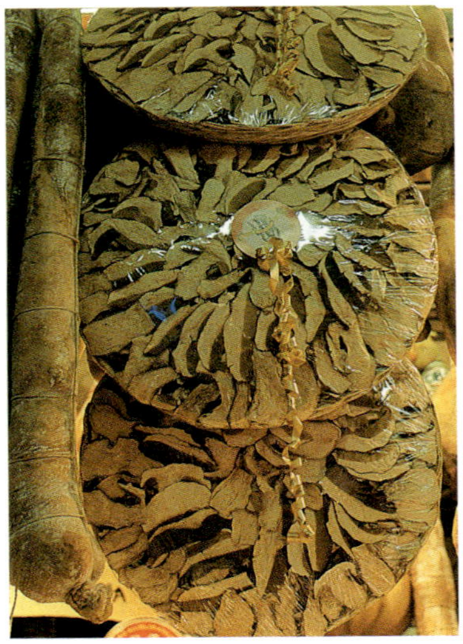

LEFT: DRIED MUSHROOMS

ventures because the demand for it is so great. All are situated near the growing areas, so that the time between collection and transportation is as short as possible. The best source for the mushrooms is the hilly part of Emilia-Romagna, but they can also be found easily all over Piedmont, Lombardy, Veneto and Trentino, Tuscany, Umbria, Lazio, Campania, Marche, Abruzzi, Calabria, the Altipiano della Sila, Basilicata, Puglia and Sicily. They are also in evidence, although less prolific, in Emilia-Romagna and Sardinia. All these regions have developed industries, which specialize in preserving the mushrooms, either by preserving them in oil or by drying them.

Because the demand is so high, *porcini* are also imported from countries as far away as Poland, Russia, Turkey, Romania and Yugoslavia – even Morocco and Tunisia. However, these foreign introductions can never match the fragrance and flavour of the home-grown variety, so Italian families tend to preserve their own so that they can be sure of the quality.

In the kitchen, the *porcino* has a position of honour. When it is in season, specialist restaurants feature it cooked in many ways. The large, but still young, caps are always grilled over charcoal, or cut into slices, dipped in beaten egg and breadcrumbs and then deep-fried. It is probably the only mushroom that stays creamy white even after cooking and the texture and taste are unmatched. *Porcini trifolati* (see the recipe for Orecchiette Trifolate on page 198) is a fantastic dish, but *porcini* are also wonderful in stews or soups, in sauces for pasta or as an accompaniment for polenta, as well as in risottos or as a side dish to meat and, sometimes, fish.

The smallest and firmest *porcini* make a wonderful salad. First clean and finely slice the *porcini*, then arrange them on a plate and sprinkle with extra-virgin olive oil, lemon juice, salt and pepper and serve with grissini. If you want to store them in the freezer, the best way is to cut them into slices about 5 mm (1/4 inch) thick and sauté them with a little chopped onion and lots of butter for 10 minutes. Divide the mixture into small trays, allow it to cool and freeze. When frozen, the butter will insulate the mushrooms from the ice.

Prataiolo / Field Mushroom *Agaricus campestris*

The common button mushroom is mainly commercially cultivated in dark humidity- and temperature-controlled rooms. The spores are mixed with sterilized straw and dung and spread over large trays. After 2 or 3 days they start to shoot and are then cut by hand when they reach the required size. They are grown all the year round, regardless of the season. This commercially produced mushroom, tasteless as it is, has many uses in the kitchen on a daily basis.

The wild version of the *prataiolo*, or field mushroom, which the French call *rose de pré* (field rose), is very delicate and enjoyable. It appears from August through to November, growing close to the ground among short grass in pastureland, especially where there are horses.

The *prataiolo* is part of the *Agaricus* genus, which includes many other edible varieties that grow in very similar conditions. Among the best are the *Agaricus silvicola*, which grows among conifers, and the silvery white *A. macrosporus*, which prefers high-altitude pastureland and has a ring or skirt around the stem and pinkish gills that darken with age. Another mushroom in the family that has been successfully cultivated is the *A. bisporus*, which can grow a cap up to 10 cm (4 inches) in diameter and is slightly brown on top. The largest in the group is the *A. arvensis* or the horse mushroom,

LEFT: PRATAIOLI

which is a real giant – growing a cap of up to 30 cm (12 inches) in diameter, with the same ring around the stem and the typical pink gills that turn almost black with age.

If you pick any of these mushrooms yourself, take care to avoid the very similar *Agaricus xanthodermus*, which has the same white colour, ring or skirt around the stem and the same pink gills. As its English name 'yellow stainer' indicates, however, it colours yellow when touched. You can also spot it by the yellow stain at the base of the stem. One of the reasons why it is important not to cut mushrooms but to twist them gently without pulling up the mycelium or root is that you can check this sort of detail.

Field mushrooms are very versatile in the kitchen and have a wide range of uses, from raw in salads to being sautéed in butter, in an omelette, or *al funghetto* (pan-fried with garlic and parsley). The only thing I would never do is peel them, otherwise all the taste is lost; instead, wipe them with a damp cloth and cut away the earthy or sandy base with a knife.

PRUGNOLO / ST GEORGE'S MUSHROOM *Lyophyllum georgii, Tricholoma gambosum*

This is one of the earliest mushrooms to appear and for this reason is called St George's mushroom in English, because it usually makes its first appearance around the 23rd of April, St George's Day. It grows on old pastureland that has not been disturbed by cultivation for many years, and has a tendency to grow in a circle like the *gambe secche*, fairy ring champignons. In fact, they often share the same ring because the mycelium or root spreads in a circle beneath the earth, thereby expanding the diameter every year.

Another of its names, *gambosum* (like a big leg), refers to its tight bulky stem thinning towards the top where it carries a compact cap. It is off-white in colour, with dense flesh, and has a slightly flowery scent and a very subtle flavour. It is an excellent mushroom, which can be found in large numbers.

To find it, look for circles of dark green as this is one of the best indicators that the mushrooms are hidden in the grass, allowing them to be spotted at a distance. It mostly grows on the slopes of the hilly Pre-Alps or in lush fields, and is mostly used in the north of Italy. It is delicious sautéed in butter with a little garlic and some chopped parsley or chives, in tomato sauces to dress pasta, or parboiled and then dressed with extra-virgin olive oil and lemon or plum *aspretto* (vinegar) in a salad.

SPUGNOLA, GIALLA, ELATA / MOREL *Morchella conica, M. esculenta*

RIGHT: SPUGNOLI

This is a fairly sophisticated mushroom and, although it is not as popular in domestic kitchens as many others, it is much used and loved by professional chefs and connoisseurs. The only exception is in Emilia-Romagna where no such division exists. One of the reasons for the uncertainty about its pedigree could be the fact that it belongs to a family of mushrooms that include potentially poisonous varieties. Two are poisonous when raw, but are perfectly safe when cooked, but a third, the *Gyromitra esculenta*, is very poisonous even after it has been cooked.

The curious sponge-like texture and unusual taste of the morel make it highly prized, especially in France. The first of the three varieties of morel is the *Morchella conica*, which has a small, conical cap made up of a dark brown, honeycombed or spongy flesh. Varying from 5 cm (2 inches) to as much as 15 cm (6 inches) in height, its stem is white and it grows in mixed scrubland or hills near pine woods, where the soil is fairly bare. Because it is hollow inside, it sometimes collects stones or pine needles as it grows. Unlike true mushrooms, morels belong to the Ascomycete family, producing spores inside the spongy cells, called asci. The second of the three varieties is the *M. esculenta*, which is very similar to the *conica* except that the spongy cap is slightly lighter in colour, making it more highly valued by the cook than its darker counterpart. The third member of the family, is the toxic *Gyromitra esculenta*, which differs from the other two in having a more irregularly shaped dark brown cap. As all three are so similar, be sure to get the advice of an expert to avoid picking the poisonous one. If you buy your morels, however, you can be sure that they will be the right ones.

Morels need to be particularly thoroughly cleaned to get rid of the stones and earth they collect inside their caps. The best method is to blanch them in hot water for a minute, as this washes away not only the dirt but also any latent toxins. Being hollow, the morel is ideal for stuffing, but is also delicious in sauces for pasta, in risottos, with scrambled eggs and as an accompaniment for game and poultry. One of the most useful features of the morel is that it can be dried very successfully and, once rehydrated, will return to its original shape and size.

STECCHERINO DORATO / HEDGEHOG MUSHROOM *Hydnum repandum*

This mushroom is one of the oddities of nature, a wonderful fungus that has neither gills nor pores and does not belong to the

Ascomycetes family either. Instead it has underneath its cap spikes which produce spores, hence its Italian name *steccherino* from *stecchi* meaning 'little sticks' and *dorato* meaning 'gilded', and its English name of hedgehog.

It grows from summer through to autumn in moist, shady places, under trees in woods where there is short grass or moss. It can be bought from markets in Northern and Central Italy. The cap is pale orange, irregularly shaped and quite meaty. The stems are also very uneven, with tight and very fragile spikes running from the cap to the base. These spikes are only loosely attached and fall off if touched. The flesh, which is slightly paler than the colour of the skin, is similar to that of chanterelles and can be cooked in the same way.

TARTUFO / TRUFFLE *Tuber aestivum, T. melanosporum, T. magnatum pico*

Romans used to think that this subterranean fungus, called a tuber, was the fruit of lightning, since it grew under or in the proximity of trees. They could not find any other explanation for something so delicious that even pigs were inebriated by it.

For centuries afterwards, this has been seen as a food that only cultured people could enjoy and not like other fungi. Indeed, the aura surrounding this fungus has been so elevated that it has become an elitist food to be enjoyed only by those with money. In Italy, however, even with the high prices, almost every Italian eats truffle at least once a year, even if it is only a few shavings on a plate of pasta.

There are three varieties of truffle; all belonging to the same genus:

Tartufo bianco, *Tuber magnatum pico* (white Alba truffle)

The Lange area of Piedmont is the capital of the white truffle, or Alba, as it is known in Italy. Although it also grows in Emilia-Romagna, the Marche, Umbria, Tuscany and Calabria, these cannot compare with the Piedmontese Alba, with its intensely pungent scent. Because it is the best and most sought-after truffle, it is also the most expensive, costing up to 5,000,000 lire or £2,500 per kilo.

It is only ever eaten raw, thinly shaved with a special cutter called a *mandolino*, and lightly sprinkled over a dish to give a hint of its precious flavour. Indeed, it is so intense that if placed in a refrigerator its scent will impregnate all the food in it. I keep a white truffle in the cellar together with fresh free-range eggs, so that after a day or so the eggs will have absorbed so much of the aroma that they will taste of truffle.

Along with the majority of

LEFT: WHITE TRUFFLES PRESERVED IN BRINE.

recipes for truffle, a cheese dish has been developed in Piedmont – where the truffle is king – known as *fonduta*, a sort of creamy hot mixture of egg, milk and Fontina cheese over which truffle is shaved before the whole mixture is scooped up with bread, like a Swiss fondue. Other classic dishes in which truffle features include risottos, on pasta like tagliolini, baked or fried eggs, raw beef salads and porcini salads. Truffle is also used to flavour oils (see page 217) and butter, as well as to make truffle cream for

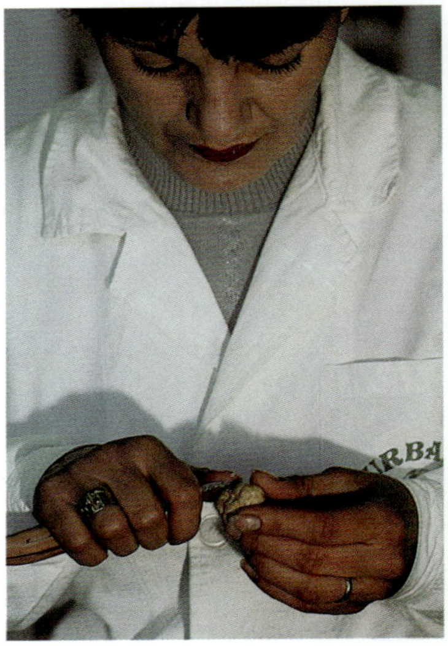

LEFT: DORIANA CLEANING TRUFFLES.

FAR LEFT: TARTUFI BIANCHI D'ALBA

crostini and, indeed, any other savoury dish you might want to try it with.

Tartufo nero di Norcia or **Invernale,** *Tuber melanosporum* (winter, black or Périgord truffle)

This tuber grows from winter to late spring in Umbria and specifically around Norcia, as well as in Piedmont and Emilia-Romagna and Calabria. A similar truffle can be found in Campania around Bagnoli Irpimia, but unfortunately it has a strong smell of carbolic acid and so is not much sought after (although it is eagerly consumed by the locals).

The *melanosporum* has much smoother skin than its summer counterpart, but it is its scent and taste for which it is valued. It is hunted down by trained dogs (mostly mongrels), who are rewarded with biscuits to prevent them from eating the bounty themselves. In the past, pigs were used to track down truffles, but pigs were so fond of them that it was difficult for the truffle hunter to persuade them not to eat the truffle themselves.

It has recently been discovered that it is possible to encourage cultivation by impregnating the roots of selected young oak trees with the spores. It still takes ten to twelve years before they can be collected though, a long time to wait and remember where the truffle should be growing. Despite this innovation to increase production, the prices stay high, as demand escalates beyond the reach of what nature is capable of supplying.

It can be used shaved like the white truffle, but it is mostly used in sauces, pâtés and dishes *en croûte*, to keep the maximum flavour. In Umbria, they cook it chopped in butter as a sauce for pasta.

Scorzone, *Tuber aestivum* (summer truffle)

Called *scorzone* (bark-like) in Italian because of its tough, warty black skin, this tuber grows harmoniously on the roots of trees like chestnuts, beeches and hazelnuts. It first appears in the early summer and continues until late winter. One of the main problems with this truffle, as with all others, is that it is difficult to find and then only by dogs. However, it does sometimes grow near the surface so that its knobbly skin and other protuberances extend above the soil. The skin has pyramidal warts, but its flesh is creamy, maturing to brown with white veins. Due to its poor scent and taste it does not have a great commercial value. This poor cousin among truffles is often used in tandem with truffle oil to boost its flavour.

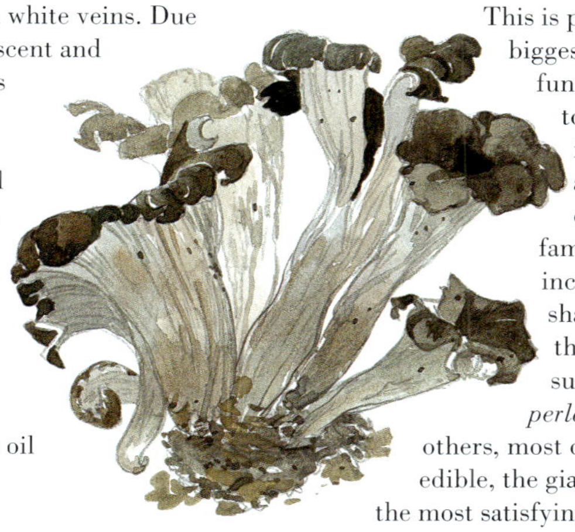

RIGHT: TROMBETTA DEI MORTI

TROMBETTA DEI MORTI, CRATERELLO / HORN OF PLENTY *Craterellus cornucopioides*

The macabre Italian name *trombetta dei morti*, meaning 'trumpet of death', is a poor indicator of the beauty and flavour of this funnel-shaped, thin and fragile fungus. Black on the inside and greyish black outside, it is very delicate and grows only a few centimetres high. It is easy to find, though, as it grows prolifically in little groups in mixed woods and on almost bare ground from summer through to autumn.

To clean it, cut away the base of the fungus until you can see through the funnel to any trapped leaves and insects. It can then be sautéed gently in butter and used to accompany steamed fish, especially in a dish of poached fillet of sole, where its black colour and delicate scent and flavour give the most dramatic contrast to the white fish. It is popular with professional chefs and can be used in the same way as the chanterelle.

RIGHT: PRESERVED BLACK TRUFFLES PACKED FOR FOOD MANUFACTURING COMPANIES.

VESCIA MAGGIORE, LOFFA / GIANT PUFFBALL *Lycoperdon* or *Langermannia gigantea*

This is perhaps the biggest of all the fungi, growing up to 60 cm (2 feet) in diameter. Of all the members of the puffball family, which includes the pear-shaped *piriforme*, the pearly-surfaced *perlatum* and many others, most of which are edible, the giant puffball is the most satisfying because, if in good condition, its firm white flesh will feed an entire family.

It can be found among nettles, in pastureland and sometimes in woods and even flower borders – I once found one in Hyde Park in London, hidden among the flowering shrubs. It grows from summer to autumn, depending on the weather. It is usually attached to a single root that you should take care not to damage when you pick it. If it is very fresh and young it gives a satisfying deep hollow sound when tapped gently with your fingers. Be careful to avoid the inedible common earth ball (*Scieroderma citrinum*), which is often found on footpaths.

It can be used in many ways, including cut into cubes and sautéed in butter, or sliced then dipped in egg and breadcrumbs and fried or, as I like it, cut into large slices or simply halved, brushed with garlic-flavoured olive oil, and grilled over charcoal for a couple of minutes on each side, then served sprinkled with salt and finely chopped parsley.

TAJARIN AL TARTUFO

TAGLIERINI PASTA WITH TRUFFLE

FOR 8

- 300 G ($1^3/_4$ LB) FRESH OR DRIED TAJARIN PASTA (SMALL RIBBONS ABOUT 3 MM / $^1/_8$ INCH WIDE
- 125 G ($4^1/_2$ OZ) BUTTER
- 85 G (3 OZ) WHITE ALBA TRUFFLE, CUT INTO SHAVINGS
- 85 G (3 OZ) PARMESAN CHEESE, GRATED
- $^1/_2$ GARLIC CLOVE
- SALT

The simpler the better, they say. This is not only better, it scores highly for simplicity and sophistication.

Cook the pasta in a large pan of boiling salted water until *al dente*.

Meanwhile, rub a frying pan with the halved garlic clove. Put the butter and a few truffle shavings in the pan and heat gently.

Drain the pasta, reserving a little of the cooking water. Add the pasta to the butter and truffle, mixing well, then add salt to taste. Stir in some of the pasta cooking water if the mixture is too dry. Add the Parmesan cheese, mix well and serve topped with the remaining truffle shavings. Serve immediately.

PORCINI SOTT'OLIO

PORCINI IN OIL

MAKES ENOUGH TO FILL TWO 500 G (1 LB) JARS

- 1.5 KG ($3^1/_4$ LB) VERY FRESH, FIRM, YOUNG BOLETUS EDULIS MUSHROOMS
- 2 LITRES ($3^1/_2$ PINTS) STRONG (6%) VERY GOOD-QUALITY WHITE WINE VINEGAR
- 1 LITRE ($1^3/_4$ PINTS) WATER
- 60 G (2 OZ) SALT
- 10 FRESH BAY LEAVES
- 10 CLOVES
- 20 BLACK PEPPERCORNS
- 1 CHILLI
- GOOD OLIVE OIL (NOT VIRGIN), TO COVER

The art of pickling mushrooms so they can be eaten out of season is very widespread in Italy. Using either own-gathered or bought mushrooms, almost every family makes at least one jar to be saved for grand occasions such as Christmas. They are served as part of an antipasto *and people don't mind the vinegary taste, which takes most of the initial mushroom flavour.*

I must stress that when preserving mushrooms at home it is important to take precautions against botulinus, *a deadly bacterium which can develop in the centre of food that has not been properly cooked or preserved. Vinegar and salt are ideal preserving agents and I devised this recipe using both to ensure perfect preservation. However, home preserving is subject to variations, so I cannot assume responsibility for any unfortunate little incidents. But my friends and I are still alive and enjoying fungi!*

Thoroughly wash the preserving jars and dry them in a low oven. Scrupulously clean the mushrooms to remove all the impurities (see page 185). Cut them open to check for maggots. Cut any large *porcini* in half so they are all the same size.

Put the vinegar, water, salt, bay leaves, cloves, peppercorns and chilli in a pan and bring to the boil. Add the mushrooms and cook for 20 minutes from the moment the mixture comes back to the boil, then drain. Put the mushrooms on a very clean linen cloth and under no circumstances touch them with your hands. Using a sterilized spoon, put the mushrooms (without the bay leaves etc) in the sterilized jars so that they are quite tightly packed but not pressed down. Pour in enough olive oil to cover the mushrooms by 1 cm ($^1/_2$ inch), making sure it reaches every surface of the mushrooms. Seal the jars tightly. The porcini will keep like this for a month but should be refrigerated once opened.

OPPOSITE: TAJARIN AL TARTUFO

Funghi Conciati

CURED MIXED WILD MUSHROOMS

For 4

- 600 g ($1^1/_4$ lb) mixed wild mushrooms
- 4 tbsp white wine vinegar
- 125 ml (4 fl oz) extra-virgin olive oil
- 2 garlic cloves, sliced
- 1 chilli, finely chopped
- 2 tbsp finely chopped flat-leaf parsley
- salt

For this recipe a good mixture of whatever you find in the market – or in the woods if you are a knowledgeable mushroom lover – will do. Chanterelles, field mushrooms, hedgehog or some oyster mushrooms are all welcome.

Carefully clean the mushrooms (see page 185) and cut any large ones in half. Bring a large pan of water to the boil with the vinegar and 15 g ($^1/_2$ oz) salt per litre ($1^3/_4$ pints) of water. Add the mushrooms and boil for 8–10 minutes, then drain and leave to cool.

Heat the oil in a pan, add the garlic and chilli and fry gently for a minute or two without letting the garlic brown. Add the mushrooms, stir well and then add the parsley and salt to taste. Serve cold as a salad or starter, or with cold meats.

Capretto ai Cardoncelli

BAKED KID WITH CARDONCELLI

For 6

- 500 g (1 lb) cardoncelli mushrooms
- 125 ml (4 fl oz) extra-virgin olive oil
- 1 large onion, finely sliced
- 1 chilli, coarsely chopped
- 1 leg of kid, weighing about 1.5 kg (3 lb 5 oz), cut into chunks
- 400 g (14 oz) ripe pomodorini or polpa di pomodoro (see page 118)
- sprig of rosemary
- small sprig of wild marjoram
- salt
- flour for dusting

This recipe is from Apulia, where both kid and mushrooms are commonly available in season. Cardoncelli *can be replaced by oyster mushrooms or shiitake.*

Preheat the oven to 180°C/350°F/gas4. Carefully clean the mushrooms (see page 185) and cut any large ones in half.

Heat the oil in a casserole and gently fry the onion and chilli until the onion is translucent. Dust the meat with flour, add to the oil and brown on all sides. Stir in the mushrooms and cook gently for 10 minutes, then add the tomatoes, rosemary, marjoram and some salt. Cover the casserole with a lid, transfer to the oven and bake for 45 minutes, until the meat is tender.

Orecchiette Trifolate

JUDAS EARS SAUTÉED WITH GARLIC AND PARSLEY

For 4

- 400 g (14 oz) fresh Judas ear mushrooms
- 60 g (2 oz) butter
- 1 garlic clove, finely chopped
- 1 small chilli, finely chopped
- 125 ml (4 fl oz) chicken stock
- 2 tbsp coarsely chopped flat-leaf parsley
- salt

These mushrooms are also called Judas ears, from the Latin Auricola judae. *They are remarkable gelatinous fungi, growing mostly on old elder trees. If you cannot find fresh ones, you can rehydrate the dried version. This is available from Chinese food stores and is known as black fungus.*

Carefully clean the mushrooms (see page 185) and cut any large ones in half.

Put the butter in a pan with the garlic and chilli. Allow it to melt and then add the mushrooms. Stir-fry for 1 minute, then add the stock and cook gently for 15 minutes or until most of the liquid has evaporated. Stir in the parsley and salt and then serve, either as a starter or to accompany chicken, meat or game.

Cappelle di Funghi alla Griglia

GRILLED PORCINI CAPS WITH GARLIC

1 LARGE PORCINO MUSHROOM PER PERSON
GARLIC, CUT INTO THIN STRIPS
OLIVE OIL FOR BRUSHING
SALT
CHOPPED FLAT-LEAF PARSLEY, TO GARNISH

Remove the stalks from the mushrooms and discard. Make small incisions in the mushroom caps and insert the strips of garlic. Drizzle with olive oil and place under a hot grill for about 10 minutes, until tender. Sprinkle with salt and chopped parsley, then serve.

Insalata di due Tuberi

TWO-TUBER SALAD

For 4

600 G ($1^1/_4$ LB) WAXY POTATOES
45 G ($1^1/_2$ OZ) WHITE ALBA TRUFFLE
SALT AND PEPPER
EXTRA VIRGIN OLIVE OIL

The potato is a tuber in its own right, whereas the truffle is actually a fungus but is also called a tuber – in this case Magnatum pico, *the white Alba truffle.*

Peel the potatoes and boil them until tender but still quite firm. Slice thinly and place on a serving dish. Drizzle over some olive oil, season with salt and pepper and then shave over the white truffle. Serve immediately, while still hot.

Ovoli in Insalata con Tartufo

SALAD OF CAESAR'S MUSHROOMS WITH TRUFFLES

For 4

- 6 still-closed (in the shape of an egg) caps of ovoli (Amanita caesarea) mushrooms
- 45 g (1½ oz) Parmesan cheese, in a piece
- 90 ml (3 fl oz) olive oil
- juice of ½ lemon
- 45 g (1½ oz) white Alba truffle, brushed and ready to be sliced
- salt and pepper

I include this recipe with the knowledge that you will find it difficult to come by the two main ingredients outside Italy. The ovolo (Amanita caesarea) *and the white truffle are both in season in Italy around September/October and only very good restaurants offer this rather sophisticated but wonderful simple dish. Serve as a starter with* grissini.

Clean the mushrooms of earth with a knife and rub them with a wet cloth if they are still dirty. Cut the mushrooms in very thin slices directly on to each serving plate, displaying the beautiful orange colour and the shape of the gills. Shave the Parmesan on top very thinly.

Mix together the olive oil, lemon juice and some salt and pepper to make a dressing and pour it over the salad. Finally, shave the Alba truffle on top and enjoy a dish fit for kings! (Caesar was very fond of this mushroom.)

Finferli al Liquore

CHANTERELLES PRESERVED IN SWEET VERMOUTH

Makes enough to fill a 500 g (1 lb) jar

- 1 kg (2¼ lb) fresh chanterelle mushrooms
- 1 litre (1¾ pints) sweet vermouth
- small piece of cinnamon stick
- pinch of salt
- 2 tbsp caster sugar
- apricot liqueur, to cover

This recipe is for mushroom fanatics who would have mushrooms even for dessert. Well, here is an idea which can serve as a decoration for panna cotta, *tiramisu and other cream-based desserts. The best chanterelles to use for this preserve are very firm and not too large. Bear in mind, however, that they reduce in volume by half when cooked.*

Carefully clean the mushrooms (see page 185). Put the vermouth in a pan with the cinnamon, salt and sugar and bring to the boil. Add the mushrooms and keep them pressed down with a wooden spoon to ensure they are submerged in the liquid. Boil for 15 minutes or a little longer if necessary, depending on size. They must be completely cooked; taste one to see if it is cooked in the middle.

Drain the mushrooms (the vermouth, unfortunately, has to be discarded) and put them on a very clean cloth to cool and dry. Try not to touch them with your hands (bacteria!). Put them in a sterilized preserving jar with a sterilized spoon, pressing them down gently with the spoon. Pour over enough apricot liqueur to cover the mushrooms completely and then seal the jar.

Once opened, keep them refrigerated and always under liquid. Use just a few to decorate puddings.

Crostini ai Funghi

MUSHROOM CROSTINI

For 4

- 500 G (1 LB) MUSHROOMS (SEE RIGHT)
- 60 G (2 OZ) BUTTER
- 1 GARLIC CLOVE, CRUSHED
- 4 SAGE LEAVES
- 2 TBSP VIN SANTO OR EQUIVALENT WINE (NOT TOO SWEET)
- 1 TBSP COARSELY CHOPPED FLAT-LEAF PARSLEY
- 8 SLICES OF PANE DI CAMPAGNA (COUNTRY-STYLE WHITE BREAD), TOASTED
- SALT AND PEPPER

Porcini *mushrooms or other* boleti, *such as bay or birch mushrooms (see pages 187 and 191), are best for this recipe, but a mixture of these would do. You could also use cultivated mushrooms with the addition of dried porcini for flavour.*

Carefully clean the mushrooms (see page 185) and then chop them finely. Melt the butter in a pan, add the garlic and the sage leaves and fry gently for 2 minutes. Add the mushrooms and sauté, stirring from time to time, until they are tender and most of their moisture has evaporated. Add the wine and some salt and pepper and stir-fry for a couple of minutes. Stir in the parsley and spread the mixture on the toasted bread.

Zuppa di Finferli con Canederli

CHANTERELLE SOUP WITH DUMPLINGS

For 4

- 150 G (5 OZ) SMALLISH, FRESHLY PICKED CHANTERELLE MUSHROOMS
- 1 SMALL SHALLOT, FINELY CHOPPED
- 30 G (1 OZ) BUTTER
- 1.5 LITRES (2$^{3}/_{4}$ PINTS) CHICKEN STOCK
- SMALL BUNCH OF CHIVES

For the dumplings:

- 150 G (5 OZ) FRESH WHITE BREADCRUMBS
- 3 EGG YOLKS
- 2 TBSP FINELY CHOPPED FLAT-LEAF PARSLEY
- 60 G (2 OZ) PARMESAN CHEESE, GRATED
- 1 SLICE OF SPECK (SEE PAGE 84), CUT INTO STRIPS FIRST, THEN INTO VERY SMALL CUBES
- SALT AND PEPPER

This typical South Tyrolean or Alto Adige recipe reflects the Austrian culinary influence. The dumplings may be varied but are usually based on stale breadcrumbs and egg. Here they accompany chanterelles in a delicate broth.

To make the dumplings, mix the breadcrumbs with the egg yolks, parsley, Parmesan cheese, speck and some salt and pepper to give a pliable consistency. Shape them into balls the size of a large olive.

Carefully clean the mushrooms (see page 185) and cut any large ones in half. Sauté the shallot in the butter and as soon as it starts to colour, add the chanterelles. Sauté for 5 minutes, then add the stock and bring to the boil. Add the dumplings to the boiling soup. Simmer for 5 minutes and then serve topped with the chives, cut into small tubes with scissors.

Funghi in Tegame

Sautéed Wild Mushrooms

For 4

800 g ($1^3/_4$ lb) mixed wild mushrooms, such as ceps, chanterelles, horn of plenty, bay boletus, shaggy inkcap, oyster mushrooms
45 g ($1^1/_2$ oz) butter
2 tbsp extra-virgin olive oil
1 garlic clove, finely chopped
1 small chilli, finely chopped
2 tbsp coarsely chopped flat-leaf parsley
salt

Whether you are a knowledgeable fungi gatherer or buy them in specialized shops, you can use any sort of wild mushroom for this dish. Sometimes I cook ten different varieties and the result is always stunning because of the wonderful combination of flavours. Serve sautéed mushrooms alone as a starter, with scrambled eggs, or as a side dish to accompany meat or poultry.

Clean the mushrooms by scrubbing them with a small, soft brush. Don't wash or peel them unless absolutely necessary. Cut them into bite-sized pieces.

Heat the butter and oil in a large frying pan and briefly fry the garlic and chilli. Add the mushrooms and stir-fry over a high heat. Once they begin to soften, add some salt and the parsley and serve immediately.

OILS, VINEGARS, HERBS, SPICES & FLAVOURINGS

OLI, ACETI, ERBE, SPEZIE E SAPORI

Whenever I travel abroad, the first place I visit in any town or village is the marketplace, because it reveals so much about the gastronomic life of any area or culture. In some of the countries that I have visited, like India, Bali, Turkey, Egypt and Morocco, the spice markets are separate from those selling other food products. I do not fully understand the subtleties of the combinations of the spices in the recipes from these countries, but it seems to me that certain flavours predominate. In Indian food it seems to be cumin, while in Chinese cooking it is soy sauce and ginger, and in Thai cooking lemon grass, coriander and chilli. If I had to classify the central flavours of Italian cooking in the same way it would have to be garlic and basil, with some rosemary and oregano.

Spices used to be called *droghe* (drugs) in Italy, because medicines, like spices, were also made from the seeds, flowers and berries of plants and used to be sold in *drogherie* (drugstores cum grocers) which specialized in *coloniali*, indicating products originating from the colonies. Spices first came to Europe from India and China many centuries ago. Italian cuisine, however, seems to have concentrated more on the herbs and spices grown domestically, allowing the exception of cinnamon, nutmeg and cloves. Other spices like saffron were adapted to its climate and are grown in Italy, even though it this is not their natural home.

Salt is probably the most used flavour enhancer and preservative in cookery. It is an essential ingredient in almost every kitchen. Its position was once so valuable in Italy that it was handled by the government and was sold exclusively at tobacconists, along with tobacco and quinine (when malaria was common in Italy). In fact the English word 'salary' comes from the practice of the Ancient Romans paying their soldiers with salt. Salt is mostly produced in Trapani, Sicily, by the evaporation of sea water. Today, sea salt is sold in its traditional coarse form, as well as in more refined varieties

so it can be poured into food rather than ground over it or added in its crystal form.

The most common companion to salt is, of course, pepper. As well as being ground into almost everything we eat, it is also used whole or crushed. Today, pink and green peppercorns have become fashionable. Despite their popularity, though, it is black peppercorns that are still the most often used and these are among the most valued spices in Italian cooking.

Rosemary and sage are also commonly used all over Italy and are even sold – or even given away – by some butchers along with particular cuts of meat. Many Roman dishes include rosemary along with mint. The Neapolitan courgette dish, *zucchini alla scapece* would be nothing without fresh mint (and garlic). In spring, Sicily produces a lot of wild fennel, which is mainly used in Pasta con le Sarde (see the recipe on page 166). Fennel seeds are also frequently used throughout the whole of the south of Italy, sometimes being added to sausages to make the Tuscan speciality *finocchiona*. They are also used with good olive oil in the South to make *taralli*, little round crunchy savoury biscuits to accompany *antipasti* instead of bread.

Peperoncino, hot chilli pepper, is a popular spice in southern Italy and Calabria in particular. There, it is used in the simple but delicious *pasta all'arrabbiata* (with tomatoes, chilli and garlic) and *aglio, olio e peperoncino* (garlic, oil and chilli), and in stews and sausages, as well as salami – a tradition also shared by Campania and Puglia.

The Italian classics, however, are still basil and garlic, which with the addition of pine nuts, Parmesan and extra-virgin olive oil make the famous pesto sauce. Basil and tomatoes, another traditional combination of flavours whether raw or cooked, is difficult to beat. Of the other herbs used in Italian cooking, parsley is the most widely used and has a central role in the making of Salsa Verde (see page 224), a sauce that has become very fashionable abroad, much like *rucola* or wild rocket, which has become a central ingredient in today's green salads, although it is also eaten on its own and with tomatoes as well as being a component in various types of *carpaccio*. *Foglie di sedano* (celery leaves) are used to add a marvellous aroma to chicken or beef *brodo*, and in various types of summer salads.

Oregano is perhaps the most misused herb outside Italy, because although it is associated with Italian cooking, it is not often used in the same dishes abroad as it is in Italy. Italians use spices and herbs to improve good quality ingredients, while cooks in countries where the natural ingred-ients are not of such a high quality use the powerful flavour of oregano to hide or pep up flavours.

Of the other flavourings used in Italian cooking, the most important are the oils and vinegars and of the oils, the one that epitomizes Italian cooking is olive oil. The olive was first cultivated in Iran about

TOP LEFT: AN OLIVE GROVE IN LIGURIA.

LEFT: MARIA, A CALABRIAN WOMAN, PUTS HER HARVEST OF CHILLIES TO DRY IN THE SUN.

Above: the 'secolari' thousand-year-old olive trees in the grounds of the Masseria San Domenico, Puglia.

5,000 years ago, and from there spread to Italy. The climatic conditions in Italy mean that the olives grown produce very fine olive oil and Italy is one of the largest producers of it, second only to Spain. Italian olive oil is subject to strict legislation to guarantee its quality and purity. Olive oil's international status has recently been secured by the recognition that it is one of the most beneficial fats available, even helping to keep blood cholesterol levels low. A major contributor to the Mediterranean diet, it is used in the southern European countries as butter is used in the north. Italians have in their larders at least two types of olive oil – virgin for dressing salads and an ordinary olive oil for sauces and other cooking – together with one seed oil for frying.

The other indispensable condiment is vinegar, which is mostly made from wine but has more recently begun to be made from anything containing alcohol, including cider and beer. All this is only possible thanks to a bacterium called *acetobacter aceti* which when introduced into the beverage transforms the alcohol into vinegar. As well as being delicious in salad dressings, vinegar gives a distinctive flavour to marinades, and like salt, sugar and alcohol, makes an excellent preservative. Vinegar can be used to pickle a large number of vegetables, including artichokes, mushrooms, aubergines, courgettes, tomatoes, sun-dried tomatoes, peppers, asparagus and many others, to make wonderful additions to the classic Italian *antipasto*.

A-Z of Oils, Vinegars, Herbs, Spices & Flavourings

Aceto / Vinegar

Vinegar is produced by a bacteria called *acetobacteri aceti* which turns alcohol into acetic acid. A lot of oxygen is needed to aid this process, which is why a bottle of low-alcohol wine left open turns quite quickly into vinegar. In Italy a good vinegar has, by law, to have a minimum of 6% acetic acid and a maximum of 1.5% alcohol residue. Vinegar can also be produced using a colony of bacterial fungi, called a mother, which looks like a gelatinous mass and builds up on the bottom of vinegar-making containers.

Vinegar has various uses in the kitchen mainly to preserve food. A vinegar with 6% acidity is strong enough to preserve vegetables and fruit, although it does have the disadvantage of leaving behind a strong flavour, which either needs to be washed off or watered down or the food stored in oil after being cooked in the vinegar. Vinegar can also be used in small quantities to sharpen sauces, or in marinades for fish and meat. More unusually, there are parts of Italy where vinegar is poured over strawberries and sugar to lift the flavour and where it is added to water and sugar to make a refreshing summer drink.

Aceto Balsamico / Balsamic Vinegar

This special vinegar was once used to cure illness, hence its name *balsamico*, meaning 'like a balm'. It is probably the most expensive vinegar in the world, partly because of the complex and lengthy process needed to make and mature it, and partly because only a small quantity is produced each year. *Aceto Balsamico Tradizionale di Modena* is the name given to the only genuine balsamic vinegar, brewed by 30 or 40 families in the Modena area who only produce 8,000 litres a year. Together, these families form

LEFT: 'BATTERIA' OF WOODEN CASKS FOR THE AGEING OF ACETO BALSAMICO TRADIZIONALE DI MODENA IN THE WONDERFUL ATTIC OF SIGNORA GIACOBAZZI IN SPILAMBERTO, MODENA.

the *Consorzio*, a special association that safeguards the quality of the vinegar. It is sold at a high price in small specially designed bottles, each containing only 10 cl, and should have been aged for at least 30 years.

It is made by reducing down the must of the white Trebbiano grape until it achieves a deep brown colour and syrupy consistency called *saba*. This liquid is poured into open-topped oak barrels and left to mature in well-ventilated attics, where the seasonal extremes of cold and heat encourage the evaporation of the vinegar, so concentrating the flavours. The reduced liquid is transferred, using a process called *solera*, into successively smaller barrels each year of the maturing process. The first is made of chestnut wood, the next smaller barrel is made of cherry wood, the third of ash, then one of mulberry. This cycle is repeated until the vinegar has been aged for the requisite period. Some vinegars are aged for up to 50 years, to become rich and treacle-like. The batteries of barrels used are precious components of the estates of the producing families, and are accordingly traditionally left to the eldest sons.

Due to the explosion in demand for balsamic vinegar, an inferior product also called *aceto balsamico di Modena*, but without the all-important *Tradizionale* label, has been created. This second-class version, however, is still quite good, having been aged for a minimum of 5 years and sometimes up to 10, 15 or even 20 years for the best. If you want to be sure of the quality, depend on the price for guidance; the cheapest can be no more than a normal vinegar with burnt sugar syrup added for colouring. Try to spot the differences.

Balsamic vinegar can be used for marinades, for brushing foods to be grilled, or to make vinaigrettes for salads or to add to sauces. I like just to savour it by itself in small quantities – a few drops are excellent on a piece of fresh Parmesan or on boiled vegetables or on steamed lobster.

Aceto di Frutta, Aspretto di Frutta / Fruit Vinegars

Modern cooks have shown a great interest in exotic vinegars made with fermented fruit such as plums or berries. Such vinegars are expensive, however, because of the need to ferment the fruit first to make a wine before then turning it into a vinegar, which then in turn requires a lengthy ageing process of up to 6 months. It is stored in barrels in cold cellars hewn out of rock, where the temperature means that the wine reaches only 4-5% oxidation. The addition of essence made from the fruit enhances the flavour.

These fruit vinegars can give extra

BELOW: TASTING ACETO BALSAMICO TRADIZIONALE DI MODENA.

flavour to salads, although care should be taken to choose the right type, for example raspberry vinegar is wonderful on a salad of bitter leaves. One of the best ways to use them is in sauces to accompany game. Try pouring fruit vinegars over grilled meat or combining them with melted butter for fish.

ABOVE: THE LABEL FOR A BOTTLE OF ACETO BALSAMICO TRADIZIONALE DI MODENA.

Aceto di Vino / Wine Vinegar

Today, almost the whole production of wine vinegar is undertaken by large manufacturers mainly for use in the preservation industry. White or red wines can be used to make wine vinegar, called *aceto di vino bianco* or *aceto di vino rosso*. You can buy wine vinegars that have been made with just one variety of grape, but this has more to do with being able to charge a higher price than producing a better product. If the vinegar has been properly made, allowing the alcohol in the wine to oxidize to 6% acidity, then the type of wine used is not important.

Wine vinegars are generally used to make salad dressings and Italians tend to make their wine vinegars into *aceti aromatici* by adding herbs or other flavouring ingredients, like rosemary, dill, basil, tarragon, bay, garlic, shallots and chilli.

Acqua di Rosa / Rose Water

The petals of the highly perfumed wild red *Rosa canina*, are imported from Arabic countries, Romania and Bulgaria to make rose water, which is used to flavour biscuits and pastries. It is also essential for the preparation of Rosolio, a gentle and old-fashioned liqueur which has recently become fashionable again.

Agrodolce / Sweet-and-Sour

This term describes a method of cooking which imparts a sweet-and-sour taste to certain types of food. The sweetness is usually provided by sugar or honey and the sourness by vinegar or lemon juice, in combination with other flavourings like garlic, herbs and spices. Vegetables like onions, aubergines, artichokes (see Carciofi in Agrodolce. page 129), courgettes and cauliflower are often give this treatment, as are some sauces for meat and game.

Alloro, Lauro / Bay

The aromatic leaves of the evergreen sweet bay tree (*Laurus nobilis*) have always been a popular herb in the kitchen. Bay plays an important part in *aromi* (the Italian version of bouquet garni, see right), court-bouillon and soups. My mother used to use a sprig of bay to pierce liver before it was wrapped in caul fat for frying. I use bay leaves when boiling chestnuts and in marinades for fish and meat. Try to get fresh leaves as they have a stronger flavour than dried.

Aneto / Dill

Dill is a relative newcomer to Italian cuisine. Because of its physical similarities to fennel, is it is known in Italy as *finocchio fetido* or *bastardo*. It has thin bushy leaves and an intense aroma, whether used fresh or dry, and is used in sauces for fish and vegetables as well as with preserved gherkins to give them a distinctive flavour. I like dill finely chopped in a salad with peeled and thinly sliced cucumber, a little salt and pepper, some olive oil and some milk.

Anice / Aniseed

Aniseed comes from a plant very similar to fennel (*Pimpinella anisum*), that bears bunches of greenish-yellow flowers which produce the seeds when mature. Indeed, it is difficult to distinguish between both plants growing in the wild. The essential oil of the seeds, called *anetolo*, has an intense flavour which is used in the making of liqueurs and confectionery, as well as medicinally. The seeds are much used in baking, especially the famous Sardinian sweet biscuits called Anicini (see the recipe on page 288), and are to be found with baked dried figs in Campania and Puglia. They are also used to flavour some savoury dishes, particularly salads and grilled fish.

Anice Stellato / Star Anise

The star-shaped fruit of this Oriental plant, quite unrelated to aniseed, produces seeds which have an intense aniseed flavour – about 20 times as strong as aniseed itself. Because of its potency, it is imported for use in the preparation of liqueurs like Sambuca, as well as in the confectionery and pharmaceutical industries. The ground seeds are an ingredient of Chinese five-spice powder, so popular in Asian duck and pork dishes.

Aromi / Bouquet Garni

The togetherness of a few flavours like herbs and spices is called *aromi*, being the equivalent of bouquet garni. A *mazzetto di aromi* or *mazzetto odoroso* usually consists of a mixed bunch of parsley, rosemary, sage, thyme, bay and sometimes marjoram, tied up in a bundle so that they may be easily discarded after use. *Aromi* are often sold in fruit and vegetable shops, and are used to enhance soups, sauces, marinades and stews.

ASCOLANA, SEE OLIVA

Basilico / Basil

In my opinion this is by far the best of the herbs. Although originally

RIGHT: BASIL GROWING IN LIGURIA.

LEFT: LIGURIAN BASIL BEING GROWN FOR THE MAKING OF PESTO IN FINALE.

from India, since the Romans brought it from Greece it has been adopted throughout Italy to take up a central position in Italian cuisine. The bushy annual with small leaves grows up to 50 cm (20 inches) high on a tall stem. To keep the growth bushy and the flavour of the leaves sweet, nip off the flower at the top of the plant. I think it should always be used fresh or preserved, as when it is dried it loses much of its character. To preserve basil, take just the leaves, unwashed and completely dry, and keep them under olive oil in an airtight jar. My father used to add salt and chilli too. Basil leaves can also be used to flavour extra-virgin olive oil, and this can be then used to make dressings for salads.

LEFT: PACKING BASIL AT A LIGURIAN GROWER.

There are two types of basil grown in Italy, mainly in Liguria, home of the famous pesto sauce (see page 228). One variety has small, very pungent leaves and the other has larger leaves and is grown in the summer (and under glass in Campania). Basil is principally used in tomato sauces, on pizzas and in salads.

BORRAGINE, BORAGINE, BORRANA / BORAGE

This unusual plant, with its pretty pale blue and yellow flowers (used for decorating salads and desserts) and large deep green, hairy leaves, is very popular in two Italian regions, Campania and Liguria. In Campania it is used as a vegetable like spinach. I like to boil the leaves until tender, then sauté them briefly in extra-virgin olive oil, with garlic and a little chilli, and sprinkle them with lemon juice just before serving. In Liguria, where borage grows freely with many other herbs, it is cooked in a similar way and is an essential part of *preboggion*, a mixture of wild herbs used as a filling for Pansôti (see the recipe on page 167).

CACAO / COCOA

It was Hernando Cortés, the Spanish conquistador, who first brought back the precious cocoa bean from South America at the beginning of the 15th century. The fruit containing these seeds grows on trees found mainly in Central South America and Equatorial Africa. They are grouped in pods embedded in a yellow pulp which is allowed to ferment before the beans are removed in order to develop the flavour. After drying in the sun, the beans are then sent to chocolate factories where they are roasted and milled to produce a thick deep brown paste ready for further refinement to produce chocolate or treated with alkalis to remove much of the fat, or cocoa butter, and make it into the soluble powder we know as cocoa. Cocoa is widely used as a flavouring in cake- and pastry-making, as well as in confectionery and in drinks.

CAFFÈ / COFFEE

One of the most remarkable happenings at the beginning of the Perestroika era in Russia was the sanctioning of the opening of Western-style cafés in Moscow, and Gorbachev personally endorsed the enjoyment of having an espresso from a Gaggia machine. That the café could become a symbol of Western culture and be politicized is indeed remarkable. The exciting drink which Italians consume in vast quantities is obtained by infusing a powder of a roasted bean produced by an evergreen plant. Coffee was brought into Italy by the Arabs in the 16th century, and the first coffee shop was opened in Venice in 1640, where Turkish-style coffee was available. Indeed the term *caffè* in Italian refers to both the drink and the place.

The coffee plant is tropical, originally from East Africa but now cultivated also in Costa Rica, Honduras, Colombia and – above all – Brazil, where it was established by European settlers to make the country the largest producer in the world. It is necessary to blend various types of beans to get the right flavours, generally most are blends of the arabica and robusta varieties. How the beans are roasted dictates the different style of coffee. The Americans like a light roast, producing a pale brown drink with light aroma and full of caffeine (a potent stimulant that can be toxic if abused). The general European roast is darker, giving a better aroma with less caffeine content. Italians love their coffee

BELOW: BICERIN CHOCOLATE AND COFFEE AT THE BARATTI E MILANO CAFFÈ IN TURIN.

ABOVE: A FANTASTIC COFFEE POT, CREATED BY ARCHITECT RICCARDO D'ALISI FOR AN EXHIBITION OF NEAPOLITAN COFFEE POTS.

beans roasted to a very dark brown colour, almost burnt, giving a very concentrated flavour and a certain bitterness, which is balanced by added sugar. The dark roasted Italian-style coffee has less caffeine content because caffeine is reduced during the longer and hotter roasting process.

There are several ways of brewing coffee: either simply in a jug like tea, or by allowing hot water to percolate through the coffee grounds or with pressure produced by boiling the water in a *caffettiera* with a screw top, or in the modern systems by very high pressure steam in a special machine.

RIGHT: A CAFFETTIERA.

Coffee is used in various forms in the kitchen, especially in baking and confectionery. It is a delight in summer to order a *granita di caffè* in any bar in Southern Italy and you will be presented with a small glass full of iced coffee. In a concentrated form, coffee is used in liqueurs, to fill chocolates and in powdered form in some pastries, like Cannoli alla Siciliana (see page 256). Instant coffee is not much used in Italy, where the fresh espresso and cappuccino are taken for breakfast and at any time of the day, but especially after meals – perhaps *corretto* with a dash of grappa in the North and a dash of anis in the South.

CAMOMILLA / CAMOMILE

This herb is commonly found growing on open fields. The centres of its small flower are used to make tisanes and teas which have a calming effect, aiding sleep and digestion. Italians often take a cup of camomile tea after a meal.

CANNELLA, CINNAMOMO / CINNAMON

The Italian name for this spice comes from *canna*, meaning 'little cane', indicating the fact that cinnamon comes from a piece of bark. Cinnamon comes from India, Sri Lanka, and China. The Chinese variety is often considered to be the best, with a stronger aroma and flavour. Cinnamon first found its way to Europe many centuries ago from the Far East via travellers and explorers. It is used all over Italy in savoury dishes, such as sauces for meat and game, and even in risottos (see the recipe for Risotto all'Isolana on page 226). It is also familiar in mulled wine and as a flavouring in sweets like Cannoli alla Siciliana (see page 256) and cream fillings for sweet flans. Ground cinnamon is also sprinkled over fresh fruit.

CAPPERO / CAPER

The caper is a bud of a plant with very pretty thick round or oval shaped leaves. The harvesting of the buds starts in late springtime in Sicily, when the weather is already hot. The little islands of Lipari and Pantelleria, south of Sicily, produce capers of excellent quality and in sufficient quantities to be able to export as well. The smallest capers are the most sought after, because of their pungent flavour and tenderness. The larger they grow, the less taste they have.

Like olives, capers are bitter and inedible when raw and need first to be cured before being eaten. They can be cured in either vinegar, brine or dry salt. I think the best preserving medium is either brine or dry salt. If using brine, make a solution of 20% salt, add the capers and leave them to soak for a couple of days, then drain them and layer them in a jar with coarse sea salt, finishing with a top layer of salt. When you want to use them, soak them in a bowl of water for about 15 minutes.

The best way to use capers is to add them to a dish, either chopped or whole, towards the end of the preparation, so that they keep their flavour and do not turn bitter. Capers can be used to flavour salads, tomato sauces, pasta or cooked vegetables like artichokes or broad beans. They can also be used to add piquancy to tuna fish sauces, as in Vitello Tonnato (see page 87), and to make a butter and lemon juice sauce for steamed fish.

RIGHT: CAPERS GROWING IN LIPARI.

CAPSICO, SEE PEPERONCINO

CARDAMOMO / CARDAMOM

This exquisite spice is mainly used in the cooking of India and the East, but was popular in Amalfi, Pisa, Genova and Venice during the time of the Doges. The flavour of the cardamom comes from the black seeds inside the pale-green oval pod. However, in Italy it is mostly used in the form of an oily liquid extract in the manufacture of liqueurs and confectionery, as well as in the speciality called Panforte di Siena (see pages 281 and 296) which dates back to the Middle Ages. I myself often make a cardamom-flavoured ice-cream.

CERFOGLIO / CHERVIL

The leaves of this delicate plant, which looks like flat-leaved parsley except that it is much smaller and paler, are used all over Italy during the summer when it grows freely. Chervil is very aromatic when fresh and is especially good with steamed vegetables, on salads, in delicate soups such as *stracciatella* (a broth with egg beaten into it), and in other egg dishes, especially scrambled eggs. It should always be used uncooked and only added to hot dishes just before serving.

CHIODI DI GAROFANO / CLOVES

Brought to Italy around the time of the Crusades, cloves are still popular in Italy. The clove (from the Latin *clavus*, like the Italian *chiodi*, meaning 'nail') is an unopened bud of the *Eugenia carophillata*, an evergreen tree that grows up to 15 metres (45 feet) high. The buds are picked and dried in the sun so that they keep their pungent aroma, and are used in many recipes, including *vino brûlé* (mulled wine), roast meats, game sauces, marinades, stocks, cooked fruit, and when preserving fungi and gherkins. Clove powder and oil are also widely used both in the pâtisserie industry, and as a medicine (for their anaesthetic qualities).

CINNAMOMO, SEE CANNELLA

CIOCCOLATO / CHOCOLATE

Chocolate, the substance that has the power to make both children and grown-ups equally happy, is made from the cocoa bean (see Cacao). Lots of refinement and blending, plus the possible incorporation of milk, cream, sugar, vanilla essence and more cocoa butter (the fat extracted from the cocoa bean) are made either industrially or on an artisanal basis. Italy is quite famous for good chocolate, the industry and artisans are spread in all the regions and they mostly use the best-quality cocoa beans from Ecuador, the Ivory Coast and Ghana. A company in Turin, Peyrano, still imports the cocoa beans and makes the very lengthy transformation to

produce bars of *cioccolato* or *cioccolatini* (small chocolates), with the addition of all sorts of flavourings, such as orange, mint, vanilla and many more. The chocolate is poured by hand into classic moulds, allowed to cool and wrapped in multicoloured metal foil. For specially shaped chocolate, like Easter eggs or bunnies, or Father Christmas, best bitter chocolate is needed to prevent the figures breaking or melting too easily.

As well as for confectionery, chocolate is also used in and on desserts and cakes, and in the South with baked figs or to coat crystallized fruit like clementines, cherries, walnuts and hazelnuts. The chocolate used for this is called *copertura* (couverture) and comes in big blocks which are melted down for use. Sweetened drinking chocolate called *cioccolata* is very popular in Italy and is at its best when served in one of the beautiful old cafés of Turin.

CORIANDOLO / CORIANDER

Italians only use the seeds of this herb and not the wonderfully aromatic leaves so common in the cooking of Southeast Asia. Coriander seeds are added to salamis, such as mortadella, and are used to make syrups for the manufacture of liqueurs and by the baking industry.

CREN, RAFANO / HORSERADISH

This curious plant *(Armoracia rusticana)* grows wild all over Italy during the summer. It is harvested for its pungent tap root late in the season so it can be kept through the winter. The strong leaves can be easily confused with those of the dock, and the thick root – which can grow up to 35 cm (18 inches) in length – has to be dug out carefully to avoid breaking it. It is very hard and has be grated for use. When doing this, take care to wear glasses or goggles of some sort as the juices in the radish are very pungent and will irritate the eyes if they get into them.

Horseradish is mainly used in Veneto, Trentino and Alto Adige, where there is a cookery tradition influenced by the southern Tyrol in Austria. As well as simply being used as a condiment and in sauces for boiled meats like pork, chicken, veal and beef, and with fish (particularly smoked) and on salads, it is often mixed with a potato purée together with double cream. I particularly like it freshly grated on rare T-bone steaks called (see Bistecca alla Fiorentina, page 70).

CRESCIONE / WATERCRESS

Watercress grows wild at the banks of small rivers, but is mainly grown commercially. It is in season from spring to autumn, when the weather is mild. This herb, which has only recently found a place in Italian cuisine, has a peppery flavour which is delicious in soups and salads.

CUMINO / CUMIN

Cumin is a very aromatic spice that comes from the fruit of a plant called *Carum carvi*, which is similar to aniseed. It grows in the summer around the edges of fields and is used to flavour breads, potato dishes and sauerkraut. It is only used in the north-east of Italy, in Trentino, Friuli and Veneto.

DIAVOLILLO, SEE PEPERONCINO

LEFT AND TOP: TRADITIONAL CHOCOLATE PACKAGING.

How Chocolate is Made

At the Peyrano chocolate factory in Turin, the raw dried cocoa beans are picked over and then toasted over olive wood.

The toasted beans are then milled between huge rotating cylindrical stones and the resulting chocolate liquor is chilled to produce solid blocks of raw chocolate.

This is then subjected to a long series of further refining and blending processes, mixing in sugar and other flavourings, including Piedmontese hazelnuts when making the gianduiotti (see overleaf) shown.

The chocolate is poured by hand into the classic moulds and, when set, wrapped and packed – again by hand.

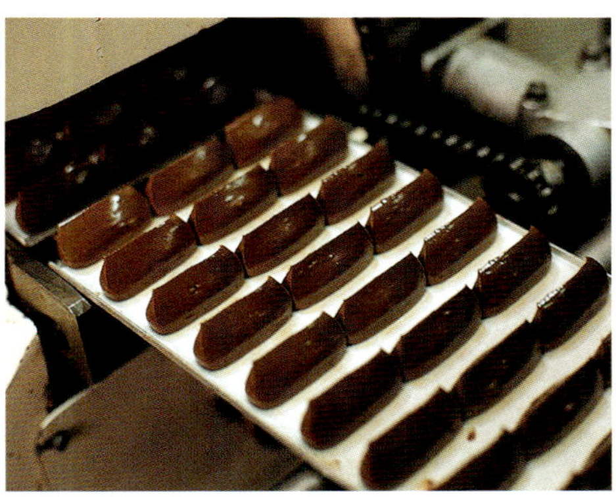

LEFT: WILD FENNEL GROWING IN SICILY.

DRAGONCELLO, SERPENTARIA, ESTRAGONE / TARRAGON
This strongly flavoured summer herb with long narrow leaves is nowadays much used in modern Italian cooking, probably as a result of French influence. It mainly features in sauces for fish, eggs and poultry, although it is also used in salads and as a garnish. A typical sauce based on melted butter, lemon juice and finely chopped tarragon is ideal with poached trout or boiled chicken. Added to vinegar, tarragon imparts a distinctive flavour to any salad dressing. Based on a French idea, I have created a sorbet made with lemon juice, water, sugar and plenty of finely chopped fresh tarragon.

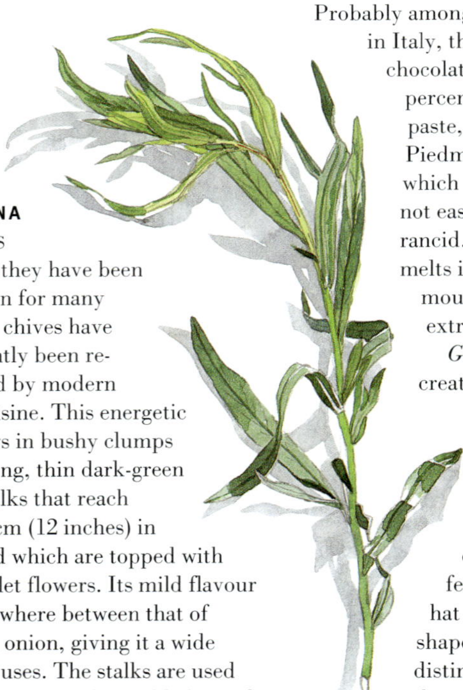

LEFT: DRAGONCELLO

ERBA CIPOLLINA / CHIVES
Although they have been well known for many centuries, chives have only recently been re-discovered by modern Italian cuisine. This energetic herb grows in bushy clumps and has long, thin dark-green hollow stalks that reach about 30 cm (12 inches) in height and which are topped with pretty violet flowers. Its mild flavour falls somewhere between that of garlic and onion, giving it a wide variety of uses. The stalks are used finely cut in egg dishes, added to soft cheeses, salads, consommés and on *crostini* with tomato.

FINOCCHIO / FENNEL
As well as using the bulb as a vegetable (see page 112), both the leaves and seeds of the fennel plant are widely used in Italy, where it can be found growing wild in the South beside country roads. Its flavour is less sweet than that of the very similar aniseed, to which it is related. The seeds are longer and a distinctive pale green when dried.

Fennel is popular in the cooking of Tuscany and the South, to flavour pork dishes and the famous Tuscan salami called *finocchiona*, as well as other fresh and preserved sausages. In Puglia and the South it is much used to make *taralli*, the local savoury biscuits, as well as bread and sweet biscuits.

GIANDUIOTTO / HAZELNUT CHOCOLATE
Probably among the best produced in Italy, these little triangular chocolates contain a high percentage of hazelnut paste, produced from Piedmontese hazelnuts which are celebrated for not easily becoming rancid. The chocolate melts instantly in the mouth and has an extremely fine flavour. *Gianduiotto* was created to celebrate the local folkloric figure called Gianduja, who is used to represent the city of Turin at carnivals and other festivities. Gianduja's hat is triangular in shape, hence the distinctive shape of the chocolates. A famous speciality called *bicerin* – said to be the favourite drink of the hero of Italian unification, Cavour – can be tasted in the wonderful classic Turin cafes. A *gianduiotto* is added to a cup of hot espresso coffee, resulting in a deliciously rich beverage.

GINEPRO / JUNIPER
This common plant, similar to the pine but much more prickly, grows mainly around the coasts in Italy as well as on the Tuscan Apennines, Sardinia and the Nordic Pre-Alps. The juniper berry is green, ripening to black, and has a slightly resinous flavour that is at its best when the berries are fresh and lightly crushed before use. Well-known for its use in the distillation of gin, it is widely used in marinades and meat dishes, especially game.

ABOVE: WILD FENNEL BUNDLES IN FLORENCE MARKET FOR DRYING.

LAURO, SEE ALLORO

LIQUIRIZIA / LIQUORICE
In Italy this perennial plant grows mostly in the south. In Sicily and Calabria it is harvested after about 4 or 5 years of growth, when it has reached a height of about 1 metre (3 ft). Its flavour is extracted commercially by cooking down the root until it forms a black syrup which is then mixed with sugar and starch to make the sweet liquorice, mostly used in the confectionery industry. I remember when I was quite young I used to buy small batons of liquorice root, which we children chewed to extract the sweet juice.

MACIS, SEE NOCE MOSCATA

MAGGIORANA / MARJORAM
A close relative of oregano, marjoram is enjoyed in most Italian regions for its minty fragrant aroma, but is especially popular in Liguria where it grows freely in the hills. It is used to savour the famous stuffed breast of veal, *cima alla genovese*, and Torta Pasqualina (see the recipe on page 301) as well as other roast meats and stews, especially with rabbit, and in salads. Marjoram is

also the predominant herb in *preboggion*, a paste of mixed herbs used to fill Pansôti, ravioli dressed with a walnut sauce (see the recipe on page 167). Marjoram is also easily cultivated and is often grown on windowsills and in pots on balconies.

Menta, Mentuccia, Nepitella, Nepetella / Mint

Italians use three of the many varieties of mint available and further confusion arises from the fact that the same name has been given to two types of mint grown in different regions. The most common form of mint is peppermint, *Mentha piperita*, a very invasive plant that grows up to 1 metre (3 feet) high and has dark green oval, pointed leaves. This plant does not propagate by seeding but via its roots, which spread so quickly over the ground that it has to be contained by delimiting the area with stones pushed deep under the earth. The other commonly used variety is the small-leafed mint called *mentuccia* (*M. romana*) which is often confused with *nepitella* (*Calamintha nepeta*), a slightly less popular small-leafed mint, the wild version of which is known as *nepetella*. Only in Tuscany and Umbria is the *nepitella* used in cooking, mainly with mushrooms and stews.

Oils extracted from mint are used in the making of sweets, syrups, sugar candies and chewing gum. Mint syrup added to ice makes a particularly refreshing granita. It is also infused in water or milk to make refreshing drinks. My mother used to put mint leaves in 95% pure alcohol for a couple of days so that she could make a wonderful drink made up of two parts sugar dissolved in equal parts of the mint liqueur and water. We children were only allowed a thimbleful of this drink which had to be further diluted with fresh water for us, but even so it was wonderful.

As well as sweets and drinks, mint is also used in salads (especially of fish), with tripe, or with fried courgettes (see the recipe for Zucchini alla Scapace on page 124) and artichokes, as in *carciofi alla giudea*. Today, mint is as much loved by modern Romans as it was the ancients, who stuffed it in chickens and use it to savour cooked beans and, as they also do in Umbria, leafy vegetables.

Miele / Honey

As everyone knows, honey is made by bees from the nectar of a variety of flowers and is the oldest sweetener known to mankind. Most honeys are made from the nectar of all the flowers within the range of the hives and these are called *millefiori* (thousand flowers). However, some honeys are made by bees who have collected nectar from only one type of flower. These are called monofloral (single-flower) and are generally more expensive than ordinary honeys and have more delicate aromas and flavours, reflecting the qualities of the flowers used.

Right: bee hives in Piedmont.

The most common single-flower honey is acacia and this is common in the region of Veneto. Acacia honey does not crystallize or cloud when used. It is popular in the confectionery industry but is also delicious eaten on buttered bread. *Fior d'arancio*, orange blossom honey, is a speciality of Calabria and Sicily and has an intensive bitter-sweet taste which is popular in Sicily for making sweets similar to the Arabic speciality, Turkish delight.

Castagno or chestnut honey is a very dark and heavily scented honey with a slightly bitter flavour, which is made all over Italy when the chestnut tree is in bloom. Piedmont, with its hilly terrain, produces a lot of good-quality chestnut honey, and this makes delicious Croccante di Nocciole (see the recipe on page 280).

Lavanda or lavender honey is an extremely delicate and highly perfumed honey that is mainly produced in Liguria, where wild and cultivated lavender grows abundantly. In Tuscany, *rosmarino* or rosemary honey is specially made, with producers regularly moving their beehives to areas where rosemary is abundant. In addition to these specialities, there are honeys made with the nectar of almond blossom, thyme and cloves, although only in very small quantities.

Honey is easily digestible and includes many nutritionally valuable trace elements and proteins. It is mostly used in the preparation of biscuits and creams, and to sweeten drinks. I add it to sauerkraut and spread it on roast pork to caramelize the skin. It is, however, at its most delicious in the Neapolitan speciality Struffoli (see the recipe on page 306).

Nepetella, Nepitella, see Menta

Noce Moscata, Macis / Nutmeg, Mace

The nutmeg is the seed of the tropical tree *Myristica fragrans* that grows up to 12 metres (35 feet) in height and which is native to the Molucca Islands of Indonesia, but is now mostly cultivated in the West Indies. It produces a yellowish fruit, similar to an apricot. The brown seed, which looks like an oval nut, is dried in the sun. The outer skin, or aril, which shrinks to a lacy covering and turns dark orange, is known as mace. This is usually ground to a powder and used for flavouring in the same way as nutmeg, although it has a subtly different flavour.

The actual dark brown nutmeg, although it is also sold ready-ground as a powder, is better freshly grated over food so that its intensive aroma can be fully appreciated. Since the introduction of nutmeg by Arabs during Roman times, it has always been part of Italian cooking, especially in the north where it is used to savour roasts, stews, sauces, mashed potatoes and stuffings for ravioli.

LEFT: A TRADITIONAL NEAPOLITAN OLIVE OIL CAN USED IN THE MAKING OF PIZZAS.

OLIO / OIL

Oils are made by pressing fruit, seeds and nuts through a special press or extracted using a chemical process. In the past, oil production in Italy centred on olive oil, with the result that the country has gained the reputation for producing some of the finest quality olive oil in the world. However, many other oils are now produced in Italy, including *arachidi* (groundnut), *semi di girasole* (sunflower), *semi di soya* (soya), *mandorle* (almond), *noci* (walnut), *nocciole* (hazelnut), *ravizzone* (rape seed) and *vinaccioli* (grape seed).

Olio di arachide, groundnut (or peanut) oil came to be used in Italy at the same time as margarine was introduced from America. It is used for frying because it takes high temperatures well and is cheaper than olive oil. Like groundnut oil, *olio di mais* (corn oil) is widely used in Italy as a cheap alternative to olive oil for frying.

LEFT: A SIGN OUTSIDE A SHOP IN NORCIA, UMBRIA.

OLIO D'OLIVA / OLIVE OIL

This miraculous product is made by mincing and pressing the pulp of the olive, itself the fruit of an amazing tree. Olive trees are native to Mediterranean countries and Italy is no exception. In the last 2,000 years, olive oil has become a symbol of Italian agricultural skill and expertise. It is not so much the quantity of the oil, although Italy is the largest producer of oil in the world after Spain, but the unique characteristics that make it the best-known olive oil in the world. With the exception of Piedmont and Lombardy, where the climate and soil are unsuitable, all of the other 18 Italian regions grow olive trees and these produce millions of tonnes of olives, which in turn go towards making about 824,000 tonnes of oil, half of which is extra-virgin.

For the olive trees to produce this kind of quantity they need a great deal of care, especially as 58% of the total area of 1,176,000 hectares devoted to them is on hilly slopes. One of the most difficult provinces for growing olive trees is Liguria, where, high in the hills, the trees have to be planted on terraces and can only be reached on foot. The Ligurian oil is one of the lightest and it is produced exclusively from one type of olive, the Taggiasca, a relatively small olive which is collected from around December to January, when the olive is almost ripe.

They are immediately transported to the *frantoio* or olive mill (of which there are about 9,000 in Italy) where they are reduced to a pulp by two huge rotating millstones. The pulp is then evenly spread on round mats which are laid on top of each other, like a huge sandwich, and crushed by hydraulic presses until the last drop of oil is extracted. The liquid is collected in huge containers where it separates naturally into cold green oil on top of water from the olives. (About 30% of the total liquid collected is oil and the rest is water.) The oil is separated from the water and filtered to remove any impurities. Olive oil is sensitive to sunlight, which can reduce the quality of the oil, so it is kept in complete darkness until it is bottled, usually in dark glass containers.

Olio di Oliva Extra Vergine (extra-virgin olive oil)

By law, an oil can only be called 'extra-virgin' if it has less than 0.5% acidity. This can only be guaranteed if the olives are collected by hand when still unripe to prevent any bruising which would cause the veins carrying the oil to be exposed

ABOVE: EXTRA-VIRGIN OLIVE OILS FROM TUSCANY, UMBRIA, LIGURIA AND PUGLIA.

to the air and result in oxidation. Also to avoid oxidation, it is paramount that the olives reach the mill in the shortest time possible and that they are milled immediately by a process of cold-pressing. This need for careful treatment goes some way to explaining the high price of extra-virgin olive oil. Cooking damages the proteins in extra-virgin olive oil, so it is better used cold as a dressing or in dishes such as Pinzimonio, Fettunta and Bruschetta (see pages 223, 226, and 224).

RIGHT: LEMON-FLAVOURED OLIVE OIL AND OLIVE OIL FROM PUGLIA FOR COOKING.

Tuscan oil is made with Frantoio, Leccino, Maurino and Puntino olives, and is quite different to Ligurian olive oil. Tuscans like their oil fairly peppery and herby. Tuscan olives are collected as early as October, when they are still very green and their acidity especially low. Because the olives are so young, however, they do not reach full size and so the yield of Tuscan olives is lower than that of those grown in other regions. As a result, the quantity of oil produced is also quite low, making it especially precious, and it is valued all over the world for its exceptional quality. In a bid to market their oil more aggressively, a group of producers has created a special bottle for it, called *laudemio*. In my opinion these oils are not superior to others, although they are of a very high quality.

Tuscany has hosted the first world congress for olive oil producers, called Oleum, where experts from all over the world meet to discuss their problems and achievements. There are also many professional oil tastings organized to try to discover which is the best olive oil. The Pugliese, who are the largest producers of oil in Italy, have been a little jealous of these Tuscan initiatives regarding olive oil, but are pleased that it has led to general guidelines being drawn up to help eliminate dubious production methods and products.

Pugliese oil is made from Corantina, Frantoio, Oliarola Barese and Leccino olives, although it is not always a combination of the oil from all four varieties and is sometimes a mixture of just two or three. Whatever the combination, however, Pugliese oil usually has a sharp, fruity flavour because it is made with fully ripened olives whose acidity is at the highest permitted level, due to the fact that they are picked as late as January.

In Sicily, olive oil is made from Nocella Etnea, Tonda Iblea and Bianco Lilla olives, which produce an oil very similar to the Pugliese variety, whereas the Marche uses a wide variety of olives – Frantoio, Moraiolo, Leccino, Rosciale, Maurino, Pendalino and Carbonella – to blend their distinctive oil, which is considered to be one of the best in Italy.

Olio Vergine di Oliva (virgin olive oil)
Virgin olive oil is produced in the same regions as extra-virgin, using more mature olives and giving a greater yield. It has a higher acidity level and a lower price. It is mainly used for light cooking where the oil is not overheated, and for mayonnaise and vinaigrettes. It is an excellent oil and can be mixed with extra-virgin olive oil when a richer colour and taste are required.

Olio d'Oliva (olive oil)
This is the simplest of the oils, usually made using a hot pressing method to extract the oil and sometimes using the 'cake', the crushed cold-pressed olives that remain after the extraction of extra-virgin olive oil. It is frequently used for cooking as it is suitable not only for preserving but also for frying, as it maintains its qualities when heated to a high temperature. *Fritto misto alla piemontese* and *fritto misto di mare* are always fried in olive oil to give the dishes extra flavour. The rest of the 'cake', which after the hot pressing is called *sansa*, is passed on to commercial producers who chemically extract the remaining 5-10% oil from it for cosmetic and other purposes.

In the last few years there has been a growing demand for oils flavoured with truffle to make *olio al tartufo*, which is used to dress cold meat dishes, fish and egg dishes. Other ingredients that are also used to flavour olive oil include chilli (*olio al peperoncino*), garlic (*olio all'aglio*), rosemary (*olio al rosmarino*), and mixed herbs (*olio alle erbe*). All of these oils, except the truffle oil, can be made at home simply by adding the relevant ingredients to a bottle of olive oil, although care should be taken with the garlic which will need to be discarded after a day or two.

OLIVA / OLIVE

If you were to eat an olive picked straight from the tree you would discover that it is extremely bitter; whether ripe (black) or unripe (green), it is inedible. It is the salt-curing process that makes olives palatable.

Olives grown for consumption are generally different varieties from those grown for oil production, with the exception of Taggiasca which is grown in Liguria for both. Edible olives, called '*da tavola*', are mostly grown in the south and include varieties such as the fairly large green Ascolana in the Marche, the Pugliese Cerignola, Maiatica and Molellara, and in Sicily, the Bella di Spagna, Santa Agostino and Santa Caterina from Spain, all of which are

RIGHT: OLIVES GROWING IN PUGLIA.

picked when green and unripe but which turn from deep violet to black when ripe.

Olives are cured by fermentation, which usually takes place naturally courtesy of the micro-organisms in the skin, called lactic bacteria, preserving the olive from decay. The oldest method of preserving small green olives is by soaking them in water for ten days, changing the water daily, and then preserving them in salt water and storing them in a cool place. Larger olives, such as the Ascolana and Cerignola, are treated with caustic soda and lime before they are preserved in brine to sweeten them.

Left: Pugliese olives in the Florence market.

A Sicilian olive called Olive Bianche goes through a prolonged curing process with a very strong salt solution which leaches the colour from the olives. They are then repeatedly washed to clean away all the salt and stored in a light brine. Commercial producers of olives pasteurize, or even sterilize, them before selling them cheaply in large cans. Olives are sold in this way either whole, stoned or stuffed with peppers or pimentos. Black Baresane olives are also sweetened with caustic soda and lime, before being sterilized and canned.

Famous for its sharpness and very widely used in Italian cooking is the *oliva di gaeta*, a black olive cured in water for one day and in salt for another day, then soaked in water for 40 days and finally kept in a boiled mild brine. These olives are excellent for *antipasto*. One of my favourite olives is the small black cured variety which are baked (or dried in the oven) for a more concentrated flavour.

Italian markets sell a huge range of olives, sometimes more than 20 different varieties, whole and stuffed. Most are eaten with bread as part of an *antipasto*, but some are only suitable for cooking in one of the countless Italian recipes employing olives, especially those from Sicily where the olive is an indispensable ingredient in famous dishes such as Caponata (see the recipe on page 135).

Some olives can be stuffed at home, and the range of possible fillings includes mincemeat or tuna fish with capers, parsley, breadcrumbs and beaten egg. The stuffed olives are then dipped in beaten egg and rolled with breadcrumbs before being deep-fried until golden (see the recipe for Olive Ascolane on page 223). Recently, recipes such as olive pâté have been developed, and this is used to boost the flavour of sauces and as a topping for bruschetta.

Origano / Oregano or Wild Marjoram

This small-leaved, long-stemmed herb grows up to 70 cm ($2^1/_2$ feet) high and produces bunches of bushy pinkish flowers when mature. This typical Mediterranean plant can be found growing wild on hillsides, although it is now often commercially cultivated. It has a strong minty flavour and is one of the few herbs that is actually improved by drying. Most recipes that include oregano come from the South, where it is almost as popular as basil.

It goes particularly well with aubergines, especially the preserved variety, and with tomatoes as part of the famous Pizzaiola Sauce (see the recipe on page 57). It is also added to breads and biscuits, sprinkled over pizzas and used to flavour olives. However, contrary to the widespread belief outside of Italy that it makes the sauce more Mediterranean, it should *never* be added to Bolognese sauce.

Panpepato / Peppered Bread

Panpepato is a sweet bread that is made in a number of Italian regions and was the predecessor of Tuscan *panforte*. It gets its name from the addition of copious amounts of ground black pepper to the more usual ingredients of almonds, hazelnuts, walnuts, pine nuts, candied orange and lime peel, wheat flour and honey. The bread is then cooked in a medium oven for 40 minutes and allowed to cool. Sometimes the loaf is also covered in a layer of dark chocolate. (See the recipe on page 230.)

Paprica, Paprika, see Peperoncino

Pepe / Pepper

Of all the exotic spices, pepper is the one that has been most enthusiastically received in Italy. It is believed that Alexander the Great brought it back from India, where it is still grown today. The corns are the fruit of a vine-like plant that climbs up to a height of 10 metres (30 feet), although it is usually cut back to 4 metres (12 feet) so that it is easier to pick and so that it produces compact clusters, each bearing 70-80 peppercorns. India, Pakistan and Indonesia are all producers of pepper.

White peppercorns are mainly used in pale sauces and in dishes where the distinctive flavour is needed. To make white peppercorns, the corns are collected from the trees, then soaked in water to loosen the outer skin. When it is soft, the outer skin is rubbed off and the corn is left to dry in the sun. To get black peppercorns, the fresh corns are fermented with the skins on, then drained before being dried

Right: a variety of chillies strung for drying.

in the sun. Green peppercorns are simply fresh or preserved peppercorns and do not have as much flavour as the dried versions. A fourth variety, the pink peppercorn, is not in fact a real peppercorn at all, but comes from a different tree and lacks the pungent, sharp flavour of real pepper.

To make the most of pepper, it is important to grind it as you need it, because it loses its delicate aroma and piquant taste if stored ready ground. It is also important to buy the best quality peppercorns possible, and to store them correctly. The best white pepper comes from Madras in India, while the best black is from Moluccan Islands and the best green peppercorns from Madagascar.

In Italy, pepper is used whole in salami to add spice, and on hams, such as the air-cured rolled bacon pancetta *arrotolata*, which is covered in coarsely ground pepper. It is also used in stocks and soups, where the long cooking of the whole corn helps to develop flavour. Ground pepper is added to most sauces and is delicious on slices of *lardo di arnaz*, cured pork fat, grilled until translucent and then eaten on a piece of bread. Pepper is the main ingredient of a sauce called Peverada (see the recipe on page 228), which is a speciality of Treviso, and is heroic in Panpepato (see the recipe on page 230).

Below: peperoncini

Peperoncino, Capsico, Diavolillo, Pepe di Cayenna / Chilli Pepper, Cayenne Pepper

It is thought that chilli was brought back from America by Christopher Columbus. It quickly became known as *la droga dei poveri*, 'the poor man's drug', because of its powerful taste that could flavour any food, however dull. It also had the extra benefit of stimulating digestion as well as acting as a disinfectant. In Italy, chilli is very popular in the South, where it is used as a condiment and offered on the tables of restaurants along with the salt and pepper.

Peperoncini are part of the Capsicum (sweet pepper) family, but instead of producing the large mild peppers, the plants bear small fruits of green or fire-red in the shape of little horns. The smallest chillies, called *diavolilli* (little devils) in Abruzzi, are the hottest, while other varieties include the round cherry-shaped red chilli, the long, fat chilli called *sigarette* and the very common cayenne, a small pointed chilli which is dried and powdered to make *pepe di cayenna* or *pepe d'India* (cayenne pepper), much like the Hungarian spice paprika only hotter.

In Italy, chilli is used in a number of recipes, including *spaghetti aglio, olio e peperoncino* (spaghetti with garlic olive oil and chilli), and *penne all'arrabbiata* (pasta quills with 'angry sauce', a chilli-hot tomato sauce). Until recently, chilli has only traditionally been used in the South and the islands. Today, however, it has been embraced by the cooks of every Italian region with more or less enthusiasm. Piedmont uses it in Tumin (Tomino), a small fresh cheese that is preserved in vinegar and oil with garlic and lots of chilli. In fact, it is so hot that is it sometimes called *Tomino elettrico* because it feels like an electric shock on the tongue – hotter still is an explosive version called *atomici*!

Chilli is also used in *tofeia*, a dish of beans and pork cooked with chilli in a special terracotta pot, as well as in Salsa Verde (green sauce, see the recipe on page 224). The further south you go, the more this powerful 'drug' is used. The peppers can often be seen hanging in long strings from people's balconies and windows, ready to be added liberally to sauces, salamis, sausages, stews and vegetables.

Prezzemolo / Parsley

There are two different types of parsley, both of which are used a great deal in every Italian kitchen, but especially those on the coast because of the herb's affinity with fish. The tightly curled type of parsley is usually used as a garnish, while the common *gigante d'Italia* – with its small, flat leaves – is the variety used for flavouring a large number of recipes.

Parsley is often used combined with garlic as the base of a number of sauces for pasta and seafood. It is also used in seafood salads and with sautéed kidneys, fried sweetbreads, soups, stocks and vegetables such as braised artichokes, carrots and sautéed mushrooms. Parsley is also the main ingredient in the Piedmontese recipe Salsa Verde (see the recipe on page 224) and is a crucial flavouring in aubergine fried *al funghetto*.

Rafano, see Cren

Rosmarino / Rosemary
This evergreen herb grows in all the coastal regions of Italy and most families with a garden or balcony grow a small bush for their own use. The aromatic rosemary needles, with an underside of velvety grey, are carried on woody branches and the plant has an attractive blue flower in the summer.

The herb goes particularly well with any roasted meat. It can also be used, finely chopped, in marinades and in sauces, although it should be used carefully to avoid over-flavouring. If grilled over charcoal, rosemary gives a wonderful smoky flavour to meat and fish. It is best when used fresh as once dried the taste changes slightly.

Left: rosmarino

Ruta / Rue
This bushy little plant (*Ruta graveolens*) has pretty grey-blue leaves which may be used in salads, but with caution because of its sharp bitterness. A branch of rue is sometimes put into grappa to add to its digestive qualities.

Sale / Salt
Salt was the first preserving agent used by man and as a result was extremely valuable, in fact the word 'salary' comes from *salario* meaning that part of people's earnings which used to be paid in salt. Salt is most notably used in the preservation of fish such as cod, anchovies and herrings. However, it is also used to preserve capers and, above all, for curing of all the many and varied pork products.

There are three types of salt, the refined commercial salt, coarse treated sea salt and very coarse untreated sea salt. Sea salt is still made in Trapani in Sicily and in Sardinia by flooding flat areas with sea water and letting this evaporate in the sun. The resulting salt is then treated and refined to make it edible. Some Italians use coarse sea salt when cooking pasta but I like it best on focaccia, when it gives the bread a lovely crunchy quality.

Salvia / Sage
Along with basil, oregano, rosemary and parsley, sage is one of the most popular herbs in Italian cooking and is used in every region. It is a perennial plant with evergreen oval leaves that are velvety to the touch. The grey-green leaves contain a fragrant oil that is delicious with white meat like veal, pork and chicken. Among the most popular ways of using sage are with calves' liver sautéed in butter and in ravioli or tortellini, along with meat and vegetables and Parmesan.

Left: salvia

Senape / Mustard
Around May and June the fields of mustard start to turn deep yellow as the mustard plant flowers. After this, the seed pods form and fill with little black or white seeds, which are then milled and reduced down to a yellow or brown powder. This is then mixed with vinegar, wine or sometimes garlic and anchovies to make a paste that can be used in cooking or as an accompaniment for meats, salamis and fish. Some mustards are flavoured with tarragon or other strong spices and are used in the making of sauces for game. I like the little broccoli-like, unopened flowers of the mustard heads briefly boiled and then savoured with olive oil and lemon juice.

Timo / Thyme
This very popular perennial herb grows wild all over the Mediterranean region. In Italy it is almost easier to find it growing wild on most hills than it is to buy it fresh in shops. The flavour of the very small leaves of this little evergreen plant is quite intense. It suits all meat dishes, especially used in marinades made to tenderize the meat, but is especially suitable for lamb, pork and game. It is part of the *aromi* and has to be used sparingly because of it strength of flavour. Thyme is also used in the preparation of liqueurs such as Strega and Cent'erbe.

Above: timo

Vaniglia / Vanilla
Vanilla comes mostly from the tropical rain forests of Mexico and Central America. It is produced by a perennial vine that climbs to the top of huge trees of up to 30 metres (100 feet) in height. The thin pods, about 15 cm (6 inches) long, contain a

ABOVE: PINUCCIA, OWNER AND CHEF AT THE RISTORANTE S. GIOVANNI IN CASARZA, LIGURIA, WITH HER OWN DRIED HERB MIXTURE.

sticky brownish substance that holds millions of tiny seeds. Before it can be used, the pod has to be cured and fermented for up to six months, then dried before it gives off any flavour or aroma. At this stage, however, it has developed a strong sweet smell.

To make the most of the flavour, the pod should be split open along its length in order to expose the seeds, which are scraped out and used for flavouring. If you cannot get hold of vanilla pods, then look for good quality vanilla essence, which is very expensive and strong and should be used with care. There is also a powdered version for dishes where the seeds and colour of the vanilla are not wanted. Synthetic versions of vanilla essence and powder are far weaker than the real thing.

Vanilla is used almost exclusively in the making of sweets, chocolate, creams, ice-creams, custards and patisserie. It is also possible to use the pods to flavour sugar by placing one or two pods in an airtight jar until the sugar has absorbed the scent. This vanilla sugar can then be used for making custards, or for *panna cotta*, or added to all sorts of puddings and cakes.

ZAFFERANO, ZAFFERANONE / SAFFRON

Saffron has enjoyed a reputation as the king of spices since Egyptian times and was used as currency for trading by the Doges of Venice. Its high price is due to the fact that it has to be picked by hand and that it takes the stigmas of half a million *Crocus sativus* (which only flowers for two weeks) to make a kilo of saffron. Once picked, the stigmas are dried over a low heat, and this reduces their overall weight by eighty per cent. This, combined with the fact that it is widely used in medicine and as a dye makes it extremely rare and very valuable.

The saffron stigmas are sold in small packets of just 1 gram in weight or reduced to a powder. It is best to get the strands as they give the best flavour and colour. To use saffron, soak the strands in water to release the colour and taste before adding them to the dish with the soaking liquid. Saffron is used very parsimoniously in Italian cooking, the most famous recipe being the Milanese Risotto allo Zafferano (see page 178). It is also used in fish sauces and soups, which are really lifted by the warm colour and aroma imparted by the spice. I have developed an ice-cream based on saffron to celebrate the Doges of Venice (see the recipe on page 231).

RIGHT: SUGAR AT THE PFATISCH BAR IN TURIN.

Most saffron is grown in La Mancha in Spain, but Italian saffron comes from the Abruzzi region, and more recently Sardinia, where the longest, richest-coloured stigmas of outstanding quality can be found. There is a much cheaper version of saffron called *zafferanone* which only has a fraction of the aroma of the real thing, but the same colouring properties.

ZENZERO / GINGER

The Romans tried unsuccessfully to bring this root to Europe from the Middle East, although it originates from Asia. In the Middle Ages it started to be used in Tuscany, along with many exotic spices like cardamom, nutmeg, coriander, cinnamon and others to make a bread called Panpepato (see the recipe on page 230) and this recipe is still used today to make *panforte*. The ginger plant, which has only a few leaves and pretty pink or red flowers from a cane-like stem, is cultivated in Africa, China, India, Jamaica and Japan, although the best comes from Australia.

ZUCCHERO / SUGAR

Sugar occurs naturally in almost all foods, although there are a few where it appears in a very high concentration and it is from these that sugar is extracted. Sugar cane, a perennial grass, *Saccharum officinarum*, originated in India before spreading all over the world and now it is mainly grown in the West Indies and Southeast Asia. Other principal sources of sugar are roots like sugar beet, which are cultivated all over Europe and now produce a respectable quantity of sugar.

Making caramel from sugar is a science in itself and requires a fine judgement of both temperature and cooking time, to make sweets like Croccante di Nocciole (see the recipe on page 280) or burnt caramel for Crema Caramello (Crème Caramel).

RIGHT: SUGARED ALMONDS IN TURIN'S BARATTI E MILANO CAFFÈ.

Pinzimonio

CRUDITÉS WITH EXTRA-VIRGIN OLIVE OIL

For 4

2 bunches of spring onions, trimmed
4 small tender artichokes, outer leaves removed, cut into eighths
2 young fennel bulbs, cut lengthwise into eighths
inner tender stalks, plus hearts, of 4 young heads of celery
8 small new carrots
1 ramekin or small dish per person full of extra-virgin olive oil
salt and pepper

Pinzimonio, *also called* cazzimperio *in Rome, is the surprise put on your tables in good trattorias in Tuscany when the first tender vegetables of springtime are available and the newly pressed olive oil is still at its full, peppery strength.*

Put the vegetables in a large bowl containing ice cubes and a little water and place on the centre of the table. Add to each dish of olive oil a teaspoon of salt and a teaspoon of pepper, which will collect at the bottom.

Each guest takes a piece of vegetable, dips it in the oil while trying to collect a little of the salt and pepper, and eats it accompanied by good bread.

Olive Ascolane

STUFFED OLIVES

Makes 48–50

55 g (1¾ oz) butter
300 g (10½ oz) minced pork
300 g (10½ oz) minced beef
grated zest of ½ lemon
1 glass of dry white wine
1 tbsp tomato paste
100 g (3½ oz) salami, very finely chopped
55 g (1¾ oz) mortadella, very finely chopped
55 g (1¾ oz) black truffle, cut into fine shavings (optional)
55 g (1¾ oz) Parmesan cheese, grated
2 tbsp chopped flat-leaf parsley
5 eggs
48–50 very large green olives (preferably Ascolane olives – see page 217)
salt and pepper
freshly grated nutmeg
flour for dusting
breadcrumbs for coating
olive oil for deep-frying
lemon juice, to serve (optional)

Quite a lot of preparation is required for this dish but the result is extremely tasty and most useful for drinks parties or to serve as an antipasto.

Heat the butter in a pan, then add the minced meat, lemon zest and some nutmeg, salt and pepper and fry for a few minutes. Stir in the white wine and tomato paste and cook gently for 30–40 minutes. Leave to cool and then stir in the salami, mortadella, the truffle if using, plus the Parmesan, parsley and 2 of the eggs. Put the mixture in a blender to obtain a fairly soft paste that still has a little texture.

Using a very sharp curved small knife, cut the flesh of each olive from the stone in a spiral fashion to obtain a loose case; the olive should open up like a continuous strip of peel. Stuff each olive case with a little of the filling, reshaping it as a large olive.

Beat the remaining eggs together. Dust the stuffed olives in flour, then coat them with beaten egg and roll in breadcrumbs. Deep-fry in olive oil; to avoid using a lot of oil, do this in a small pan and fry them in small batches. If serving them hot, sprinkle with some lemon juice; otherwise they can be eaten cold.

BRUSCHETTA

MAKES 6

- 1 LOAF CIABATTA BREAD, CUT INTO SLICES 5 CM (2 INCHES) THICK
- 2 LARGE GARLIC CLOVES, PEELED
- 8 TBSP EXTRA-VIRGIN OLIVE OIL
- 2 LARGE RIPE BEEF TOMATOES, VERY FINELY CHOPPED
- BASIL LEAVES
- SALT AND PEPPER

Originally from Abruzzo, this basic dish has conquered all of Italy and it would also seem that its sway is spreading all over the world. From the dialect word, bruscare, *meaning 'to grill' or 'to toast', the slice of very good toasted country bread is rubbed with a clove of garlic and savoured with the best extra-virgin olive oil available. The addition of tomatoes, basil and salt makes it more than a bread to accompany* antipasti.

Preheat the oven to 200°C/400°F/gas6. Place the ciabatta slices on a baking sheet and bake for about 10–15 minutes, until golden brown.

Take out of the oven and immediately rub the garlic cloves over the hot bread. The garlic should melt into the bread. Drizzle about half the olive oil over the bread, then sprinkle the tomatoes on top and add a leaf of fresh basil. Season with salt and pepper and then drizzle over the rest of the olive oil.

Serve immediately while still warm or serve cold as a party snack.

SALSA VERDE

GREEN SAUCE

FOR 4–6

- 6 SALTED ANCHOVY FILLETS, SOAKED IN WATER FOR 10 MINUTES AND THEN DRAINED
- 25 G (3/4 OZ) SALTED CAPERS, SOAKED IN WATER FOR 10 MINUTES AND THEN DRAINED
- 2 GARLIC CLOVES
- LARGE BUNCH OF FLAT-LEAF PARSLEY
- 4 BASIL LEAVES
- EXTRA-VIRGIN OLIVE OIL

At the Trattoria Italia in Castelletto Stura, Piedmont, this unusual salsa verde *is put on each table regardless of whether or not it has been ordered. It is one of those trattorias one always hopes to find, with the mother (Ghibaudo Marianna) cooking the most delicious local specialities. Father and son serve in the restaurant and the rest of the family works behind the scenes. A huge bowl of impeccably cleaned vegetables is also presented to your table with a knife so you can prepare your own salad!*

Chop the anchovies, capers, garlic, parsley and basil very finely with a knife (not in a food processor). Stir in enough olive oil to make a very dense sauce.

It can be eaten with buttered bread or grissini as an *antipasto*, or served with Bollito Mistó (see page 92), also a local speciality.

FRITTELLE DI BORRAGGINE

BORAGE FRITTERS

OR 4–6

- 00 G ($10\frac{1}{2}$ OZ) BORAGE LEAVES AND TOPS (WITH FLOWERS)
- 00 G ($3\frac{1}{2}$ OZ) PLAIN FLOUR
- INCH OF SALT
- EGGS, BEATEN
- LITTLE MILK
- LENTY OF OLIVE OIL FOR FRYING

Borage is not very much used in Italy. A borage soup is made in Naples, otherwise it is added to beans. These fritters are excellent served with aperitifs.

Blanch the borage in boiling salted water for 3 minutes, then drain thoroughly and leave to cool. Sift the flour and salt into a bowl. Whisk in the eggs and enough milk to make a batter with a fairly liquid consistency. Dip a few borage leaves in the batter at a time and shallow-fry in plenty of hot olive oil until golden. Drain on paper towels. Best served warm but they are also good cold.

SALMORIGLIO

DRESSING FOR BOILED FISH

Mix together 3 parts extra-virgin olive oil and 1 part lemon juice. Add some freshly chopped parsley and pour over boiled fish.

RISOTTO ALL'ISOLANA

RISOTTO ISOLA-STYLE

FOR 4

300 G (10½ OZ) LUGANIGA SAUSAGE (SEE PAGE 77)
1 ONION, FINELY CHOPPED
85 G (3½ OZ) UNSALTED BUTTER
400 G (14 OZ) VIALONE NANO OR ARBORIO RICE
L LITRE (1¾ PINTS) CHICKEN STOCK
1 TSP GROUND CINNAMON
60 G (2 OZ) PARMESAN CHEESE, GRATED
SALT AND PLENTY OF FRESHLY GROUND BLACK PEPPER

Isola, south of Verona, is the area from which this remarkable risotto comes. The unique use of cinnamon reflects the influence of nearby Venice, which imported spices from the East during the Middle Ages.

Take the sausagemeat out of its skin and crumble it. Gently fry the meat and onion in 55 g (1¾ oz) of the butter until the onion is translucent and the meat is slightly browned.

Prepare the risotto in the usual way (see page 175), then remove from the heat, add the cinnamon and the rest of the butter and stir to mix well. Serve topped with the Parmesan cheese.

FETTUNTA

TUSCAN TOASTED BREAD

FOR 4

8 SLICES OF TUSCAN COUNTRY-STYLE UNSALTED BREAD
1 GARLIC CLOVE, PEELED
6 TBSP TUSCAN EXTRA-VIRGIN OLIVE OIL
SALT AND PEPPER

From fetta *(slices) and* unta *(oiled), this is exactly what it says. The Tuscans eat it with* antipasti *or by itself as a snack. In Lazio and other parts of the South it is called* bruschetta, *not to be confused with the tomato version on page 224.*

Toast the bread on both sides, then gently rub with the garlic. Drizzle over the olive oil, sprinkle with salt and pepper and eat warm.

PATÉ DI OLIVE NERE

BLACK OLIVE PASTE

MAKES 400 G (14 OZ)

500 G (1 LB) FIRM BLACK OLIVES
25 G (¾ OZ) SALTED CAPERS, SOAKED IN WATER FOR 10 MINUTES AND THEN DRAINED
4 ANCHOVY FILLETS
1 TSP FRESHLY GROUND BLACK PEPPER
1 SMALL CHILLI, CHOPPED (OPTIONAL)
PINCH OF FRESH OR DRIED OREGANO (OPTIONAL)
125 ML (4 FL OZ) EXTRA-VIRGIN OLIVE OIL

This makes a welcome spread for crostini *or is served with bread as an* antipasto. *The paste can also be made with green olives, although the anchovies are then replaced by ground almonds.*

Stone the olives, taking care that no hard fragments remain.

Put all the ingredients except the oil in a liquidizer. With the motor running, add the oil a little at a time until you have a spreadable paste. No salt is necessary because of the olives, capers and anchovies, which are already salted. If you include the chilli, reduce the amount of black pepper.

Penne all'Arrabbiata

PENNE WITH ANGRY (CHILI-HOT) SAUCE

For 4

90 ML (3 FL OZ) EXTRA-VIRGIN OLIVE OIL
1 SMALL ONION, FINELY SLICED
FRESH OR DRIED CHILLI, AT YOUR DISCRETION AND TASTE
1 GARLIC CLOVE, COARSELY CHOPPED
600 G ($1^1/_4$ LB) TOMATOES, PEELED, DESEEDED AND FINELY CHOPPED (OR THE EQUIVALENT OF POLPA DI POMODORO – SEE PAGE 118)
6 BASIL LEAVES OR 3 TBSP COARSELY CHOPPED FLAT-LEAF PARSLEY
400 G (14 OZ) PENNE RIGATE
SALT

This sauce has gained worldwide popularity through the multitude of Italian restaurants and trattorias. It is also eaten in every region of Italy. Arrabbiata *means angry, and the sauce is so-called because of the abundance of chilli it contains. Penne is the usual pasta for serving with it.*

Heat the oil in a pan, add the onion, chilli and garlic and fry for 1 minute. Stir in the tomatoes and cook, not too violently, for 6–8 minutes, then add the basil or parsley and some salt.

Cook the pasta in boiling salted water until *al dente*. Drain and mix with the sauce, allowing it to absorb the flavours for a minute. No Parmesan cheese here!

ARRABBIATA SAUCE READY TO BE ADDED TO THE PASTA.

Peverada di Treviso

TREVISO PEPPER SAUCE

For 4–6

- 4 tbsp extra-virgin olive oil
- 1 onion, very finely chopped
- 1 carrot, cut into very small cubes
- 100 g (3½ oz) speck (see page 84), cut into strips, then into small cubes
- 3 anchovy fillets, finely chopped
- zest of ¼ lemon
- 300 g (10½ oz) very fresh chicken livers, cleaned and very finely chopped
- 5 tbsp dry white wine
- 1 tbsp white wine vinegar
- 1–2 tsp black pepper, not too finely ground
- 100 ml (3½ fl oz) chicken stock
- 2 tbsp finely chopped flat-leaf parsley
- salt

In and around the town of Treviso in Northern Italy, this sauce, not to be confused with the totally different peara *of Verona, is a must for serving with chicken, guinea fowl, pigeon and most game. It comes in many versions but the abundant use of black pepper is its main characteristic. If you simmer it to evaporate the moisture it can also be used as a spread for* crostini.

Heat the oil in a pan, add the onion, carrot and speck and fry for a few minutes until the onion becomes translucent. Add the anchovies, lemon zest and chicken livers and stir-fry for 5 minutes, then add the wine, vinegar, black pepper and some salt and cook, stirring from time to time, for 5 minutes. Add the stock, reduce the heat and simmer for 5 minutes.

Just before serving, stir in the parsley and adjust the seasoning with salt and pepper.

Pesto alla Genovese con Trofie

PESTO WITH TROFIE PASTA (SEE PAGE 167)

For 4

- 400 g (14 oz) trofie pasta

For the pesto:

- 45 g (1½ oz) freshly picked basil leaves, preferably Ligurian small-leafed basil
- 10 g (⅓ oz) coarse sea salt
- 25 g (¾ oz) pine nuts, toasted
- 2 garlic cloves, roughly chopped
- 55 g (1¾ oz) Parmesan cheese, grated (if you prefer a stronger sauce, use pecorino instead)
- 125 ml (4 fl oz) Ligurian extra-virgin olive oil

One of the most famous Italian sauces, pesto is served with pasta, minestrone and other dishes. Here it is accompanied by trofie, a type of pasta twirl which is still hand-made in Liguria; elsewhere the commercially produced version is very good. Another typical Ligurian pasta, trenette, is sometimes cooked with a few potatoes and green beans and then dressed with pesto. Many versions of this sauce exist; this is representative of them all.

You could put all the ingredients for the pesto in a food processor and after a few seconds it is all over. However, the taste of real pesto is obtained using a pestle and mortar. Put the dry basil leaves in a mortar with the salt, pine nuts and garlic. Rotate the pestle to grind all the ingredients, using the salt at the bottom of the mortar to help break them down. Work like this for a while until you see a pulp starting to form. Still working with the pestle, add the cheese a little at a time and pound until it has all been absorbed and a thick paste has formed. Now start to pour in the oil a little at a time and work with the pestle until it has all been absorbed.

Cook the pasta in boiling salted water until *al dente*, then drain, keeping 2 or 3 tablespoons of the cooking water. Put the pesto in a pan, dilute with the reserved cooking water and just warm through. Mix with the pasta and serve.

Fegato al Balsamico

CALVES' LIVER WITH BALSAMIC VINEGAR

FOR 4

8 THIN SLICES OF CALVES' LIVER
45 G ($1\frac{1}{2}$ OZ) BUTTER
4 TBSP BALSAMIC VINEGAR
SALT AND PEPPER
FLOUR FOR DUSTING

This delightful dish is very popular in the North, especially in Emilia-Romagna where balsamic vinegar is made.

Dust the slices of liver with flour and shake off any excess. Melt the butter in a large pan. As soon as it is hot, increase the heat and fry the liver very briefly – about $1\frac{1}{2}$ minutes on each side. Add the vinegar and stir to scrape up the sediment from the base of the pan. Season the liver with salt and pepper and serve immediately.

Patate al Rosmarino

POTATOES WITH ROSEMARY

FOR 6–8

1.5 KG ($3\frac{1}{4}$ LB) WAXY POTATOES
A FEW SPRIGS OF ROSEMARY
4 SAGE LEAVES
ABUNDANT TUSCAN EXTRA-VIRGIN OLIVE OIL FOR FRYING
SALT

Rosemary has such an intense flavour that it should be used carefully. Potatoes, however, can take strong flavours, especially when combined with peppery Tuscan olive oil, as in this recipe. Potatoes cooked in this way can accompany any meat dish.

Peel the potatoes and boil them in lightly salted water for 10 minutes. Drain and cut into 2 cm ($\frac{3}{4}$ inch) cubes.

Put a good layer of olive oil in a large frying pan over a medium heat and add the potatoes. Cook until tender and brown, stirring often to ensure that the potatoes brown on all sides. Add the rosemary and sage half way through cooking and season with salt just before serving.

PANPEPATO

PEPPERED BREAD

MAKES 1 LOAF (SERVES 6–8)

- 85 G (3 OZ) ALMONDS, BLANCHED, SKINNED, TOASTED AND CHOPPED
- 85 G (3 OZ) HAZELNUTS, TOASTED AND SKINNED
- 85 G (3 OZ) WALNUT HALVES
- 55 G (1¾ OZ) PINE NUTS
- 55 G (1¾ OZ) MUSCAT RAISINS, LEFT TO SOAK IN A FEW TBSP VIN SANTO FOR 30 MINUTES, THEN DRAINED
- 60 G (2 OZ) BITTER COCOA POWDER
- 100 G (3½ OZ) MIXED CANDIED PEEL, CUT INTO SMALL CUBES
- ½ TSP GROUND CINNAMON
- ½ TSP GROUND CORIANDER
- ½ TSP FRESHLY GRATED NUTMEG
- 1 TSP FRESHLY GROUND BLACK PEPPER
- 125 G (4½ OZ) ACACIA HONEY
- PLAIN FLOUR TO BIND

This is another ancient speciality based on spices. In this case the name comes from the predominance of black pepper. Various versions exist in different regions but Tuscany still remains the main consumer of this delightful cake. This recipe comes from a pâtisserie in the town of Gubbio.

Preheat the oven to 160°C/325°F/gas3. Mix all the ingredients together in a bowl, adding enough flour to obtain a fairly stiff mixture. Shape with wet hands into a round loaf and place on a buttered baking tray. Bake for 30 minutes, then leave to cool before serving.

GELATO ALLO ZAFFERANO

SAFFRON ICE-CREAM

FOR 6

600 ML (1 PINT) MILK
PINCH OF SAFFRON POWDER
8 EGG YOLKS
125 G ($4^1/_2$ OZ) CASTER SUGAR
175 ML (6 FL OZ) DOUBLE CREAM

This is more my own contribution to the ice-cream world more than a traditional speciality. It was my aim to celebrate saffron, one of the most sought after and expensive spices in the world. I believe it constitutes an expression of modern Italian cooking without being too clever.

Bring the milk to the boil in a pan and add the saffron. Beat the egg yolks and sugar together in a bowl until foamy and then gradually pour in the milk, stirring all the time, to obtain a velvety mixture.

Pour the mixture into a bowl set over a pan of very hot water, making sure the water is not touching the bowl, and cook, stirring, until it begins to thicken.

Add the double cream, mix well, then transfer to an ice-cream maker and freeze. If you do not have an ice-cream maker, pour the mixture into a shallow bowl and place in the freezer for about 1 hour, until it is beginning to solidify around the edges. Whisk it well with a fork, then return to the freezer. Repeat this process 3 times and then freeze until firm.

DAIRY PRODUCTS

LATTE E DERIVATI

Milk is the first food mammals receive when they are born, and it continues to give warmth and nourishment until the youngster is able to take solid food. Today, I still dip bread into a bowl of milk when I want a comforting snack. The amazing transformation of milk into cheese is almost as old as humanity. It is a miracle that is brought about by a coagulating agent, either from the stomach of a milk-fed calf or an artificial chemical or vegetable coagulant from the flower of the cardoon, or the milk of the fig plant or even from some fungi. When the coagulant is added to the milk, the whey separates from the curds, producing a mass which can be strained, pasteurized, fermented or aged, until it turns into what we know as cheese.

Everyone in Italy consumes quite a lot of milk daily. Children have their *scodella di latte* with biscuits, and either at home or at a bar before going to work adults have a cappuccino with a brioche for breakfast. Some of the milk is used fresh, some is turned into yoghurt, the rest is turned into cream, butter and cheese. Lately cream has become very popular in cooking. Although it is pleasant to eat, I find it makes everything taste the same. In my restaurant, cream is not used widely. Cream is, however, important for pâtisserie and very important in the making of ice-cream, a product of which the Italians are very fond and knowledgeable about. Italian soft cheeses like mascarpone, which is over 60% fat, are much used in desserts.

Each Italian region produces their own distinctive dairy products, which are hardly known in other regions. For example, on the Eastern part of the Italian Riviera *quagliata* (or as they call it in Ligurian dialect, *prescinsoeua*), a coagulated milk similar to junket, is used mixed with pesto sauce or eaten on its own sweetened with sugar. While in other parts of Italy *cagliata*, a sort of Italian unfermented yoghurt, is eaten with fruit.

One of the images of my childhood in Piedmont is the exodus of the cows to the mountains as soon as the snow had melted, the herds accompanied by a smiling and brown-faced cow-boy or girl. The cows would return in the autumn after having spent a very productive summer. With their huge bells hanging around their necks, you can hear them far away in the valley. Everybody in the village turns out to see the spectacle of hundreds of cows, led by the *reine* – or Queen – and the major bull, both decorated with flowers and bows in the colours of the Italian flag. They really looked liked they were coming back from their holidays, and I can still smell the

ABOVE: SHEEP GRAZING ON SPRING PASTURE IN SICILY.

strong-scented leftovers on the road which people collected to put in their geranium pots!

Fortunately, the inhabitants of the Aosta Valley still have their sense of tradition in annually pursuing, among other festivals, *La Bataille des Reines*. It takes place near Aosta between the more belligerent cows, not the bulls. This demonstration of their determination is not a cruel spectacle; the farmers place bets on which cow will win – the losing cow just abandons the fields.

If, by chance, you find yourself in Aosta Valley in the Valle di Champoluc, take the cable car to the crest and visit my very good friend Nina Burgai. You cannot possibly miss her, she is one of the three inhabitants of this wonderful tranquil spot, where she runs a small hotel. As soon as you arrive she will probably offer you a coffee, into which she may put a knob of her own butter (as she always does for me). The butter is made locally at 2,000 metres, where Nina's happy cows roam. The creamy milk is put in a large copper bowl and then into a small storehouse that sits over the burbling cold mountain stream. The butter has a unique fragrance and is like a light and foamy cream when it is in the

coffee; it is not oily and fatty as you might imagine. The taste and smell of all those minty grasses and herbs of the high mountain pasture are reflected in the foam – a unique experience.

Of course, the most important category of dairy products is cheese. During the cheese-making process and depending on the kind of milk used and the results required, the cheese can be drained in perforated baskets made out of willow, plastic or stainless steel and the resulting mass pressed together. It can then either be immersed in brine, or salt can be added directly to the cheese as a preservative, before it is left to age.

Because of its geographical position and its array of different landscapes, Italy has a great history of cheese-making. Starting from the luscious North, some of the Alpine slopes are carpeted with the juiciest and most aromatic pasture imaginable. Farther down towards the Po, is the region of Emilia-Romagna, which is the home of what is perhaps the most prestigious – and certainly most famous – Italian cheese, Parmesan. From Liguria towards the Apennines, the vegetation becomes sparser and sparser until in Puglia and Calabria, Sicily and Sardinia, the type of farming is totally different, and sheep's and goats' milk gradually replaces cows' milk in cheese-making. Most of the cheeses are hard for grating, but you will also find soft fresh cheeses such as ricotta, caciotta and many others.

Just south of Rome and in the Naples region, were originally buffalo territory and here are to be found hundreds of small artisanal producers of specialities using buffalo milk. Now, however, delicious buffalo mozzarella is produced all over Southern Italy, as well as industrial versions using cows' milk made in the North.

As the Italian dairy industry has grown, laws have had to be implemented to safeguard the good quality and the origin of the best cheeses. *Consorzi*

TOP RIGHT: (LEFT TO RIGHT) MATURE PECORINO SARDO, FRESH PECORINO, PECORINO WITH PEPPER, ACCOMPANIED BY FRESH BROAD BEANS.

RIGHT: GOATS ON THEIR WAY TO MARKET IN SICILY.

FAR LEFT: CHEESES AND BUTTERS OF THE LANGHE IN PIEDMONT: INCLUDING CASTELMAGNO, TOMA, RASCHERA, BIANCO SOTTO BOSCO, TOMINI AND CAPRINI, WITH CHESTNUTS AND RED VINE LEAVES.

LEFT: CHEESES FROM BATTIPAGLIA IN CAMPANIA: INCLUDING BURRINO, PROVOLETTA, SCAMORZA AFFUMICATA, MOZZARELLA AFFUMICATA, RICOTTA SALATA, RICOTTA FRESCA, MOZZARELLA FARCITA, MOZZARELLA, BOCCONCINO WITH MASCARPONE.

are cooperatives or agencies of the producers of the same type of cheese. Their self-imposed systems of production control ensure that each member uses only the best local milk and makes the cheese in the traditional manner, in some cases by methods that have been followed for centuries. These cheeses are DOC (*Denominazione di Origine Controllata*), protected in just the same way as fine wines, the equivalent of France's *Appellation Contrôlée*.

Usually DOC cheeses have their own brand or stamp on the rind and in many cases the cheeses are numbered and dated so that their authenticity can be checked more effectively. In the case of such cheeses, the milk that is used to produce them has to be from a certain type of cow. For example, the original brown cows whose milk was used to make Parmesan cheese could only be milked by human hands (I don't blame them), rejecting the much more convenient but soulless machines. This is just one of the many reasons why Parmesan is so expensive.

Italian cheeses are classified first by the milk used and then by their consistency, and sometimes by the methods used in their manufacture. Starting with milk, there are four different varieties:

Cows' milk: mostly available in the North and used for most of the familiar soft and hard cheeses, like mascarpone, Gorgonzola and Parmesan.
Buffaloes' milk: produced almost exclusively in the regions of Lazio, Campania, Puglia and Calabria, and almost all of it used to make mozzarella. The most famous *mozzarella di bufala* is made in the Battipaglia near Salerno. Nowadays, however, buffalo milk is either mixed with – or totally replaced by – cow's milk in much mozzarella manufacture, to make a more economical (but not necessarily better-quality) cheese.
Goats' milk and *sheep's milk*: the areas in which these milks are more widely produced are Tuscany, Lazio and the entire South, including Sicily and Sardinia. There is a return to their production, due to increasing popular demand for pecorino and caprino.
The main cheese consistency categories are:
Formaggi a pasta molle (soft cheeses), which include all fresh cheeses. They have a content of more than 40% water and must be consumed soon after production as they are best when eaten fresh. Cheeses in this group include mascarpone, mozzarella, formaggella and robiola.

RIGHT: SHEEP BEING GATHERED TO GO UP TO GRAZE ON THE MOUNTAINS IN PIEDMONT.

Formaggi a pasta dura (hard cheeses), to which *stagionati* or aged cheeses belong, have a water content of less than 40%. The longer hard cheeses age, the more water evaporates and the harder the cheese becomes. It is then used grated for sprinkling on top of dishes and in cooking. Obviously, cheeses like Parmesan and pecorino belong to this category.

Fat content categorizes cheeses further with: *formaggi magri* (low-fat cheeses), with a fat content of less than 20%; *formaggi semi grassi* (half-fat cheeses), having a fat content of 20-42%; *formaggi grassi* (full-fat cheeses), with a fat content of over 42%. The fat content is determined by the milk used, which can be either *scremato* (skimmed), *parzialmente scremato* (semi-skimmed), *inero* (full fat) or *con aggiunta di panna* (with added cream).

Cheese can also be either pasteurized, indicating that it has been heat-treated to kill any bacteria, or left unpasteurized to make *pasta cruda*, cheeses that continue to develop as they age. *Formaggi fermentati*, fermented cheeses, belong to this second group and include cheeses such as caciocavallo and provolone, both of which are made with partially pasteurized milk.

Some cheeses are made for eating on their own and are called *formaggio da tavola* or table cheeses, while others are made for use in cooking and are called *formaggio per cucina*. When buying cheese for the table, you should always buy from the best shop so that you can be sure of good quality. If you are not sure, ask for information about how to keep or serve a cheese. If you are having a formal lunch, either serve one exceptionally good cheese or a selection of six cheeses, of which three should be soft and three semi-hard, including at least one blue cheese.

Cheese should be served when it is at the peak of its maturity, with a variety of breads and grissini, and a few curls of butter, toasted hazelnuts, walnuts, small bunches of red grapes, pieces of fresh pear and celery. Keep cheese in the least cold part of the refrigerator and take it out at least an hour and a half before serving. I personally only keep the very fresh cheeses like ricotta and mozzarella in the refrigerator.

BELOW: MILKING EWES BY HAND IN PIEDMONT.

A-Z of Dairy Products

Asiago
This cheese has been made since medieval times, although it has only been eaten all over Italy since the beginning of this century. There are three varieties: asiago d'allevo, asiago pressato and asiago grasso di monte.

The first, asiago d'allevo, is a half-fat hard cheese with a smooth crust made from cows' milk. Quite a compact cheese with holes in the paste, it has a light straw colour and a sweet flavour. The milk for this cheese comes from the cows that graze on the Altopiano di Asiago, the Alpine pastures of Veneto. Formed into rounds with a diameter of about 30-36 cm (12-14 inch), 9-12 cm (4-5 inch) in height and weighing 8-12 kg (18-27 lb), it is one of the region's most interesting cheeses. It is aged for varying amounts of time: for six months, when it is known as *mezzo anello*; 12 months, when it is known as *vecchio*; 18 months, when it is called *stravecchio*; and finally for 2 years, when it is known as *vecchio di montagna*. Only *mezzo anello* is eaten at the table, otherwise the cheese is used for cooking and grating, especially with polenta, pasticciata, raviolini and *sopa acquada*, amongst other dishes.

The second variety of asiago is asiago pressato, a semi-cooked, full-cream cows' milk with a fat content of 44 per cent which comes in drums with a diameter of 30-40 cm (12-16 inches), weighing 11-15 kg (24-33 lb). It takes between 20 and 40 days to mature and is mainly eaten at table. It is made in the whole of the Veneto area and so does not carry the guarantee of quality conferred by the DOC label.

The third variety of this cheese, asiago grasso di monte, is a full-fat soft cheese made only between June and September in the Altopiano di Asiago, from the full-cream milk of cows that graze on pastures 1,000 metres (3,000 ft) above sea level.

Bagosso, Bagoss, Bagolino
In the Caffaro Valley in the province of Brescia (Lombardy), cows' milk is used to produce these half-fat round cheeses, weighing about 14-16 kg (32-36 lb), which can be eaten fresh at 3 months or aged up to 24 months and used for grating or cut into slices and grilled. It is very much the local *formaggio da tavola*.

Bel Paese
This is probably the first cheese to be commercialized on the grand scale. Produced by the company Egidio Galbani around the turn of the century, Bel Paese (meaning 'beautiful land') is a soft cows' milk cheese with a creamy yellow colour and a fat content of 45%. Used initially as a table cheese, it is now widely used for cooking because of its melting properties, especially in pasta timbales or in the modern *toast al formaggio e prosciutto* (ham and cheese toast). Due to the increasing popularity of other cheeses, the Bel Paese is disappearing more and more from Italian cheeseboards and restaurants.

Left: Bel Paese

Bitto
From the province of Sondrio in Lombardy, comes this well-known half-fat cooked cheese which is mostly used for grating or for cooking, depending on its age (up to 1 year). The cheeses weigh between 18 and 25 kg (39 and 55 lb), and their taste is mellow and fragrant. Bitto is used in making Pizzoccheri (see the recipe on page 181), but it is also eaten as a table cheese, accompanied by the famous local wines, like Sassella and Grumello.

Bocconcino
From the diminutive of *boccone* meaning 'mouthful', this term is used in various connections but always regarding food. Bocconcino has been generally adopted to indicate a small mozzarella, the size of a walnut, which is used for party food or for salads with tomatoes.

Bra
This semi-hard, half-fat (32%) cheese made with semi-skimmed cows' milk comes from the town of Cuneo in the province of Piedmont. Its name is taken from the little town of Bra, which is reputed to be the commercial centre of the production of the cheese. The cheese is sweet-tasting, mild and flavoursome, with little holes in the paste and a white centre. There are two versions: the fresh cheese, which is matured for 45 days and used as table cheese and for cooking; and the aged one, which is matured for one year, to produce a semi-hard cheese which is good for grating. Bra comes in rounds with a diameter of 30-40 cm (12-16 inches), 7-9 cm ($2^3/_4$-$3^1/_2$ inches) high and weighing around 6-8 kg (13-18 lb).

Branzi
This country cheese from the Brembana Valley in Bergano, Lombardy, is made from cows' milk and comes in two varieties: one made with full-cream milk mixed with semi-skimmed and the other with just full-cream milk. The best is produced between June and July, when the cow have grazed on lush mountain grass.

The curds are twice cooked at 45°C (113°F), then broken. The curds are put into wooden moulds 40-45 cm (16-18 inches) in diameter and 9-12 cm ($3^1/_2$ - $4^3/_4$ inches) high, and pressed to squeeze out the whey. The moulds are then topped up before being put into a salt brine for 3-4 days. The ageing takes place in a temperature-controlled room at 10-13°C (50-55°F) and the cheeses

Above: a traditional way of shaping butter.

are turned every second day for 3 to 6 months.

Branzi is an excellent semi-soft cheese of exceptional quality and is mostly used at table or for cooking delicately flavoured dishes.

Bris, Brôs, Brüs, Brussu

This cheese is a speciality of Piedmont, made with a variety of cheeses that are cut up into small pieces and then put into a jar to ferment for a few days. After this time, grappa is added to the jar and this is then left to age for couple of weeks to make a creamy cheese for spreading on bread or polenta (see the recipe on page 252). Because it is a preparation made by individual families, there is a great deal of variation of the exact recipe, with the addition of other flavourings like oil, pepper, wine and chilli. I think that the sharp tang of this cheese has been deliberately created so that it has to be washed down with the local wines, Barolo or Barbera.

Burrata

This is one of the most delicate fresh cheeses to have been developed in the last eighty years and, thanks to the family in Puglia that have created it, it now supports a whole cottage industry. It is similar to mozzarella although slightly creamier, being a soft ball made up of layers of cows' milk cheese. It should be eaten within 24 hours of being made. This full-fat cheese is eaten as a dessert, served with a little salt, pepper and sometimes a little extra-virgin olive oil.

Burrino, Butirro

This ancient method of preserving butter was developed because the high temperatures in the South would otherwise only allow butter to be kept for day or two. The principle in burrino, or butirro as it is called in the area of Avellino and Sorrento, is to include the butter in a sealed envelope of cheese.

A round casing is made with a *pasta filata* of cows' milk, as with provolone and mozzarella. The curds are worked initially by hand, as in the making of mozzarella, to spin it into strings which will result in layers in the finished cheese. When shaping the pear-shaped cheeses, an opening is left on top to allow the insertion of a ball of butter 3-4 cm ($1^{1}/_{4}$ - $1^{1}/_{2}$ inches) in diameter. This is then sealed and the cheeses put to dry by hanging them in pairs on a cane. After one week the exterior will have hardened a little and the butter inside will confer a wonderful soft taste. Each pear can weigh from 200-400 g (7-14 oz) and can be kept for a month or two. The cheese is eaten cut into slices with bread, and the butter used as such.

Burro / Butter

Butter is obtained by collecting the cream off the top of the milk. After allowing the cream to undergo a little natural fermentation to develop flavour, it is put in a revolving container and churned until a clotted mass of the fat results, and the excess water discarded. This mass is then pressed into rectangular shapes for packaging.

Right: a shop selling dairy products in Cocconato.

Italian butter is generally unsalted and is especially flavoursome, particularly when made with Alpine milk. Butter is very much used in the making of cakes, biscuits and tarts, but is used in general cooking mainly in the North. Even there nowadays, however, it is suffering in competition with Southern olive oil for reasons of health. Butter is the dairy product with the highest fat content, at least 82%, and highly saturated.

Cacio / Cheese

Cacio is a generic term for cheese, coming from the Latin *caseum*, mostly used in Tuscany. However, various cheeses take this initial name, as in Caciotta, Caciocavallo or Cacioricotta (see below), to identify a slightly aged ricotta almost turned into cheese.

Caciocavallo

Originally from Naples, caciocavallo is an uncooked cheese made with cows' milk. Using the *pasta filata* method (see page 244), the curds are worked when hot into a stringy mass, which is moulded by hand into a pear shape, then hung to dry. Like burrino, they are tied in pairs (a *cavallo*, from which it possibly gets its name) over a stick. These are then hung from the ceiling for 3 to 12 months, depending on whether they are to be eaten fresh or grated, until dried and matured. The finished cheese weighs around 1-2 kg ($2^{1}/_{4}$-$4^{1}/_{2}$ lb).

Caciocavallo is a speciality of southern provinces like Campania, Abruzzo, Puglia, Calabria and Sicily, although it is also made in the north. In Sicily there is a special variety of caciocavallo made in Ragusa using cows' and sheep's milk which is salted then aged for up to one year. It is used grated as a substitute for Parmesan.

Caciofiore

This cheese from Central Italy is made from full-fat sheep's milk using a vegetable rennet from wild artichokes. It is a soft fresh cheese, sometimes coloured with saffron, to be eaten after 2 weeks, or to be used for cooking.

Cacioricotta, Ricotta Salata / Salted Ricotta

A speciality from Puglia, this is a salted ricotta used for grating on Pugliese dishes. Cacioricotta is a hard, dense cheese that is used locally grated on pasta dishes instead of Parmesan or to make *calzone di cipolle*, an onion *calzone*.

CACIOTTA

Caciotta is a semi-soft cheese made in various regions of Italy, using cows', ewes' or goats' milk. It is round and weighs about 1 kg ($2\frac{1}{4}$ lb). When young and fresh it has a very mild flavour which makes it ideal for children: if matured for about a month, the rind yellows slightly but the cheese stays white although it has a stronger flavour. The most important regions for caciotta are Tuscany, Marche, Lazio, Umbria and Puglia, although the cheese from Tuscany is the best-known and most sought-after. In many regions this name is used to describe a different product, but always one to be eaten as a very young table cheese or for cooking. Caciotta is ideal to eat together with fresh broad beans, accompanied by good bread and a glass of red wine.

LEFT: HAND-MILKING A GOAT IN PIEDMONT.

CAGLIATA, SEE QUAGLIATA

CANESTRATO

Canestro, meaning 'basket', is named after the mesh used to strain the curds. For thousands of years this mesh was made with woven straw or rush, but now it is unfortunately made of plastic. Mainly produced in Puglia, Sicily and Sardinia, canestrato is a semi-cooked cheese made with cows' and ewes' milk and then pressed by hand into the basket. Round in shape, it weighs about 2-3 kg ($4\frac{1}{2}$ - $6\frac{1}{2}$ lb) and is imprinted with the weave of the basket. It is salted in brine then aged for 2 to 6 months, or even longer depending on whether it is to be used fresh or matured for grating. It is used in the same ways as caciotta, and has a mild flavour which strengthens with age.

CAPRINO / GOATS' CHEESE

Italian goats' cheeses are either made from raw goats' milk or with semi-cooked milk. The latter is left to mature for 2 or 3 months and is then used as it is. However, in Liguria and more especially in Piedmont, it is traditional to immerse the cheese in vinegar and oil, sometimes with added chilli. In Alba, there is a new development where the little round cheeses 4 cm ($1\frac{1}{2}$ inch) across and 2 cm ($\frac{3}{4}$ inch) high are preserved in oil with truffle.

There is also an aged version of *caprino* which has a slightly yellower skin but the same white centre and delicate flavour. In the south and in Sardinia, where the tough dry grass is ideal for goats and produces a strong and flavoursome milk, a version called meridionale is made. It comes in little drums with a diameter of 8-18 cm ($3\frac{1}{2}$ -$7\frac{1}{4}$ inches), 4-13 cm ($1\frac{3}{4}$ - $5\frac{1}{4}$ inches) high and weighing 1.3 to 5 kg ($2\frac{3}{4}$ - 11 lb), and is only aged for 20-30 days. This very white cheese with little holes has a hard rind. Formaggini or robiolini is another caprino from the area around Como in Lombardy, but the most famous comes from Valsassina and Montevecchio in the Lambro Valley in Lombardy.

CASTELMAGNO

One of the most popular Piedmontese cheeses, this blue cheese is made in the area around the town of Castelmagno in the province of Cuneo. A semi-hard cheese with only 34% fat content, it is made from cows' milk and a little partially skimmed ewes' milk. The initial curd is hung for 24 hours in cloth to allow the whey to drain out. It is then placed in a large wooden container for 4 to 5 days before being divided into moulds to mature. Each cheese weighs between 3 and 7 kg ($6\frac{1}{2}$ and $15\frac{1}{4}$ lb) and has a diameter of 15-25 cm (6-10 inches) and a height of 12-20 cm ($4\frac{3}{4}$ - 8 inches). It is kept in stone cases at a constant temperature of 10-12°C (50-54°F) for between 4 and 6 months, during which time it develops its unique nutty flavour. It is an excellent white cheese, dotted with green mould, that is mostly eaten as a table cheese.

CASUMARZU / SARDINIAN ROTTEN CHEESE

Sardinian casumarzu is a type of pecorino. You certainly need a strong stomach to enjoy it, because its major characteristic is that it contains little white maggots which are considered to be a delicacy. The maggots are added to a matured pecorino cheese through a little hole in the top, then a few drops of fresh milk are added as well. The cheese is left to develop at room temperature and, when it is ready, the maggots (tasting of pecorino) can be scooped out with bread.

CRESCENZA

It takes 100 litres (22 gallons) of full-cream pasteurized cows' milk to make between 15 and 17 kg ($32\frac{1}{2}$ and 37 lb) of full-fat (48%) crescenza cheese, depending on how long it has been drained. This typical Lombardian soft cheese was at one time made only in the winter months because of its tendency to turn sour. With the help of today's new technology, however, it can be produced all the year round. Crescenza is made by an elaborate procedure which takes place strictly at room temperature. The finished cheese is sold in 18-20 cm ($7\frac{1}{4}$ - 8 inches) squares, 4-6 cm ($1\frac{1}{4}$ - $2\frac{1}{2}$ inches) high and weighing 1.8 - 2 kg ($3\frac{3}{4}$ - $4\frac{1}{2}$ lb), although it is also sold in 200-g (7-oz) chunks enveloped in a special waterproof paper. It should be eaten 5-8 days after it has been made. It has various roles in the kitchen, especially in the speciality of Camogli in Liguria called *focaccia al formaggio*, a delicious thin focaccia stuffed with melted Crescenza. It also makes an excellent dessert cheese.

BELOW: FRESH GOATS' CHEESES WITH HERBS, PEPPER AND ASH.

Above: gelati misti in the Gambrinus Caffè, Naples.

Dolcelatte / Soft Blue Cheese
Literally translated, dolcelatte means 'sweet milk' and the cheese is simply a much milder version of gorgonzola, created by an Italian commercial cheese-making company. It does not have an official denomination, but is one of the best-known Italian cheeses throughout the world.

Fior di Latte / Mozzarella-type Cheese
This cheese, similar to mozzarella, is industrially produced in the north of Italy while mozzarella is made in the south. The main difference between fior di latte and mozzarella is that the former is made from cows' and the latter from buffaloes' milk (see Mozzarella). Fior di latte is sold in 150-200 g (5-7 oz) portions in plastic packets, together with a small amount of its own whey to keep it moist and fresh. It should be used as soon as it is removed from the whey and can be eaten not only raw in salads, like mozzarella, but also on pizzas and pasta.

Fontal
Fontal is the industrial copy of Fontina cheese (below), a very similarly shaped cheese with similar technical characteristics, but with only half of the flavour of fontina. It can be made anywhere outside the Aosta Valley, using cows' milk coming from any other areas.

Fontina
Fontina cheese is synonymous with the Aosta Valley in Piedmont. The tradition of its manufacture is very ancient and it has been produced since the twelfth century. The region is extremely proud of this product, which literally brings the fragrance of the pastures to the table. It is produced by a cooperative of Fontina-makers from 74 towns in the valley.

The cows used to produce the milk come from the Val d'Aosta area and they are very carefully controlled to make sure the cheese maintains a high standard. The milk from these herds has to be used immediately, at most 2 hours after being collected, which is why milk from cows high up in the Alps is transported to a central storage area in Aosta for distribution.

After it has been pressed, it is carefully aged in temperature-controlled cellars. The cheeses are stored on slats and turned every day. The white mould that grows on its surface is cleaned off with a cloth and the cheese is dipped in a saline solution every other day.

Fontina is a full-fat, semi-soft cheese sold in wheels 35-45 cm (14-18 inches) in diameter, 8-10 cm ($3^1/_4$ -4 inches) high and weighing 8-18 kg (18-39 lb). It has a strong orange-brown rind, 2 mm ($^1/_{12}$ inch) thick, while the cheese itself is a soft, elastic pale yellow sprinkled with copious holes. It takes 2-6 months to mature, depending on the maker. Its very sweet flavour makes it ideal for cooking, while its melting quality means it is ideal for fondue, although it can also be eaten raw. It has a high fat content of 45%, one of the highest for an Italian cheese.

Gelato / Ice-Cream
The practice of preserving snow in caves was brought to Sicily by the Arabs. There also snow was mixed with citrus fruit pulp to make early sorbets. The Romans then developed the techniques of mixing snow and ice with fruit and honey. In 1533, Caterina de Medici took this, among many other culinary novelties, with her to France when she married Henri II.

It was, however, a Sicilian, Francesco Procopio, who opened a café in Paris at which new techniques were used to produce real ice-cream, based on cream, eggs and sugar, as we know it today. However, the invention of this product has actually been credited to a French chef of the British King Charles 1, in 1650.

Today ice-cream is synonymous with Italy, where the best artisanal ice-cream is produced. The most famous *gelaterie* are still to be found in Campania and Sicily. Also, like *pizzerie*, you can find Italian-run ice-cream parlours all over the world.

Gorgonzola / Blue Cheese
Thousands of years old, this blue (*erborinato*) cows'-milk cheese originates from the town of Gorgonzola in Lombardy, although today it can also be made in Novara, Vercelli, Pavia, Cuneo Mortara, Milano, Brescia, Como, Cremona and Bergano. It is a full-fat cheese (48%) and comes in a drum 25-30 cm (10-12 inches) in diameter, 16-20 cm ($6^1/_4$ - 8 inches) in height and 6-13 kg (13-28 lb) in weight. The milk used to make it comes from herds that graze the nearby Alps. It was once produced by locals using unpasteurized milk, but today it is commercially made using pasteurized milk with fermentation aids and a selection of moulds called *Penicillium glaucum*, which give the typical blue marbling and unique flavour. It is aged in temperature-controlled caves at 4-5°C (39-41°F) over 2-4 months.

Gorgonzola is an excellent table cheese, but can also be used in

Right: gorgonzola

sauces for pasta or gnocchi, or simply with plain polenta. Torta di san gaudenzio consists of alternating layers of gorgonzola and mascarpone.

Grana Padano, Parmigiano Reggiano / Italian Hard Cheese

It is almost impossible to divide these two cheeses, but the differences between the two are many. Although technically both cheeses are made in almost exactly the same way, there is a perceptible difference in flavour. The history of parmigiano and grana goes back to the twelfth century, when the Po Valley was turned from waterlogged soil to fertile land suitable for the grazing of cows and sheep.

Parmigiano reggiano used to be made only between 1 April and 11 November, but today both types of cheese can be produced throughout the year. However, the cows that produce the milk for parmigiano reggiano can only be fed on grass and hay, but the cows producing the milk for grana padano can be fed on many other foods as well. In general, it takes longer to age parmigiano reggiano than grana padano, and parmigiano reggiano does not contain any additives to aid fermentation.

Parmigiano reggiano can only be made in Parma, Reggio Emilia, Modena, Mantova on the right of the River Po and Bologna on the left of the river Reno. Grana padano is made in the provinces of Alessandria, Asti, Cuneo, Novara, Torino Vercelli, Bergamo, Brescia, Como, Cremona, Mantova on the left of the River Po, Milano, Pavia, Sondrio, Varese, Trento, Padova, Rovigo, Venezia, Verona, Vicenza, Bologna on the right of the river Remo, Ferrara, Forli, Piacenza and Ravenna. In other words parmigiano reggiano can only be made in Emilia-Romagna while regions such as Piedmont, Lombardy, Veneto, Trentino and parts of Romagna are all allowed to make grana padano.

Because they are so dense, Parmesan and grana padano cannot be cut, but are rather forced apart with special knives. If the cheese is well made, a precise line will give a clean breaking point. Parmesan is not only grated over most Italian pasta dishes, except fish ones, but it is also used to flavour omelettes, grated and added to other ingredients as a filling, cut or shaved into slices and sprinkled on carpaccios and into salads. It is also delicious eaten with fruit such as pears, grapes, figs, walnuts or hazelnuts, or even dressed with a few drops of balsamic vinegar.

Manteca

This is the Pugliese version of the butirro, a scamorza cheese filled with butter. See Burrino.

Mantecare

This is a term especially used in Veneto and Lombardy for an operation involving the addition of a knob of butter and some grated Parmesan at the end of making risotto, to make it creamy and shiny. It probably comes from the Spanish for butter *mantequilla*.

Marzolino

Produced in the area around Sienna by Sardinian shepherds who traditionally migrated to Tuscany, this fresh soft cheese similar to caciotta was at one time made from ewes' milk given after the first fresh grass feeding in March. In the past, also, a vegetable rennet made from a wild thistle was used to firm the curds; today, however, animal (sheep) rennet is now employed. The cheese is still oval in shape, weighing 500-600 g ($17^1/_2$-21 oz), with a full and fragrant flavour and it is mostly eaten as a table cheese. A similar cheese, called Baccellone, is produced in the area around Pisa and is made in the spring when the broad beans, with which the cheese is traditionally eaten, are young and sweet (see also Pecorino).

Mascarpone, Mascherpone / Cream Cheese

Initially only made in southern Lombardy, in the province of Lodi, mascarpone is now produced in various Italian regions. Made within 24 hours from pasteurized cream coagulated with citric or 5% tartaric acid, it is a very soft cheese which once it is made has to be consumed immediately. One hundred litres (22 gallons) of cream produce 40-50 kg (90-110 lb) of mascarpone with a fat content of 50% and above.

Mascarpone is seldom used as cheese, but is extremely valuable as an ingredient for sweets and desserts, one of the most famous being tiramisu. It is also used, together with herbs, as a filling for ravioli or as a thickener for sauces. In the past it was packed in small fabric containers, but it is now sold in jars or plastic containers.

Montasio

A DOC cheese from the Friulian region in the north-east corner of Italy, montasio is also made in the provinces of Belluno, Treviso, Padova, Venice (with the main area of production around Pordenone), Gorizia and Trieste. Its name comes from the area around the Montasio Massif in the Roccolone valley. It is made using the milk from Red Pezzata and Alpine Brown cows, which are kept in immaculate pens on the steep hills in the area and away from any pollution from roads.

This hard cheese can be eaten fresh after just a two-hour maturation period, or semi-fresh after four months ageing or fully matured after 12 months. It is a smooth cheese of creamy yellow with medium-sized holes and comes

LEFT: THE REGION OF EMILIA-ROMAGNA ONLY PERMITS THE WARRANTY STAMP ON PERFECT PARMESAN WHICH HAS BEEN AGED FOR A MINIMUM OF 18 MONTHS.

How Parmigiano Reggiano is Produced

The milk is filtered and then left overnight so the cream can rise to the surface and be skimmed off. This skimmed milk, still 1.8-2.1% fat, is mixed with the unskimmed morning milk and then poured into huge double-walled copper cauldrons which allow steam to circulate, thereby regulating the temperature of the milk. The milk is brought to 32°-33°C (90-91°F) and stirred continuously while the rennet is added, and it turns into curds within 10 minutes. Each cauldron contains 1,000 litres of milk, producing about 60-70 kg (130–150 lb) of curds.

The curd is then cut or broken into tiny pieces each the size of a grain of corn and then cut even smaller. Throughout this procedure, the curds and whey are continuously stirred by a mechanical arm. They are then heated to 43°-44°C (109-111°F) for a few minutes and then the temperature is raised to 54°-56° (129-133°F). This process takes 45-50 minutes. The mixture is heated again for another 45 minutes to allow the curds to collect before they are lifted and placed in a large linen cloth still bathed in the whey. The curd is then divided into two even cakes, each of which is put into a new cloth, placed in a metal mould and covered with a round wooden lid that is weighed down to squeeze out any remaining liquid.

The cloth is changed again an hour later, the cheese turned over and the curds reshaped in the mould. This process of turning is repeated every two hours, four or five times until a crust forms. The cheeses are then put into a saline solution, where they are left for one day for every kilogram of weight and turned over every day. After about three days, the cheese is set on wooden slats to dry. After being cleaned of any mould, it is left to develop a crust before being set in a temperature-controlled room at 22°C (72°F) for 6-7 days. The cheese is then heaped into piles, divided by wooden boards, and left in large, airy, high-ceilinged rooms called 'cathedrals' for 6-7 months to dry. During this time, each cheese is turned over every 4-5 days. For the following 6-7 months, it is turned only every 10-12 days. This long ageing process goes some way to explaining the expense of the cheese.

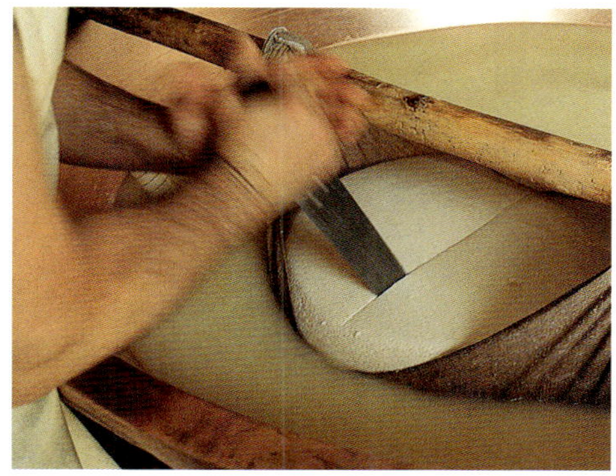

Making Mozzarella Cheese

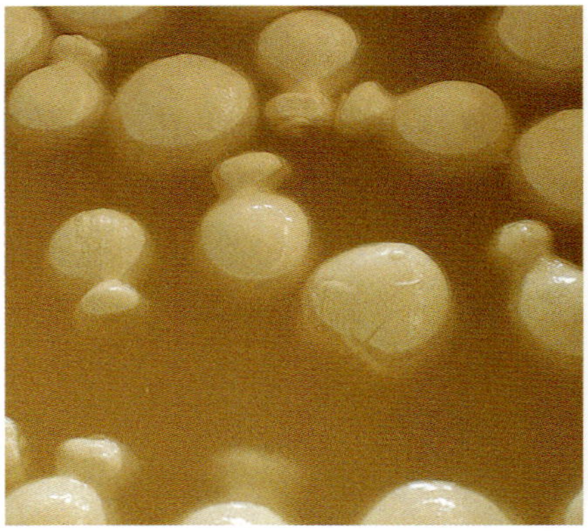

Mozzarella is a fresh soft cheese which should be consumed within 3 or 4 days of being made. The milk is heated to 33-34°C (91-93°F) and the rennet added so that the milk forms into curds and whey. The curds are then left to rest for twenty minutes before being cut into four. After a further ten minutes, the curds are further cut or broken into walnut-sized pieces and left in the warm whey to mature. When a piece of curd placed in almost boiling water breaks into strands (pasta filata), the curds are now ready for spinning.

The curd is taken out of the whey and left to drain on a special table. It is cut into small strips and immersed in water heated to 90°C (194°F). It is then spun by hand and shaped into individual portions varying in weight, including bocconcini (morsels) weighing 30 g (1 oz), ciliegine (little cherries) which are tiny, up to large 600 g (1 lb 5 oz) rounds or long plaits. It may even be wrapped round a stuffing, like that of olives and mushrooms shown. Once it has been shaped, the mozzarella is placed in cold water to cool and harden a little before being placed in salt brine for 30 minutes. Each piece of cheese is then packed in waterproof containers along with some salted water or a little milk and water so that it stays moist. A smoked version, called provola, has a harder yellowish-brown skin.

in small round drums 30-40 cm (12-16 inches) in diameter, 6-10 cm (2½ - 4 inches) in height and weighing 5-7 kg (11-15 lb). It is used at table, but also has a prominent place in Friulian cuisine, where it is grated over various dishes including polenta and carpaccio.

MOZZARELLA / BUFFALO-MILK CHEESE

This southern Italian cheese is named after the technique of tearing apart or cutting (*mozzata*) the whey with the fingers to form balls of cheese. It is mainly produced in Battipaglia in the province of Salerno, but is also made in Caserta and the provinces of Naples, Puglia and Lazio. Authentic buffalo-milk cheese is traditionally produced by only a few specialists, as there is not enough buffalo milk to meet the demands of commercial production.

What makes mozzarella so special is its unusually low fat content. The richness of flavour of the buffalo milk, with only 7 to 7.5% fat content, also gives mozzarella its distinctive taste. The cheese has been made since the thirteenth century and the same techniques used then are still used today. It is said that, in the past, in order to increase milk production the buffaloes were milked one by one to the tune of a lullaby and each one was individually named – real VIP treatment.

Fresh mozzarella has a sweet, nutty and slightly salty flavour and is perfectly white. It should also have a few holes inside, where tears of whey seeped out when the cheese was cut. In Lazio, especially around Rome, another version of mozzarella, called provatura, is made with a mixture of whole cows' milk and pasteurized sheep's milk. It is similar to the original cheese but is harder in texture and with a yellowish colour. A smoked version, called scamorza, is produced in Campania, Abruzzo and Molise. Scamorza is also used to make butirro, see page 239.

Mozzarella is delicious eaten uncooked and sliced, dressed with a little salt and pepper and a trickle of extra-virgin olive oil, and with slices of tomatoes and a few basil leaves in Mozzarella Caprese (see page 137). It can also be used cooked on pizzas and in timbales of pasta.

MURAZZANO / SHEEP'S-MILK CHEESE

This tasty soft fresh full-fat (50-56%)

RIGHT: BUFFALO IN CAMPANIA.

cheese is made mostly with ewes' milk around the area of Murazzano, in Cuneo in the province of Piedmont. Formed into a cylindrical shape 10-15 cm (4-6 inches) in diameter, 3-4 cm (1¼ -1½ inches) high and weighing about 300-400 g (10½ -14 oz), it is white and does not have a crust, because it is immersed in brine before being eaten, which should be within 6-10 days of being ready. It is an exquisite table cheese and is delicious served with olive oil, salt and pepper, or in hot sauces.

PAGLIERINA

This soft full-fat cheese from the area around Turin in Piedmont, is made from cows' milk and is shaped into rounds 10-20 cm (4-8 inches) in diameter and 1-2 cm (½ - ¾ inch) in height. The little discs are briefly left to mature on little straw mats, or *paglia*, from which the cheese gets its name. Paglierina should be eaten as soon as it is ready and makes a wonderful table cheese, especially when served dressed with olive oil and vinegar.

PANNARONE, PANNERONE, PANERONE

This full-fat sweet-flavoured soft cheese from the Lodigiano area in Lombardy is known as 'white gorgonzola', because it has a similar flavour and shape as the famous blue cheese, as well as being made by a similar method although without the mould. It gets its name from *panera*, which is Lombardian for the top of the milk from which it is made. Formed in drums 25-30 cm (10-12 inches) in diameter, 18-20 cm (7-8 inches) in height, weighing 8-12 kg (18-26 lb), it has a smooth, thin, slightly yellow crust and a creamy-white paste. This is one of the very few unsalted cheeses and it should be eaten as soon as it has matured, at about 8-10 days. It is an excellent table cheese that is generally only eaten locally.

PARMIGIANO REGGIANO, SEE GRANA PADANO

PECORINO / SHEEP'S-MILK CHEESE

This cheese is so popular that almost every region makes its own version, each one adapted to suit local ingredients and culinary traditions. Wherever it comes from, pecorino is made in the same way. The difference in flavour between each one comes from the qualities in the local milks and the ageing processes. Pecorino is a semi-cooked hard cheese made with full-fat milk. The drums are about 20-30 cm (8-12 inches) in diameter, 14-22 cm (5½ - 8¾ inches) high and weigh 6-22 kg (13-48 lb). It is a compact, white cheese which is aged for at least 8 months before being eaten at table or grated like parmesan.

By law, pecorino romano can only be made in Lazio in the provinces of Rome, Frosinone, Grosseto, Latina and Viterbo. Exceptionally romano-style pecorino is also made in Sardinia, in the provinces of Cagliari, Sassari and Moro, where three-quarters of all pecorino romano-style cheeses are produced.

Sardinia's own pecorino is called *fiore sardo* or *cacio fiore* and is produced in the same way as other pecorinos, except that it is formed into much smaller rounds, weighing 1.5-5 kg (3¼ - 11 lb). It is ready to be eaten at table after only 2-3 months, although it needs to be aged for 6 months if it is to be hard enough for grating. Sardinian pecorino is very popular in Liguria, despite the fact that Liguria makes its own pecorino, where it is used to make pesto sauce. One pecorino, which is produced in the province of Ragusa, has whole black peppercorns in it.

Prescinsoeua, see Quagliata

Primo Sale / Fresh Cheese

Similar to caciotta, primo sale (meaning 'first salt') is a fresh cows'-milk cheese made in several regions in Italy, including Liguria and Savona. It has to be eaten when extremely fresh and just after it has been through the salting process. In Sicily and the south there is a similar fresh cheese also called primo sale, the only difference being that it is made with ewes' milk.

Provatura

This large mozzarella-type cheese is made to be aged slightly, for a couple of days at least to obtain a stronger flavour and texture. It is sometimes smoked and eaten as a table cheese, or used in cooking. See also Mozzarella.

Provolone, Provoletta, Provoloncino

This peculiar cheese originated in the Basilicata in the province of Potenza and from there it spread all over southern Italy and eventually to the north, where it now flourishes.

It is a compact full-fat cheese made of cows' milk. After the rennet and relevant fermenting agents have been added, as with caciocavallo, the curds are spun in hot water and worked into a large pear-shaped or cylindrical cheese, weighing at least 5.9 kg (13 lb). They can, in fact, reach 1.4 m (4 ft) in height and a weight of anything between 60 and 100 kg (130 and 220 lb). After they have been shaped, they are placed in giant containers and immersed in brine before being hung and bound by special strings which give them their distinctive shape.

The maturing process takes about 12 months, depending on whether the cheese is to be eaten fresh (*tipo dolce*) or aged for grating (*piccante*). The matured cheese is covered with a thin layer of wax to prevent it from being contaminated by bacteria. It is also known as provoloncino or provoletta, as well as many other names depending on the region.

Provolone is eaten as a table cheese and is used in cooking, added in small cubes to stuffings for vegetables and pasta timbales, and also grated on pasta. It has a distinctive texture and flavour, the *tipo piccante* sometimes tasting quite sharp.

Quagliata, Prescinsoeua

This coagulated milk similar to junket is enjoyed all along the Eastern part of the Italian Riviera (in Ligurian dialect, it is known as *prescinsoeua*). It is used there mixed with pesto or eaten on its own sweetened with sugar. In other parts of Italy *cagliata*, a sort of Italian unfermented yoghurt, is eaten with fruit. I remember my grandmother sun-drying milk with a little lemon juice to produce her own.

Quartirolo

This soft, full-fat cheese is made exclusively in Lombardy, in the areas of Como, Milano, Bergamo, Brescia and Pavia. The best, called Quartirolo di Monte, come from Valsassina (Sassina Valley) and from the Quartirolo, and are square in shape like taleggio.

The cheese is made with the milk from cows fed on the fragrant grass of the high pastures of the Quartirolo. The unpasteurized milk is coagulated in small copper cauldrons using rennet and milk enzymes. After the curds have formed, they are put in square moulds, where the whey is drained off. The salting of the cheese takes place after a few days' maturation, when a white mould has formed. For the next 6 to 8 days, the cheese is repeatedly rubbed all over with salt, after which the cheese is ready.

When ready to eat, each cheese weighs about 1.5 kg ($3^1/_4$ lb) and they are then sold in quarters. The compact white cream cheese has a delicate and fragrant flavour reminiscent of mushrooms.

Ricotta / Soft Cheese

As is suggested by its name, meaning literally 'cooked again', this cheese is the product of other cheeses using the residue left after the curd has been lifted. Fresh milk is added to this residue to give a higher yield and then the mixture is brought to the boil. An acidic agent like lemon juice or rennet is then added, and when casein froth forms on the surface it is scooped off and allowed to drain. This froth is the cheese, and there are many types of it made all over Italy.

Ricotta forte: this ricotta from Bari in the province of Puglia is made in the basic way except that salt is added before it is put in wooden containers to cool and dry. Over the next couple of months, the ricotta is moved from one container to another, being worked by hand each time, until all the excess liquid has been forced out. It has a distinctive sharp flavour and is yellow in colour. It is used in a variety of ways, including in calzone mixed with onions.

Ricotta romana: this is cooked a little longer than most others to give a more compact and refined ricotta that can be used in a variety of savoury or sweet dishes.
Fior di Ricotta: this is made with full-cream sheep's milk instead of the cheese residue, to produce a richer ricotta, higher in fat, which

Above: Umbrian ricotta in husks of wheat.

Left: freshly made ricotta.

may be eaten raw but is mainly baked in Pastiera di Grano (see the recipe on page 177), or used as a filling for other desserts.

Ricotta marzotica: this ricotta from Foggia in Puglia is named after the month of March because it is made, salted and aged for 15-30 days during this month. Due to the springtime freshness of the grass, this ricotta is particularly delicate and ideal for filling ravioli or just for eating as a dessert.

Ricotta calabrese condita: this is a variation on the excellent Calabrian ricotta, made in the usual way except that salt and chilli are added before it is dried in an oven to give it a very *piccante* flavour.

Making and Preserving Tomini

The curds are cut and drained, then the tomini shaped by hand into rounds about 4 cm (1/2 inches) in diameter and 2 cm (3/4 inch) in height. They can be flavoured with wine vinegar, before being bottled in oil with added flavourings such as herbs, chillies or truffles.

Ricotta infornata: similar to the Calabrese Condita, this ricotta from Sicily is also dried and salted before being covered with ground black pepper.

Ricotta salata: this salted ricotta is allowed to mature and harden, so it can be used grated on a variety of dishes.

Robiola

This soft cheese, traditionally made with unpasteurized full-cream cows' milk, is now commercially produced using treated milk. Although it is a speciality of Lombardy, it is also made in Piedmont where the cheese has an aromatic, spicy flavour. The drained curd is dipped in brine then matured for 20-30 days. It must then be eaten immediately, as a table cheese. Smaller versions of the same cheese are called robioline.

Robiola delle Langhe is a variation of the main cheese made with a mixture of cows' and goats' milk to give a very distinctive flavour. Another variation, Robiola di Roccaverano, was at one time made only with goats' milk, but is now made using only cows' milk. Robiola is one of the cheeses generally used to make Bros (see the recipe on page 252).

Scamorza

Made using the mozzarella technique, scamorza is produced industrially using mostly cows' milk. It is more consistent in texture than mozzarella and shaped in a way that allows it to be tied with a string or raffia. The cheeses always come tied in pairs, which are hung and sometimes smoked. It is eaten fresh as a table cheese one to three days after it is made. Scarmorza is often also filled with butter for ageing as in butirro.

Taleggio

One of the best-known Italian cheeses, taleggio is eaten at table all over Italy as well as abroad. It is made in the Italian Pre-Alps, in the Taleggio Valley north of Bergamo, where the pastures are particularly juicy and aromatic, and in Savoy there is a consortium of producers who safeguard the quality of the cheese. However, this full-fat cheese (48%) is also made in Brescia, Como, Cremona, Milano, Pavia, Novara and Treviso.

It is matured for 40-45 days, during which time it develops a pinkish crust. It is then sold in squares of 20-30 cm (8-12 inches) about 6 cm (2½ inches) high. The cheese itself is very soft, containing many tiny holes and has a creamy white colour. It should be eaten quite fresh, as it becomes increasingly acidic as it ages.

Toma, Tometta, Tomino

This hard cheese, made with unpasteurized full-fat or semi-skimmed cows' milk, is produced in Piedmont, the Aosta Valley and Liguria. The cheeses are shaped into cylindrical rounds 10-20 cm (4-8 inches) in diameter and 4-8 cm (1½ - 3¼ inches) in height, with an average weight of 2-4 kg (4½ - 9 lb). After it has been salted in brine, it is aged for 30-70 days.

It is essentially a table cheese, with all the flavours of Alpine pastures. When it is fresh it is called tometta and is sold in rounds of a similar shape to the toma and, like paglierina, 12-15 cm (4¾ - 6 inches) in diameter and 2-3 cm (¾ - 1¼ inches) high. The most famous of these cheeses are the carmagnola of Pratonevoso and the caprella, which is made with goats' milk.

Tomino is another fresh toma that is sold in rounds 4 cm (1½ inches) in diameter and 2 cm (¾ inch) in height. It can be flavoured with wine vinegar before being submerged in oil and spiced with either herbs or chilli. The resulting cheese is called *tomini elettrici*, because of its strong flavour. In the Langhe region, tomini are also immersed in oil before being flavoured with Alba truffle to produce an exquisite cheese. The most famous of these preserved tomini are from Chiaverano near Ivrea.

Fonduta con Tartufo

CHEESE FONDUE WITH TRUFFLE

For 4

- 400 g (14 oz) fontina cheese, cut into small cubes
- about 250 ml (9 fl oz) milk
- 6 egg yolks
- 30 g (1 oz) butter
- 45–55 g ($1^1/_2$–$1^3/_4$ oz) white truffle
- salt and pepper

Farmers in Piedmont used to dip bread in this heavenly-tasting sauce made with local ingredients: fontina cheese from the Aosta Valley (irreplaceable for this dish) and white truffles. Due to the incredibly high prices for truffles, this dish is now available only in the finest Piedmontese restaurants. A most elegant and delicious starter, it is very simple to make but needs care.

Put the cubes of fontina cheese in a bowl, pour over enough milk to cover and leave to soak for 2–3 hours.

Place the bowl over a pan of hot but not boiling water, making sure the water is not touching the base of the bowl. Stir gently until cheese melts to form a smooth mixture. At this stage add the egg yolks, butter, a pinch of salt and some pepper. Continue to stir until the mixture thickens to a creamy consistency.

Distribute between 4 small hot bowls. Shave some truffle over and eat with toasted slices of bread cut into strips.

Asparagi alla Emiliana

ASPARAGUS EMILIAN-STYLE

For 4

- 800 g ($1^3/_4$ lb) green asparagus (I prefer the green to the white)
- 100 g ($3^1/_2$ oz) Parmesan cheese, grated
- 85 g (3 oz) butter, melted
- salt and pepper

Asparagus is a wonderful vegetable which goes extremely well with dairy produce. In Emilia-Romagna, and especially in Parma, you can't get away from using the local produce such as butter and Parmesan. This dish announces the arrival of summer.

Peel the lower stem of the asparagus, discarding all the stringy parts. Boil in lightly salted water until the stalks are just tender but still *al dente*, ensuring that the tips are intact.

Drain the asparagus, then arrange the spears all pointing in the same direction on serving plates and sprinkle over the Parmesan cheese. Season with salt and pepper to taste, then pour the hot melted butter over the tips and serve immediately.

Opposite: Fonduta con Tartufo

Torta Rustica di Ricotta

SAVOURY RICOTTA CAKE (SEE PAGE 304)

For 6

- 25 G (3/4 OZ) BUTTER
- 3 TBSP BREADCRUMBS
- 500 G (1 LB 1 1/2 OZ) VERY FRESH RICOTTA CHEESE, PREFERABLY SHEEP'S-MILK RICOTTA
- 4 EGGS, SEPARATED
- 45 G (1 1/2 OZ) PARMESAN CHEESE, GRATED
- 55 G (1 3/4 OZ) PLAIN FLOUR
- 100 G (3 1/2 OZ) MIXED MELTING CHEESES, SUCH AS PROVOLONE, PECORINO, SCAMORZA, ETC, CUT INTO VERY SMALL CUBES
- 100 G (3 1/2 OZ) PARMA HAM, SALAMI, SPECK, ETC, VERY FINELY CHOPPED
- SALT AND PEPPER

Ricotta is a wonderful vehicle for both sweet and savoury flavours. It is very convenient because it is fairly low in fat and mixes perfectly with eggs to produce a delightful and not too heavy result. My mother used to conceal any leftover salami and cheese in this savoury ricotta cake. It was our favourite!

Preheat the oven to 200°C/400°F/gas6. Use the butter to grease a 20 cm (8 inch) ovenproof dish and dust with the breadcrumbs.

Put the ricotta in a bowl. Beat the egg yolks with the Parmesan cheese, flour, a little salt and plenty of freshly ground black pepper. Fold this mixture into the ricotta and then add the cheese and ham.

Beat the egg whites until stiff and fold them gently into the ricotta mixture until it is smooth and light. Pour it into the prepared dish, smooth the top level and bake for 30–40 minutes or until a nice crust has formed.

Turn out on to a serving dish and eat warm. It is also good cold.

Gnocchi alla Bava

GNOCCHI PIEDMONTESE-STYLE

For 6

- 300 G (10 1/2 OZ) 00 (DOPPIO ZERO) FLOUR
- 300 G (10 1/2 OZ) BUCKWHEAT FLOUR
- 2 EGGS
- ABOUT 3 TBSP MILK
- 150 G (5 OZ) FONTINA CHEESE, THINLY SLICED
- 150 G (5 OZ) FRESH TOMA CHEESE, THINLY SLICED
- 55 G (1 3/4 OZ) PARMESAN CHEESE, GRATED
- 60 G (2 OZ) BUTTER
- SALT AND PEPPER

There are many variations on this dish, most of them from Piedmont. Alla bava *means that when you lift the gnocchi from the plate with a fork they should form strings of melting cheese. Most gnocchi are made from ingredients such as potatoes and semolina; unusually these are made from two types of flour.*

Preheat the oven to 200°C/400°F/gas6. Put the flours into a bowl, then mix in the eggs and enough milk to obtain a firm dough. Roll a small part of the dough at a time into a cigar shape. Cut into small chunks about 3 cm (1 1/4 inches) long and run them lightly over the tines of a fork to leave an indent, rolling them off the fork on to a clean cloth. Cover and leave to rest for 30 minutes.

Bring to the boil a large pan of lightly salted water (about 5 litres/9 pints) and cook the gnocchi in it for a minute or two. They are ready when they swim to the surface. Scoop them out with a slotted spoon and arrange them in layers in an ovenproof dish with the fontina, Toma and a little of the Parmesan. Sprinkle the remaining Parmesan over the top, dot with the butter and bake in the oven for 10 minutes. Serve immediately.

Mozzarella in Carrozza

FRIED MOZZARELLA SANDWICH

For 1

- 2 THICK SLICES OF PANE DI CAMPAGNA (COUNTRY-STYLE WHITE BREAD)
- 1 LARGE SLICE OF BUFFALO MOZZARELLA
- MILK
- 2 EGGS, BEATEN
- SALT
- FLOUR FOR DUSTING
- OLIVE OIL FOR FRYING

Originally from Naples and generally from Campania, this dish has spread all over Italy and is to be found mostly in bars as a lunch-time snack. It is delicious when freshly made and still crisp.

Dip the slices of bread in milk for a few seconds but do not soak them. Drain, then place the mozzarella on one piece of bread and put the other on top to make a sandwich. Dip in flour seasoned with salt, then the egg. Shallow-fry in a good quantity of oil for 5 minutes until golden, turning once. Serve immediately.

Formaggio al Tartufo

TRUFFLED CHEESE

For 6

200 g (7 oz) ricotta cheese, preferably sheep's-milk ricotta
55 g (1 3/4 oz) Parmesan cheese, grated
200 g (7 oz) mascarpone cheese
25 g (3/4 oz) fresh Alba truffle, grated (or use fresh black truffle and a few drops of truffle oil)
salt and pepper

If you cannot get hold of truffled cheese it is easy to make yourself – provided you have the most important ingredient, the truffle.

Mix all the ingredients together very well, adding just a little salt and pepper, and leave for a couple of hours for the flavours to infuse.

Formaggio Conciato (Bros)

CURED CHEESE

Makes enough to fill a 1 kg (2 lb 3 oz) jar

800 g (1 3/4 lb) mixed cheeses such as robiola, fresh toma, goats' cheese, fresh pecorino or even gorgonzola
1 chilli, very finely chopped
4 tbsp grappa
1 1/2 tsp freshly ground black pepper
100 ml (3 1/2 fl oz) extra-virgin olive oil
2 tbsp red wine vinegar

This is a typical Piedmontese speciality, made mostly at home. There is an infinite number of combinations but the idea is to use up leftover cheese, which is macerated in oil, grappa and spices for some time to obtain a 'hell of a cheese', as I call it. It is usually eaten either on toast or with sliced polenta. In Apulia there is a similar dish made with ricotta, called ricotta forte.

Put all the cheeses into a bowl and break or cut them into small pieces. Add all the other ingredients and mix well. Put in a jar and then seal. Keep in a cool place and stir every 2 or 3 days. Do this for a couple of months until you have a hot, strong cheese paste which can be kept for a long time. Good luck!

Crocchette di Patate

MOZZARELLA-STUFFED POTATO CROQUETTES

For 4

800 g (1 3/4 lb) floury potatoes
4 tbsp freshly grated Parmesan cheese
3 egg yolks
1 tbsp finely chopped flat-leaf parsley
300 g (10 1/2 oz) buffalo mozzarella, cut into fingers
olive oil for deep-frying
1 egg white, lightly beaten
salt and pepper
dried breadcrumbs for coating

These little croquettes are stuffed with mozzarella cheese. A similar recipe uses rice instead of potatoes and is called suppli *or* arancini *(see page 179).*

Boil the potatoes in their skins until soft. Drain and peel while still warm. Pass them through a sieve to make a purée, then add the Parmesan cheese, egg yolks, parsley, and salt and pepper to taste. Mix well to give a fairly soft dough.

Cover the palm of your hand with the potato mixture. Put a mozzarella finger in the middle and cover it completely with more potato. Shape into a cylinder, making sure the mozzarella is in the centre. Repeat with the remaining potato mixture and mozzarella. Dip each croquette in the egg white, then roll in the breadcrumbs and deep-fry for a few minutes until crisp and brown. Serve warm.

Ravioli Fritti Sardi con Miele

FRIED SARDINIAN PECORINO RAVIOLI WITH HONEY

Makes 8

- 200 g (7 oz) pecorino cheese, thinly sliced
- olive oil for frying
- chestnut honey or other honey, to serve

For the pastry:

- 300 g ($10^1/_2$ oz) flour, preferably 00 (doppio zero)
- 3 eggs
- 100 g ($3^1/_2$ oz) caster sugar

These little pastries filled with pecorino cheese are a Sardinian speciality, served with honey. They are delicious after a light meal.

Sift the flour, make a well in the centre and add the eggs and sugar. Gradually draw in the flour to make a smooth dough, similar to pasta dough. Roll it out to 3 mm ($^1/_8$ inch) thick and cut out 16 circles about 12.5 cm (5 inches) in diameter.

Divide the pecorino cheese between half the pastry circles. Brush the edges of the pastry with water and cover with the remaining pieces of pastry, pressing down gently around the edges to seal.

Heat a generous quantity of olive oil in a large frying pan and fry the pastries until golden brown on both sides. Serve hot with honey.

PANNA COTTA

BAKED CREAM

FOR 4-6

1 LEAF OF GELATINE
500 ML (18 FL OZ) SINGLE CREAM
45 G (1½ OZ) SUGAR
1 VANILLA POD
1 TSP VANILLA ESSENCE
1 TBSP DARK RUM
STRIPS OF CANDIED ORANGE PEEL OR FRESH BERRIES TO DECORATE

This is one of the most fashionable desserts both in Italy and abroad.

Soak the gelatine leaf in a little cold water until soft.

In a heavy-based pan, mix the cream with the sugar and vanilla pod and essence. Bring to the boil. Take off the heat and add the soaked gelatine leaf and the rum. Stir well until the gelatine has dissolved. Pass through a fine sieve and pour into 4-6 dariole moulds. Put in the refrigerator to set.

To serve, decorate with small pieces of candied orange peel or, if you prefer, with fresh berries.

Marroni al Mascarpone

CANDIED CHESTNUTS WITH MASCARPONE

For 4

- 2 egg yolks
- 100 g ($3^1/_2$ oz) caster sugar
- 1 tsp vanilla sugar
- 2 tbsp whisky
- 4 tbsp single cream
- 400 g (14 oz) mascarpone cheese
- 12 whole chestnuts in syrup or marrons glacés
- 12 fresh bay leaves

This is a dessert with abundant calories, to be served mainly in winter after a very light meal.

Beat the egg yolks with the caster sugar, vanilla sugar and whisky to obtain a smooth cream. Beat the single cream into the mascarpone to soften it and then carefully fold in the egg yolk mixture. Put the mixture into a piping bag and pipe 3 equal dollops on to each dessert plate. Top with the chestnuts and then decorate with the bay leaves.

Parmigiano con le Pere e Noci

PARMESAN CHEESE WITH PEARS AND WALNUTS

For 4

- 200 g (7 oz) parmesan cheese
- 4 ripe williams pears
- 100 g ($3^1/_2$ oz) fresh walnuts, peeled
- good pane di campagna (country bread), to serve

This combination is ideal for when new-season walnuts are available and are fresh enough to peel. The skin should come off easily in your fingers. Not really a recipe, this is just an idea for a dessert and one that is very popular in Emilia-Romagna, where the famous cheese comes from.

Break the Parmesan cheese into splinters. Peel, core and slice the pears. Assemble the cheese, pears and walnuts on each plate and serve with the bread.

Tiramisu

For 6

- 3 egg yolks
- 100 g ($3^1/_2$ oz) caster sugar
- 1 tsp vanilla sugar or a few drops of vanilla extract
- 100 ml ($3^1/_2$ fl oz) single cream
- 500 g (1 lb) mascarpone cheese
- 6 cups cold strong espresso coffee
- 4 tbsp coffee liqueur, such as Kahlúa
- 20 savoiardi biscuits (see page 299)
- cocoa powder for dusting

Another Italian speciality that has emigrated to Italian restaurants all over the world, this can be prepared in minutes, is not cooked and yet has a high degree of sophistication and appeal. The name means 'pick me up', and could well be a reference to the number of calories this pudding contains. Whoever invented it must have been in need of quick energy. There are many variations on tiramisu but I prefer this very simple one.

Beat the egg yolks with the caster sugar and vanilla sugar until thick and mousse-like. Beat the single cream into the mascarpone to loosen it, then carefully fold in the egg yolk mixture.

Spread half the mixture over the base of a large shallow serving dish. Mix the espresso coffee and liqueur together in a shallow dish and briefly dip in the savoiardi biscuits one by one, putting them immediately on top of the layer of mascarpone. When you have used up all the biscuits, spread the rest of the mascarpone mixture on top to cover them completely and then chill. Before serving, dust the tiramisu generously with cocoa powder. You could make individual portions in glasses, cups or other small containers.

CASSATA

FOR 4

250 G (9 OZ) MARZIPAN (SEE PAGE 279 OR USE READY-MADE)
1 ROUND OF PAN DI SPAGNA (SEE PAGE 294), ABOUT 20 CM (8 INCHES) IN DIAMETER AND 5 MM (1/4 INCH) THICK
2 TBSP MARSALA
375 G (13 OZ) RICOTTA CHEESE
100 G (3 1/2 OZ) CASTER SUGAR
1/2 TSP VANILLA EXTRACT
25 G (3/4 OZ) CANDIED ORANGE PEEL, CHOPPED
25 G (3/4 OZ) CANDIED CITRON PEEL, CHOPPED
25 G (3/4 OZ) PLAIN CHOCOLATE, CHOPPED
ICING SUGAR FOR DUSTING
ANGELICA AND EXTRA CANDIED PEEL, TO DECORATE

FOR THE ICING:
125 G (4 1/2 OZ) ICING SUGAR
1 EGG WHITE
1 TSP LEMON JUICE
15 G (1/2 OZ) PLAIN FLOUR

There are two versions of cassata, both of which originate from Sicily. One is a cake made with marzipan, ricotta and candied fruit, while the other is a later development made with ice-cream. Cassata originates from an Arab word, qas'at, *meaning a small bowl used to give the shape to the dessert. The sloping sides of the container ensure that when the contents are turned out they have a conical shape. It was originally produced by nuns during Holy Week but is now available all year round. At Christmas, however, the cake is often made in a heart-shaped mould. A smaller version of cassata called* cassatina *is a common sight in Sicilian bars, cafés and pastry shops.*

Dust with icing sugar a 20 cm (8 inch) diameter pie dish with sloping sides. Divide the marzipan in two and knead one half to a smooth dough, then roll this out until it is 5 mm (1/4 inch) thick. Use it to line the sides of the dish, cutting it to fit. Take the pan di Spagna and place it on the bottom of the dish, trimming around the edges if necessary to make it fit. Sprinkle the Marsala over it.

Put the ricotta in a bowl and crush it with a fork. Add the caster sugar and vanilla extract and mix until it becomes slightly moist and binds together well. Pass the mixture through a sieve, then stir in the candied peel and chocolate. Spoon the ricotta mixture over the sponge in the dish.

Knead the remaining marzipan, roll it out and use to cover the filling. Turn the cassata upside down on to a serving plate so that the sponge that was at the bottom is now at the top.

To make the icing, sift the icing sugar into a bowl and mix in the egg white and lemon juice. Add the flour gradually to thicken it slightly. Mix well and pour immediately over the cassata to cover the top and sides. Decorate with candied peel and angelica, then leave for a couple of hours for the icing to set.

CANNOLI

SICILIAN RICOTTA PASTRIES

MAKES 15

15 G (1/2 OZ) LARD OR BUTTER
1 TBSP SUGAR
3 TBSP DRY WHITE WINE
1 TSP WHITE WINE VINEGAR
150 G (5 OZ) 00 (DOPPIO ZERO) FLOUR
1 TBSP COCOA POWDER
1 EGG, BEATEN
VEGETABLE OIL FOR DEEP-FRYING

Cannoli are probably the best-known Sicilian dessert. Nowadays they are eaten all year round, not only after meals but also as a snack. They are special pastries, wrapped around a piece of cane and deep-fried, hence the name cannolo, *from* canna. *The cane is removed after frying and the pastry filled with a mixture of ricotta cheese, sugar, candied fruit and chocolate. This used to be made only at* carnevale *(carnival time), and especially for the feast day of San Carlo. You will need 15 pieces of cane, 2.5 cm (1 inch) in diameter and 15 cm (6 inches) long, for this recipe.*

Beat together the lard or butter and sugar until light and creamy, then mix in the wine and vinegar. Fold in the flour and cocoa powder and knead to form a dough.

For the filling:
- 600 g (1 lb 5 oz) ricotta cheese
- 300 g (10 1/2 oz) caster sugar
- 55 g (1 3/4 oz) candied citrus peel, chopped
- 55 g (1 3/4 oz) dark chocolate, chopped into small pieces

Cover with cling film and leave to rest in the refrigerator for 30 minutes.

Roll out the dough into a large sheet about 2 mm (1/12 inch) thick and cut into 15 rectangles about 10 x 6 cm (4 x 2 1/2 inches). Wrap each piece of pastry around a length of cane, sealing the join with beaten egg.

Heat the oil in a large deep pan, making sure there is enough to cover the cannoli. When the oil is very hot, add the cannoli, a few at a time, and deep-fry until crisp and golden brown. This normally takes only 1 1/2 –2 minutes. Drain on paper towels and leave to cool. Remove the canes, leaving a hollow pastry to be ready to be filled.

To make the filling, sieve the ricotta cheese and beat with a fork. Mix in the sugar, candied peel and chocolate. Fill each cannoli with the ricotta mixture. Serve cool but do not refrigerate.

A selection of cakes and pastries in Maria Grammatico's shop in Erice, Sicily: (clockwise from the top left) Cannoli, marzipan apples, almond biscuits, Cassata and little baby cassatina.

FRUIT & NUTS

FRUTTA FRESCA E SECCA

When I was a child, one of the most exciting times of the year was the beginning of summer. Not only was it school holiday time, but there was also a sense of anticipation that the first of the summer crops of fruit were ripening. Having gone through the long winter eating pears and apples and preserved fruit in the form of *composta*, or compote, it was exciting to consider eating the new season's cherries for dessert instead.

These days, many fruits are available all year round. They are imported from all over the world, from Chile and Bolivia to South Africa. Unfortunately, this fruit is usually harvested when it is unripe so that it can ripen on its journey. What this means, however, is that it often lacks flavour and the fruit lacks that sun-ripened scent that comes only from fruit eaten a day after it has been picked.

Fruit is bought on a daily basis in Italy because it is ripe when it goes to market. This explains why stall-holders are so anxious to sell their goods; it is almost essential to have sold out before the end of the day, as the fruit will be past its best if kept until the next. Street markets are very colourful in Italy, with the vendors shouting the praises of their wares as loudly as they can so they can beat off the competition. The atmosphere of the markets is electric and the customer benefits enormously from the wide choice of produce on sale.

Italians eat lots of fruit in many ways, fresh, preserved or dried, and Italian meals usually end with fruit as the dessert. By happy accident, the regular consumption of fresh fruit – and lots of it – complies with modern attitudes to a healthy diet. I have the feeling sometimes that all Italians should live for hundreds of years if they eat like this. Unfortunately, other factors such as stress and man-made pollution work against this, so that a natural balance is maintained. Perhaps Italians enjoy life more, though, and that is already something!

When I was a teenager I would return from school only to be sent straight off by my mother to buy the fruit for the evening meal. I knew which would be at market before I got there, as the local farmers always told us which fruits were about to ripen. I also knew who grew the best fruit, so our table was always graced by the most impeccable specimens. If I ever bought sub-standard fruit, the family would complain to me, an occurrence which definitely encouraged me to develop the art of buying and bargaining for the best.

Cooked fruit in the form of jam is also popular in Italy and it is often eaten at tea time, known as *merenda*, with fresh bread and butter. It is also used to make jam tarts called *crostata di frutta*, a shortcrust pastry shell, baked blind then filled with jam and covered with a lattice of pastry and baked again until the lattice strips are cooked. This too is eaten for tea or for dessert during the winter months, when little fresh fruit is available.

During a filming trip to Turkey I came across a way of preparing uncooked jam. Considering that all the vitamins contained in ripe fruit are usually lost during cooking, this should be the best way to preserve them. The only handicap is that the sun has to be very strong and continuous for a few days. You just take very ripe fruit, like peaches or plums, weigh them, liquidize them and stir in an equal amount of sugar – then leave this in the sun, stirring a couple of times a day until you see that most of the liquid has evaporated and so you are sure that the sugar concentration is sufficient to keep the sun-cooked jam. In a similar way, my grandma used to produce a six-times concentrate of tomatoes, the principle being the same, but with different ingredients. Try to make the jam yourself if you are in a hot country, it is delicious.

Frutta candita, or candied fruit, is also very much used in the preparation of Italian cakes and sweets. In Calabria there is a large industry and artisanal manufacturing of all sorts of candied citrus peel due to the local abundance of tangerines, oranges, lemons and citrons. These *candite* are important ingredients in all sorts of traditional dishes, from Milanese *panettone* to the various Tuscan spicy biscuits and *panforte*, but above all in the Sicilian *cassata*, *cannoli* and many other sweet dishes. In Lombardy, Emilia-Romagna and Veneto, there is a curious but wonderful variation on candied fruit, in which all types of fruit are cooked in a heavy, sharp and sweet mustard syrup. This *mostarda di Cremona* is served as an accompaniment to boiled meats. Finally, in Piedmont there is also the production of candied chestnuts, which are given a lengthy processing in a vanilla-flavoured sugar syrup to become *marroni canditi* or *marrons glacés*.

The production of *frutta secca*, or dried fruit, was originally an ancient means of preserving bumper crops of fruit. In all the regions of modern Italy, however, it has become quite an important element in the renaissance of artisan industries. Fruit like apricots, pears, peaches, plums and figs are dried either in the sun or in ovens, to be eaten as they are – as chewy nutritious snacks – or rehydrated by cooking in water or fruit juice, together with added spices like cinnamon, to make tasty desserts. Dried fruit is also cut into small pieces and used in the production of spicy breads and cakes.

More important even are dried nuts, which contain a very high degree of protein and fat, and are used in so many ways. For example, Piedmont and Campania offer the best climatic and soil configuration to cultivate the highly prized hazelnut. These have various uses in the confectionery industry, where they are incorporated in *torrone* (a nougat made of egg white, sugar and

Left: Angelo the gardener with his lemons in Naples.

Above: a terraced lemon grove on the **Amalfi** coast.

hazelnuts) or even turned into a paste to produce the Piedmontese chocolate called *gianduja* (see Gianduiotto, page 214).

Emilia-Romagna and Campania are also the largest producers of walnuts, which are eaten as they are and also used in the making of cakes and biscuits. The incomparable flavour of these walnuts finds one of its best expressions in Liguria where it is used to make a sauce to savour pasta (see Preboggion, page 167). When picked still green, they are also used to make a liqueur called Nocino, a speciality of Modena.

The almond is the most important of nuts for the South, where it is cultivated especially in Sicily. The Arab influences in the area have left a rich legacy of use of the highly nutritious almond. As well as being eaten as a nut, reduced to a paste with added sugar and egg white it becomes *pasta reale* ('royal paste') or marzipan. Biscuits, cake fillings, *cassata*, *torrone* and *croccante* (nuts covered with melted sugar) are also made with almonds, as are the curious Sicilian *frutta di marturana*, marzipan shaped and coloured like different types of fruit. Among the most famous of the almond products are the *amaretti* biscuit, now renowned all over the world, and the *panforte di Siena*, a spicy bread containing the entire array of nuts and dried fruit, which dates back to the Middle Ages.

The best example of the value put on fruit and nuts is at Christmas, where at the end of a long and rich festive meal appear the special biscuits which have taken the last few weeks to prepare, together with tangerines, lots of nuts, walnuts, *torrone* and *marroni canditi*.

A-Z of Fruit & Nuts

Actinidia / Kiwi Fruit

Italy has only discovered the kiwi fruit in the last 10 years or so, during which time the country has become the biggest producer of the fruit in the world, as several regions have the ideal growing conditions of frost-free springs and autumns and rich, well-aired soils. The kiwi is most successfully cultivated in Piedmont, Veneto, Emilia-Romagna (the biggest producer), Campania, Lazio, Puglia and Basilicata.

The most popular variety is the Hayward, but the Bruno, Kovyorch and others are also popular. The overnight success of this fruit is partly due to its vitamin content. Kiwis contain seven times more vitamin C than a lemon and do not need sugar to make them palatable. This wonderful fruit is shaped like a large egg and is about the same size, and has rough brown skin and a brilliant green pulp. It is mainly eaten raw as a table fruit, or used in fruit salads and on fruit tarts, but a large proportion of the crop also finds its way to the drink and confectionery industries.

Agrumi / Citrus Fruit

This is the generic term for all citrus fruits, such as lemons, limes, oranges, tangerines, grapefruit, etc., which are so much a part of the Italian culinary tradition. Many were first introduced by the Arabs in the South, where they are now grown extensively.

Albicocca, Armelline / Apricot, Apricot Kernel

Left: Albicocca

Apricots were brought to Italy from China by the Arabs. It is a fruit with many varieties, including Cafona and Reale d'Imola. It ripens over the three months between June and September, depending on the variety. The velvety orangey-yellow-skinned and large-stoned fruit has a juiciness and flavour rivalled only by the peach. Italy produces about 200,000 tonnes of apricots every year, making it one of the largest producers in the world. It is grown in the warm sunny regions of Campania and Emilia-Romagna, two of the most fertile regions of Italy, as well as in Piedmont, Basilicata and Sicily.

Apricots are mainly eaten fresh, but are also used to make a drink called Nektar, and are preserved in alcohol or in syrup, and made into jam which is used in pâtisserie as a glaze and to cover fruit tarts (see Crostata di Cugna on page 277). It can also be dried and eaten in winter as a part of a compote. Finally, the kernel of the stone, called *armellina*, is used for its intense bitter almond flavour in Amaretti and in the making of marzipan.

Amarena, Marasca, Visciola, Ciliegia Acida / Morello Cherry, Maraschino Cherry, Montmorency Cherry, Sour Cherry

Even when ripe, the morello cherry still tastes sour, although it leaves a wonderful flavour in the mouth. It is this very bitterness that makes these cherries ideal for preserving and for making syrups and jams that are used in the making of pastries, drinks and ice-cream. The famous Maraschino liqueur is made with a variety of the sour cherry called Marasca. The best variety is the Montmorency, which is cultivated in the hilly regions of Italy and exported to Germany where it is used to make the liqueur Kirsch.

Anguria, Cocomero / Watermelon

This refreshing summer fruit has almost no nutritional value, with ninety-five per cent of the flesh being water and most of the rest sugar. A few successful varieties have been introduced to Italy from the Nile Valley in Egypt, from where they originate. They come in a variety of shapes, oval, oblong and round, and a range of colours from dark to pale green. The fruit is usually eaten as a refreshing dessert or as a snack on the hottest of days, turned into ice-cream or sorbet, or simply liquidized and served with ice as a drink.

Arachide / Peanut, Groundnut

Peanuts are grown in Italy, mainly in Puglia and Campania, to be eaten toasted and salted with drinks. The majority of the peanuts grown in Italy are used to make groundnut oil for frying, while those used in the confectionery industry to make *torrone* are imported from Africa, India and America.

Above: Oranges growing in Sicily.

Arancia / Orange

Oranges have a relatively short history in the Mediterranean and it was only in the last century or two that the culture of oranges began in Sicily and Campania – now two of the main areas of production in Italy. For successful cultivation oranges need sub-tropical temperatures, and well-drained and rich organic soil with a modern system of irrigation.

The orange is an extremely versatile fruit which can be eaten fresh on its own or squeezed for its juice. Certain varieties of orange can be turned into jam, and orange skin is used by the perfume and essence industries for its precious aromatic oils, as well as being candied for use in cakes and confectionery. Scented orange flower water is used in

RIGHT: ROASTING CHESTNUTS WITH BAY LEAVES.

baking, especially in Pastiera di Grano (see the recipe on page 177). In Sicily, oranges are combined with smoked herring to produce an interesting salad, Insalata di Aringhe, Arance e Pompelmi (see the recipe on page 29).

Of the many varieties, the best are Biondo Comune, Navel, Bella Donna and Valencia Late, which is much used in the jam and confectionery industry, although the bitter Seville orange is best. The main varieties of blood orange are the Tarocco, Sanguinello and Moro, which all have a deep-red pulp.

ARMELLINE, SEE ALBICOCCA

AVELLANA, SEE NOCCIOLA

BERGAMOTTO / BERGAMOT

Not to be confused with the flower of the same name, the bergamot is a citrus fruit which looks like a small, slightly pear-shaped orange. The small tree is grown only in Calabria and Sicily, and produces a bitter fruit. The skin of the fruit is candied for use by the pâtisserie industry and its oils to scent and flavour tea and liqueurs, and in the blending of perfumes – indeed, it is the main constituent of eau-de-cologne.

CACHI, KAKI, CACHI-MELA, LOTO / PERSIMMON, SHARON FRUIT

I adore this tree, which can be found in most gardens in northern Italy, especially in Campania and Puglia where it is mostly cultivated for local use. The trees grow up to 10 m (30 ft) high and have thick, round, dark green leaves which fade before the fruit ripens. The round green apple-like fruit matures into a rich orange as it ripens and inside its very thin skin there is a gelatinous but very juicy sweet pulp with 2 or 3 large oval seeds.

BELOW: CACHI

The fruit is only palatable when it is very ripe but before this it has a strong taste that is heavy with tannin. It is full of vegetable proteins and sugar, and rich in vitamins A, B1 and B2. One variety, called *cachi-mela, loto* and *legno santo* ('holy wood') is cultivated in southern Italy, but originated from Israel where it is called sharon fruit. Unlike the variety grown in the north, it is edible when it is still hard and green and never gets soft like the other variety.

The *cachi* is almost exclusively eaten ripe as fruit. Some people do make jam with it, but its mildness of flavour means that it is not otherwise much used in cooking.

CANDITO / CANDIED FRUIT AND PEEL

Candito is the name given to fruit or citrus rind that has been impregnated with a flavoured sugar syrup. In the lengthy and complicated procedure, the sugar slowly replaces the water in the fruit, both preserving it and turning it into an edible sweet morsel. *Canditi* are used to make pastries in every Italian region. All sorts of fruit flans employ candied fruits of all types, including cherries, strawberries, chestnuts, pears, apricots, whole clementines, and even certain varieties of pumpkin.

The most important candied peel, however, is that of the citrus fruits, like oranges, mandarins, lemons, and especially *cedro* or citron. Candied fruit, called *frutta candita*, is often served at the end of meals to be washed down with a little liqueur.

CASTAGNA / CHESTNUT

No walk in the mountains during the months of October and November is complete without collecting a few pounds of chestnuts. This nut grows on huge trees that are also valued for their precious wood by the furniture industry. The sweet chestnut tree is common in the Apennines and Pre-Alps and when the nuts are in season they are either roasted or boiled and consumed in huge quantities.

As well as the common chestnut, there is another variety called *marroni* which is much used in the kitchen. *Marroni* have a spiky shell and grow singly, whereas ordinary chestnuts grow in clusters. They are used to make *marroni canditi* (*marrons glacés* or candied chestnuts), which are very popular at Christmas time. *Marroni canditi* are very expensive because in the process of making them many get broken and only the whole ones are eventually sold.

In the past, chestnuts were used by the Italian peasant to enrich everyday meals such as soups, as well as being eaten as a vegetable or fruit. Because the chestnut has a rather neutral taste, it can be used in many ways, including being boiled and puréed for savoury stuffings, and with milk, sugar and whipped cream in the famous dessert, *montebianco*, which can be further enriched by the addition of Chantilly cream and alcohol. One of the classic recipes in which chestnuts are used is *caldallessa* or *ballotta*, a dish of freshly boiled chestnuts served with wine in Northern Italian trattorias or *enoteche* (wine bars) on 2 November. The nuts may also be simply boiled with a few bay leaves for 40-45 minutes, then peeled and eaten on their own.

Chestnuts can also be roasted (*caldarroste*), either in a pan over charcoal or in the oven. Whichever method you use, make sure you make a small incision in the tough skin before cooking them to prevent the chestnuts from exploding. If you roast them in a pan, you will need a special roaster with holes in the bottom. Turn the chestnuts over the heat from time to time so that they roast evenly and do not burn, although if they develop a few black spots it will give them flavour. Charcoal-roasted chestnuts are often sold on street corners in the winter. If you cook them in the oven, they will get an overall browning and will be easier to peel. Do not cook them for too long, 30 minutes in a hot oven should be enough, or they will become hard and inedible.

Dried chestnuts need to be soaked for a day before being cooked in milk until soft, when they can either be eaten with salt as a savoury side dish or with vanilla, sugar and cinnamon as a dessert. Ground dried chestnuts can also be made into a flour which is used to make an unleavened cake called Castagnaccio (see page 282), for the thickening of soups, and is sometimes mixed with wheat flour in the making of certain types of pasta. Chestnut flour is also mixed with water, sugar and vanilla to make *crema di castagne*, a filling for sweet ravioli.

CEDRO / CITRON

This citrus fruit looks like a large lemon and can weigh up to 1 kg ($2^1/_4$ lb) and its rind can reach up to 3 cm ($1^1/_4$ inches) in thickness. It is grown in Calabria, Campania and Sicily for its peel, which is rich in aromatic oils and is mainly candied for use by the confectionery industry. The candied peel is also used in the famous Italian cakes *panettone* and *panforte*, in Cassata and Cannoli (see the recipes on page 256), as well as in a filling made of ricotta and granules of *pastiera di grano*, in a tart and to make a drink called *cedrata*. The flowers of the citron plant produce a concentrated essence that is used to flavour confectionery and in the making of perfumes.

LEFT: AUTUMN FRUITS

LEFT: CITRON BEING SOLD BY THE ROADSIDE IN AMALFI

CILIEGIA / CHERRY

Cherries are mostly grown in Campania, Puglia, Emilia-Romagna and Veneto, all four regions exporting a huge number all over Europe. The main varieties grown are Durone Nero, Durone Nero di Vignola, Durone Nero di Anella and Amarena. Their need for particularly well-drained soil and hand-picking at harvest time makes them one of the most expensive fruits available. As well as being eaten on their own as a delicious fruit, cherries can also be preserved in pure alcohol or candied and coloured for use in confectionery. Cherries are also cooked with sugar and vanilla to make a dessert, as well as being used to make sauces for poultry and game.

CILIEGA ACIDA, SEE AMARENA

CLEMENTINA, SEE MANDARINO

COCOMERO, SEE ANGURIA

CONFETTO / ALMOND SWEET

These sweets are used in the celebration of baptisms, first communions and weddings, to be offered to the guests. The most common is an almond covered with hard white sugar in an oval shape. Confetti may also have an interior of hazelnut or chocolate – even a small aniseed, producing a round sweet – and may also be coloured pink, red, silver or gold.

CONFETTURA, MARMELLATA / JAM, MARMALADE

As in Britain, the Italians make a preserve similar to marmalade that uses oranges, lemons, tangerines, mandarins, clementines, grapefruits or limes. To earn the name *marmellata*, the preserve must only be made with the pulp, juice and rind of the fruit. By contrast, *confettura*, or jam, is made only with the pulp and juice of the fruit. The two are often confused, but to add to the problem there is a third type of preserve called *gelatina*, a fruit jelly made with the strained juice of the fruit.

To make perfect jams and marmalades it is essential that the balance of sugar and the ripeness of the fruit are right, so it is important to use the ripest and the most perfect fruit you can find. If you add less sugar than the fruit needs, more water is extracted from the fruit in the cooking process, making it stronger in flavour but also more prone to fermentation and turning mouldy. My mother used to make a jam called *mostarda* (or *cugnà* in Piedmontese) from freshly pressed red grape juice and pears, prunes, peaches, quinces and even walnuts. The fruit was mixed with sugar and vanilla and then cooked until it resembled a deep brown jam with a thick consistency. The taste was heavenly and we used to spread it liberally on buttered bread and Crostata di Cugna (see the recipe on page 277) for *merenda*.

CORBEZZOLO / STRAWBERRY TREE

A typical Mediterranean evergreen, this bushy strawberry tree grows wild around all the southern Italian and Sardinian coasts. The round and beautifully red fruit is covered with little red bumps that give it a spiky look. Although it is not used commercially, the fruit of the strawberry tree is both attractive and tasty. It is mostly used as fresh fruit and sometimes for jam.

Cotogna, Cugna, Mela, Pera, Cotognata / Quince, Quince Paste

In the past, the quince was much used in the kitchen, especially to make sauces for roasted meats. Today, although it is still cultivated and is available on the market stalls of Italy in the autumn, it no longer holds the culinary position it once enjoyed. The small trees, with their regularly shaped leaves, bear pear- and apple-shaped fruit (hence the names *mela* or *pera*), with downy yellow skin that rubs down to a shine. It has a wonderful scent, although its flesh is too sour to eat raw and once cut it discolours rapidly, so a few drops of lemon juice need to be sprinkled over it.

It is possible to buy a commercially produced quince paste called *cotognata*, but it can be made at home by simply peeling the fruit, quartering it and cooking it in a little water with the zest of a lemon until the water has evaporated and the fruit is very soft. It may then be liquidized or mashed to a purée, mixed with the same quantity of sugar and reheated over a medium heat, stirring all the time to prevent it from sticking, until it turns a lovely reddish-brown. Spread the mixture on a flat surface and allow it to cool and dry for a couple of days, before cutting it into cubes and rolling it in coarsely crushed sugar. It can also be cooked with less sugar, orange juice and cinnamon to make a compote or jam. In Veneto they add mustard seeds and syrup to quince to make a preserve that is eaten with boiled chicken, see Mostarda.

Croccante, see Nocciola

Dattero / Date

The date tree, which came originally from North Africa, can only be grown for fruit in very warm climates. The trees we see decorating gardens in Southern Italy produce only very small fruit which never mature. Dates, which have a sugar content of 70 per cent and are rich in vitamins A, B, and C, are among the most nutritious fruits available.

Although dates are not grown in Italy, they are often sold dried, especially at Christmas with nuts, figs and other preserved fruits. They are also eaten at other times of the year, both fresh and dried. The Ancient Romans were very fond of dates, consuming them among the exotic delicacies served during their famous banquets, but also using them to flavour meat dishes. Today they are used in pâtisserie, usually filled with marzipan, but also as part of Tuscan spicy breads like *panforte*.

Right: figs in the Palermo market.

Fico / Fig

The finest figs are those eaten ripe from the plant, a rarity these days as so much fruit is picked unripe for long transportation – a particular issue with figs, which are extremely perishable. Originally from Syria, the fig was spread all over the world by the Romans and it is now grown in Italy in the regions of Puglia, Calabria and Sicily, where a few of the 700 available varieties are grown and eaten, either raw or preserved.

Figs can be either round or pear-shaped and some of them reach a considerable size, weighing up to 55-60 g ($1^3/_4$ - 2 oz) each. The skin is very delicate and the inside of the fruit is made up of thousands of pods that produce a very sweet syrupy substance, giving the fruit its succulence. The best-known varieties grown in Italy are the Gentile Bianco, a Genovese variety which grows in Liguria, the Verdello, Brogiotto Bianco and Ottato. Fresh figs are very popular eaten simply as a fruit, with Parma ham (*prosciutto e fichi*) and in fruit salads and tarts.

Full of vitamins, the fig contains five times more calories by weight when dried than it does when fresh, and it is easier to transport and keep. Dried figs are obtained by drying the mature fruit in the sun, in an oven or in an air-drier, where all the water in the fruit is evaporated. Another way of preserving them is in a honey syrup, and these are exceptionally good eaten with a touch of cream as a dessert.

My favourite recipe for dried figs is baked in the oven until brown in colour, then cut in half and served with peeled almonds or other nuts. Figs soaked in a syrup of orange juice and honey and then boiled for about 5 minutes are also delicious, as are figs covered with chocolate.

Fico d'India / Prickly Pear

This fruit, which originates from Latin America, can often be seen on postcards from southern Italy and Sardinia. The fruit is grainy and slightly scented, with a skin that is covered in tiny sharp spikes, which give it its name of prickly pear. The whole peeled fruit can be eaten, including the little seeds. There are a number of varieties which can come in a range of colours, from yellow and white to red. As well as being eaten as a fresh fruit,

prickly pears are also used to make alcoholic drinks.

FRAGOLA, FRAGOLA SELVATICA OR DI BOSCO / STRAWBERRY, WILD STRAWBERRY

The strawberry grows outside, from spring through to autumn, but is now cultivated all year round in greenhouses. It perishes very quickly and should not be handled too much as it bruises easily. The best types of strawberry are the Gorella (a conical variety that is available from May), the rounder Pocahontas, the long and pointed Belruby and the Aliso, which grows mostly in the South, Emilia-Romagna, Piedmont, Veneto and Campania.

Wild strawberries, called *fragole di bosco*, grow in woodland areas. They are much smaller than the cultivated variety and have a much stronger flavour. They fetch a much higher price than commercially grown strawberries and, despite attempts to cultivate them, the real thing still cannot be beaten. Wild strawberries only need a little sugar and a few drops of lemon juice or balsamic vinegar as an accompaniment if they are eaten on their own, but they are also wonderful in fruit tarts and in all the same recipes using cultivated strawberry, such as confectionery, liqueurs, preserves, jams and gelatines. Strawberries may also be candied and used as a filling and decoration for many cakes, sweets and desserts.

FRUTTA SECCA / DRIED FRUIT

This is the generic term for all dried fruit, such as plums, peaches, pears, apples, apricots and figs, as well as nuts like hazelnuts, walnuts, peanuts and almonds.

GELSO, SEE MORA DI GELSO

KAKI, SEE CACHI

LAMPONE / RASPBERRY

The fruit of a bushy plant that grows in the hills of Italy at an altitude of up to 1,500 metres (4,500 feet), the raspberry needs a cool climate to grow well. Like strawberries, they are perishable and delicate, and should be handled as little as possible. They are made up of a collection of tiny pods, each of which contains a seed. The berry is attached to a conical white stem from which it can only be pulled cleanly when the fruit is quite ripe.

The flavour of the raspberry is so intense that it is mostly used to make syrups and jellies for the confectionery industry, but they are also delicious raw on tarts, on meringues, in fruit salad or, best of all, on their own. If cooked with sugar they make a wonderful sauce for ice-cream or creamy desserts, as well as making wonderful sorbets themselves. Agricultural and technological advancements have made commercial cultivation of this fruit easier and much of the new abundant crop is frozen to make sauces, syrups and gelatines.

LIMA, LIMETTA / LIME

This citrus fruit has only recently gained access to Italy, especially in Sicily where they are being grown experimentally. Smaller than a lemon, the lime has a smoother dark green colour and a highly scented rind which is used to savour drinks, as well as sauces for fish. The juice is less pungent than that of the lemon and is used in delicate dishes, again especially with fish. Very recently, also, a liqueur has been produced using the very intensely perfumed oils extracted from the skin.

LIMONE / LEMON

Originally from Asia, the lemon found its way to Europe via the Middle East and was probably introduced by the Arabs. Sicily produces 90 per cent of Italy's lemons (650,000 tonnes per year), and the other ten per cent are grown in Calabria and Sardinia, with some of the best coming from the Amalfi coast in Campania. Lemon varieties have quite funny names, like Femminello, Femminello di Santa Teresa, Monachello and Interdonato.

Lemons are well known for being rich in vitamin C and they are so acidic that their juice can corrode iron and be used as a disinfectant. In the kitchen, however, it is the ability of the lemon to flavour and to sour, as well as to prevent oxidation, that is most valued. Lemon juice is used to heighten the flavour of both sweet and savoury sauces and to establish a good balance between fat and acid. It is also used instead of vinegar to dress salads and is almost always

LEFT: PRICKLY PEARS GROWING IN SICILY.

LEFT: LAMPONE

LEFT: STRAWBERRIES IN TURIN MARKET.

squeezed over grilled, fried and boiled fish to bring out the flavour of the fish. It is an indispensable acid agent for curing raw foods such as meat tartares (see Carne all'Albese, page 86), and for marinating fish.

The aroma and flavour of the lemon is at its strongest in the skin. The drinks, confectionery and bakery industries make good use of the oils extracted from the skin in juices, jams and extracts. I often use lemon rind infused in hot water to make *canarino*, which is a wonderful tonic.

LOTO, SEE CACHI

MACEDONIA DI FRUTTA / FRUIT SALAD

This term is used of salads of fresh fruits, cut into pieces and left to macerate in orange or lemon juice with a little added sugar and perhaps a splash of liqueur, usually Maraschino. *Macedonia* can also consist of vegetables, either raw or cooked, and dressed with vinaigrette or mayonnaise.

MANDARINO, MANDARANCIO, CLEMENTINA, MANDARINETTO / MANDARIN, SATSUMA, CLEMENTINE

The mandarin has been joined by two very similar fruits, the satsuma and the clementine, but neither can match the flavour and juiciness of the seedless flesh of the thin-skinned original. This popular citrus fruit comes from China and is now cultivated with great success in Calabria and Sicily, which together produce 75 per cent of the national yield. The rest is grown in Campania, Basilicata, Puglia and Sardinia, although it is now being replaced, at least in part, by the new hybrids.

The clementine is smaller and satsuma larger than the mandarin, and both have a wonderful, deep-orange skin and are rounder than the mandarin. The best-known varieties of mandarin are the Avena, Tardivo di Ciaculli, Tardivo della Conca d'Oro, while the best-known clementine varieties are Comuni, Clementine Monreales, Clementine di Nules and Clementine Orovales. The satsuma – a seedless version of the tangerine with more compact pulp – is used in the same way as the mandarin. Its culture is fairly recent in Italy.

RIGHT: BOTTLES OF LEMONCELLO, A LIQUEUR MADE WITH AMALFI LEMONS, IN NAPLES.

The technique used in the culture of mandarins of continually watering the plants on a drip system means that the fruit can be adequately irrigated. The fruit is harvested between November and January, for consumption about a month later. A variety of commercial operations have grown up around the cultivation of mandarins, including the making of juices, aromatic oils, pulp and candied peel, all for use in the drinks, confectionery and cosmetic industries. The fruit itself is generally eaten during the winter months, especially at Christmas.

The smallest variety of mandarin, called *mandarinetto*, used to be candied whole, resulting in a delicious confection with a slightly resilient skin and a very sugary centre.

MANDORLA / ALMOND

Common all around the Mediterranean and in Asia, the almond was introduced into Italy by the ancient Greeks, along with the vine and the fig tree. The almond tree has many similarities with the peach tree, with leaves of the same shape and the same type of wood. When it is growing and forming, the nut is contained within a pointed oval stone that is encased within a thick green outer skin, called *mallo*.

Due to its combination of proteins, minerals and high fat content (50 per cent), the almond has been a valuable food for thousands of years. A number of varieties, including Tuono, Filippo Ceo and Ferrangnes, are cultivated in Sicily, Veneto, Puglia, Campania and Sardinia.

There are two types of almond: the sweet and the bitter. The bitter almond is the smaller of the two and has the typical almond taste, which is used to boost the flavour of all products made with sweet almonds. It has to be heat-treated before use, however, as otherwise it is toxic.

Among the best-known almond products is marzipan (see Marzapane, overleaf, and Pasta di Mandorle, pages 279 and 297), which is much used in the south. The almond is particularly favoured in Sicily, where it is used to make the famous Cassata (see the recipe on page 256), as well as biscuits and *torrone*.

The very precious oil from almonds is used both in pâtisserie to flavour sweets and in medicines and cosmetics for its softening properties. There is also a kind of milk that is extracted from the almond which is used to make a drink called *latte di mandorle*. It resembles coconut milk and is extremely delicious.

Almonds are also used in the making of Amaretto, a famous liqueur, and Amaretti biscuits (see the recipe on page 279). Both of these products require a large number of bitter almonds and fewer of the balancing sweetness of the other variety. In the kitchen, almonds are often paired with trout. I sometimes use ground almonds instead of flour to thicken sauces. There is a term *mandorlato* which indicates the presence of almonds, as in *torrone mandorlato*.

MARASCA, SEE AMARENA

MARMELLATA, SEE CONFETTURA

MARRONI, SEE CASTAGNA

LEFT: A MARZIPAN HEART FOR CHRISTMAS IN ERICE, SICILY.

MARZAPANE, PASTA REALE / MARZIPAN

This paste of sugar, almond flour and egg white is widely used in Sicily to make *cassata siciliana* and to bake a variety of biscuits. It is also used as filling for tarts and dates. Marzipan has a sweetish taste, only sometimes betraying a hint of the bitter almonds or *armelline* added to enhance the almond flavour. In certain parts of the South, marzapane is called *pasta reale* ('royal paste'), indicating the regard with which it was held. A Sicilian variation called *frutta di marturana* is based on marzipan shaped into all types of fruit which are then given the original colours.

MELA / APPLE

By far the most frequently eaten fruit in Italy – probably in Europe – is the apple. Of the total weight of 100 kg (220 lb) of fruit eaten by each Italian every year, at least half is apples. There are over 250 varieties of apple, a fruit that is considered to be one of the healthiest, with its high level of fibre, vitamin C and acidity.

Fifty per cent of Italian apples are cultivated in the Trentino Alto Adige, with Emilia-Romagna, Veneto, Piedmont, Lombardy and Campania contributing the remaining half. Apple trees need cool temperatures and little wind, which is why they are cultivated in tranquil valleys and the flatlands of the north. The varieties grown in Italy meet local requirements, so they may be different to those grown in other parts of the world.

The first harvest in July includes varieties like Gravenstein, Ozark Gold and the succulent Golden Red apple. These are followed in autumn by Golden Delicious, Red Delicious, the very red Stayman, the extremely green Granny Smith and the huge Imperatore. My favourite apple is the Reneste/Reveste, a rusty yellow apple with a yellowish pulp and a very developed flavour, which stays juicy and firm all winter. Most apples keep for quite a long time, up to a month if stored in a well-ventilated, temperature-controlled room.

LEFT: PLASTER MOULDS FOR MARZIPAN EASTER LAMBS.

LEFT: IMPERATORE APPLES

As well as being eaten on its own, the apple is much used in the making of sauces, compotes, pies, tarts and other baking, as well as in juices and in the manufacture of brandy.

MELA COTOGNA, SEE COTOGNA

MELAGRANA, GRANATA / POMEGRANATE

The pomegranate tree, with its pretty red blossom and fruit, is now largely grown for its ornamental beauty, although in the Middle Ages it was used to make sauces and for stuffing game. The fruit used to be regarded as sacred because it was a symbol of fecundity. Although it is still grown all over Italy, it makes a minor commercial contribution in Sicily where it is cultivated to serve the syrup industry. Especially in Renaissance times, *melagrana* was used in Tuscan cuisine as a flavouring in game and poultry dishes. Today it is mostly used as a table fruit, but is sometimes pressed for juice to produce sorbet and as an addition to fruit salad.

The pomegranate is round, with a tough orange-red skin and a little crown on top where the stalk of the tree was attached. Inside, its flesh is divided into segments by a large number of yellow membranes and each segment holds many transparent containers of juice along with a little seed. As a result it is quite difficult to eat and I tend to eat it with a spoon. First of all, make four lengthwise cuts through the skin with a knife as if cutting an apple into quarters. Then start to loosen the sections, collecting the fruit and juice in a bowl and discarding the bitter yellow membranes. The pink fruit is sweet with a slightly acidic aftertaste and a granular texture.

MELONE, POPONE / MELON

Originating from southern Asia and Equatorial Africa, the melon comes from the same family of plants as the pumpkin and courgette. The plant spreads its tentacles over a wide area, feeding the round or oval fruit with the moisture it needs to

LEFT: MELAGRANE

reach up to 1 kg ($2^1/_4$ lb) in weight. There are many varieties of melon, some growing and maturing in summer and others in autumn, with the later fruit possibly being kept for the winter months. Among the latter are the Invernale Giallo and Verde varieties, oval melons shaped like rugby balls, with a very thick yellow or green skin and a white, not-too-sweet pulp. They are mostly grown in Emilia-Romagna, Lazio, Puglia, Campania and Sicily, and can be kept for several months.

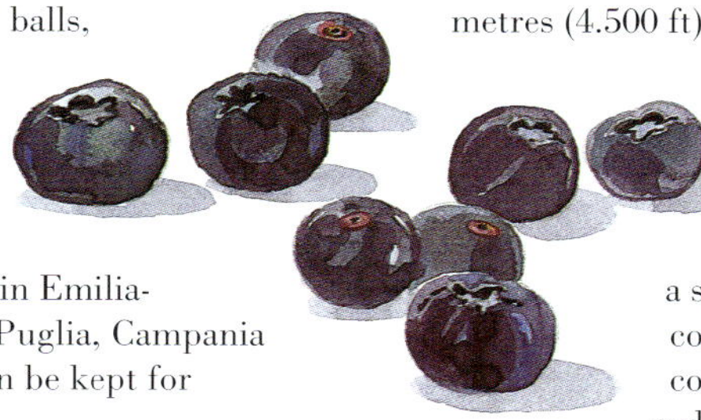

RIGHT: MIRTILLI

Summer melons tend to be round with an orange skin, which can be either smooth or rough, with a net of raised green veins all over it. The summer varieties of Cantaloupe and Retato are round in shape, with a smooth green grey skin and a net-covered yellowish skin respectively, and both containing an extremely juicy dark orange highly flavoured sweet pulp. They are grown in Emilia-Romagna, Campania and Puglia.

Choosing a ripe melon can sometimes be a little difficult, but the best way to judge is to see if the centre of both top and bottom are slightly soft and are giving off a definite aroma. The weight is also a good indication of a ripe melon, so the heavier it is the juicier and riper it will be.

Melon is almost always eaten on its own or as part of a fruit cocktail, but it can also be used to make sorbet or a refreshing drink if liquidized. It can also make a lovely chilled summer soup if pulped with some lemon juice, salt, pepper and some chives. The best way of eating melon, though, is with a few slices of Parma ham, accompanied by a good white wine, eaten beneath a pergola – that is what summer is all about.

MIRTILLO / BLUEBERRY

Pollution has made this berry difficult to find growing in the wild and there is little interest in hunting out the few that are left, which means that the only blueberries you can get are the larger commercially cultivated ones. These are available all year round but they lack the flavour of the real thing. In the wild, the blueberry grows through the summer into the autumn in the hills and mountains over 1,500 metres (4,500 ft) high. The blue-black berries are very small and a special wooden comb is used to collect them in order to avoid damaging the structure of the plant.

The cultivated blueberry from America is much bigger, with a more distinct bluish tinge to the skin and paler flesh. They can be eaten on their own or with other wild berries in the fruit salad known as *sottobosco*, or to fill fruit tarts. They are also used to make a sauce for game and poultry, a jam called *confettura di mirtilli*, a sweet sauce for pâtisserie and, finally, a liqueur.

MORA DI GELSO / MULBERRY

The mulberry bush, Chinese in origin, is mostly grown for its leaves which are used to feed silk worms. The berries come in two colours, white and black. Both are made up of a series of tightly bunched pods, but the black berry is longer and has a deep-red juice that is slightly sour but has a wonderful flavour. The mulberry is mostly grown on the plains of northern Italy and is only used locally as it not sold commercially. It can be eaten on its own or as part of a fruit salad, as well as being used to make syrups and jams.

RIGHT: MOSTARDA DI CREMONA

MORA DI ROVO / BLACKBERRY

In summer, it is common to see Italians making their way through thorny brambles to collect wild blackberries. Agricultural progress means that it is now possible to buy cultivated blackberries, grown on thornless bushes for easy picking. Although it is less flavoursome than the wild variety, the cultivated blackberry is still good in fruit salads and as a topping for fruit tarts, as well as making delicious jams, compotes, juices and syrups for use in the liqueur, pâtisserie and confectionery industries. It is a very perishable soft fruit and should be eaten as soon as it is picked.

MOSTARDA DI CREMONA / MUSTARD FRUITS

This speciality of the city of Cremona in Lombardy consists of fruit, such as cherries, pears, figs and apricots, candied for a long time in a heavy sugar syrup flavoured with essence of mustard. The result is very piquant fruit used to accompany boiled meat like capon and Bollito Misto (see the recipe on page 92).

In Veneto there is another version of *mostarda* in which the fruit is minced together, resulting in a paste which is used in the same way. The *mostarda* made in Piedmont has a totally different use and is made in a different way (see Cotogna, page 265).

NESPOLA COMUNE / Medlar

The medlar is a round, walnut-sized, rusty coloured fruit, borne on an ancient plant between the end of

LEFT: NESPOLE COMUNE

October and the beginning of November. The fruit cannot be eaten when it is harvested but needs to be kept in a well-ventilated area to 'rot' for a fairly long period of time, when it matures into a sweet and juicy fruit. It can be used to make a delicious, hard gelatine or cheese like quince (see Cotogna). The medlar is not commercially grown but, like the pomegranate, it is often planted in Italian gardens for its looks.

NESPOLE DEL GIAPPONE / LOQUAT

A popular fruit in Italy, the loquat is available during the spring and summer. The tree has long and distinctive dark-green leaves that make it popular in the gardens of the coastal regions, and there is some commercial cultivation of the fruit in Campania, Calabria, Sicily, Puglia and Sardinia. The loquat can be oval or round, depending on the variety, and is pale orange, with a very smooth, thick skin that peels easily when the fruit is ripe. Its flesh is extremely juicy and sweet, but with enough acidity to lift the flavour. It is a very pleasant fruit to eat on its own, but can also be used to make jam and sorbet.

NOCCIOLA, AVELLANA / HAZELNUT

The city of Avellino in Campania takes its name from the product for which it is celebrated, the hazelnut. The hazelnut tree comes from Turkey, but has been successfully adapted to grow in various part of Italy. More than half of the 100,000 tonnes produced each year come from Campania. The rest comes from Lazio, Piedmont and Sicily, where the nuts are particularly good. The variety called Tonda Gentile delle Langhe grows in the same area as the white truffle and it is said that the truffles which grow beside hazelnut trees are the best. Other varieties include Mortarelle, Gentile Romana and Nostrale di Sicilia.

LEFT: HAZELNUTS AND GREEN AND DRY WALNUTS.

Hazelnuts ripen in autumn. The round kernel is encased in a tough wooden husk so it keeps for a long time although, like all foods that contain fat, it will turn rancid and go bad if it is badly kept. The nuts are very nutritious, containing a balance of fat (600 calories per 100 g/3½ oz), protein, vitamins and minerals.

In Piedmont, the best hazelnuts are roasted then ground into an extremely fine paste to make nougat and Gianduiotti chocolate, while in Campania they are used to make Croccante di Nocciole (see the recipe on page 280). They are also used in a huge number of biscuits and cakes all over the country.

NOCE / WALNUT

The best Italian walnuts come from the Sorrento area in Campania and the best variety is the eponymous Sorrento, a large nut with a thin, easily breakable shell and very tasty nut. Other good varieties include the late-ripening Sorrento Giovanni and a French variety called Franquette.

The nut grows in bunches from large trees that came originally from Asia and are as much sought after for their wood as their fruit. The nut is formed inside a fleshy green outer skin called *mallo* which peels open when the nut is ripe, around September or October, allowing the nut, protected by its hard, wrinkled casing, to fall to the ground. Inside, the nut is divided into four sections, called *gherigli*.

Fresh walnuts are delicious, as long as you remove the nut from the bitter yellow skin surrounding it. To enjoy the full flavour of the walnut, however, it is better to wait until it is completely dry, when the nut will have shrunk inside the shell and the yellow skin turned brown and papery. The best nuts are those of the last crop before the oils in the nut turn rancid.

Around Modena in Emilia-Romagna, a speciality called *nocino* is made with unripe walnuts. They are collected when the nut is unformed, usually around 23 June, Saint Giovanni's day. The green walnuts are then quartered, put in a glass container and covered with pure alcohol flavoured with cinnamon then left to marinate in the sun for 40 days. The resulting liquid, once diluted with water and mellowed with sugar is dark brown and about 30-40 per cent proof, and is drunk as a digestif. It is available commercially, but it is much more fun producing it by yourself.

Walnuts are also used to make biscuits, cakes and confectionery. In Liguria, there is a pasta sauce based on olive oil, minced walnuts, garlic and Parmesan cheese (see the recipe for Pansôti al Preboggion on page 167). Walnuts are also served at Christmas time with dried fruits such as dates, hazelnuts and apricots. Finally, the oil extracted from the walnut is used to make tasty salad dressings.

Above: small Martin Prus pears.

Pasta Reale, see Marzapane

Pera / Pear

The pear originated from the area around the Caspian Sea and was introduced into Europe about two thousand years ago. Today there are around 5,000 varieties, and Italy is one of the biggest producers in the world, cultivating about 10 varieties. Nearly two-thirds of all the pears cultivated in Italy come from Emilia-Romagna, with Campania, Veneto, Lazio, Sicily, Lombardy and Piedmont making up the balance.

Early varieties, maturing around July, include Coscia, Butirra Morettini and Guyot, all of which have a juicy flesh and yellow skin. In August the red or yellow Williams pear ripens and is followed by the winter varieties such as the Abate, the orangey-yellow Kaiser and the large Decana del Comizio or Comice, and finally the largest and longest-keeping, green-yellow pear, Passa Crassana. While these are all grown commercially, the small and delicious rusty-coloured St Martin pear from Piedmont is worth looking out for. Winter varieties can be kept for a few months if properly stored, but summer fruit should be eaten when ripe.

Pears are usually eaten on their own or in fruit salads, but they can also be cooked, either in red or white wine with spices, lemon zest and sugar or just with sugar and water to make compote, or baked in the oven with wine and sugar. They can be candied or air-dried and used to make jams, syrups and sweets. They are even distilled to make William liqueur and William Schnapps, after the German tradition, based on a spirit distilled, naturally, from the William pears. The area where this speciality is made is the Trentino Alto-Adige, but these drinks are popular all over Italy as *digestifs* after dinner.

Finally as in the old Italian proverb '*Al contadin non far sapere come e' buono il cacio con le pere*', meaning 'don't let the farmer know how good it is to eat fresh pears and cheese', there is no nicer way to finish a meal.

Pera Cotogna, see Cotogna

Pesca, Pescanoce / Peach, Nectarine

The Mediterranean region, and Italy in particular, seems to be ideal for growing peaches and their cousins the nectarines. The tree was originally brought to the area from Persia by Alexander the Great, but now Italy produces about 80 per cent of Europe's total consumption, despite being avid consumers of the fruit themselves. There are two major types of peach, although there are many varieties. The first type is Pesca Comune di Pasta Bianca, the common peach, an apple-sized fruit with a thin downy skin and a white, juicy and deliciously scented flesh. The second variety is much like the first but has a yellow flesh and a reddish-yellow skin.

Other types of peach include the Percoca, a peach from the south with a yellowy-green skin and a firm flesh that is widely used by the preserving industry, and the wild Pesche di Vigna that grows alone in the vineyards of Italy. The latter has a very intense flavour and is usually white-fleshed with a green-and-red skin. This lovely peach can be prised into two halves and popped straight into your mouth because it is so small. Vineyard owners try to keep these peach trees, with their beautifully scented pink flowers, hidden away so that they can enjoy their fruit fresh or preserved in syrup for Christmas.

The nectarine is not a hybrid, but a true variety of peach. It is very similar to the peach but has a completely smooth and shiny skin. Again, there are two main types, one with white and the other with yellow flesh, and countless varieties have been developed to crop from May to September. In the end, however, the peach has much more flavour.

Peaches and nectarines are mostly eaten on their own or in fruit salads, but peaches are more widely used in the kitchen than nectarines. In Piedmont peaches are sliced, dipped in red wine and sprinkled with a little sugar before being eaten. They can also be halved, stuffed with a mixture of beaten egg, crumbled amaretti, cocoa powder and sugar, then baked in the oven. Peaches are pulped to make *succo di pesca*, which is mixed with champagne to make the famous Bellini cocktail.

Peaches are also used to make jam and a solid paste rather like *cotognata* called *pasta di frutta*, as well as being dried for long keeping.

Right: pesca

PINOLO / PINE NUT
The pine nut or kernel is the seed of the pine tree. It is held in the familiar pine cone, made up of a series of wooden tongues. The creamy-white kernel is about 1 cm (1/2 inch) long and slightly pointed at one end. The seed can only be gathered from the cones of mature trees at least 70 years of age, which is why the nut is not cultivated on a large scale. The trees themselves are part of the Ombrella family and are typical of the landscape of the coastal regions of Tuscany, Campania and Sicily. The kernel can only be harvested if the cone is completely open when it is collected, although a short spell in a hot oven will encourage it to open to release the seeds.

Despite its high fat content, the pine nut is very nutritious, having a high proportion of proteins, vitamins and minerals. Always make sure you buy fresh pine nuts as their fat can turn rancid, making them inedible. The pine nut has been popular as an ingredient since Biblical times and is often used along with raisins as a flavouring for meat, and to make stuffings for meat and poultry. This is a reminder of Arab influences on Southern Italian cooking. In Liguria, pine nuts are an essential ingredient for the famous Pesto sauce (see the recipe on page 228) and it is also use to make biscuits (see the recipe for Panpepato on page 230), and as decoration for other cakes and sweets.

PISTACCHIO / PISTACHIO NUT
The pistachio is the fruit of a wonderful little tree that is typical of the southern Mediterranean and unique in Italy to the island of Sicily, the only region with the right climatic conditions for its growth. The nuts grows in bundles enclosed within a fleshy red pod that bursts open to reveal the nut bulging out of its woody envelope. Inside, the pistachio is actually bright green, which makes it ideal for decorating cakes, biscuits and other sweets. It is also used as a stuffing for meat, and even finds its way into the salami, Mortadella. The nut is also ground into a powder and used as the base for a very tasty ice-cream and, to prove its versatility, it is also popular eaten salted as a snack with drinks.

POMPELMO / GRAPEFRUIT
The largest of the citrus fruits, the grapefruit is full of vitamin C, contains little sugar and no protein or fat, and is extremely juicy. It is mainly cultivated in Sicily, Calabria and Liguria, where the mildness of the climate favours its growth. The slightly bitter scent and flavour of the yellow Pompelmo Giallo is ideal for marinades and makes a perfect fruit juice. The pink or red varieties are much sweeter than their yellow cousin and are delicious eaten on their own as a fruit. Choose grapefruit by their weight; the heavier the better. I like to serve pink grapefruit in segments, stripped of their membranes and with orange juice poured over.

POPONE, SEE MELONE

PRUGNA, SUSINA, PRUGNA SECCA / PLUMS, PRUNES
In Italian, the words *prugna* and *susina* are both used to refer to plums, while *prugna secca* is the name given to prunes. The plum originates from Asia but grows very successfully all over Europe, as well as many other parts of the world. Italy produces about 150,000 tonnes a year, concentrating on Regina Claudia (greengages, my preference), Prugna d'Italia, Precoce die Guignao, Formosa, Dane Aubert, Santarosa Stanley, Blue Gestetter and California Blue, as well as greengages with their sweet flesh and green skin. The main regions for plum cultivation are Emilia-Romagna, Campania, Morele, Alto Adige and Piedmont.

ABOVE: PRUGNE

As well as being eaten fresh on their own, they can be baked in sweets or simply stewed with sugar or made into jam. The dried version of the fruit, the prune, is used in confectionery and for baking. They are wonderful preserved in brandy, when they can be eaten with ice-cream or with creamy desserts, or simply soaked in water as an accompaniment to pork or game dishes. They are also used to make slivovitz, a well-known Yugoslavian type of schnapps.

RIBES / BLACKCURRANTS, REDCURRANTS, WHITE CURRANTS
These soft summer fruits come from a bushy plant that can be found in the wild. The translucent black, red or white berries are collected in small bunches. The blackcurrant is used by the drinks industry to make an alcoholic syrup that can be diluted with wine or spumante to make kir or for making jams. In jam-making, because of their high pectin content, *ribes* are often added to low-pectin fruit like strawberries, cherries and peaches. They are used in pâtisserie, in fruit tarts, and for decorating sweets. Along with other berry fruit, they are used to make summery fruit salads called *macedonia sottobosco* or *frutti di bosco*.

ROVO, SEE MORA DI ROVO

LEFT: PINE CONES FOR KERNELS IN CAMPANIA.

SORBO / SORB APPLE
This little tree, common in the hills all over Italy – especially Sardinia – produces a small apple-like fruit that turns from yellow to red, indicating that it is ripe and ready for eating. It is not grown commercially and can only be found in the wild, although it may be sold in specialist fruit shops towards the end of the summer.

SOTTOBOSCO / WILD BERRIES
This is a fairly recent term used to describe all the wild soft fruit one may find in the woods, such as wild strawberries, wild raspberries, wild blackberries, etc. It is also applied to a salad made of such fruit, or sauces incorporating the fruit for use in and with cakes and tarts. The term has even found use in the language of wine-tasting, to evoke flavours reminiscent of woodland like moss and fungus.

ABOVE: SOTTOBOSCO

SULTANINA, SEE UVA

SUSINA, SEE PRUGNA

TAMARINDO / TAMARIND
Originally from India, the tamarind tree produces a beautiful brown fruit. Although it is not grown in Italy, the tamarind is widely used in Italy to make a soft drink, a syrup and confectionery.

UVA, UVA DA TAVOLA, UVETTA, SULTANINA / GRAPE, RAISIN, SULTANA
There is an unbelievable variety of grapes grown in the world; some are cultivated exclusively for wine making, while others are for eating as a fruit – *uva da tavola* or table grapes. While it is possible to eat wine grapes at the table, table grapes cannot be used to make wine, however.

The vine is a climbing plant, introduced to Italy thousands of years ago from the area around the Caspian Sea. The Romans took this vital plant with them everywhere they went, introducing it to France and many other countries as they conquered Europe. Italy is now the biggest producer of grapes in the world, followed by Spain and France. The majority of these grapes are used to make wine, with the most frequently used grape being the thin-skinned white, pink or red *Vitis vinifera*. The best-known and most successful table grape is the Italia, which – thanks to new techniques for delaying ripening – is available from August to December. It is much appreciated in Italy and Europe, where it is exported in large quantities to Germany and France. Other varieties include the Uva Regina, the Red Cardinal, Primus and Baresana.

More than half of the grapes grown in Italy come from the fertile region of Puglia, with Sicily, Abruzzi, Lazio, Basilicata, Calabria and Sardinia making up the difference. Together they produce 1,400,000 tonnes of grapes a year, of which 450,000 are exported. In Piedmont, Veneto and most of the other wine-grape-producing regions, wonderfully ripe grapes like Uva Americana, Fragola (with the scent of strawberries) and the very sweet Moscato are often sold locally. I think the only variety worth eating is the Muscat. Bunches are hung on strong string until they turn from golden yellow to a wrinkled golden brown, when they become intensely and deliciously sweet. In Italy it is considered to be good luck to eat grapes on New Year's Eve and, although I am not superstitious, I still do it now (sadly, however, not with the same quality of grapes).

More and more foreign varieties are taking over, including the popular seedless Thompson variety. Today, the vast quantity of winter grapes sold lack flavour. Table grapes are eaten raw as dessert, or in fruit salads, or to cover fruit tarts. Some of the grapes are preserved in alcohol and served in a little bowl with a little of the liquor.

When they are dried, grapes turn into *uvetta* or raisins and *sultanina* or sultanas, which are often made with seedless grapes. The largest sultana is the pale-blonde Malaga, which has a few seeds, and the smallest raisin is the seedless blue-black Corinth, which is imported from the Middle East. Both raisins and sultanas are used in pâtisserie, featuring in a range of recipes from Panettone to Panpepato (see pages 218 and 230), as well as being used with ricotta in sweet fillings for tarts and cakes. In Naples, Sicily and Liguria they are also mixed with pine nuts as a stuffing for meat and game. They also make a delicious snack when soaked in brandy or rum.

Probably the most sought-after raisin to eat by itself is that made from the Zibibbo grape, the fruit of a vine grown in Italy for the making of the famous Moscato di Pantelleria. The raisins are dried still attached to the stalks and sold like this.

UVA SPINA / GOOSEBERRY
This spiky bush is related to the red currant. The berries are delicious when golden-yellow and ripe, but are only grown privately in Italy. They can be eaten in pies, cooked with sugar and puréed as a dessert, and used to make gooseberry fool.

VISCIOLA, SEE AMARENA

RIGHT: UVE DA TAVOLA

Melecotogne in Composta

MELECOTOGNE IN COMPOSTA

QUINCE COMPOTE

FOR 10

- 1 KG ($2^1/_4$ LB) QUINCES, QUARTERED, PEELED AND DESEEDED
- 1 LEMON, PREFERABLY ORGANICALLY GROWN
- 400 G (14 OZ) CASTER SUGAR
- 1 CINNAMON STICK (OPTIONAL)

The quince never ripens to a satisfactory point and so needs a great deal of sugar to preserve it.

Put the quinces in a large pan and add enough water to reach a third of the way up the fruit. Add the sugar and squeeze in the juice from the lemon, then add the squeezed-out lemon halves and the cinnamon stick, if using. Bring to the boil, cover and simmer for about 15 minutes, until the quinces are soft but still hold their shape. Check by inserting a knife from time to time. Remove the lemon halves and leave to cool. Serve chilled with some double cream or mascarpone or even with plain yoghurt.

CONFETTURA

JAM

All jams in Italy used to be called marmellata *until recent EU regulations decreed that they should be known as* confettura *– except ones made with citrus fruit, which would remain* marmellata *in line with British terminology. Below are recipes for three of my favourite* confetture.

CONFETTURA DI PERE COTOGNE

PIEDMONTESE MIXED FRUIT JAM

MAKES 5 KG (11 LB)

- 2 LITRES ($3^1/_2$ PINTS) FRESH RED GRAPE JUICE
- 1 KG ($2^1/_4$ LB) QUINCES, PEELED, CORED AND CHOPPED
- 1 KG ($2^1/_4$ LB) RIPE PLUMS, STONED AND CHOPPED
- 500 G (1 LB) PEARS, PEELED, CORED AND CHOPPED
- 1 CINNAMON STICK
- FINELY GRATED ZEST OF 2 LEMONS
- 200 G (7 OZ) WALNUT HALVES
- 2 KG ($2^1/_4$ LB) CASTER SUGAR

In various parts of Piedmont, where I grew up, this was also known as cugna, *from* cotognata *meaning quince, or* mostarda *because it contained many other fruits as well as quince. It was made in the autumn during the grape harvest so freshly pressed grape juice and other autumnal fruits could be used. It is delicious, and the taste still lingers in my memory from when Mamma would give us a slice of white bread covered with* cugna *for our afternoon snack. It is also served with Bollito Misto (see page 92) or used to make Crostata di Cugna (see page 277). Ideally you should make your own fresh grape juice for this from red grapes.*

Put the grape juice, fruit, cinnamon stick, lemon zest and walnuts into a large pan, preferably a copper preserving pan. Cook slowly for 1 hour, then add the sugar and cook over a gentle heat for a few hours, stirring often to prevent sticking, until the mixture is very thick and almost brown in colour and all the fruit has dissolved. Put in sterilized jars and cover with waxed paper discs. Leave until completely cold, then seal.

Confettura di Lamponi

RASPBERRY JAM

Makes 1 kg (2 lb 3 oz)

700 g (1½ lb) raspberries
700 g (1½ lb) caster sugar

This is probably the most delightful of jams for taste and colour. In the mountainous regions of northern Italy it is still possible to pick your own wild raspberries and they have a remarkably intense flavour, particularly good in this jam. You may also be able to buy them in a market, which will certainly be easier although they will not taste as good.

Put the fruit and sugar in a heavy-based pan over a low heat and stir with a wooden spoon to break up the fruit. Increase the heat slightly and, when it begins to boil, skim off the foam from the surface. Simmer for about 30 minutes, then check the setting point by putting a teaspoonful on a small plate: if it solidifies when cool, it is ready. Put into sterilized jars and cover with waxed paper discs. Leave until completely cold and then seal.

Confettura di Castagne

CHESTNUT JAM

Makes 2 kg (4 lb 6 oz)

1.25 kg (2½ lb) fresh chestnuts
a few bay leaves
1.25 kg (2½ lb) caster sugar
200 ml (7 fl oz) water
1 vanilla pod, slit open lengthwise

My granny used to make this jam and we children would eat it by the spoonful. It was sometimes served with double cream as a pretty calorific dessert.

Slit the skins of the chestnuts, boil for 5 minutes and then peel while still hot, removing both the outer and thin inner layer of skin. Cook the peeled chestnuts with the bay leaves in lightly salted boiling water for 30 minutes, then drain and leave to cool. Remove any remaining pieces of skin with the tip of a knife. Pass the chestnuts through a sieve to obtain a fairly dry purée.

Put the sugar, water and vanilla pod in a heavy-based pan and stir over a moderate heat until you get a pale, translucent syrup. Discard the vanilla and add the chestnut purée to the syrup. Cook gently, stirring often, for 30 minutes. Pour the jam into sterilized jars and cover with waxed paper discs. Leave until completely cold and then seal.

Salsa di Noci

WALNUT SAUCE

In Genoa, where this recipe comes from, it is called *tocco de noxe* and is mainly used with pansôti or other pasta. See page 167 for the recipe.

Crostata di Cugna

MIXED FRUIT JAM TART

For 6–8

- 500 g (1 lb $1^{1}/_{2}$ oz) 00 (doppio zero) flour
- 200 g (7 oz) soft butter, cut into small cubes
- 5 egg yolks
- 200 g (7 oz) caster sugar
- 1 tbsp vanilla sugar
- grated zest of $^{1}/_{2}$ lemon
- pinch of salt
- 350 g (12 oz) Confettura di Pere Cotogne (see page 275) or other favourite jam

The Italian equivalent of English tea at 4 or 5 o'clock in the afternoon is the merenda, *when most children eat a slice of what every Italian mother can make – jam tart. It is usually filled with a good home-made jam such as peach, apricot, cherry or prune. Here Confettura di Pere Cotogne (see page 275), also known as* cugna, *is used. It can also be made with fresh or cooked fruit on a blind-baked shortcrust pastry base.*

Pile the flour up on a work surface into a volcano shape, made a well in the centre and add the butter, 4 of the egg yolks, caster sugar, vanilla sugar, lemon zest and salt. Gradually draw in the flour and then with the palm of your hand knead quickly and lightly to obtain a smooth dough. Wrap in cling film and leave to rest in the refrigerator for 1 hour.

Preheat the oven to 180°C/350°F/gas4. Take three quarters of the pastry and roll it out on a lightly floured board until it is large enough to fit a 25 cm (10 inch) round flan tin or a rectangular baking tray. Butter the tin or baking tray and line with the pastry, trimming off the excess. Fill with the jam, then roll out the remaining pastry and cut it into long strips with a pastry wheel or a sharp knife to make a lattice for the tart. Brush with the remaining egg yolk and bake for 30 minutes. Leave to cool and then serve.

FICHI AL FORNO

BAKED FIGS

FOR 4

- 12 RIPE BUT FIRM, LARGE FRESH FIGS, PEELED
- 300 G ($10^{1}/_{2}$ OZ) CASTER SUGAR
- ZEST AND JUICE OF 1 LEMON
- MASCARPONE OR LIGHTLY WHIPPED DOUBLE CREAM, TO SERVE (OPTIONAL)

This great classic dessert is made with very simple ingredients indeed. However, the figs have to be impeccably ripe and of good quality.

Preheat the oven to 250°C/475°F/gas9. Put the figs closely together on a small baking tray and cover them evenly with the sugar. Sprinkle the lemon juice over them and half the lemon zest, cut into thin strips. Finely dice the remaining lemon zest and set aside. Bake the figs for 20 minutes, until the sugar is foaming, then spoon a little of the caramelized sugar on to each fig and sprinkle over the remaining lemon zest. Put back in the oven for another 5 minutes.

Remove and transfer to a nice porcelain plate, pour the cooking juices over and leave to cool, then refrigerate. Serve with a dollop of mascarpone or lightly whipped double cream, if desired.

Pasta di Mandorle

MARZIPAN

Makes about 1.25 kg (2¾ lb)

1 kg (2¼ lb) fresh sweet almonds
400 g (14 oz) icing sugar
½ tsp vanilla extract
cornflour for dusting

This is a sweet paste based on ground almonds, used by pastry chefs to make cakes and petits fours. It is mostly used in Southern Italy and Sicily, where almonds grow in abundance. Pasta di mandorle *is also known as* marzapane *or* pasta reale. *Another type of almond paste called* marturana *was originally made by nuns in a convent at Marturana in Palermo, Sicily. This paste is used as a base to model various shapes and figures, for example fruit, animals, etc, which are then painted.*

Needless to say the combination of almonds and sugar is a highly calorific mix that should be eaten sparingly if you do not want to damage your waistline! Pasta di mandorle *is very simple to prepare and home-made tastes much nicer than the ready-made variety. My advice, however, is to use fresh almonds and grind them yourself rather than buy ready-ground almonds, which dry out quickly and lose their flavour.*

Put the almonds in a large pan of boiling water and simmer for 5 minutes. Drain and leave to cool, then peel them. The skins should come off easily. Grind the almonds in a food processor to obtain a slightly coarse mixture. Stir in the icing sugar and vanilla extract, then turn the mixture out on to a work surface and knead to a dough, dusting with cornflour to prevent sticking.

At this stage you can roll out the almond paste and make it into shapes, dusting your hands and the work surface with icing sugar to prevent sticking, or you can store it in an airtight container in the fridge until required. Should you want to colour the marzipan, use good non-synthetic food colouring.

Amaretti

ALMOND BISCUITS

Makes 40

275 g (10 oz) sweet almonds
30 g (1 oz) bitter almonds, blanched and skinned, then toasted until dry but not coloured
500 g (1 lb) icing sugar
4 egg whites
55 g (1¾ oz) caster sugar

There are two versions of these famous little almond biscuits. One is for soft amaretti *(see page 288) and the other, this recipe, for dry and crumbly ones.*

Preheat the oven to 220°C/425°F/gas7. Reduce the sweet and bitter almonds to a coarse flour either with a pestle and mortar or in a food processor. Gradually incorporate the icing sugar and egg whites until you obtain a firm mixture. Roll this with your hands to a sausage shape about 3 cm (1¼ inches) in diameter and cut it into slices 1 cm (½ inch) thick. Place well spaced apart on a buttered baking sheet. Sprinkle with the caster sugar and bake for about 15 minutes, until pale brown and crunchy. Leave to cool on the baking sheet.

Croccante di Nocciole

Hazelnut Crunch

Makes 1 kg (2 lb 3 oz)

- 400 g (14 oz) caster sugar
- 100 g ($3^1/_2$ oz) honey
- zest of 2 tangerines, cut into strips, then into very small dice
- 500 g (1 lb) hazelnuts, toasted and skinned
- a few sheets of rice paper
- 1 lemon, cut in half

This is a popular sweet at every village festa (fête), especially in the South, and one that announces that Christmas is approaching. It can be made with almonds (as in the photograph on the right), pistachios or mixed nuts but toasted hazelnuts are my favourite.

Melt the sugar and honey in a heavy-based pan over a gentle heat. Raise the heat slightly and, when the sugar begins to go a blondish-brown colour, add the tangerine zest. Stir for a minute with a wooden spoon, then add the hazelnuts. Heat a little, stirring, until the hazelnuts are coated with the sugar syrup.

Pour the very hot mixture on to the rice paper and use the lemon halves to spread it out to about 2.5 cm (1 inch) thick (lemons are ideal for this because they do not stick to the mixture). As soon as it has cooled down, but is still warm, cut into cubes with a large knife. They will still be attached at the bottom. Wait until they are completely cold, then break the cubes apart. Put them in an airtight jar and enjoy them when you feel like it. At Christmas they are served at the end of the meal.

Torta di Nocciole e Cioccolato

Hazelnut and Chocolate Cake

For 6–8

- 300 g ($10^1/_2$ oz) hazelnuts, toasted and skinned
- 6 eggs
- 500 g (1 lb) caster sugar
- 2 tsp baking powder
- 300 g ($10^1/_2$ oz) butter, melted
- 150 ml ($^1/_4$ pint) milk
- 375 g (13 oz) 00 (doppio zero) flour
- 100 g ($3^1/_2$ oz) bitter chocolate (at least 70% cocoa solids), cut into small cubes

I can't resist any hazelnut cake. I find the taste of the nuts, especially roasted, highly attractive. I hope you will agree with me.

Preheat the oven to 180°C/350°F/gas4. Put the hazelnuts in a food processor and reduce to a coarse flour. Using an electric mixer, beat the eggs with the sugar and baking powder until the mixture is mousse-like and thick enough to leave a trail on the surface when drizzled from the beaters. Gently but thoroughly fold in the melted butter and milk, then fold in the flour and hazelnuts, followed by the chocolate.

Pour the mixture into a buttered and floured 25 cm (10 inch) cake tin and bake for 45 minutes, or until a skewer inserted in the centre comes out dry. Leave to cool before serving.

PANFORTE

TRADITIONAL TUSCAN CAKE

FOR 10

- 250 G (9 OZ) ALMONDS, BLANCHED, SKINNED AND TOASTED
- 150 G (5 OZ) WALNUTS OR PECAN NUTS
- 55 G (1¾ OZ) CANDIED CEDRO (CITRON PEEL), CUT INTO SMALL STRIPS
- 250 G (9 OZ) CANDIED PUMPKIN, CUT INTO SMALL CHUNKS
- 2 TSP GROUND CINNAMON
- 2 TSP GROUND CORIANDER SEEDS
- ½ TSP FRESHLY GRATED NUTMEG
- 200 G (7 OZ) PLAIN FLOUR
- 200 G (7 OZ) ICING SUGAR
- 200 G (7 OZ) HONEY (ACACIA IS BEST)
- A FEW SHEETS OF RICE PAPER
- 2 TBSP VANILLA SUGAR

This Tuscan speciality has been eaten since the Middle Ages, when the first spices were imported from the Mediterranean. Sienna is the city that assumed paternity of this 'strong bread', now famous all over the world. The recipe includes candied pumpkin, which is easy to find in Italy but not so easy elsewhere. It can be replaced with candied citrus peel, although the flavour will not be the same. You could try looking for candied pumpkin in Turkish and Middle Eastern shops.

Preheat the oven to 160°C/325°F/gas3. Mix the almonds, walnuts or pecans, candied peel, pumpkin and spices together in a bowl. Add the flour and mix in very well. Put the icing sugar, honey and a tablespoon of water in a heavy-based pan and heat gently until dissolved. Increase the heat so that the mixture bubbles and then stir with a wooden spoon until it forms a dense, pale-brown caramel. Pour it on to the flour and nuts and mix until smooth.

Use the rice paper to line a 20 cm (8 inch) cake tin, 4 cm (1½ inches) deep. Spread the mixture in it, levelling the top with a spatula. Bake in the oven for about 30 minutes, then remove and leave to cool in the tin. Dust with the vanilla sugar. It can be kept for a long time but I doubt you will be able to!

CASTAGNACCIO

CHESTNUT CAKE

FOR 8–10

750 G ($1^3/_4$ LB) FRESH CHESTNUT FLOUR
PINCH OF SALT
6 TBSP CASTER SUGAR
6 TBSP VIRGIN OLIVE OIL
3–4 SPRIGS OF ROSEMARY
150 G (5 OZ) ZIBIBBO RAISINS (SEE UVA, PAGE 273) OR ORDINARY RAISINS

There exist various versions of this seasonal dish, which is made with the flour of new autumn chestnuts. Chestnut flour tends to become stale quite quickly, which is why it is best used fresh. This is the one of the simplest and most tasty ways of cooking it.

Preheat the oven to 180°C/350°F/gas4. Mix the flour, salt and sugar with enough cold water to obtain a soft but not too runny mixture. Put the oil in a deep 30 x 40 cm (12 x 16 inch) baking tray and spread evenly, then pour in the batter. Sprinkle with the rosemary and raisins and bake for 20 minutes, until golden. Cut into squares to serve. It's best served hot but can also be eaten cold.

ORZATA

ALMOND MILK DRINK

FOR 4

165 G ($5^1/_2$ OZ) SWEET ALMOND PASTE (SEE PAGE 267)
600 ML (1 PINT) WATER

This wonderfully refreshing summer drink was originally made with barley, but now a thick, sugared almond paste is more likely to be used. It is also called latte di mandorle, *or almond milk.*

Put the almond paste and water in a liquidizer and blend until it forms a white, milky fluid. If it is too strong, dilute with a little more water.

FRUTTA SCIROPPATA

FRUITS IN SYRUP

MAKES ENOUGH TO FILL A 1.5 KG (3 LB 5 OZ) JAR

1 KG ($2^1/_4$ LB) FRUIT (SEE RIGHT)
800 G ($1^3/_4$ LB) CASTER SUGAR
1 LITRE ($1^3/_4$ PINTS) WATER
1 VANILLA POD

This is half way between a compote and crystallized fruit. The secret is to achieve a degree of sugar concentration in the liquid so that it functions as a preservative. The fruit should keep its shape. Ripe peaches, plums or kumquats are all ideal. It is often served with ice-cream or panna cotta.

If using peaches, blanch them briefly in boiling water, then skin and halve them and remove the stone.

Put the sugar, water and vanilla pod in a large pan and heat gently until the sugar has completely dissolved. Add the fruit and cook gently until just tender – anything from 25 minutes for the softest fruit to 40 minutes for harder ones. Remove the fruit with a slotted spoon and set aside. Increase the heat and boil the liquid until reduced in volume by a third. Reduce the heat again, put the fruit back in the pan and cook over a very low heat for another 30 minutes. Transfer to a sterilized jar, seal and store in a cool place until needed.

Frutta Sotto Spirito

FRUIT IN ALCOHOL

It is best to use very high spirit (95 per cent alcohol) for this, which is readily available in Italy but not everywhere (see page 310). You should always use ripe fruit no larger than a small tangerine. Grapes, cherries, apricots, and dried fruits such as raisins are ideal. Soft fruits such as berries are not suitable. Pack the fruit tightly into a sterilized preserving jar, then pour over the alcohol and seal the jar. The rest is done by time, and 3 months is the minimum it should be left. Serve the fruit in small glasses either on its own or accompanied by cream or ice-cream. It should not be given to children; this is a serious grown-up affair!

BREADS & BAKING

PANE E CIBI DA FORNO

The origins of baking, especially that of bread baking, go back to at least 2,000 years before Christ, and the Egyptians seem to be the first to have had any expertise in the field. Since then bread has spread all over the world to become, after rice, the principal element of human nutrition. Every country or race has chosen different ways to produce it, using the most favourable local grains and utensils. Basically, however, it is the same for everybody. Flour of various grains is combined with water, a little salt and yeast, this dough is left to rise through the action of yeast and then it is baked for immediate use.

As a small child in Castelnuovo Belbo, my brother Carlo used to head off on his bike with a huge willow basket balanced on the handlebars. This basket was lined with an immaculate linen cloth, containing a huge lump of fresh bread dough that my mother had prepared to send to the local bakery to be baked into loaves for the family's needs. She used to knead the dough for a long time before letting it rise and then she placed it gently into the basket and covered it. Carlo then had the task of cycling to the bakery in the village, where the dough was divided into various large portions and baked. The result was stunning! This was bread made with love and had a fragrance that even impressed the baker, who always wanted to keep a piece for himself.

The function of a bakery, especially one in a small village, wasn't only the baking of bread. All sorts of things lovingly prepared at home, like roasts, tarts, biscuits, and various other things, like loaves of bread cut into slices to be biscuited (see Frisella, page 293), were brought by the villagers on trays to be baked once the actual bread baking was finished for the day, but while the oven was still hot. The fragrance of those dishes, mingled with the wonderful smell of the burnt wood, was something out of this world!

This was at the end of the war, when we were very lucky to have many ingredients which were otherwise hard to find. My father had obtained two big sacks of sea salt which he bartered for merchandise such as wheat, etc. I will never forget the slice of bread eaten for *merenda*, the Italian equivalent of high tea, topped with *mostarda* jam – also made by my mother.

The way of baking today has changed completely. It is rare to find a bakery still with a wood-burning oven to impart the full flavour to the bread. Everything is industrialized in the name of progress but, in my opinion, only in the name of commercialization that does not understand real quality. I really feel sorry for the younger generation in this respect, because with every baker closing down a piece of artisan culture has probably gone forever.

A little revival of this art does, however, seem to be underway, thanks to some nostalgic people reviving the old ways of making bread. These artisans prepare all sorts of specialities from the past, like *pane di segala*, dark hard rye bread as they used to make in the Aosta Valley for long keeping, which is edible only when dipped in water or in milk. All sorts of other interesting breads, made using wholemeal flour in response to modern dietary demands, as well as bread made with half maize flour and half wheat flour, are on offer to help us rediscover some of the textures and tastes of bygone times.

Industrially produced bread is absolutely diabolical, keeping its freshness and crispiness for only a few hours and tasting mostly of cotton wool. Unfortunately, even the Italians – who usually make a big fuss about the quality of food – seem to have accepted this sort of bread for the sake of convenience. The only real use of a wood-fired oven today is usually the making of pizzas, which have taken the world by storm. Even in that industry, however, wood-fired ovens are in the minority, as commercialization dictates more economical ways.

RIGHT: TUSCAN FIELDS, NEAR MONTALCINO, PREPARED FOR GRAIN.

LEFT: A RANGE OF SICILIAN BREADS.

A-Z of Breads & Baking

AMARETTO / MACAROON BISCUIT
There are many varieties of this popular biscuit, the most well-known being the crispy *amaretto di Saronno*, a pair of small *amaretti* wrapped in paper and served with coffee in almost every Italian restaurant or trattoria. It takes its name from the town of Saronno, where it has been made for the last hundred years by Lazzaroni. *Amaretti* can be found all over Italy, however, ranging in texture from dry and crisp to moist and soft, depending on the recipe and cooking time. The most sought-after are those of Mombaruzzo, a small town in Piedmont. These *amaretti* are soft and each one is wrapped by hand in characteristic oiled paper.

Making Amaretti Biscuits

To make your own moist and soft amaretti (see page 279 for a recipe for crisp ones), mix 500 g (1 lb $1^{1}/_{2}$ oz) peeled and freshly ground almonds with 150 g (5 oz) ground bitter almonds or armelline (ground apricot kernels, see Abicocca, page 262).

Carefully fold 500 g (1 lb) caster sugar into 4 lightly beaten egg whites, then add the ground almonds and the grated zest of $^{1}/_{2}$ lemon.

Place the mixture in a piping bag and pipe round discs of it on a buttered baking tray. Dust with some coarsely crushed sugar, then place in an oven preheated to 190°C/375°F/gas5 and bake until brown.

ANICINO / ANISE BISCUIT
These Umbrian biscuits are a testimony to the popularity of aniseed in Italy. The biscuits are a speciality of Orvieto, although they are also made in Sardinia and can be eaten either on their own or dipped in wine like *cantuccini*. In Sardinia they are dipped into the local strong wine, Monica di Sardegna. As a variation, the biscuits can be made with olive oil instead of the usual hard fats, making them tastier and healthier.

BABA / RUM BABA
This typically Neapolitan sweet is said to have been introduced to the area by the French during their invasion, although the exact origin is not known. What is certain, though, is that Neapolitans are very fond of it, especially when it is drenched in rum. The round cake sponges can also be served with cream and fruit, but the original recipe is the best (see page 309).

BACO DI DAMA / BISCUIT, LADY'S KISS
This Piedmontese biscuit gets its name from the fact that the two circles of shortcrust biscuit, sandwiched together with plain chocolate, look like a pair of lips. To make them: mix together 150 g (5 oz) finely ground almonds with 150 g (5 oz) 00 flour, 150 g (5 oz) caster sugar, 150 g (5 oz) soft butter, a little grated lemon, orange or lime zest and 3 egg yolks. Work the mixture until well combined, then form it into little balls and place on a buttered baking tray and bake in an oven preheated to 190°C/375°F/gas5 until golden brown. Allow the biscuits to cool, then sandwich them together with a little melted chocolate.

Making Bignole

To make bignole: place 500 ml (18 fl oz) of water, a pinch of salt and 200 g (7 oz) butter in a pan and place over a high heat. As soon as it comes to the boil, take the pan off the heat and add 300 g ($10^{1}/_{2}$ oz) plain flour. Mix well, then leave to cool before adding 6 whole eggs and 4 egg yolks, and 30 g (1 oz) sugar. Mix thoroughly, then place the mixture in an icing bag fitted with a plain nozzle. Pipe small dots of dough on a buttered baking tray, and cook for about 20 minutes in an oven preheated to 200°C/400°F/gas6. When they are done, remove them from the oven and leave to cool. They should have puffed up to 3 or 4 times their initial size and be hollow so they can be filled with cream or zabaglione (see the recipe on page 65). Dip a part of each bignole in a lemon-flavoured glacé icing, leave to set, then serve.

BARCHETTA / LITTLE BOAT, BARQUETTE
Little boat-shaped biscuits, made from shortcrust pastry, *barchetta* may be filled with fruit, jam or *crema pasticcera* and eaten as a dessert. They can also be filled with shrimps, scrambled egg and caviar, and served as canapés.

LEFT: AMARETTI

BASTONE / STICK, BAGUETTE
This long stick of white bread is similar to the French baguette (see Pane).

BIGNÈ, BIGNOLE / PROFITEROLE
Bignè refers to any cake made with choux pastry, including profiteroles and eclairs among others. Piedmont has moved even closer to France, with the creation of *bignole*, little balls of choux pastry filled with

cream or zabaglione, then partially dipped in glacé icing.

BIOVA, BIOVETTA / PIEDMONTESE BREAD

This Piedmontese bread is now eaten in most of the northern regions of Italy. It is made with *pasta dura*, a hard, unproved dough that is worked well to get rid of air bubbles and to make it softer. The crust of the cooked bread is quite crispy, while the centre is very dense and white. It is often formed and cut into the most incredible shapes, or it can be bought in loaves, the small ones being called *biovetta* and the larger *biova*.

BISCOTTO / BISCUIT

Originally a slice of bread, as the name suggests, twice baked to achieve dryness. The *biscotto* was originally a means of conserving bread by drying it, for later reuse by adding moisture again in the form of water or milk (see Frisella). Today the *biscotto* is more a kind of true biscuit, which can be made of eggs and flour with the addition of sugar, honey and yeast and other ingredients like almonds, chocolate, etc., or a combination of these. *Biscotti* can also be savoury, like Taralli or crackers to take the place of bread. *Biscotti* are made both for immediate use or for long keeping, the best examples of each being fresh and dry *amaretti*. Italians use a great deal of *biscotti* of any kind, mostly sweet and mainly to dip into *caffè latte*, the morning breakfast drink.

BELOW: A RANGE OF BISCUITS FROM PFATISH IN TURIN: ALUMETTI, CANNONCINI ALLA CREMA, BACI DI DAMA, BISCOTTINI DA GELATO, BISCOTTINI FROLLINO OVALE, LINGUE DI GATTO AL CIOCOLATTO, BISCOTTO NOVARA.

BOMBOLONI, SEE KRAPFEN

BRUSCHETTA

Bruschetta is a slice of toasted bread flavoured with oil, fats or garlic, to be eaten on its own as a snack or served with *antipasto*. The most common way of serving *bruschetta* is brushed with a clove of garlic and drizzled with a little extra-virgin olive oil. Another method is to spread the toast with good-quality pork lard or goose fat. In Lazio and Abruzzi, olive oil is drizzled over and a little chopped tomato and basil added. In Tuscany, *bruschetta* is called *fettunta* or *panunto*, meaning 'greased slice of bread' and it is usually made with an unsalted bread called *pane sciocco* (see Pane).

RIGHT: BRUSCHETTA

BUCCELLATO LUCCHESE / LUCCHESE CAKE

This simple cake, looking more like a bread than a cake, is a speciality of Lucca in Tuscany; however, a much more complicated version is made in Sicily, based on eggs and including candied peel. Both cakes are eaten in the same way, though, as dessert or for breakfast, dipped in milk. They keep very well if stored in an airtight tin.

BUGIE, SEE CENCI

CALZONE / FOLDED PIZZAS

Calzone, from the word for 'trousers', is made with the same dough as pizzas, and is folded into a pocket around stuffing. The Neapolitans fill theirs with Provolone cheese, mozzarella, hot Neapolitan sausage or salami, all cut into cubes and mixed with beaten eggs. Other recipes include one from Puglia that includes braised sliced onions, ricotta forte, eggs and Parmesan; and cooked Swiss chard or spinach with eggs, Parmesan and Pecorino cheese. Whatever combination of ingredients is chosen, to make the pocket of dough, roll out the dough and place in a 30 cm (12 inch) pizza dish, then sprinkle your mixture of ingredients on top. Fold over, seal and bake for 40 minutes in an oven preheated to 220°C/425°F/gas7. Smaller envelopes of filled dough can be fried in olive oil and are good eaten both hot and cold.

CANAPÉ

Canapés are slices of bread that have been cut into small squares, triangles or rectangles, then spread with butter or mayonnaise and topped with a range of meat, fish or salad combinations. They are usually served as an appetizer with drinks. If warm they are known as

MAKING BUCCELLATO LUCCHESE

To make buccellato lucchese: mix together 500 g (1 lb 1½ oz) plain flour with 175 g (6 oz) caster sugar, 60 g (2 oz) soft butter, 2 beaten eggs (keeping back enough for brushing over the finished cake) and a tea cup of milk with 25 g (¾ oz) fresh brewers' yeast, or the equivalent of dry. Combine together all the ingredients until you have a fairly soft dough, then add 60 g (2 oz) raisins, 15 g (½ oz) aniseed and a pinch of salt. Mix well and leave to rise for about 2 hours. Cut off chunks of dough and form into sausage shapes with your hands. Using a knife, cut a few diagonal slashes in the top of each sausage, then brush with the reserved beaten egg and leave to rest for an hour. Bake in an oven preheated to 190°C/375°F/gas5 for 1 hour.

crostini, and are particularly popular in Tuscany.

Canapés are served all over Italy at receptions and private parties, but they are never too substantial as they are usually followed by a full meal. The toppings can be made from a whole range of ingredients, but the most popular are anchovies, smoked salmon, salami, and tomato and mozzarella. The bread used is *pane in cassetta*, a square slice of special white bread with a very thin crust.

CANNOLO / FILLED SWEET PASTRY TUBE

Cannoli is probably the best-known Sicilian dessert and gets is name from the fact that it is deep-fried around a piece of cane (*canna*). It used only to be made for *Carnevale* (carnival) and for the feast day of San Carlo. Now it is eaten all year round, not only after meals, but also as a snack. The special pastry is filled with a mixture of ricotta, sugar, candied fruits and chocolate (see the recipe on page 256).

CANNONCINO / LITTLE CANNON, PUFF PASTRY HORN

A popular pastry in Italy, the pastry horn is made from a rectangular piece of puff pastry, about 30 cm (12 inches) in length and 3-4 cm ($1^1/_4$ - $1^1/_2$ inches) wide. It is rolled very thin, then wound tightly around a metal cone to make the horn shape. The pastry is then brushed with beaten egg and baked on a buttered baking tray in a hot oven for 20 minutes. When the horns are cool the metal cone is removed and the pastry filled with flavoured creams or zabaglione.

CANTUCCI, CANTUCCINI / TUSCAN ALMOND BISCUITS

In Tuscany, it is common to finish a meal with these biscuits, dipped in a glass of the strong wine, Vin Santo. It is such a pleasurable way of finishing a meal, that the custom has spread all over Italy, as well as to other countries. The biscuits come from Prato in Tuscany and so they are also known as *cantucci di prato*.

To make them: beat 300 g ($10^1/_2$ oz) caster sugar with 3 eggs and 3 egg yolks until you have a well-amalgamated foam. Add 500 g (1 lb $1^1/_2$ oz) 00 flour, 200 g (7 oz) lightly toasted unpeeled almonds, a pinch of salt, 1 teaspoon orange essence and 1 teaspoon bicarbonate of soda or baking powder. Mix gently until you have a soft dough. Divide into longish sausages and place on a buttered baking tray, pressing each one until it is flattened to about 2 cm ($^3/_4$ inch) high and 4 cm ($1^1/_2$ inch) wide. Make sure the dough sausages are far enough apart to give them room to rise as they bake. Brush each one with a little beaten egg and bake in an oven preheated to 190°C/375°F/gas5 for 15 minutes. Remove from the oven and cut each biscuit diagonally into 2 cm ($^3/_4$ inch) wide strips and return to the oven until completely cooked and dry, about 10 minutes. Remove from the oven and allow to cool, before storing in an airtight jar or tin until needed.

CARTA DA MUSICA, PANE CARASAU / FLAT SARDINIAN BREAD

This very thin, flat, crispy bread, which resembles old parchment or music manuscript paper (hence its name), is difficult to make and is usually bought now rather than made at home. It is sold in piles of 10 or 20 slices, which are carefully packaged because of their fragility.

The dough is made with two-thirds durum wheat fine semolina and one-third plain flour, mixed with yeast, water and a little salt. All the ingredients are mixed together very thoroughly and worked until smooth, the dough is then left to prove for 6 hours, after which time it is knocked back, kneaded again and left to rise for a second time. The dough is then formed into balls and rolled thinly to fit a dish that is just 2 mm deep. All the filled dishes are piled up on top of each other, with linen cloth separating them. A weight is placed on top of the pile and the dough is then left to rest for 2 or 3 hours. The dishes are then placed in an oven, traditionally wood-fired, and baked briefly until they puff up.

While they are still warm, each disc of dough is cut into two even thinner discs, placed into even shallower dishes and piled up as before to keep them flat until completely cooled. They are then baked again, one by one, in a hot oven until they are slightly coloured and crispy. They keep for about a month, which is why farmers used to go to such lengths to make the bread.

Sardinians eat this bread either soaked in water and served with ripe tomatoes and grated Pecorino cheese or brushed with oil and briefly heated in a hot oven until very crisp. After being softened in

LEFT: CARTA DA MUSICA

LEFT: CANTUCCI AL MIELE

water, it can also be layered, like lasagne, with a tomato sauce, cheese and meat *ragù*, sprinkled with Parmesan and baked.

CASATIELLO, CASATELLO / NEAPOLITAN EASTER BREAD
This special savoury bread is made in Naples for Easter, usually in batches of two or three, so there are always spare loaves to give as presents to friends.

CASSATA
Cassata gets its name from *qus'at*, the Arab word for the small conical container in which the dessert is traditionally made. It used to be made only by nuns during Holy Week, but is now available all year round. There are two versions of the dish, both of which come from Sicily, where it was created. The first is a cake made with marzipan, ricotta and candied fruit; and the second, a later development, made with ice-cream. A smaller version of *cassata*, called *cassatina*, is often sold in Sicilian bars, cafés and pastry shops.

CASTAGNACCIO, SEE PAGE 282

CENCI, CHIACCHERE, BUGIE / PASTRIES
Cenci, meaning 'rags', are usually made for *Carnevale*, but are now available all year round. They are made from a dough of 00 (*doppio zero*) wheat flour with the addition of butter, sugar, eggs and a little Vin Santo. The pastry is rolled out, then cut into ribbons and deep-fried, possibly in lard but also sometimes in olive oil. They are dusted with icing sugar when cool.

CHIFEL, SEE CORNETTO

CIABATTA / BREAD
One of the most popular breads in Italy and around the world, *ciabatta* is made with type 0 wheat flour and is characterized by its softness and moisture, both of which are due to the long raising time of 6 hours, when the large air holes are formed. Its soft crust is the result of cooking the bread in ovens where water is allowed to evaporate as the bread cooks (see Pane).

CIALDA / WAFER
To make wafers you need a wafer iron. Wafers are made from a smooth dough called *cialda* or *cialdone*, made with 350 g (12 oz) plain flour, 1 egg and 2 egg yolks, 100 g (3½ oz) sugar, 60 g (2 oz) butter and a pinch of salt. Mix all the ingredients together until you have a fairly soft dough, adding a little water if the consistency is not loose enough. Heat the wafer irons until they are very hot, brush with a little oil or fat and put a tablespoon of the dough on one side of the iron, press the other side of the iron on top and bake on both sides for a few minutes. Open the iron and peel off the hot wafer. While it is still warm, shape it into a cone or leave it to cool flat, depending on how you want to use it. Fill with cream or ice cream and anything else you like, or eat on their own.

RIGHT: CIABATTA

CIAMBELLA, CIAMBELLONE, CIAMBELLINA / RING-SHAPED CAKE
There is a proverb in Italy '*Non tutte le ciambelle riescono con il buco*', which translates as 'not every *ciambella* comes with a hole', meaning not everything can be perfect. The *ciambella* is made from a dough that is baked in a ring mould or simply shaped into a ring. It can be either savoury or sweet, depending on the ingredients added to the basic dough mixture. *Ciambellone* is a larger cake and *ciambellina* a smaller one.

One of the most frequently made recipes consists of 350 g (12 oz) 00 flour, 200 g (7 oz) caster sugar, 3 eggs, 75 g (2¾ oz) soft butter, 3 tablespoons dark rum, the grated zest of a lemon, a pinch of salt, 1 sachet of yeast and enough milk to make a soft dough. Mix all the ingredients together thoroughly, then place in a buttered ring mould and bake in an oven preheated to 190°C/375°F/gas5 for 40-50 minutes.

COLOMBA / EASTER DOVE
This cake, made in the shape of a dove, is an Easter offering representing peace. Like *panettone*, it is now eaten all over Italy and sold abroad in specialist shops. It is quite different to *panettone*, in that it does not include raisins and has a higher proportion of eggs and butter and includes candied orange peel. It is covered in a sugar-and-almond icing and is eaten as a dessert, ideally with a glass of Moscato or any other sparkling dessert wine.

CORNETTO, CHIFEL / HORN BREAD
Cornetto is a bread shaped like the French croissant, made with a 00 (*doppio zero*) flour dough folded to create layers of pastry, much like puff pastry. It is sometimes made with *pane all'olio*, a dough made with oil or butter to make it more crumbly. A similar bread, called *chifel*, is made in Trentino-Alto Adige.

CROSTATA, SEE THE RECIPE ON PAGE 277

CROSTINI DI PANE / TUSCAN TOASTED BREAD
Crostini have recently become very fashionable all over the world. Originally from Tuscany, they are made with slices of unsalted Tuscan bread that is toasted and spread with

a pâté of chicken livers, a wild boar *ragù* or vegetables. Tuscans eat this canapé with aperitifs, but selections with various toppings are now also served as a first course. The finest *crostini* are spread with a pâté and topped with a slice of truffle.

FARINATA / UNLEAVENED BREAD

The most ancient methods of making breads used just flour and water, with no raising agent. A wide range of flours, including those of wheat, rye and barley, can be used, but an old and unusual bread that is still made today in Piedmont and more particularly in Liguria, is based on chickpea flour.

The bread is made as follows: mix 1 part fine chickpea flour with 4 parts lukewarm water and a pinch of salt to make a very thin batter and leave to rest for about an hour. Sprinkle a baking tray with some very good extra-virgin olive oil and then pour in the mixture until it is about 2 cm (3/4 inch) in depth. Stir the mixture in the tray to distribute the oil evenly and bake in an oven preheated to 230°C/450°F/gas8, until golden brown. *Farinata* has to be eaten hot, cut into small squares and dusted with freshly ground black pepper.

A delicious variation used in Palermo is *panella*, in which fennel seeds and freshly chopped parsley are added to the flour-and-water mixture. When cooked, the soft bread is laid on an oiled surface to cool, then cut into oblongs or squares and fried in oil. A similar, but much more complicated method, is used when making Castagnaccio, a bread made with chestnut flour (see page 282).

FAVE DEI MORTI / ALMOND BISCUITS

On 2 November, Italians celebrate the Day of the Dead. *Fave dei morti*, which literally translates as 'broad beans of the dead', is the name given to the biscuits eaten during the festival in Piedmont, Lombardy and in many other regions.

They are based on a mixture of 250 g (9 oz) finely ground almonds, 2 eggs, 125 g (4 1/2 oz) plain flour, 55 g (2 oz) softened butter, 100 g (3 1/2 oz) sugar and 2 tablespoons good honey, a pinch of salt, 55 g (1 3/4 oz) coarsely chopped pine nuts, toasted hazelnuts or toasted almonds, a pinch of cinnamon powder and 2 tablespoons grappa. Combine the ingredients thoroughly and make a paste that can be cut into small pieces, each of which will be shaped like a broad bean. Place each 'bean' on a buttered baking tray and bake in an oven preheated to 200°C/400°F/gas6 for 20 minutes. They keep for some time in an airtight jar.

LEFT: A VARIETY OF FOCACCIA FROM CAMOGLI, INCLUDING FOCACCIA AL FORMAGGIO AND FOCACCIA STUDDED WITH OLIVES.

FOCACCIA / FLAT BREAD

Focaccia is also known as *pinza* in Veneto, *pitta* in Calabria, *pizza* in Naples, *pissalandrea* in Genova, *schiacciata* in Emilia-Romagna, *fitascetta* in Lombardy, *sardenaria* in Liguria, and *stiacciata* in Tuscany. Whatever it is called, however, this bread has the same basic characteristics, being a flat bread made with a bread dough (see the basic recipe on page 301) mixed with olive oil and salt. A simple version of *focaccia* was eaten by the Romans and over the centuries has developed until now there is a multitude of varieties, both salted and sweet, depending on taste and the availability of local ingredients.

Before it is cooked, the dough is pressed flat in the tin and little indentations are made with the fingers so that the olive oil that is drizzled abundantly over the dough collects in them to give the dough a wonderful flavour. Coarse salt is then sprinkled sparingly on top and the dough baked until it is golden brown.

Focaccia is eaten on its own as a snack and used to make sandwiches, when it is particularly good filled with mortadélla. *Focaccia* has given rise to the pizza in Naples (see pages 298 and 303) and the savoury and sweet version of pizza, *pinza*, in Veneto and Emilia-Romagna, using polenta flour to make the dough.

There are a huge number of different varieties of *focaccia*, including the *smacafam* from Trentino, a type of *focaccia* using buckwheat flour. The dough has onions in it and is topped with sausage meat and baked in a larded baking tray. The Calabrian *pitta* is similar to the Middle-Eastern bread, except that it is formed into a ring, cut open and filled, while still hot, with *ciccioli* (pork fat, see page 73), oil and chilli or grated Pecorino. In Lombardy, especially around Como, they make *fitascetta*, a *focaccia* bread topped with a jam of red onions and salt or sugar, while the Tuscans make *stiacciata*, a proved dough that is mixed with sugar, eggs and spices before being baked in a hot oven for 40 minutes. Finally, the Ligurian speciality, known variously as *pizzalandrea* or *pissadella*, and *sardenaria* in Genovese, is related to the French onion tart, *pissaladière*.

Perhaps the tastiest version of them all is the *focaccia al formaggio*, a speciality of Camogli, an enchanting fisherman's town near Genova. Two very thin layers of dough made of plain flour, water, oil and yeast, are worked in a similar way to strudel dough. The layers are filled with plenty of stracchino cheese, drizzled with olive oil and baked until the cheese has melted, see the photograph opposite.

RIGHT: GRISSINI

FRISELLA, FRESELLA, FRISEDDA, PAN BISCOTTO / BISCUIT BREAD
Frisella was born of the necessity to create a completely dry bread without moisture that would not be susceptible to mould. It was widely used, first of all, by the army and navy because of its keeping qualities. The bread, made mostly with durum wheat flour, is partially baked then removed from the oven and, while still warm, cut into thick slices or, as with the Campanian and Pugliese *frisella*, which are shaped like a small *ciambella*, they are cut in two. The sliced bread is then put back in the oven until all its moisture has evaporated and it has become crisp like a biscuit. Before it is used, it is put under running water for a few seconds so that it is not too hard to eat. It has its own special flavour and is often served with ripe tomatoes, olive oil, salt and basil. Once a favourite snack of farmers, it is now enjoyed by everyone.

FROLLINO / SHORTCRUST BISCUIT
Made with shortcrust pastry (see Pasta Frolla), these biscuits come in various shapes and sizes and are produced and sold all over Italy. They are often eaten dipped into milk and coffee for breakfast.

GALLETTE / BISCUIT
This biscuited hard bread is specifically baked for long conservation. It used to be produced for the army and navy, and the only way to eat it was to dip it in water to make it edible.

GRISSINO / BREADSTICK
Grissini, crisp thin breadsticks made using type 0 flour, water, yeast and sometimes a little olive oil, originally came from Turin but are now eaten all over the world. The long sticks of bread can reach up to 70 cm (28 inches) in length and are still handmade by stretching a piece of dough until it is round and thin before baking it until crispy and dry. To achieve an even more crumbly texture, oil or butter are added to the dough. They are also commercially made and those wrapped in cellophane can keep for many months. *Grissini* can be eaten with any food, but are mostly served with *antipasti*, or as a substitute for normal bread during a meal. They can also be wrapped in a thin slice of Parma ham to make a delicious snack.

GUASTEDDE / SICILIAN BREAD
This special bread roll is sold filled with a variety of ingredients, but most famously the local delicacy of fried spleen sold at Vucceria market in Palermo. The bread roll is made with a leavened dough of plain and semolina flour, yeast and water, sprinkled with sesame seeds. They are cut in half and filled with the spleen which has been boiled then thinly cut and fried, along with *ciccioli* (pork fat, see page 73), in lard and spices. The whole thing is sprinkled with Pecorino cheese to make a wonderful and unusual snack.

KRAPFEN / DOUGHNUT
As the name suggests, this deep-fried sweet is German in origin. An Italian version, called *bomboloni*, is very popular in Emilia-Romagna. It is made of a leavened dough formed into balls which are deep-fried until brown. *Bomboloni* are usually dusted with sugar, but may also be filled with jam, like apricot or cherry, or with custard.

LIEVITO / RAISING AGENT
There are two types of yeast, one natural and one synthetic. They both have the task, through their fermentation, of producing bubbles in the combination of flour and water, or other ingredients, in order to raise and aerate the mixture and thus obtain a softness in the baked goods. Bread without yeast would be flat and hard and inedible. The best yeast is a by-product of making beer. The pinky brown substance is diluted with water and mixed with whatever is to be baked. It is important to allow the fermentation to take place in a warm place, before putting the dough in a hot oven. Synthetic yeast does not need such pre-fermentation.

MARITOZZO / SWEET ROMAN BREAD
This sweet brioche-type bread is traditionally eaten during Lent in Lazio and Umbria, although today it is available all year round. It is made with a sour dough that requires a long process of proving before ingredients such as eggs, sugar, olive oil and salt are added. The dough is then left to rise again for about four hours, before further kneading and the addition of more ingredients such as flour, raisins, orange peel, more eggs and a little milk. It can then be divided into small pieces and baked.

MARTURANA, MARZAPANE, SEE PASTA DI MANDORLE

MOLLICA DI PANE / BREAD DOUGH, FRESH BREADCRUMBS
The internal soft part of the bread, called *mollica*, is used in Italy as an ingredient for the stuffing of vegetables (see Peperoni Ripieni, page 126) or meat. See also Pane Grattugiato.

LEFT: MOSTACCIOLI WITH MARSALA WINE IN ERICE, SICILY.

MOSTACCIOLO, MUSTAZZOLI / MUST BISCUITS

One of the most common of the Italian biscuits, *mostacciolo* (or *mustazzoli* in Sicilian) are made and eaten in many regions, although there are usually slight variations on the basic recipe.

The hard dry biscuits, which used to be made by the Ancient Romans, consist of a mixture of plain flour, cooked grape juices (the product of wine-making called must) or honey, and spices like cinnamon, clove and nutmeg; but they do not contain either yeast or eggs. When the mixture has been worked into a firm dough, it is rolled out to a height of 1 cm ($\frac{1}{2}$ inch), cut into lozenge shapes and baked in a moderate oven for about 25 minutes. When they are removed from the oven they are brushed with a glaze made up of 2 parts sugar to 1 part water and left to dry and cool.

They are a speciality of Erice in Sicily, and are eaten after meals dipped in sweet dessert wines, such as Moscato, Passito di Pantelleria and Marsala. They were probably brought to Italy by the Arabs, and spread through Italy via Sicily and the southern regions.

PAN BISCOTTO, SEE FRISELLA

PAN DE MEI, PAN MEINO / SWEET LOMBARDIAN BREAD

A small, sweet bread made with a combination of maize and wheat flour, *pan de mei* is typical of Lombardian cuisine. The simple recipe consists of 200 g (7 oz) each sugar, soft butter, polenta flour and wheat flour, all of which are mixed together with 3 eggs and 35 g ($1\frac{1}{4}$ oz) brewer's yeast dissolved in a little milk. Once all the ingredients have been well combined, allow the dough to rise, until about doubled in volume. Then divide it into small chunks and shape them into rounds. Place each roll on a buttered baking tray, brush with beaten egg then put in an oven preheated to 200°C/400°F/gas6 and bake for 20-25 minutes.

PAN DI RAMERINO / ROSEMARY BREAD

Pan di Ramerino is a sweet bread made and eaten at Easter in Tuscany. As the name suggests, the dough includes rosemary oil, together with the more usual sweet ingredients of sugar, raisins and butter. It is shaped into small loaves or rolls, placed on a baking tray and baked at 200°C/400°F/gas6 for 25 minutes.

PAN DI SAN GIUSEPPE / DECORATIVE BREAD

This bread, skilfully modelled into a variety of shapes and symbols, is used to decorate altars before being offered to the Holy Family and given to friends as a good omen on San Giuseppe's day. The bread is a reminder of the legend of the saint, who is celebrated annually with a special meal, *la cena di San Giuseppe* (the supper of St Joseph) in the village of Salemi, a small village built on top of a high hill near Trapani in Sicily.

LEFT: PAN DI SAN GIUSEPPE

The story that inspires this celebration is that of a fisherman and his wife who lived in the village. One day, as the fisherman went off on a fishing trip, his wife promised that should he survive his next fishing trip she would invite the entire village to dinner. However, the fisherman and his wife were so poor that when he suddenly returned, all she had to feed to her guests was flour and water, which she made into bread in the shape of the food she would have dearly loved to have given and of Christian symbols.

PAN DI SPAGNA, PASTA MARGHERITA, PASTA MADDALENA / PASTA VIENNESE / SPONGE CAKE

Pan di spagna is a basic soft, sweet sponge cake, made by beating together 6 egg yolks with 250 g (9 oz) caster sugar until you have a foamy mixture. Add to this the beaten whites of the six eggs and a pinch of salt. Slowly add 150 g (5 oz) fine 00 (*doppio zero*) flour and 150 g (5 oz) potato flour, stirring carefully with a wooden spoon. Add a few drops of vanilla essence or the seeds of one vanilla pod, and the finely grated zest of $\frac{1}{2}$ lemon. Pour the mixture into a high-sided baking tray that has been buttered and dusted with flour. Bake for 30 minutes at 180°C/350°F/gas4, then remove and allow to cool. Cut in half and fill with cream, jam, custard or chocolate.

PANDOLCE / SWEET BREAD

Like *panettone* is for the Milanese, *pandolce* is the centrepiece of the Christmas feast for the Genovese. It is a much smaller and heavier cake than panettone, as it contains so much candied fruit, raisins and nuts as well as special flavourings like orange water or aniseed. It takes quite a long time to bake, because of the amount of time it takes for the dough to rise.

PANDORO / VERONESE CHRISTMAS CAKE

Literally translated, *pandoro* means 'golden bread', because of its deep

MAKING PANDOLCE

To make Pandolce: mix together 55 g ($1^3/_4$ oz) sour-dough (fermented bread dough) with 250 g (9 oz) 00 flour and a little warm water, until you have a soft, silky dough. Cover and leave the dough to rise in a warm place for 12 hours. Then mix together a separate dough of 650 g (1 lb 7 oz) 00 flour, 200 g (7 oz) caster sugar, 150 g (5 oz) soft butter, 1 small glass of Moscato or Vin Santo and 2 tablespoons of orange flower water, until well combined and soft. Mix the two doughs together and knead well, before adding 3 tablespoons finely diced candied citron peel, 30 g (1 oz) sultanas and 1 teaspoon aniseed or fennel seeds. Knead again until all the ingredients are perfectly combined and the dough has a soft and elastic texture. Put the dough in a well-greased and floured high-sided cake tin, making sure that the dough does not come more than one-third of the way up the sides of the tin. Leave to rise again for a further 12 hours, or until the dough has doubled in volume. Bake for 50-55 minutes in an oven preheated to 200°C/400°F/gas6. Allow to cool before removing from the tin.

yellow centre, due at least in part to the number of free-range eggs included in the cake along with 00 (*doppio zero*) flour, sugar, butter and yeast. It is an extremely light, moist and spongy cake, made by the Veronese and Venetians at Christmas. Due to the lengthy method, taking several days and requiring three proving stages, the Veronese no longer make it at home, preferring to buy commercially made versions. This tall cake is traditionally made in an eight-pointed star-shaped mould. It is usually eaten on its own, although I like it buttered then grilled so that the sugar in it caramelizes slightly.

PANE / BREAD

One of the basic elements of the Italian diet is bread. Italians eat a great deal of bread on a daily basis, of all types and shapes according to the regional resources of grain and the type of food with which it is to be eaten.

The most common flour used for breadmaking in Italy is wheat, which is milled to make a very fine white flour. The flour is graded as 00 (*doppio zero*) and is also used to make, among other things, fresh egg pasta. Slightly less refined flour is graded 0, and so on until wholemeal flour, called *integrale*, containing the husk of the grain. It is, of course, well known that wholemeal flour is more nutritious and is a better source of roughage than white flour, but white flour and white bread are still more popular than the brown in Italy. In southern Italy, 00 (*doppio zero*) flour is mixed with durum wheat semolina to give the bread a much more solid consistency than the more delicate bread made in other parts of Italy. There are many other flours used to make bread, each of which gives a special quality to the finished product. Other flours used to make bread in Italy include rye, maize and cornflour, which is mixed with white flour for a more developed taste and more digestible bread.

The North prefers very white bread and mostly in small shapes, Liguria prefers *focaccia*, Emilia-Romagna *pane a pasta dura*, a type of white bread with a hard consistency, and a flat bread called *piadina*. Tuscany has a saltless bread called *pane sciocco*, to accompany its various savoury dishes, salami and spicy preserves. Rome loves the *sfilatino*, a short baguette also called *bastone*, or 'stick'. The entire South is definitely much happier with more substantial bread, like the *pugliese*, which is made of hard durum wheat and keeps fresh for a longer period of time. The round loaves can be gargantuan in size, to satisfy large families.

Special breads are also made using a wide variety of flavouring ingredients, including lard, butter, olive oil, sun-dried tomatoes, herbs, olives, nuts, and a whole range of seeds.

Because it has to be fresh, bread is mostly bought on a daily basis. This is true especially in the North, because white bread rolls don't keep for more than a day. There are, however, various recipes containing stale bread which is turned into soups, salads and other specialities.

PANE A CASSETTA, PAN CARRÉ / SANDWICH BREAD

This white bread, made from type 0 flour, water and yeast, is baked in a special mould called a *cassetta*, which keeps the bread compact and dense, limiting the amount it can rise when baked and this giving it an even square shape and thin crust. This means that, after the crust has been removed, it can be cut into smaller squares and stamped into circles to make *tartines*, canapés and sandwiches, or cut into small cubes and fried to make croutons for salads and soups.

RIGHT: TRAMEZZINI (SANDWICHES) IN THE CAFFÈ MALISSANO, TURIN.

PANE CARASAU, SEE CARTA DA MUSICA

PANE CON L'UVA / FRUIT LOAF

The Milanese make this bread with a sweet dough, including butter, sugar, and lots of raisins or currants. It is shaped into small loaves or rolls, which are left to rise for half an hour before being baked at 200°C/400°F/gas6 for 25 minutes. It is usually made as an Easter treat.

PANE GRATTUGIATO / DRIED BREADCRUMBS
Leftovers of good-quality bread (never artificially coloured or spiced) are further baked in the oven at a lower temperature to drive off all the moisture but not let it colour. The breadcrumbs produced from this are called *grattugiato* (meaning 'grated') because, before the existence of food processors, the pieces of bread were grated to obtain the crumbs.

Breadcrumbs are widely used in Italian cooking; for example Sardine Ripiene (page 31), Arancini (page 179), Fritto Misto alla Piemontese (page 89) are all specialities coated in breadcrumbs before being deep-fried. Breadcrumbs are also used to thicken stuffings and sauces.

PANETTERIA, PANETTIERE / BAKER'S SHOP, BAKER
Usually the term *panetteria* was used to indicate a bread shop where the bread was baked on the premises. You could discover the location following the irresistible smell of freshly made bread inviting you to buy. Unfortunately many of these shops keep the name, but are only outlets for selling all sorts of baked goods like bread, cakes, etc., made elsewhere.

I have a very fond memory of going to the baker to buy fresh bread in the morning. The bread was sold by the kilo and the hand-made loaves didn't always reach that weight. To make it up the baker would just cut a piece of bread from another loaf, called *l'aggiunta*, which regularly ended up in my watery mouth before arriving home.

To be a *panettiere* you have to have considerable experience; in fact it is truly a vocation, because in order to have the freshly made bread available to the public in the morning the baker has to get up at about 2 am and work through the night. It is a highly appreciated artisan craft, which is unfortunately sadly disappearing with the advent of huge commercial bakeries.

PANETTONE / MILANESE CHRISTMAS CAKE
The most widely made and eaten of the regionally based Christmas cakes in Italy, *panettone* or 'the big bread' is the tallest and largest cake of all; a result of the lengthy procedure required to make it, including many proving periods. It is a difficult cake to make at home because it involves the mixing of two sets of dough – one made with flour, yeast, butter and sugar that needs to prove for about 10 hours, and the other a mixture of flour, butter, eggs, sugar, salt, cubes of candied citron and orange peel, and raisins, which has to be mixed with the first dough and the whole thing left to prove for another 4 or 5 hours. It is then baked in precise, temperature-controlled ovens, which allow the cakes to mushroom up and gently cook until they are dark brown but not burned, leaving the insides wonderfully fluffy and moist. Like the other traditional Christmas cakes, *panettoni* are only baked from October until November.

The most important thing to look for when buying your *panettone* is the quality of the fats used in making it, as this will determine the flavour of the cake. It is also worth checking the date, as the freshest are the best.

In response to consumer demands, many cakes are now covered or filled with chocolate or sabayon sauce. However, the simple classic cake is still the best.

PANFORTE / FRUIT AND SPICE CAKE
This typical Tuscan speciality dates from the Middle Ages, when the first spices were imported from the Mediterranean. Sienna is the city that assumed the paternity of this 'strong bread', now famous all over the world. See the recipe on page 281.

PANPEPATO, SEE PAGES 219 AND 230

ABOVE: SIGNOR GARELLO, THE BAKER IN TURIN'S VIA MADDALENA.

LEFT: PANETTONE TRADIZIONALE

PANZANELLA, PAN BAGNATO / SOAKED BREAD
Similar to the specially dried bread, *frisella* (see page 293), *pan bagnato* is simply stale or dry bread that is soaked and eaten in soups, dipped in milk or softened with the juice of freshly cut tomatoes. In Tuscany, salted bread is used; the custom being to top the water-softened bread with chopped tomatoes, sweet onions, celery leaves, basil and a little trickle of olive oil.

My mother's *panzanella* was made with leftover bread, which she broke into pieces and put into a bowl with very ripe and juicy tomatoes. This was left to soak for a while and then she would mix it with her hands until it broke into small pieces. She would then add extra-virgin olive oil, salt, finely chopped sweet onions, capers and sometimes a little finely chopped garlic, along with a little basil or oregano, like the Neapolitans and Sicilians do. It looked like chicken feed, but it tasted delicious and I still make it in the same way today.

PARROZZO / ALMOND CAKE
A speciality of Pescara in the Marche region, this simple cake is made with flour, eggs, sugar and yeast, enriched with ground almonds and covered with chocolate.

PASSATELLI / BREADCRUMB NOODLES
As well as all the usual ways of using breadcrumbs, Emilia-Romagnans also mix them with beaten egg, Parmesan cheese, salt and pepper,

to make a soft dough, which is then pushed through a special utensil with holes (you can use a colander) over a pot of boiling water or soup to make *passatelli*, little noodles or dumplings. Boiled in water, they can be used in the same way as pasta, dressed with a simple sauce.

PASTA DI MANDORLE, PASTA REALE, MARZAPANE, MARTURANA / MARZIPAN

A sweet paste based on ground almonds and sugar, marzipan is used by pastry chefs to make cakes and petits fours, and is especially popular in the South and Sicily, where almonds grow in abundance. Another special almond paste called *marturana*, was originally made by nuns in a convent at Marturana in Palermo, Sicily. It is used to make figures and various shapes like fruit and animals, which are then coloured and used to decorate cakes and other desserts.

Pasta di mandorle is very simple to make and tastes much nicer if homemade. To get the best results, grind the almonds yourself using fresh nuts, as pre-ground almonds tend to dry out quickly and lose their flavour. (See the recipe on page 279.)

PASTA FROLLA / SWEET SHORTCRUST PASTRY

The easiest pastry to make, shortcrust pastry is used in a large number of different sweet dishes. To make about 1.25 kg ($2^{3}/_{4}$ lb): mix together gently but quickly 500 g (1 lb $1^{1}/_{2}$ oz) 00 (*doppio zero*) flour with 5 eggs, 250 g (9 oz) soft butter, 250 g (9 oz) caster sugar, a pinch of salt and the grated zest of a lemon. Then let this dough rest for at least 1 hour in a cool place, before using it to make biscuits and other sweets. It can be refrigerated for a few days, if necessary, but before using it make sure the pastry has first come back to room temperature. Shortcrust pastry usually needs 30 minutes in a medium to hot oven, and is cooked until it is a light golden brown. *Pasta sable*, a richer sweet shortcrust pastry from the French tradition, contains more butter. It is crumblier than *pasta frolla*, but can be used in much the same way and is especially good in fruit tarts.

PASTA MARGHERITA, PASTA MADDALENA, SEE PAN DI SPAGNA

PASTA REALE, SEE PASTA DI MANDORLE

RIGHT: TYPICAL MARZIPAN BISCUITS IN THE SHOP OF MARIA GRAMMATICO IN ERICE, SICILY.

PASTA SFOGLIA / PUFF PASTRY

Puff pastry is the only pastry you need to see being made to learn the art and, if you cannot do this, then the easiest way to get puff pastry is to buy it ready-made, especially as the quality is so good nowadays.

Puff pastry is made by putting butter, or other fats like lard, between sheets of pastry and rolling and folding it until the pastry is built up into many layers with fat separating each one. The difficulty lies in trying to roll out the pastry with the hard fat beneath it without allowing the fat to break through the pastry. It also takes some time to make, as the pastry has to be left to cool and rest between rollings. The end result, however, is a pastry which, when baked, puffs up as each sheet is cooked and separated by the layers of fat. It is used to make both savoury and sweet tarts, pies and biscuits, and can be combined with cheese to make tasty snacks.

PASTA VIENNESE, SEE PAN DI SPAGNA

PASTICCERIA, PASTICCINI / PASTRY SHOP, PASTRIES

Italians are very fond of *pasticcini*, small cakes like *bignole*, *bignè*, and various tarts, which are eaten with coffee or tea, or with hot chocolate, or even with a glass of Moscato Spumante. The *pasticceria* is the place where such *pasticcini* are produced, but very often functions also as a café, where you can sit and enjoy *pasticcini* with your coffee. At lunch-time, the *pasticceria* may also serve *salatini*, small savoury snacks like mini pizzas, small breads filled with truffle butter, anchovy rolls or small canapés with smoked salmon, etc.

PASTIERA DI GRANO / WHEAT TART

Pastiera is an Easter cake, made with whole-grain wheat and ricotta to symbolize wealth; for this reason they are often made in pairs, so there is one left to give to a loved one. The preparation starts long before Easter, as the wheat has to be soaked in water for at least a week to soften it, although it is sometimes possible to buy pre-soaked wheat. See the recipe on page 177.

PIADINA, PIADA / ROMAGNAN BREAD

This unleavened bread from Emilia-Romagna is similar to the Arabic pitta bread, but tastier. It is usually eaten with the local speciality of Parma ham, stracchino cheese or even sautéed spinach, but may also be served as an accompaniment to other dishes. There are as many recipes as there are families who make this bread, but the basic recipe is to mix together 500 g (1 lb $1^{1}/_{2}$ oz) 0 flour, 55 g (2 oz) lard, a pinch of salt and just enough water to produce a soft and elastic dough (sometimes people add yeast). The dough is kneaded briefly and then allowed to rest for 1 hour, before rolling it out to a thickness of 3-4 mm ($^{1}/_{8}$-$^{1}/_{6}$ inch). It is then cut into discs about 15 cm (6 inches) in diameter.

In Emilia-Romagna there is a special tool for baking the bread, but it can also be cooked in a heavy cast-iron pan on top of the stove.

Put the bread in the pan without any fat, and dry-fry the *piadina* for 2 minutes on each side. The little burnt spots add taste to the bread, which is eaten immediately, topped with whatever you fancy and folded in half.

PISSALADEIRA / TYPE OF PIZZA

This focaccia covered with anchovies and onions is said by the Genoese to come from *pizza alla Andrea*, after Andrea Doria, the famous Ligurian sailor. It is, however, very similar to *pissaladière*, the savoury tart of neighbouring Provence. See Focaccia, page 292.

PIZZA

It is not difficult to prepare an original pizza provided you have the right ingredients, the know-how and a good oven. This type of focaccia has been developed by the Neapolitans, thanks to their imaginative way of using the best local ingredients – the good flour, good water, good tomatoes, good basil, good mozzarella cheese and good olive oil.

There are two periods in the history of the pizza: the AP period (Ante Pizza) in which the pizza was considered just a bread to accompany other foods like the Indian naan); and the PP (Post Pizza) period, when toppings were added, leading to the current idea of the pizza being a bread base for any combination of ingredients.

The optimum way of obtaining a good Neapolitan pizza dough is to produce your own sour dough starter. Mix some flour with water to a soft dough and leave this in a warm place for a day. The natural yeasts will have fermented and caused it to rise, so this will be a perfect natural starter for the pizza dough. Alternatively simply use brewer's yeast as follows.

Pizza dough, unlike its predecessor focaccia, is a bread dough made of 00 (*doppio zero*) flour. Mix 400 g (14 oz) 00 flour, a pinch of salt, 35 g (1¼ oz) fresh brewer's yeast diluted in a cup of lukewarm water, with just enough water to make a soft dough. Mix all the ingredients together thoroughly and leave to rest for a while before dividing into four round balls, each of which will be large enough to fit a 20 cm (8 inch) diameter pizza pan. Cover the balls of dough with a clean cloth and set aside in a warm place to rise for at least 1 hour. After it has doubled in volume, knock it back and knead each dough ball, then roll them out to a thickness of 5 mm (¼ inch), leaving a raised edge all the way around the border, to a height of about 1 cm (½ inch). Place these in oiled pizza pans or dishes and set on a baking tray. Add the topping and cook in a preheated very hot oven, until the topping is melted and the edges are crispy. Pizza should be eaten in quarters with your hands.

LEFT: PIZZA MARINARA

Pizza Napoletana or Margherita has a topping based on a pulp of sun-ripened tomatoes or canned tomato pulp, 2 large rounds of buffalo mozzarella cut into small chunks, salt and a drizzle of extra-virgin olive oil sprinkled on top. Just before serving, add a few fresh basil leaves. The Margherita, on which the Napoletana is based, is said to have been invented to please Queen Margherita of Italy. The Marinara is topped with extra-virgin olive oil, garlic, tomatoes, salt, pepper and little oregano. The Romana has mozzarella, tomatoes, anchovy fillets, salt, pepper, oregano and extra-virgin olive oil.

LEFT: NEAPOLITAN STREET CARRIER FOR PIZZA.

Pizza fritta or *pizzetta* is the same as a normal pizza, but smaller for easy consumption in bars. An even smaller pizza, called *stuzzichino*, is served at parties with drinks.

PUGLIESE

This term is used to describe a wide range of items made in Puglia, but perhaps nowadays here is mostly used to refer to bread. *Pane Pugliese* is a very large round bread, about 40 cm (16 inches) in diameter and 12-14 cm (5-6 inches) high, with a thick and dark crust. It is made using plain wheat flour with the addition of hard durum wheat flour, resulting in a very dense, wholesome and extremely flavoursome bread, able to last for several days.

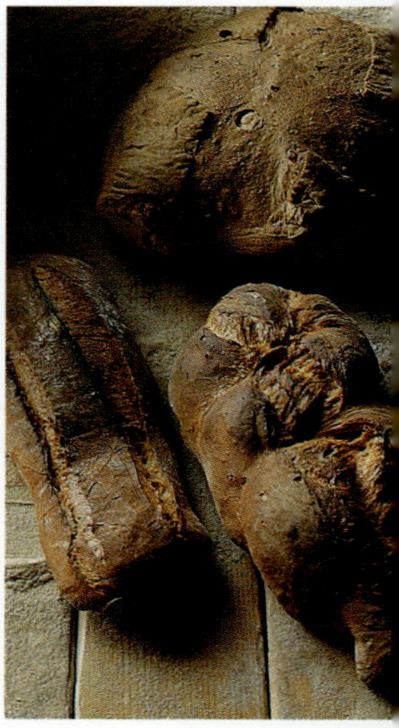

ABOVE: PUGLIESE BREAD NEAR BARI.

RICCIARELLO / TUSCAN ALMOND BISCUIT

This speciality of Sienna is a biscuit made with almonds and dusted with a large amount of icing sugar. They can be bought ready-made, but the homemade version is much better.

To make them: mix together 300 g (10½ oz) freshly ground sweet almonds and 350 g (12 oz) sugar, and work thoroughly before adding the grated zest of 1 lemon, 1 teaspoon of vanilla sugar or a few drops of vanilla essence, the beaten whites of 2 eggs and 1 tablespoon honey. Mix again to incorporate all the ingredients, then roll the dough on a surface that has been dusted with icing sugar, until it is 2 cm (¾ inch) thick. Using an oval cutter or a knife, cut out lozenges 4-5 cm (1½-2 inches) in

RIGHT: RICCIARELLI

length. Place these on a baking tray lined with rice paper which has, in turn, been covered with a 3 mm (1/8 inch) layer of icing sugar. Bake in an oven preheated to 190°C/375°F/gas5 for 20 minutes, but do not let the biscuits brown.

SALATINI / LITTLE SAVOURIES
All small savoury pastry snacks served with aperitifs are known as *salatini*. They are usually made with puff or shortcrust pastry, topped with cheese, anchovies, capers, olives, or seeds such as those of the poppy and fennel, or simply with ground pepper or salt. You can make these nibbles with frozen puff pastry and the flavouring of your choice, but in Italy they can be bought at the *pasticceria*.

SAVOIARDO / SPONGE FINGERS
These sponge-cake-like biscuits are one of the most important ingredients of the newly popularized Italian dessert, *tiramisu* in which the sponges are dipped in strong coffee or liqueur and layered with mascarpone cheese. *Savoiardi* sponges are also used to make other desserts, such as *zuppa inglese*, being favoured for their light and absorbent qualities.

To make the sponges: beat 5 egg yolks until they are white and creamy, then add 100 g (3½ oz) caster sugar, before carefully folding in 115 g (4 oz) 00 flour and 1 teaspoon vanilla sugar or a few drops of vanilla essence. Mix well, then carefully fold in the stiffly beaten whites of the eggs and 55 g (2 oz) icing sugar. Butter a baking tray and dust it with flour. Pipe the mixture into 10-12 cm (4-5 inch) long small sausages of sponge, taking care to leave enough space between them. Sprinkle over a little of the caster sugar and bake in an oven preheated to 190°C/375°F/gas5 for 20-25 minutes. When cool, store in an airtight jar.

SFOGLIATELLA / PUFF PASTRY CAKE
In Campania and Naples, *sfogliatella* is sold in bars as a rather wonderful snack. They are usually served warm, but are also very good cold. There are two varieties, one a simple pocket of shortcrust pastry and the other a much more elaborate affair involving a special puff pastry, made with a dough of lard instead of butter. The filling usually consists of cooked semolina with ricotta, sugar, eggs, chopped candied peel and a few drops of vanilla essence.

STRUFFOLI, SEE THE RECIPE ON PAGE 306

TARALLO, TARALLUCCIO, TARALLINO / ROUND SAVOURY BISCUIT
This round savoury biscuit was traditionally made in Campania, but from there it spread to Puglia, then Calabria and finally Sicily. It is loved for its flavour and crunchiness, as well as for the fact that it is so easy to make and keeps so well in an airtight jar. It can be eaten on its own as a snack or with *antipasto*.

To make the biscuit: mix 500 g (1 lb 1½ oz) type 0 flour with 125 g (4½ oz) lard, 55 g (2 oz) brewer's yeast and spices like pepper, salt, fennel seeds, chilli and anything else you fancy. Add enough water to make a workable dough, then mix again until all the ingredients are well blended. Take small pieces of the dough and shape each one into a small sausage. Then join all of them together to form a circle. Sprinkle with oil and place on a baking tray to rise for an hour or so. Bake for one hour in a low oven preheated to about 150°C/300°F/gas2. Allow the biscuits to cool, when they become crumbly and dry.

TARTELETTA / TARTLET
Although these pastry cases originate from France, the Italians have taken them into their own cuisine with enthusiasm. They are used as containers for jams, fruit, nuts, sauces etc., and they are eaten for dessert or with tea in the afternoon or in bars as snacks. Generally made with shortcrust pastry, these mini pastry cases can come in any shape, square, round or rectangular.

TARTINA / SNACK
Using *pan carré* or *pane a cassetta* (see page 295), *tartine* are small savoury snacks filled with any combination of ingredients including butter and anchovies, capers, smoked salmon, pâtés or cheese. They are usually eaten with drinks and are often served in bars.

ZEPPOLA / CHOUX PASTRIES
This Southern speciality, usually produced for the celebration of San Giuseppe's Day, is made with eggs, yeast, 00 (*doppio zero*) flour and lard. The dough, deep-fried in oil, is usually extruded by a syringe, giving a round shape similar to that of *ciambella*. The cooked pastries are then dusted with icing sugar or filled with cream, or even dipped in honey diluted with water to make them absorbent and juicy. My mother used to bake a savoury version, with a piece of anchovy in the middle of the spoonful of dough, which gave an extremely tasty result.

RIGHT: TARALLI IN PUGLIA.

Focaccia

For 6–8

30 g (1 oz) fresh yeast
about 175 ml (6 fl oz) lukewarm water
500 g (1 lb $1^1/_2$ oz) 00 (doppio zero) flour
2 tbsp olive oil, plus extra for drizzling
pinch of salt
25 g ($^3/_4$ oz) coarse salt

A classic of Italian cuisine with ancient Roman origins, this was adopted by the Ligurians first and is now popular everywhere. It is a cross between pizza and bread, with the addition of olive oil and coarse salt. You could include cheese, olives, onions or even sweet ingredients.

Dissolve the yeast in the water. Put the flour in a bowl, then add the oil, yeast liquid and pinch of salt. Mix together, adding more water if necessary to obtain a very soft and smooth dough. Knead for about 10 minutes, until elastic, then place in a bowl, cover and leave to rise in a warm place for 1 hour or until doubled in size.

Preheat the oven to 200°C/400°F/gas6. Lightly oil a large baking tray. Knock back the dough, then dip your fingertips in olive oil and gently press out the very elastic dough until it covers the whole tray. It should be about 2 cm ($^3/_4$ inch) high. Brush with olive oil and then make small indentations here and there in the dough with your fingertips. Sprinkle the coarse salt over the top and bake for 25–30 minutes, until a golden-brown crust has formed. As soon as the bread comes out of the oven, drizzle more olive oil on top; this will be absorbed, giving a wonderful flavour.

Allow to cool, then cut into squares and enjoy. It can be eaten plain or, as they do in Genoa, made into a sandwich with some mortadella while still warm!

Torta Pasqualina

EASTER TART

For 8

675 g ($1^1/_2$ lb) shortcrust pastry
4 tbsp olive oil, plus more for the tart pan
2 onions, thinly sliced
hearts of 8 fresh very young artichokes
6 eggs
100 g ($3^1/_2$ oz) Parmesan cheese
800 g ($1^3/_4$ lb) spinach, blanched and coarsely chopped
salt and pepper

There are probably as many versions of this savoury Ligurian tart, traditionally made at Easter, as there are families who live in the region. It is based on pastry, vegetables and eggs, and is eaten especially on Easter Monday, Pasquetta, when almost everybody goes for a picnic. My mother used to make it quite often, however, regardless of tradition.

Heat the oil in a heavy-based pan and fry the onions until soft. Add the artichoke hearts with a glass of water, cover and braise very gently until tender.

Preheat the oven to 180°C/350°F/gas4 and oil a 25 cm (10 inch) tart pan. Roll out the pastry and use to line the pan.

In a bowl, lightly beat the eggs. Add the Parmesan cheese, with salt and pepper to taste. Add the spinach, and the artichokes and onions. Mix well. Fill the pastry shell with the artichoke mixture and bake in the oven for 40 minutes. Serve hot or cold.

Opposite: a range of focaccia with different toppings, including olives, cheese and courgettes.

CALZONE CON CICORIA E CARCIOFI

CALZONE WITH DANDELIONS AND ARTICHOKES

MAKES 4

- 425 G (15 OZ) WILD DANDELION LEAVES, ROUGHLY CHOPPED
- 4–6 SMALL YOUNG ARTICHOKES
- 4 TBSP OLIVE OIL
- 1 ONION, FINELY CHOPPED
- 2 GARLIC CLOVES, FINELY CHOPPED
- 2 RED CHILLIES, FINELY CHOPPED
- 300 ML (1/2 PINT) WATER
- 85 G (3 OZ) STONED GREEN OLIVES, CHOPPED
- 2 TSP SALTED CAPERS, SOAKED IN WATER FOR 10 MINUTES, THEN DRAINED
- 60 G (2 OZ) PECORINO CHEESE, GRATED
- 2 EGGS
- FRESHLY GROUND BLACK PEPPER
- OLIVE OIL FOR DEEP-FRYING

FOR THE DOUGH:

- 1 TSP OLIVE OIL
- PINCH OF SEA SALT
- 15 G (1/2 OZ) FRESH YEAST
- 150 ML (1/4 PINT) LUKEWARM WATER
- 300 G (10 1/2 OZ) PLAIN FLOUR

These little turnovers make a delicious, filling snack. Choose young, tender dandelion leaves from plants that haven't yet flowered. If you don't like the bitter taste of dandelions, you could use nettles or spinach instead. However, I find that with the dandelion you get a full country taste.

To make the dough, put the oil, salt and yeast in a small bowl, add the lukewarm water and stir to dissolve the yeast. Mound up the flour on a clean work surface and make a well in the centre. Gradually pour the yeast mixture into the well, mixing with your hands until all the liquid has been absorbed by the flour. Knead the dough for 8–10 minutes, until smooth and elastic, then place in a large bowl and cover with a cloth. Leave in a warm place for at least an hour, until it has risen to three times its original size.

Meanwhile, make the filling. Cook the dandelion leaves in boiling water for 5 minutes (this takes away some of their bitter taste), then drain and squeeze out the excess water. Remove the stalks and outer leaves from the artichokes (see page 105) and cut them into quarters.

Heat the olive oil in a large pan, add the onion, garlic and chillies and fry for a few minutes, stirring all the time, until the onion has softened. Add the dandelions, artichokes and water and stir. Add the olives and capers, mix well and cook for 15 minutes. By this time, most of the liquid should have evaporated, leaving the cooked vegetables just moist. Remove from the heat and leave to cool. Add the grated pecorino cheese and season with pepper. Beat in 1 egg and mix well.

Knock down the risen dough and divide it in 4 balls. Roll them out into ovals about 3 mm (1/8 inch) thick and divide the filling between them, placing it to one side of each piece of dough. Lightly beat the remaining egg and use to brush the edges of the dough, then fold in half to make turnovers, pressing the edges together with a fork to seal. Leave to rest for 5 minutes.

Heat the olive oil in a large deep pan. Add the calzone and deep-fry for about 3–4 minutes, until golden brown. Remove from the pan and drain on paper towels. Serve hot or cold.

RIGHT: CALZONE CON CICORIA E CARCIOFI (BELOW); PASTA CON LE SARDE, PASTA WITH SARDINES (TOP LEFT) SEE PAGE 166; ASPARAGI SELVATICI, WILD ASPARAGUS (TOP RIGHT) SEE PAGE 249.

Pizzette Margherita

Makes 12-16

500 g (1 lb) tomato pulp (see page 118)
400 g (14 oz) mozzarella, thinly sliced
125 ml (4 fl oz) extra-virgin olive oil
20 basil leaves
salt and pepper

For the dough:
25 g (3/4 oz) fresh yeast
200 ml (7 fl oz) lukewarm water
500 g (1 lb 1/2 oz) 00 (doppio zero) flour
3 tbsp extra-virgin olive oil
1 tsp salt
1/2 tsp sugar

It is said that this pizza was named after Queen Margherita of Italy in 1889 and was made for her by a Neapolitan pizzaiolo. *Whatever its origins, it is the simplest of pizzas and, in my opinion, the best.*

To make the dough, first dissolve the yeast in the water. Pile the flour up on a work surface in a volcano shape, make a well in the centre and add the oil, salt and sugar. Slowly incorporate the yeast mixture, then knead the dough with your fingers and the palm of your hand until it has a silky, soft consistency. Put it in a bowl, dust with flour, then cover and leave to rise for 1 hour or until doubled in size.

Knock back the dough, divide it into 12-16 pieces, then knead each piece briefly and reshape it into a ball. Cover and leave to rise for 15 minutes. Preheat the oven to 220°C/425°F/gas7.

Above (clockwise from the bottom left): pizzette margherita, rustici (potato, ham and cheese croquettes), arancini di riso alla palermitana (page 179)

Flatten each ball of dough a little with a rolling pin, then stretch it out with your fingertips until it is about 10-12.5 cm (4-5 inches) in diameter. The dough should be slightly thicker at the edges. Place on 2 or 4 oiled baking trays. Spread the tomato pulp over the pizza bases, then distribute the mozzarella evenly over the top. Sprinkle with salt and drizzle with the extra-virgin olive oil. Bake for about 8–10 minutes, then sprinkle over the basil leaves and some coarsely ground black pepper and serve straight away.

RIGHT: CASATIELLO (LEFT); TORTA RUSTICA DI RICOTTA (RIGHT, PAGE 250)

CASATIELLO

SAVOURY EASTER BREAD

FOR 8

- 225 G (8 OZ) SOFT LARD (YOU COULD USE BUTTER, BUT LARD GIVES AN AUTHENTIC TASTE)
- 100 G ($3^1/_2$ OZ) HARD PECORINO CHEESE, GRATED
- 100 G ($3^1/_2$ OZ) PARMESAN CHEESE, GRATED
- 100 G ($3^1/_2$ OZ) PROVOLONE CHEESE, VERY FINELY GRATED
- 100 G ($3^1/_2$ OZ) NEAPOLITAN SAUSAGE, CUT INTO VERY SMALL CUBES
- 1 TBSP FRESHLY GROUND BLACK PEPPER, NOT TOO FINE
- 1 TSP SALT
- 8 EGGS

FOR THE DOUGH:

- 600 G (1 LB 5 OZ) 00 (DOPPIO ZERO) FLOUR
- 60 G (2 OZ) SOFT LARD
- 55 G ($1^3/_4$ OZ) FRESH YEAST
- 200 ML (7 FL OZ) LUKEWARM WATER

Together with Pastiera di Grano (see page 177), this is an essential part of Neapolitan Easter celebrations. Every family has its own recipe but the decoration never varies – the Easter symbol of eggs, pushed into the dough before baking. The eggs are shelled after baking and eaten with the bread, which is usually ring-shaped.

To make the dough, put the flour in a bowl and rub in the lard. Dissolve the yeast in the water, add to the flour and mix well to form a dough. Knead for 10–15 minutes, until it has a soft and silky texture, then put the dough in a bowl, cover with a cloth and leave for about 2 hours, until doubled in size.

Knock back the risen dough and knead it briefly to eliminate air bubbles. Flatten it into a rectangle about 3 cm ($1^1/_4$ inches) thick, dot half the lard, cheeses and sausage over it and sprinkle with half the pepper and salt. Fold up the bottom third of dough, then fold down the top third and knead to distribute the ingredients and work in the lard. Flatten it into a rectangle again and cover with the remaining lard, cheeses and sausage, then repeat the folding and kneading. Place the dough in a greased 25 cm (10 inch) ring mould, or lay it on a greased baking tray in a ring shape, then cover and leave to rise for another 2 hours.

Preheat the oven to 190°C/375°F/gas5. Wash the eggs and push them half way into the dough. Bake for 1 hour, then remove from the oven and leave to cool. It can be kept for a few days.

Cenci

PASTRY RIBBONS

For 8–10

350 g (12 oz) 00 (doppio zero) flour
45 g ($1^1/2$ oz) soft butter
45 g ($1^1/2$ oz) caster sugar
1 sachet vanilla sugar
2 eggs
pinch of salt
3 tbsp moscato passito or vin santo
200 g (7 oz) icing sugar
olive oil for deep-frying

These moreish pastries are supposed to be eaten during Lent and are associated with carnevale, *which takes place 40 days before Easter.* Cenci *literally means pieces of fabric, and this is what they are called in Tuscany. But with a few variations the same thing can be found in all the regions, under all sorts of names. In the South they are fried in lard instead of olive oil.*

Sift the flour into a bowl, add the butter, caster sugar, vanilla sugar, eggs, salt and wine and work together to obtain a very smooth dough. Cover and leave to rest for 1 hour.

Using a rolling pin or a pasta machine, roll out the dough until it is 3 mm (1/8 inch) thick. With a serrated pastry wheel, cut it into strips 15–18 cm (6–7 inches) long and 3–4 cm ($1^1/4$–$1^1/2$ inches) wide, then very patiently tie each one in a loose knot. Deep-fry them in olive oil, a few at a time to allow them to swim well, until golden and crisp, then put them on kitchen paper to drain off excess oil. When cold, pile them up on a tray and dust them abundantly with the icing sugar. They are irresistible!

Savoiardi

SPONGE FINGERS

Makes about 400 g (14 oz)

6 eggs, separated
125 g ($4^1/2$ oz) caster sugar
150 g (5 oz) 00 (doppio zero) flour, sifted
30 g (1 oz) icing sugar
$1^1/2$ sachets vanilla sugar
25 g (3/4 oz) granulated sugar

You can buy a special baking tin for these super-light and spongy little biscuits, which gives a deeper, more regular shape. However, they can also be piped out on to a baking tray. They are ideal for making tiramisu, zuppa inglese *and other desserts where an absorbent biscuit is required.*

Preheat the oven to 180°C/350°F/gas4. Beat the egg yolks with the caster sugar until the mixture is very thick and mousse-like. Gradually fold in the flour. In a separate bowl, beat the egg whites until stiff, then sift in the icing sugar and carefully but thoroughly fold it in. Fold this into the egg yolk mixture together with the vanilla sugar, being carefully not to knock air out of the mixture.

Put it into a piping bag and pipe on to a buttered baking sheet in little sausage shapes about 12.5 cm (5 inches) long and 3 cm ($1^1/4$ inches) wide, spacing them well apart. Sprinkle with the granulated sugar and bake for about 18 minutes. They should be dry and a wonderful golden colour.

Leave to cool on a wire rack, then store them in an airtight container.

STRUFFOLI NAPOLETANI

NEAPOLITAN FRIED PASTRIES

FOR 10

- 5 EGGS
- 3 TBSP GRANULATED SUGAR
- 500 G (1 LB 1½ OZ) FLOUR
- GRATED ZEST OF 1 LEMON AND 1 ORANGE
- PINCH OF SALT
- 1 TBSP PURE ALCOHOL (IF NOT AVAILABLE, STRONG VODKA WILL DO)
- 50 G (2 OZ) CEDRO (CANDIED CITRON PEEL)
- OIL FOR DEEP-FRYING
- 25 G (¾ OZ) LITTLE EDIBLE SILVER BALLS, TO DECORATE

FOR THE CARAMEL:

- 100 G (3½ OZ) SUGAR
- 250 G (9 OZ) HONEY

In a large bowl, beat the eggs with the sugar, then gradually mix in the flour to make a smooth dough. Add the citrus zest, the salt and the alcohol. Knead well for 3 or 4 minutes and roll into a ball. Cover and leave to rest for 2 hours in a cool place.

Taking a little bit of dough at a time, roll it with your hand into sausage shapes about 1 cm (½ inch) in diameter. Cut the sausage into small pieces about 1 cm (½ inch) long. It is quite laborious rolling out these sausages and will take you some time.

In a small pan, pour in oil to a depth of 2-3 cm (¾ -1¼ inches) and heat until moderately hot. Deep-fry the pieces of dough in the hot oil in batches until lightly browned. Remove and drain on absorbent paper.

To make the caramel: in a large heavy-based pan, heat the sugar and honey with 2 tablespoons of water until the liquid becomes clear. Add the struffoli and the chopped peel. Stir carefully until all the struffoli are coated with caramel. Arrange in the form of a crown on a serving plate, decorate with silver balls (not too many) and leave to cool.

BUDINO DI ROSA

ROSA'S PUDDING

FOR 6

- 1 LITRE (1¾ PINTS) MILK
- 300 G (10½ OZ) SUGAR
- 100 G (3½ OZ) 00 (DOPPIO ZERO) FLOUR
- 100 G (3½ OZ) POWDERED BITTER CHOCOLATE
- GRATED ZEST OF 1 LEMON
- YOLKS OF 3 EGGS
- 16 SAVOIARDI BISCUITS
- 5 TBSP AMARETTO LIQUEUR

This is not a pudding made from roses, as the title might lead you to expect, but a wonderful creation of Rosa, the pasta queen of the Ristorante Ardenga in Diolo, Emilia-Romagna. It is simple but highly effective.

Put the milk and 100 g (3½ oz) of the sugar in a pan, then stir in the flour and chocolate. Stir until smooth and bring to the boil, stirring continuously. Remove from the heat, stir in the lemon zest and egg yolks and mix well.

In a small bowl, mix the liqueur with an equal amount of water. Dip the biscuits briefly in this mixture and use them to line a pudding mould. Pour the milk mixture into the lined mould and chill to set.

When the pudding is quite cold and firmly set, about 2-3 hours, turn it over and remove it from the mould (dipping it first very briefly in hot water will help).

Dissolve the remaining sugar in 4 tablespoons of water and cook until it begins to brown to a caramel. Pour this over the pudding and leave that to set before serving.

UDINO DI ROSA

PRUSSIANI

SWEET PUFF PASTRY BISCUITS

MAKES 24-30

500 G (1 LB $1^1/2$ OZ) PLAIN FLOUR
PINCH OF SALT
175 G (6 OZ) BLOCK OF HARD BUTTER
10 GENEROUS HANDFULS OF SUGAR

Puff pastry is one of those recipes that is so difficult that it is seldom made at home; it is more likely to be the ultimate challenge in baking.

Put the flour and salt into a large bowl with 250 ml (9 fl oz) water and mix well to produce a dough. On a floured surface, roll the dough out to form a square just over twice the size of the block of butter.

Place the butter in the middle of one side of the pastry square. Fold over the other half and press down the edges with a rolling pin to make a sealed package around the butter. Turn the package so the fold is to one side and roll out the package to form a rectangle three times as long as it is wide. Fold the bottom third up and the top third down over that. Again seal the edges by pressing with a rolling pin. Wrap loosely in cling film and chill for at least an hour. Repeat this rolling, folding and chilling process 4 or 5 times more, each time giving the pastry a quarter turn clockwise before beginning.

Preheat the oven to 200°C/400°F/gas6.

Sprinkle a handful of sugar over a work surface, place the chilled pastry on it and sprinkle more sugar over the pastry. Roll out into a square, sprinkling more sugar as you roll. Fold over in half and then fold this again in half. Roll again, sprinkling it with more sugar as you go, into a long rectangular shape. Then fold this rectangle in half and repeat the rolling and folding process once more. Roll again once more into a rectangle, then fold this lengthwise to form a sausage shape. Slice this into 1 cm ($^1/2$ inch) thick circles.

Place on a baking tray well spaced apart. Place in the oven for 12 minutes, then turn the biscuits over and bake for a further 5 minutes.

RIGHT (CLOCKWISE FROM THE TOP): SFOGLIATELLI (PAGE 299), TINY BABAS, PRUSSIANS

BABA VESUVIO

RUM BABA

SERVES 10-12

25 G (3/4 OZ) FRESH BREWERS' YEAST (OR THE EQUIVALENT OF DRIED)
100 ML (3 1/2 FL OZ) LUKEWARM MILK
300 G (10 1/2 OZ) 00 (DOPPIO ZERO) FLOUR, PLUS MORE FOR DUSTING
PINCH OF SALT
85 G (3 OZ) SUGAR
100 G (3 1/2 OZ) MELTED BUTTER, PLUS MORE FOR GREASING
1 TBSP GRATED LEMON ZEST
5 EGGS
5 TBSP WARMED APRICOT JELLY

FOR THE SYRUP:

250 G (9 OZ) CASTER SUGAR
GRATED ZEST OF 1 ORANGE
300 ML (1/2 PINT) DARK RUM

This dessert harks back to the French occupation of the area. Finding a mould to make a large baba in the shape of Vesuvius was quite difficult. This symbol of Naples could also be made using any conical container. Of course, you could make it in any shape and ovenproof container you choose. Babas are traditionally made in ring moulds and served filled with fruits in syrup.

Dissolve the yeast in the lukewarm milk and gradually add to the flour, salt and sugar in a large bowl. Mix thoroughly. Add the butter and lemon zest. Mix well. Gradually add the eggs, one by one, and work well to obtain a smooth dough. Leave covered with a cloth in a warm place until doubled in size, about 2 hours.

Punch the risen dough and work with your hands to knock out the air built up during rising. Grease the mould (see above) with butter and then dust it with flour. Put the dough into it (it should only fill it about three-quarters full). Leave to rise again, until the dough reaches the top of the mould.

Preheat the oven to 200°C/400°F/gas6 and bake the baba for 40 minutes.

While the baba is baking, make the syrup: put the sugar in a pan with 600 ml (1 pint) water and the orange zest. Bring to the boil, then remove from the heat and stir in the rum.

Remove the baba from the oven and, while it is still warm, pour half of the syrup over it. Leave for a few minutes to let the baba absorb the syrup, then pour the remaining syrup over it. Place the baba on a serving dish and brush with the apricot jelly. Chill briefly and serve. It should have a springy texture.

WINES & LIQUEURS

VINI, LIQUORI E BEVANDE

ALCOL / PURE ALCOHOL In Italy it is possible to buy pure alcohol for cooking purposes, mainly to make liqueurs or to preserve fruit. Mostly it is produced from grapes but it may also be made from other fruit, and is distilled to the highest possible percentage alcohol, 95%. It is white and tasteless, and quite dangerous to use because it is highly inflammable.

AMARETTO This is the most typical of Italian liqueurs taken, mostly by ladies, as a *digestif* after a meal. Like the biscuits of the same name, it is based on bitter almonds, but the liqueur also contains other added fruit essences and aromatic herbs. With its very distinctive bitter almond taste, it can also be added to desserts, fruit salads, puddings and cocktails.

AMARO / BITTER From the Italian for 'bitter', the word *amaro* signifies a *digestivo*, which is a very popular drink in Italy. They are made from infusions of various herbs with the addition of alcohol and sugar. An *amaro* is drunk in small quantities after dinner to help the digestion, but some types of *amaro* may also be used as aperitifs (see Aperitivo) or mixed with hot water to produce soothing hot drinks. The best known *amari* are Fernet, Amaro Lucano, Amaro Averna, Amaro Varvelli and Centerbe ('a hundred herbs').

AMARONE DOC This deep ruby-red wine comes from the Valpantena in Veneto. There are two best-known types, both having as a base the Recioto della Valpolicella (see Valpolicella) made from the Corvina Veronese, Rondinella and Molinara grapes. One, usually known as Reciota della Valpolicella Amabile, is a very velvety semi-sweet red wine which is quite high in alcohol content because it is made from dried grapes. The other, dry, wine goes very well with roast meat or game and strong cheeses.

ANISETTA This liqueur probably originates from Greece, descending from the same source as ouzo. It is very much used in Southern Italy where, especially in Naples, it is diluted with water as a drink, or small quantities are added to espresso coffee, as they do in Sicily. Made from an infusion of star anise, with alcohol and sugar, it is also used as a flavouring in pâtisserie.

APERITIVO / APERITIF This word comes from the Latin *aperire*, meaning 'to open', and generally signifies an alcohol-based drink taken before a meal to stimulate the appetite. It is today more generally served as a means of marking the beginning of a celebration or a simple meal among friends.

At midday *aperitivi* are taken in Italy's numerous bars. In summer, water or soda water is often added to make refreshing drinks as well. Aperitifs are usually based on stimulating herbs, and are sometimes strongly coloured, like Campari. Other well-known aperitifs are Americano, Cordiale and Cynar (which is based on artichokes). There is also a series of aperitifs based on wine, with the addition of a little alcohol and of herb infusions. Vermouth is the most widely known, of which Cinzano and Martini are the most popular worldwide. These wines, which can be dry, sweet-white and sweet-red, are served on ice or diluted with soda water, but are also used for mixing cocktails, like negronis or martinis.

There is also a range of non-alcoholic aperitifs which consist only of herb infusions, which are then diluted with soda water. These are generally known as *aperitivi analcolici*. When you want to order one at the bar you simply say '*un analcolico per favore*'.

AQUA VITE, SEE GRAPPA

ARNEIS DOC This Piedmontese dry white wine is made with the Arneis grape in the area of Roero near Alba. It has a very intense bouquet and is often drunk as an aperitif, but also served to accompany *antipasti*.

BARBARESCO DOCG This is one of the most popular DOCG Piedmontese red wines. This status is given only to a few wines in Italy and in this case means that the wine can only come from a small area in the South of Piedmont, near Alba in the towns of Barbaresco, Neive and Treiso. With a minimum alcohol content of 12.5, the wine has a garnet red colour, with orange reflections, and a pleasant and deep scent. The flavour is well balanced, dry and velvety. It goes very well with game and all roasted and grilled red meat. Barbaresco can be called *riserva* only if it is aged for at least 4 years.

BARBERA DOC This is another classic Piedmontese wine which may only be made in that region. The grape gives the name to the ruby red wine, which is considered to be a good table wine and everybody drinks it in Piedmont. There are three areas which vie for supremacy in the making of this wine – Barbera d'Asti, Barbera D'Alba and Barbera del Monferrato, with some usual differences. The Barbera D'Asti is exclusively made with Barbera grapes, while the Alba wine can be made with a little percentage of Nebbiolo grapes and that of Monferrato can include Freisa, Grignolino and Dolcetto grapes.

There are various qualities of Barbera: from the normal, which can sometimes be quite rough, to the superior, which has been aged for at least two years. It is drunk with all the Piedmontese food, especially with Bagna Caôda and dishes accompanied by polenta. There is a dry sparkling version of it, which is wonderful slightly chilled in summer.

Bardolino DOC This wine comes from the Veneto, near Lake Garda around Bardolino. It is a light ruby red wine which, when young, is quite pinkish. It does not exceed an alcohol content of 12% and is one of the most exported Italian wines, together with Valpolicella. In fact Bardolino, Valpolicella and Chianti were the first three Italian wines to be exported successfully.

Barolo DOCG Often called the 'King of Italian wines', Barolo is made mostly with Nebbiolo grapes growing in the Piedmontese areas of Barolo, Castiglione Falletto, Serralunga D'Alba, Cherasco, Diano D'Alba, Grinzane Cavour, La Morra, Monforte D'Alba, Novello, Roddi and Verduno in the province of Cuneo. This wine undergoes serious analysis and judgement before it is put on the market in order to safeguard the very high reputation it has in Italy and abroad as one of the best wines produced by Italy. It is a very strong wine with a very deep red colour, with a bouquet of violets and roses. A full balanced velvety dry wine, it should be drunk on grand occasions.

A *riserva* has to be at least 5 years old, while the other version requires a minimum of 3 years ageing, starting from the January following the harvest. Barolo Chinato is an aperitif made with the addition of quinine (see Vino Chinato). A good Barolo goes with all traditional meat dishes. Game, such as venison or pheasant, red meat and hare always goes well with this wine. In cooking, the most important use is for Brasato al Barolo, a dish of beef cooked for a long time in the wine.

Brunello di Montalcino DOCG At an altitude of 6 or 700 metres (1,800 or 2,100 feet), the town of Montalcino in Tuscany dominates an area of vineyards which seem all to be exposed to the intense sun. Brunello is one of the grand wines of Italy and the Cooperativa dei Coltivatori di Brunello makes sure that all the wines bearing the name are worthy of it. Every year they present the new vintage to the national press and it is remarkable how every producer of Brunello would go to the barricades to defend the reputation of the wine. The Sangiovese Grosso grape used for making Brunello gives a very aristocratic wine able to age for a long time, up to fifty years. Due to the care they take to make it and to the esteemed (and valuable) reputation, the wine is produced only in the best years, omitting a year if the quality of the wine wasn't good enough. To be saleable the wine has to be at least 4 years old, of which 3 is spent in wooden barrels. The Brunello aged for 5 years can have the name *riserva* added to the label. This is an ideal and very fine wine to drink with roast and grilled meat of any kind, especially game – locally wild boar is abundant.

Cabernet di Pramaggiore DOC This magnificent deep ruby-red wine comes from the provinces of Venice, Treviso and Pordenone. With a minimum of 11.5% alcohol, its dry softness makes it an ideal wine for light meat dishes. Cabernet Sauvignon and Franc are French grapes varieties recently introduced to Italy which now form the backbone of many very good modern Italian wines.

Campari This aperitif, known worldwide, is made from an infusion of herbs, with alcohol (about 18%), sugar, water and the typical red colouring. It is drunk chilled, mixed with soda water or orange juice. It is also used to produce sorbets, like Campari and passion fruit sorbet.

Canarino Literally translating as a 'canary', this is the simplest drink ever – hot water and lemon rind. Very soothing, it is said to be excellent for the digestion and is often drunk by those who cannot drink tea or coffee.

Cannonau DOC This very well-known full-bodied Sardinian ruby-red wine comes in two versions, dry or semi-sweet. The cannonau grape may be late harvested or indeed allowed to dry on mats, in this case the alcohol content can rise to produce a wine that is dry or *amabile* (semi-sweet), which is mainly used as dessert wine. Otherwise, Cannonau is excellent with grilled meat.

Carema DOC As so often is the case, the town or village where certain grapes grow also give its name to the wine made from them. Carema is a very picturesque little village surrounded by impressive vineyards at the hilly bottom of Piedmont's Aosta Valley. This particular piece of country enjoys the sunshine for a large part of the day and the Nebbiolo grape cultivated on arduous terraces benefits fully from this situation. This wine has been known since the 16th century and it is said that Napoleon, who passed by on the way to Piedmont, particularly appreciated this excellent dry garnet-coloured wine. With a minimum alcohol content of 12% and an excellent body, it offers a soft and velvety bouquet and is ideal for the local cuisine, based on beef, veal and game.

Cartizze, Prosecco DOC This very fashionable white wine from the Veneto is made from the Prosecco grape growing in the area of Conegliano or Valdobbiadene in the province of Treviso. There are two types of white produced with this grape. The slightly sparkling *tipo frizzante* is obtained by natural fermentation and can be dry or semi-sweet. The straw-yellow *spumante*, especially the Superiore di Cartizze, is also dry or *amabile* (sweet) but pleasantly fruity. Cartizze is usually decanted into a tall glass jar to get rid of some of the sparkle! One of the most popular drinks made with this wine is the Venetian speciality, the Bellini cocktail, in which fresh peach juice is added to the wine to make a delicious summer drink.

Centerbe, See Amaro

Chianti DOCG Probably next to Barolo, Chianti is one of the best-known Italian wines. Tuscany has produced this wine for many centuries, the Frescobaldi and Antinori companies can both count more than 600 years of wine-making tradition. In all this time the wine has been made using Sangiovese and Canaiolo Nero grapes. In the last century Chianti underwent quite a complicated procedure, secured by Government decrees, to safeguard the quality and the good name. The time of finding a red liquid in the traditional raffia-covered *fiasco* is generally long gone, although some companies are still bottling the improved modern Chianti in these typical bottles, which used to decorate the walls of Italian restaurants all over the world. The better Chianti is now put in normal bottles, and they can carry the DOCG status only if they correspond to the tough and complicated legislation.

Cinque Terre DOC Only recently were roads built to the little towns of Monterosso, Vernazza and Rio Maggiore, where the famous Cinque Terre and Cinque Terre Sciacchetra are made. Indeed some of the vineyards, which are splendidly exposed to the sun in this corner of Liguria extending until La Spezia, may still only be reached by boat. The terraces on which the vines are planted are very steep indeed and most of the work can be done only by hand, and by climbing. The results are exquisite white wines produced with Bosco, Albarola and Vermentino grapes. The Cinque Terre, with 11% alcohol, has a straw-yellow colour and a dry and pleasantly delicate taste. It is ideal for the fish specialities of the Ligurian coast. The Cinque Terre Sciacchetra is a dessert wine produced with the same grapes, but the sugar in the grapes is concentrated by a short drying on mats which gives a higher alcohol content although still remains sweet. It is an ideal dessert wine, with a wonderful scent and a rich amber colour.

Cinzano, see Martini

DOC & DOCG The Italian equivalent of the French *appellation contrôlée*, DOC means *Denominazione di Origine Controllata* and DOCG *Denominazione di Origine Controllata e Garantita*. It is only since 1966 that the Italian Government has introduced legislation to control the previously chaotic production and classification of all Italian regional wines. Italy is quantitatively the biggest wine producer in the world, but qualitatively Italy has suffered for a long time of being seen as the producer, with a few exceptions, of simple wines. This is despite the fact that Italy perhaps offers the widest differentiation of types of soil, climate and grapes among all the wine-producing countries. A few far-sighted Italian wine producers, who have looked over the shoulder of their French cousins, already advanced in the method of producing exceptional wines, have in the last 30 years or so produced such improvements that Italians can count on perfectly made wines that can compete with the best in the world. The combination of the new legislation and private initiative has given birth to a new breed of wines like Tignanello, Sassicaia and Solaia.

The DOCG denomination is reserved for wines originating from a very small defined area, where only the grapes from that area are used. Of the more than 300 DOC wines in 1994, only 13 had this specification.

Curiously, Tignanello, Sassicaia, Solaia and a few others, although by name and fame the very top of the range of Italian wines, don't have a DOC denomination, but have a simple classification *vino da tavola*, table wine.

ERBALUCE DOC From Canavese in the province of Turin and Vercelli at the estuary of the Aosta Valley in Piedmont comes this exquisite white wine, of which several versions are made. Erbaluce Caluso is dry, with a straw yellow colour. Its very fine bouquet makes it suitable for all fish and delicate dishes. The Caluso Passito is also made from Erbaluce grapes, but they are put to dry after harvesting to increase the natural sugar content. This produces a wine which is dark amber in colour, with a 13.5% or 14% alcohol content, making it a wonderful aperitif wine. A third type, Caluso Passito Liquoroso, is fortified with added alcohol, making it the perfect dessert wine.

FERNET, SEE AMARO

FIANO DI AVELLINO DOC
From the centre of Campania, more precisely Avellino and the surrounding province, comes this remarkable white wine which was known even to the Ancient Romans. The Fiano grapes produce a straw-yellow wine with a dry taste and a deep characteristic bouquet. The wine is extremely drinkable with all types of dishes, delicate and less so. It is a typically robust white wine from the very fertile volcanic local soil.

FRANCIACORTA DOC
This name is given to four wines made in the province of Brescia in Lombardy. The Franciacorta Bianco (white) and Franciacorta Spumante (sparkling) are both made with a mixture of Pinot Bianco, Pinot Grigio, Pinot Noir and Chardonnay grapes. A minimum alcohol content of 11 or 11.5% is required for the production of this soft and delicate wine with an intense bouquet. The Franciacorta Rosato Spumante (sparkling rosé) is made with the Pinot Bianco, Chardonnay and Pinot Noir grapes, giving a very fragrant sparkling wine for the summer. Franciacorta Rosso is made from Cabernet Franc and Barbera or Nebbiolo grapes. Brilliant red in colour, becoming garnet with age, it has a balanced and dry taste, and being light (a minimum alcohol content of 11%), it is suitable for local meat and cheese dishes.

FRASCATI DOC From the region south-east of Rome, where the town of Frascati is situated, comes this very well-known white wine, traditionally appreciated by Roman clergy and nobility. Produced on the hills around Rome (Castelli Romani), Frascati is the result of the union of Malvasia Bianca and Trebbiano Toscano grapes. The Amabile (semi-dry) and Dolce (sweet) types, which the Romans like very much, are made with the addition of concentrated must to increase the sugar content. Straw-yellow in colour, with a delicate taste, the Frascati Secco (dry) has a minimum alcohol content of 11% and is considered the wine that best suits most Roman dishes, including Porchetta (page 80). For such a rich dish, perhaps the Frascati Superiore, with an alcohol content of 12%, is more suitable.

GATTINARA DOC The province of Vercelli in Piedmont is mainly known for rice cultivation, but where the sunny hills of the Northern part of the region start to build up to the Pre-Alps, there you will find Gattinara, an excellent garnet red wine made with the Nebbiolo grape, the same as used in Barolo. A dry and almost bitter taste characterizes this fine wine, which is excellent with game dishes, especially hare and wild boar.

GAVI (CORTESE DI GAVI) DOC This fine straw-yellow Piedmontese wine is made almost at the border with Liguria. The town of Gavi and the surrounding fertile and sunny hills grow the Cortese grape, which produces a crisp and pleasant white wine that is also suited to being turned into sparkling wine. It is a very popular wine, especially with *antipasto* and first courses.

GENEPY This speciality of the Aosta Valley is a liqueur made by infusing local herbs, especially *genzium* (gentian), in alcohol and mixing this with sugar and water. There are clear and green versions of Genepy, which has an alcohol content of 40% and over. It is a wonderful *digestivo* or winter warmer, especially après ski.

GRAPPA, ACQUA VITE
Grappa is for Italians, especially Northerners, what whisky is for the Scots. It is produced both commercially and privately. The best grappa is made by distilling with the leftovers after the grapes have been pressed, including pips, skin and stalks. The grappas made in this way are very aromatic. There are grappas made with selected grapes, tasting for example of muscat or Barolo or Chianti. Grappa is drunk at room temperature after the meal as a *digestivo*. Some people add a few drops of grappa to their espresso coffee, to make the coffee that is called *corretto* (corrected).

GRECO DI TUFO DOC From the province of Avellino, where the Fiano also comes from, this wine is made with Greco grapes and is one of the most popular Campanian wines. A golden-yellow wine, it is soft and dry, and suitable for delicate fish dishes and pale meat dishes.

GUTTURNIO COLLI PIACENTINI DOC From around Piacenza on the very fertile and sunny hills of Emilia-Romagna comes this excellent dry red wine made with Barbera and Bonarda grapes. It can be dry or demi-sec if all the sugar hasn't turned into alcohol.

LACRYMA CHRISTI DEL VESUVIO DOC The area all around Vesuvius has a rich volcanic soil on which the Coda di Volpe and Verdeca grapes grow vigorously, giving birth to the Vesuvio Bianco wine. When this has a natural minimum alcohol content of 12%, it can be called Lacryma Christi ('tear of Christ'). Pale yellow in colour, and dry with a touch of acidity, this excellent Neapolitan wine is perfect for the light local dishes. The Vesuvio Rosso (deep red) and Rosato (rosé) are made with the Piedi Rosso and Sciascinoso grapes which also grow locally. Again, if these have a minimum alcohol content of 12% they are also called Lacryma Christi.

LAMBRUSCO DI SORBARA
For the Emilians, Lambrusco is so dense it has to be eaten and drunk at the same time. This is the real Lambrusco, locally produced in Emilia-Romagna from the Lambrusco di Sorbara and Lambrusco Salamino grapes which grow in the province of Modena. Although only 11% alcohol, the intensity of this wine makes it very dense and extremely dark red, almost violet. It is naturally sparkling, which makes it foamy, and it has a very pleasant bouquet and tastes of fruit. It is most suitable for the various pork and duck dishes of the area and generally with the fairly rich local food. There are a few other varieties of Lambrusco made with slightly different grapes but with the same characteristics; Lambrusco Grasparossa, Lambrusco Reggiano and Lambrusco Salamino di S. Croce are the best known. This is a wine that does not travel too well, so it is better to drink it locally.

LOCOROTONDO DOC From the Trulli region of Alberobello, the Locorotondo is a gentle white wine with a pleasant bouquet and a dry and delicate taste. This typical Pugliese wine is made from the Verdeca and Bianco Alessano grapes. It is a typical summer wine, which goes well with the local fish dishes.

MALVASIA DOC There are various wines called Malvasia, usually followed by the name of the area from which they come. The Piedmontese types are red, not very alcoholic and slightly sparkling, due to the use of grapes like Freisa and Barbera or Grignolino. Malvasia di Casoro and Malvasia di Castelnuovo don Bosco are the best representatives of this wine. The others come from the islands of Sicily and Sardinia and are of a totally different nature. The Malvasia delle Lipari, from the island of that name is made with golden and yellow aromatic grapes which become amber after being dried. The resulting wine, called Passito, has a high total alcohol content and is still sweet. The Sardinian wine comes from Cagliari and is of similar nature, but straw-yellow to golden-yellow in colour. Another type called *liquoroso* is fortified with alcohol to 17.5%, still with a lot of sugar making it like a refined but pungent dessert wine, to be served with dry biscuits and cakes.

MARASCHINO Originally from Dalmatia in Yugoslavia, this liqueur made from Marasca (morello) cherries was adopted by Italians mainly to add to fruit salads or for cocktails or for use in pastries. It has a sweet, slightly almond taste and is produced mostly in the Veneto region, where it is produced by lengthy processing of the cherries, which are crushed, fermented and distilled.

MARSALA DOC Named after the city where most of the cellars are located, Marsala is perhaps the most famous Sicilian wine. It is produced in the province of Trapani from the Catarrato, Pignatello, Nerello, Calabrese and Grillo grapes. It comes in three different types, according to alcohol and sugar content. Ageing of Marsala in wooden casks also determines the variety and so does the addition of cooked must before fermentation, which is allowed by the law. The Marsala Fino must have a minimum alcohol content of 17% and has to age for 1 year. Marsala Superiore has a minimum 18% alcohol content with the type Ambra including 1% cooked must added, while for the Oro and Rubino type with a minimum age of 2 years no addition is allowed. Marsala Vergine with a content of 18% alcohol with an ageing of 4 years and no addition is one of the finest marsalas, only topped by the M. Vergine Stravecchio or Riserva with an age of 5 years. The degree of sweetness varies also because of the permission of adding must or alcohol to make them fortified. This wine is widely used in cooking and for the preparation of the famous Zabaglione. Scaloppine al Marsala is another classic of Italian cooking.

Today Marsala in the dry and old version is enjoying a come-back as an aperitif or after-dinner drink.

MARTINI The name of a Piedmontese family who started to produce vermouth wines in 1863. Later on, with the merger of that company with Rossi, they have grown until today they are the best-known producers not only of the well-known red, white and dry vermouth, but also of dry and sweet sparkling wines, aperitifs like China Martini and more. Martini vermouth is the base of various cocktails and drinks worldwide, but it is also widely used in cooking as, for example, in the mushroom dish Finferli al Liquore (page 201). The other slightly less famous house sharing the world vermouth market is Cinzano.

MERLOT DI PRAMAGGIORE DOC Red-to-garnet in colour, this delicious wine is made almost entirely of Merlot grapes in the province of Venice, where Pramaggiore is the main area of production. It has a deep bouquet, and a dry well-balanced taste. The alcohol content of 11.5% makes it easy to drink, especially with roast and light game.

MONICA DI CAGLIARI DOC This deep ruby-red wine, made in Sardinia from grapes of the same name, is a rare red vinous dessert wine most suitable to accompany all the local almond-based sweet pastries. It is aged for at least one year before drinking.

MONTEPULCIANO D'ABRUZZO DOC From the provinces of Chieti Aquila, Pescara and Teramo, comes this excellent red wine which is largely representative of the Abruzzo region. Made of the Montepulciano grape, it has a typical cherry-red colour, a vinous and pleasant bouquet and a dry taste. This very interesting wine should be drunk young with *antipasti*.

MOSCADELLO DI MONTALCINO DOC From the sunny and hilly area of Montalcino comes this highly regarded dessert wine made from the Moscato grape. This straw-yellow wine comes in two versions: the first a sweetish wine with only 10.5% alcohol content and a wonderful delicate but aromatic flavour. The second, called Liquoroso, is fortified to a strength of 19%. It is ideal as a dessert wine, with *cantucci* (see page 290) or other baked goods from the area.

MOSCATO DOC I can say I grew up with this wine because, as a child, I often drank the freshly pressed must – with 'dramatic' consequences! Especially in Piedmont, where I grew up, there exist at least 10 different types of Moscato, according to the provinces in which it is made. Asti is the main area, followed by Cuneo and Alessandria. The Moscato grape produces a very flavoursome wine, which is then sold as Moscato d'Asti. There is a famous sparkling version, Asti Spumante. The Moscato Naturale d'Asti is not sparkling and has a natural muscat bouquet which makes it very desirable. This is a dessert wine par excellence and its lightness makes it delightful after a large meal.

NEBBIOLO D'ALBA DOC The Nebbiolo grape gets its name from *nebbia*, the word for the fog covering the hills of Piedmont in Autumn. It grows on the hills of Alba and Langhe, in the provinces of Cuneo, famous for the white truffle. Although it is the father of such illustrious wines as Barolo, Barbaresco and Carema, it makes a fine wine in its own right.

NOCINO This liqueur, a speciality of Modena, is based on unripe walnuts, traditionally collected around the 24th of June. The nuts are cut into quarters and macerated in a mixture of alcohol, sugar, cinnamon and cloves for 40 days, until the liquid is dark brown and drinkable as a perfect *digestivo*. Nocino is now made almost everywhere in Italy and, as it is so simple to make, it is often home-made.

NURAGUS DI CAGLIARI DOC A pleasant Sardinian dry white wine made from the grape of the same name in the province of Cagliari, it is pale straw-yellow in colour and has a pleasant bouquet, making it suitable for fish dishes.

ORVIETO DOC For centuries this ancient wine was regularly served at the table of the Popes. Made in the area of Orvieto, the Southern part of Umbria, from grapes like Trebbiano, Verdello, Grechetto and Malvasia, it can be dry (*secco*) or semi-sweet (*abboccato*), depending on the proportions of each grape used. Orvieto has a straw-yellow colour, a delicate taste and a pleasant bouquet. It can be served as an aperitif and goes very well with *antipasto* and light first courses.

PASSITO This term indicates a wine made with grapes which have been left to dry on the plant, or hung in drying rooms or laid on straw mats, to achieve a better concentration of the natural sugars, resulting in strong wines that are mostly sweet dessert wines.

PROSECCO, SEE CARTIZZE

ROSOLIO An old-fashioned 'ladies' ' liqueur, based on sweetened alcohol with flavours from rose petals to strawberries, it is a very pleasant drink currently enjoying a revival. It can be drunk as a mild after-dinner drink.

SABA, SAPA, VINO COTTO *Saba* is a preparation obtained by cooling down the freshly pressed must of Sangiovese di Romagna grapes and reducing it by cooking it to a thick dark liquid, 25% of its original volume. This liquid is mainly used for making the celebrated balsamic vinegar, but is also diluted with water to be served as a drink and used as an ingredient in some types of biscuit. Equivalents exist in Puglia, there called *vino cotto* (cooked wine), and in Sardinia, there called Sapa but made with a white grape variety. As a boy I remember it being poured on a snowball to have an instant sorbet.

SALICE SALENTINO DOC From the province of Lecce deep in Puglia comes this jolly wine which comes in two versions, red and a rare rosé. As is to be expected in a truly Pugliese wine, the warmth and dryness of the red is accompanied by 12.5 degrees alcohol. The rosé version is milder, with a lasting delicate bouquet and enough power for it to be drunk on warm sunny days with roasts or grilled fish, as well as with all the roasted vegetables of the area.

SAMBUCA This typical central Italian liqueur is based on star anise seeds. It is well known in Italian restaurants because of the effect obtained by setting a coffee bean on top of it and lighting the alcohol vapours. This is more a gimmick than anything done to develop the flavour.

SANGIOVESE DI ROMAGNA DOC This wine is made from the Sangiovese grape which is cultivated in a very large area of Emilia-Romagna included in the provinces of Forlì, Ravenna and Bologna. The ruby-red wine is vinous, dry and well-balanced, and goes well with lasagne. When this wine is aged for at least two years it can be called *riserva*.

SASSICAIA, SOLAIA, TIGNANELLO (VINI DA TAVOLA) Sassicaia, together with a couple of other special wines, Solaia and Tignanello, come from precisely the same area, Tenuta S. Cristina in Val di Pesa in Tuscany. They are the result of the most modern wine-making technologies introduced into Italy a couple of decades ago. By taking Cabernet Sauvignon, Sangiovese and Cabernet Franc grapes, changing the proportion of the grapes in each wine, using the best care of the vine and the best method of vinification and ageing in *barriques* (wooden barrels) as they do in France, they have achieved three of the top Italian wines. They don't even participate to the usual DOC classification system. They are, in fact, called Tuscan Table Wines but still command the highest respect and price. With high alcohol contents (from 12.8 to 13%), these are wonderful smooth wines, ideal for red meat and game dishes.

SCIACHETRA CINQUE TERRE DOC, SEE CINQUE TERRE

SLIVOVITZ
A schnapps, or fruit spirit, of Yugoslavian origin, this is made by the distillation of plums. It has been adopted in the border area of Trieste and is used as a strong spirit.

SOLAIA TOSCANA, SEE SASSICAIA

STREGA This famous herb liqueur from Benevento in Campania is yellow in colour. It is drunk as a *digestivo*, but it is also used for flavouring puddings and many Southern pastries.

TAURASI DOC A proud representative of Campanian red, this full-bodied dry red wine is produced in the province of Avellino and Benevento from Piedirosso, Agliancico and some Barbera grapes. It has a pleasant and deep bouquet, and is excellent for many meat or very spicy dishes.

TIGNANELLO TOSCANA, SEE SASSICAIA

TORCOLATO Although a non-DOC wine, this is still very appreciated by dessert wine lovers. Made with Tocai, Vespaiolo and Garganega grapes, it has a sweet fruity taste, so it can also be drunk with a soft and creamy Gorgonzola or Dolcelatte cheese.

TORGIANO DOC An Umbrian wine of character, the Torgiano is produced in the commune of the same name in the province of Perugia and can be red or white. The red is produced with Sangiovese, Canaiolo and Trebbiano Toscano grapes. The deep ruby Torgiano red has a delicate bouquet and a dry well-balanced taste, making it excellent with game, pork and lamb dishes. The Torgiano white is straw-yellow in colour and produced with Trebbiano Toscano, Grechetto and Malvasia Toscana grapes. It has a fruity and pleasant dry taste, so it is served with first courses and pale meat or fish dishes.

TRAMINER AROMATICO DOC From the Traminer grape, grown so much in Alsace and Germany, this wine is appreciated for its extremely fruity and aromatic taste. The wine is cultivated in Alto Adige, in the northernmost part of Trentino and Friuli. Its golden green colour and its distinctive bouquet make it stand apart from the other white wines of the area. It is drunk as an aperitif, but also to accompany light first courses.

TREBBIANO DI ROMAGNA DOC The Trebbiano grape is cultivated in the provinces of Bologna, Forlì and Ravenna. The Roman legionaries were responsible for the introduction of this grape to the area. There is also a sparkling version. The grape is widely used mixed with many other grapes and in other areas. This very well-known wine is straw-yellow in colour and has a pleasant bouquet and dry balanced taste.

VALPOLICELLA DOC This wine has a long history, and was known and appreciated by the Ancient Romans, but still today has a worldwide appeal. Together with Chianti, Valpolicella has been popularized by the *trattorie* and other restaurants in Italy and abroad. Having enjoyed early commercialization, Valpolicella is made with Corvina Veronese, Rondinella and Molinara grapes growing in 19 communes in the province of Verona. Ruby-red in colour, with a delicate pleasant scent and almond taste, it is a very easy-to-drink wine. There is a version, Recioto della Valpolicella, made with partly dried grapes to impart a higher sugar and alcohol content. See Amarone.

VERDICCHIO DEI CASTELLI DI JESI DOC This very popular dry white wine, which is excellent with fish and seafood, is made in the province of Ancona, the capital of Marche, from Verdicchio, Trebbiano Toscano and Malvasia grapes. With a pale straw colour, delicate bouquet and dry balanced taste, it is bottled in a characteristic amphora-like bottle and is now strongly commercialized. It should be drunk very young because it tends to oxidize with age. A second, not dissimilar, type of Verdicchio is called Verdicchio di Matelica and is made in the province of Macerata.

VERMENTINO DI GALLURA DOC The Gallura is the northernmost tip of Sardinia, in the provinces of Sassari and Nuoro. The very dry straw-yellow white wine made with Vermentino grapes has a deep and delicate bouquet and slightly bitter aftertaste, making it ideal for fish, especially crustacea.

VERMOUTH, SEE MARTINI

VERNACCIA DI SAN GIMIGNANO, V. DI ORISTANO DOC The favourite wine of Pope Paul III comes from around the splendid Etruscan town of San Gimignano in Tuscany. It is made with San Gimignano grapes, which came originally from Greece, producing a golden-yellow wine with a deep and fine bouquet. It is a very dry, almost bitter, wine but its fresh balanced taste makes it ideal as an aperitif, or with *antipasto* and fish dishes. Another Vernaccia is no less popular. It is made with the eponymous grape in the province of Cagliari, in Sardinia. It has an amber yellow colour, a delicate bouquet and a slight aftertaste of bitter almonds. This wine is ideal as an aperitif. There is also a Liquoroso (liqueur) version which is used as a dessert wine.

VIN NOBILE DI MONTEPULCIANO DOCG
A noble wine indeed, this is extremely appreciated by connoisseurs. It is said to have been given the name because a few noble families of Montepulciano used to make it for their own use. This is a DOCG wine made with Prugnolo Gentile, Canaiolo and Malvasia del Chianti and Trebbiano Toscano grapes, all growing at an altitude of 300-650 metres (850-2000 feet) in the area of Montepulciano. The wine has a deep garnet colour becoming orange with age, and a delicate bouquet with a hint of violets. The taste is dry and it has abundant tannin, so it ages well. This brilliant wine is ideal for game and robust red meat dishes.

VIN SANTO DOC Some attribute the use of the word *santo* here to the fact that this wine is used sometimes for celebration of the Mass, others because the wine originated from Xantos in Greece. This rich aromatic Tuscan wine is a delicious dessert wine, traditionally used to dip Cantucci biscuits after a meal. It is produced from Malvasia and Trebbiano grapes which, after harvesting, are put on straw mats to dry to increase the sugar content before being turned into wine. Depending upon the fermentation, the ageing process in wooden casks for at least 3 years produces a wine that may be sweet, semi-sweet or dry. Vin Santo is also used as a flavouring in pastries and creams.

VINO CHINATO This traditional Piedmontese aperitif is made from Barolo wine with the addition of the rind of China, an Oriental evergreen plant (*Cinchona succirubra*), as well as many other herbs and spices, and is used as a flavouring in other wines and liqueurs. Vino Chinato has a dark red brown colour and is drunk either cold on ice or as punch.

VINO COTTO, SEE SABA

INDEX

The Tortia family who run the fine restaurant Cannon D'Oro in Cocconato – Paolo and Franca, Maria Grazia and Guido.

ACKNOWLEDGEMENTS

This book could not have been made without the enormous generosity of our friends in Italy, who lent us their homes, their kitchens, their families, their production and their time. THANK YOU.

Eva Agnesi, *Imperia*
All our friends at *Altesino*, Montalcino, Toscana
Adelvio and Bedullia in their garden, Umbria
Ristorante Ardenga, Diolo, Emilia-Romagna
Baratti e Milano, Torino
Famiglia Bartolini, especially Ulderico, Umbria
Famiglia Bava, Cocconato
Famiglia Battista, Lago Maggiore
Valtusciano Battipaglia
Sig. Bottera, *La Bottera*, Cuneo
Noé Bovo, Piemonte
British Airways, London
Rosalba Carluccio, Ivrea
Famiglia Carluccio, Ivrea
Cappelli Sergio e Patrizia Ranzo *Arch.*, Napoli
Dai Fratelli, Orvieto
Riccardo Dalisi, *Arch.*, Napoli
Da Marco Norcia
Dr Silvano Dametto, Roma
Gianni e Anna Daneri
Daneri (coltivazione di basilico), Liguria
Giuseppe D'Urso, Positano
Sig. Eustachio, *Nettis Impianti*, Puglia
G. Sig. Ferraris, G. Pfatisch, Torino
Guido Ferrero, *Salumificio*, Cocconato
Conca at *Fiorella*, Camogli
De Fillipi Pasta, Torino
Bitten Eriksen
Franco Fasano (pottery), Grottaglie
Ceramiche Fedolfi, Montalcino
Fiat Roma (for the loan of their Ulisse)
Antonio Fiordelisi, Puglia
Luciana Florio of Napoli
Giuseppe Garello Panificio, Torino
Antonucci Gianfranco, Foggia
Sig.ri & Sig.ra Giacobazzi, Modena
Maria Grammatico, *La Pasticceria*, Erice, Sicilia
Conte de La Gatinais, Rapitalá, Sicilia
Instituto ICE, Roma
Trattoria Italia, Castelletto Stura
Il Pane di San Giuseppe, Salemi (Giuseppe Lo Castro), Sicilia
Signor Antonio Marella, Puglia
Bar Marotta, Palermo
Masseria San Domenico, Puglia
Molisano Caffè, Torino
Carlo Montani, Umbria
Palace Hotel, Palermo
Paola Navone, Milano
Pinuccia Novara Ristorante San Giovanni, Casarza Ligure
Signor Pazienza, PAP, Puglia
Pesce Azzurro, Sicilia
Sig. e Sig.ra Bruno Peyrano, Torino
Pasticceria Revello, Camogli, Liguria
Rino, wine-maker, Altesino, Montalcino
Dr Bruno Roncarati
Louisetto Marco, Settimo Vittone, Piemonte
Giovanetto Alberto, Settimo Vittone, Piemonte
Urbani Tartufi, Umbria
Hotel Verbano, Isola dei Pescatori
Lella and Giorgio, Pistoni, Ivrea
Collezione di Vetro Antico, *Museo del Vetro*, Villa Banfi, Montalcino, Toscana
Associazione di Categoria Regionali
Quinto & Famiglia Tagliavini, Caseificio Motta, Polesine, Emilia-Romagna

Thank you as well to the team who helped to produce the book:
André Martin for his wonderful photography, Jan Martin and Jean-Christophe Moreau who assisted him, Fabrice Moireau for his beautiful and helpful illustrations, Paul Welti for designing the book, Lewis Esson for editing the text, Jane Middleton for editing the recipes, Liz Przybylski for typing all the many drafts, and – last but by no means least – Gennaro Contaldo for his help in testing recipes.